T0150378

STRATEGIES FOR MONETARY POLICY

The Hoover Institution gratefully acknowledges the following individuals and foundations for their significant support of the *Working Group on Economic Policy* and this publication:

Lynde and Harry Bradley Foundation

Preston and Carolyn Butcher

Stephen and Sarah Page Herrick

Koret Foundation

William E. Simon Foundation

John A. Gunn and Cynthia Fry Gunn

STRATEGIES FOR MONETARY POLICY

EDITED BY

JOHN H. COCHRANE
JOHN B. TAYLOR

CONTRIBUTING AUTHORS

James Bullard
John H. Cochrane
James D. Hamilton
Peter N. Ireland
Andrew Levin
Andrew Lilley
Loretta J. Mester
David Papell
Charles I. Plosser
George P. Shultz
Kevin Warsh
John C. Williams

Richard H. Clarida
Mary C. Daly
Laurie Simon Hodrick
Robert S. Kaplan
Mickey D. Levy
Thomas M. Mertens
Scott Minerd
Monika Piazzesi
Kenneth Rogoff
John B. Taylor
Volker Wieland

WITH ADDITIONAL DISCUSSANTS

HOOVER INSTITUTION PRESS
STANFORD UNIVERSITY   STANFORD, CALIFORNIA

Hoover Institution Press Publication No. 711
Hoover Institution at Leland Stanford Junior University,
Stanford, California 94305-6003

First printing 2020
27 26 25 24 23 22 21 20   9 8 7 6 5 4 3 2 1

Manufactured in the United States of America

Library of Congress Cataloging-in-Publication Data

Names: Cochrane, John H. (John Howland), 1957– editor. | Taylor, John B., editor.
Title: Strategies for monetary policy / edited by John H. Cochrane, John B. Taylor.
Other titles: Hoover Institution Press publication ; 711.
Description: Stanford, California : Hoover Institution Press, Stanford University 2020. | Series: Hoover Institution Press publication ; no. 711 | Papers presented at a conference held at the Hoover Institution in 2019. | Includes bibliographical references and index. | Summary: "As the Federal Reserve reviews its monetary policy strategy, key experts provide an in-depth discussion of the financial tools, debates, and practices that will ensure a sound US economy"—Provided by publisher.
Identifiers: LCCN 2020002140 (print) | LCCN 2020002141 (ebook) | ISBN 9780817923747 (cloth) | ISBN 9780817923761 (epub) | ISBN 9780817923778 (mobi) | ISBN 9780817923785 (pdf)
Subjects: LCSH: Board of Governors of the Federal Reserve System (U.S.)—Congresses. | Monetary policy—United States—Congresses. | LCGFT: Conference papers and proceedings.
Classification: LCC HG540 .S74 2020 (print) | LCC HG540 (ebook) | DDC 339.5/30973—dc23
LC record available at https://lccn.loc.gov/2020002140
LC ebook record available at https://lccn.loc.gov/2020002141

Contents

Preface   ix
John H. Cochrane and John B. Taylor

ONE   **Models, Markets, and Monetary Policy**   1
Richard H. Clarida
GENERAL DISCUSSION: *John B. Taylor, Michael D. Bordo,*
  Chris Crowe, Charles I. Plosser, Sebastian Edwards,
  Brian Sack, John H. Cochrane

TWO   **The Case for Implementing Effective Negative**
Interest Rate Policy   27
Andrew Lilley and Kenneth Rogoff
DISCUSSANT: *Andrew Levin*
GENERAL DISCUSSION: *Michael D. Bordo, Peter Fisher,*
  John H. Cochrane, Mickey Levy, George Selgin,
  Charlie Calomiris

THREE   **Tying Down the Anchor: Monetary Policy Rules**
and the Lower Bound on Interest Rates   103
Thomas M. Mertens and John C. Williams
DISCUSSANT: *Monika Piazzesi*
INTRODUCTORY REMARKS: *Kevin Warsh*
GENERAL DISCUSSION: *Krishna Guha, John H. Cochrane,*
  Volker Wieland, Bob Wenzel, George Selgin,
  Thomas M. Mertens, James Bullard

FOUR   **Perspectives on US Monetary Policy Tools**
and Instruments   173
James D. Hamilton
DISCUSSANT: *Peter N. Ireland*

GENERAL DISCUSSION: *Adrien Auclert, John B. Taylor,*
Jeff Lacker, John H. Cochrane, Sebastian Edwards,
Andrew Levin, Andy Filardo, James Bullard

FIVE   **Evaluating Rules in the Fed's Report**
       and Measuring Discretion   217
       John H. Cochrane, John B. Taylor, and Volker Wieland
       DISCUSSANT: *David Papell*

SYMPOSIUM:
The Interaction of Markets and Policy   259

       Introduction   259
       George P. Shultz
SIX   **The Interaction of Markets and Policy: A Corporate**
       Finance Perspective   263
       Laurie Simon Hodrick
SEVEN **The Fed and Financial Markets: Suggestions**
       to Improve an Unhealthy Relationship   269
       Mickey D. Levy
EIGHT **Market Feedback Effects of Central Bank**
       Operations under an Inflation-Targeting Regime   289
       Scott Minerd
       GENERAL DISCUSSION: *George P. Shultz, Peter Fisher,*
       John B. Taylor, John H. Cochrane

SYMPOSIUM:
Monetary Strategies in Practice   309

       Introduction   309
       Charles I. Plosser
NINE   **Optimal Monetary Policy and Inequality**   311
       James Bullard
TEN   **Monetary Policies in Practice**   323
       Mary C. Daly
ELEVEN **Discussion of Key Issues Impacting Achievement**
       of the Fed's 2% Inflation Objective   335
       Robert S. Kaplan
TWELVE **Improving Our Monetary Policy Strategy**   345
       Loretta J. Mester

GENERAL DISCUSSION: *Charles I. Plosser, Andrew Levin, John H. Cochrane, Michael D. Bordo, Bill Nelson, Brian Sack, Andy Filardo*

About the Contributors   367

About the Hoover Institution's Working Group
on Economic Policy   377

Index   379

Preface

John H. Cochrane and John B. Taylor

The chapters in this book were prepared and presented to help inform an important review of monetary policy undertaken by the Federal Reserve in 2019. Like the Fed's review, the book focuses on the evaluation of strategies, tools, and communication practices for monetary policy. The chapters address two related questions that are central to an evaluation of policy. First, can a given strategy be improved upon, for example, by altering the degree of data dependence, by reconsidering monetary tools or instruments, or by changing communications about the strategy? Second, how robust are different policy strategies? The aim of the conference and this book is to present the latest research developments and debate these crucial policy questions. It is meant to be an integral component of the monetary policy review, and of the academic and policy community's ongoing evaluation of this review and its underlying strategic issues.

The results went well beyond our expectations. The formal presentations were original and insightful. The market symposium and policy symposium were exciting, with many novel points and suggestions. And the discussions—all recorded and transcribed here—by academic researchers, market participants, members of the media, and monetary policy makers covered much new ground. All of this, in our view, adds greatly to the review of policy that the Federal Reserve began. We are also confident that the results will be useful and relevant to a similar review by the European Central

Bank, which is now currently under way, and to broader understanding of how monetary policy should be conducted.

The leadoff chapter is by Richard Clarida, vice chair of the Federal Reserve Board. He considers the impact of models and markets on the strategy of monetary policy, emphasizing the key question of data dependence. "Data dependence" states that monetary policy should react to economic events as they come along rather than follow a preannounced track, but it should react in a predictable way. Data dependence needs to be clear about what data to respond to and what reaction depends on it, or it can appear to be whimsical and introduce uncertainty into the economy.

Clarida argues that there are two forms of data dependence. The first describes how the instruments of monetary policy should react to the numerical difference between actual economic outcomes and target outcomes for inflation or unemployment. This is a normal rule-like question, and getting the right sign and size of response is essential. That the interest rate should react by more than one to one with the inflation rate is an example of rightsizing mentioned by Clarida.

The second type of data dependence considered by Clarida involves measurement of the key benchmarks in the policy rule: the equilibrium rate of interest and potential GDP, or the natural rate of unemployment. The rule in the first type of data dependence states that the deviation of the interest rate from the natural rate should react to the deviation of GDP from potential, or the deviation of the unemployment rate from the natural rate. One needs to measure those benchmarks as well as the actual unemployment and inflation rates in order to properly set monetary policy. In recent years, empirical research has suggested that both the equilibrium interest rate and the natural rate of unemployment should be adjusted down. That research has also shown, however, just how difficult it is to define and measure these quantities

Clarida emphasizes that both types of data dependence are part of rules-based monetary policy, not a reason to abandon strategies for monetary policy. Clarida does not argue for altering the degree of data dependence, but rather for making it more accurate and embedding it into a rules-based framework. The more accurate and precise is the dependence of policy on data, better the policy strategy will be.

The second chapter is also about data dependence and policy strategy. Here Andrew Lilley and Ken Rogoff make the case, as their title has it, for implementing effective negative interest rate policy. When one plugs real-world inflation or output data into policy rules for the interest rate, one sometimes finds that the rules prescribe negative interest rates. Lilley and Rogoff argue that negative interest rates are no reason to hold the rate at zero or above.

They consider regulatory changes that would allow the interest rate to go more easily to -2 or -3 percent, including steps to stop people from holding large amounts of cash, which pays a better rate, at 0 percent, and potentially undermines negative interest rate policies. They recognize, however, that regulatory lags and other resistance might prevent this change, and thus consider alternatives to negative interest rates, such as quantitative easing (QE) to drive down longer-term interest rates, helicopter money, forward guidance, and a higher inflation target. This part of the paper presents a valuable and balanced summary of the pros and cons of such "unconventional" monetary policies. The authors point out, however, that recent research indicates that quantitative easing may have had little or no effect in the United States, at least outside of the normal lender-of-last-resort role of the central bank and beyond its effect as a signal of how long the Fed is likely to keep interest rates at zero.

Lilley and Rogoff then go on to consider removing the zero or effective lower bound constraint, stating that the "elegant and effective tool to restore monetary policy effectiveness at the zero bound would be unconstrained negative interest rate policy, assuming all necessary legal, institutional, and regulatory changes were first instituted." But they stress that "no country yet has taken the steps necessary to have the kind of deeply negative rates we are discussing here (say, minus 2 percent or more)." The discussion of possible regulatory changes in insightful and valuable, as is their discussion of layering and their response to critics of negative rates, including Monika Piazzesi later in this book. Anyone interested in the zero or effective lower bound on the interest rate—which is anyone interested in monetary policy—should read and consider this chapter carefully.

In his commentary on Lilley and Rogoff, Andrew Levin agrees that "QE and other unconventional monetary policy tools are complex, opaque, and ineffectual," and he therefore proceeds to argue that reform is needed. He proposes a more extensive use of digital cash, drawing on his work with Michael Bordo, to allow negative interest rates to be used more widely.

Chapter 3 also deals with the lower bound on interest rates. Entitled "Tying Down the Anchor: Monetary Policy Rules and the Lower Bound on Interest Rates," its authors, Thomas Mertens, of the San Francisco Fed, and John Williams, president of the New York Fed, use an econometric model to evaluate alternative policy rule and find the one that works best.

Mertens and Williams consider three types of monetary policy rules: (1) a standard inflation-targeting interest rate rule in which the Fed reduces its response to higher inflation and output, in order to bias the economy toward higher interest rates and inflation and thereby reduce the probability of hitting the lower bond; (2) a rule in which the average inflation target is higher than with standard inflation targeting, though the strength of responses to deviations is unchanged; and (3) price-level targeting rules, in which the Fed allows substantial inflation after a low-inflation episode, until the price level recovers to its target, and vice versa. A variant of rule (2) has a similar flavor. It is an interest rate rule that "makes up for past missed stimulus due to the lower bound" by allowing the central bank to condition its interest on the sum of past shortfalls in interest rate cuts, as identified in earlier work by Reifschneider and Williams.

They show, by simulating the policy rules in the model, that the price-level targeting rule and the Reifschneider-Williams make-up-for-shortfalls rule work best among the alternatives. They conclude by noting that "further work is needed to evaluate their robustness by analyzing them within different economic models." They also recommend quantitative assessment of the policy with an estimated larger-scale model.

In Chapter 4, Jim Hamilton offers "Perspectives on US Monetary Policy Tools and Instruments," which points out that quantitative easing does not seem to have affected interest rates and the economy. This finding supports statements by Lilley and Rogoff and by Levin summarized above, and also comments by Peter Fisher in this book.

Hamilton presents empirical evidence in time-series charts that the longer-term interest rate rises during periods when the Federal Reserve is engaged in large-scale purchases of domestic bonds, rather than declining as the Fed expected. See especially Hamilton's figure 4.2. This finding suggests that other Fed research—presented for example at the Chicago Fed review conference—should focus on explaining this reverse impact. The policy impact of quantitative easing on long-term interest rates is a key part of the Fed's review, and a key part of its contingency plan for a future zero bound episode.

With Volker Wieland, we contribute chapter 5, which focuses on the robustness of current policy. The chapter compares the interest rate prescriptions that result from the rules published since 2017 by the Fed in its semiannual *Monetary Policy Report* with the actual path of the federal funds rate. These rules include the Taylor rule, a "balanced-approach" rule, a difference rule that responds to growth rather than levels of inflation and unemployment, and two rules that take particular account of periods with near-zero federal funds rates by implementing a forward-guidance promise to make up for zero bound periods with looser subsequent policy. The chapter evaluates these monetary policy rules in seven well-known macroeconomic models—a small New Keynesian model, a small Old Keynesian model, a larger policy-oriented model, and four other models from the Macro Model Data Base. We regard robustness across models as an essential part of the evaluation process.

The chapter reports that departures—a measure of discretion—from all the rules reported by the Fed were small in most of the 1980s and 1990s, a period of relatively good macroeconomic performance. However, such discretion began to grow again in the early 2000s, though not as large as in the 1970s, and this discretion amplified prior to the 2007–09 recession.

The chapter shows that the rules in the Fed's *Report* work well. However, some are not very robust. The first difference rule does very well in forward-looking New Keynesian models but very poorly in backward-looking Old Keynesian models. The chapter also shows that many of the Fed's reported rules are close to the inflation-output volatility curve of optimal rules. Any rule may be better than no rule.

In commenting in the chapter, David Papell notes that, in general, deviations from rules are very large in poor performance periods and very low during periods with good performance. He also shows the importance of robustness by demonstrating how results from different models are much different from one another.

An important tradition of the monetary policy conferences held at the Hoover Institution in recent years has been the inclusion of market participants and policy makers into the debates and discussions. In keeping this tradition, this book contains two fascinating symposia along these lines.

The first symposium is on the interaction of markets and policy. It brings market participants directly into the discussion, including

Mickey Levy, Scott Minerd, and Laurie Hodrick, with an overview and introduction by George Shultz. The key issue addressed by all three presenters is that policy makers must take the interaction of markets and policy strategies into account when designing monetary strategies. As Hodrick puts it: "The interaction of markets and policy is actually a full circle. Not only are firm valuations affected by Fed policy . . . but the Fed also interprets data from the economy, including stock market price levels, as additional noisy signals with which to set its policy." Levy and Minerd offer suggestions for improvement that, in our view, would improve policy outcomes and should be seriously considered by the Fed. As Levy recommends, "The Fed must take the lead to break its negative self-reinforcing relationship with financial markets by taking steps to rein in its activist fine-tuning of the economy and focus on a strategy for achieving its dual mandate." Minerd argues that the Fed should "allow more volatility in short-term rates through revised open market operations policy or setting a wider fed funds target range. This would allow short-term rates to more accurately reflect changes in the market demand for credit and reserves."

The second symposium is on monetary strategies in practice. It brings Fed policy makers into the discussion, including Jim Bullard, Mary Daly, Robert Kaplan, and Loretta Mester, with Charles Plosser as the chair.

Bullard presents a new overlapping generations model and shows how a policy rule of nominal GDP targeting is optimal. Nominal GDP targeting is similar to price-level targeting, in that it follows a period of less inflation with a period of inflation above target, and expectations of that future inflation may help to stimulate the economy during any current recession. In this logic, it is a new rationale for an old approach to policy, but one that still gets much attention. Daly addresses the lower bound on interest rates, as do Mertens and Williams, and concludes, after carefully considering alternatives, that "average inflation targeting [is] an attractive option."

Kaplan considers the main reasons that inflation has been below the Fed's inflation target of two, and he draws the implication that "we don't want inflation to run persistently below or above our 2 percent target. Sustained deviations from our inflation target could increase the likelihood that inflation expectations begin to drift or become unanchored."

Mester addresses the broadest aspects of the Fed's review of its framework and concludes that "effective communication will be an essential component of the framework. I believe there are ways we can enhance our communications about our policy approach that would make any framework more effective." She has several suggestions; the first, which seems particularly important, is that "simple monetary policy rules can play a more prominent role in our policy deliberations and communications. . . . The Board of Governors has begun to include a discussion of rules as benchmarks in the *Monetary Policy Report*. . . . This suggests that systematic policy making is garnering more support." In many ways, this recommendation and assessment, which concludes the policy panel and the whole conference, highlights the theme of this book *Strategies of Monetary Policy.*

CHAPTER ONE

Models, Markets, and Monetary Policy

Richard H. Clarida

The topic of this volume and the Monetary Policy Conference it originates from, Strategies for Monetary Policy, is especially timely. The Federal Reserve System is conducting a review of the strategy, tools, and communication practices we deploy to pursue our dual-mandate goals of maximum employment and price stability. In this review, we expect to benefit from the insights and perspectives that are presented here, as well as those offered at other conferences devoted to this topic, as we assess possible practical ways in which we might refine our existing monetary policy framework to better achieve our dual-mandate goals on a sustained basis.

This essay is not, however, devoted to a broad review of the Fed's monetary policy framework—that process is ongoing, and I would not want to prejudge the outcome—but it will instead focus on some of the important ways in which economic models and financial market signals help me think about conducting monetary policy in practice after a career of thinking about it in theory.

THE ROLE OF MONETARY POLICY

Let me set the scene with a very brief—and certainly selective—review of the evolution over the past several decades of professional

---

The views expressed are my own and not necessarily those of other Federal Reserve Board members or Federal Open Market Committee participants. I would like to thank Ed Nelson and Bob Tetlow for their assistance in preparing this speech.

thinking about monetary policy. I will begin with Milton Friedman's landmark 1967 American Economic Association presidential address, "The Role of Monetary Policy."[1] This article is, of course, most famous for its message that there is no long-run, exploitable trade-off between inflation and unemployment. And in this paper, Friedman introduced the concept of the "natural rate of unemployment," which today we call u^*.[2] What is less widely appreciated is that Friedman's article also contains a concise but insightful discussion of Wicksell's "natural rate of interest"—r^* in today's terminology—the real interest rate consistent with price stability. But while u^* and r^* provide key reference points in Friedman's framework for assessing how far an economy may be from its long-run equilibrium in labor and financial markets, they play absolutely no role in the monetary policy rule he advocates: his well-known k-percent rule that central banks should aim for and deliver a constant rate of growth of a monetary aggregate. This simple rule, he believed, could deliver long-run price stability without requiring the central bank to take a stand on, model, or estimate either r^* or u^*. Although he acknowledged that shocks would push u away from u^* (and, implicitly, r away from r^*), Friedman felt the role of monetary policy was to operate with a simple quantity rule that did not itself introduce potential instability into the process by which an economy on its own would converge to u^* and r^*.[3] In Friedman's policy framework, u^* and r^* are economic destinations, not policy rule inputs.

---

1. See Friedman (1968). Recent retrospectives on Friedman's (1968) American Economic Association address that consider its implications for monetary policy analysis include Hall and Sargent (2018), Laidler (2018), Mankiw and Reis (2018), and Nelson (2018).

2. See Friedman (1968, 8–11). At roughly the same time, Phelps (1967) derived similar results using a formal economic model.

3. Another consideration motivating Friedman's choice of rule was his concern that a more active monetary policy strategy might be difficult to formulate because of the "long and variable lags" in the effect of monetary policy (a term he had coined in Friedman 1948, 254).

Of course, I do not need to elaborate for this audience that the history of k-percent rules is that they were rarely tried, and when they were tried in the 1970s and the 1980s, they were found to work much better in theory than in practice.[4] Velocity relationships proved to be empirically unstable, and there was often only a very loose connection between the growth rate of the monetary base—which the central bank could control—and the growth rate of the broader monetary aggregates, which are more tightly linked to economic activity. Moreover, the macroeconomic priority in the 1980s in the United States, the United Kingdom, and other major countries was to do "whatever it takes" to break the back of inflation and to restore the credibility squandered by central banks that had been unable or unwilling to provide a nominal anchor after the collapse of the Bretton Woods system.

By the early 1990s, the back of inflation had been broken (thank you, Paul Volcker), conditions for price stability had been achieved (thank you, Alan Greenspan), and the time was right for something to fill the vacuum in central bank practice left by the realization that monetary aggregate targeting was not, in practice, a workable monetary policy framework. Although it was mostly unspoken, there was a growing sense at the time that a simple, systematic framework for central bank practice was needed to ensure that the hard-won gains from breaking the back of inflation were not given away by shortsighted, discretionary monetary experiments that were poorly executed, such as had been the case in the 1970s.

---

4. See Clarida, Galí, and Gertler (1999, Result 10, 1687). Monetary targeting was adopted to a limited degree by the Federal Reserve and other central banks in the 1970s and 1980s, but it did not endure. Even during the period from 1979 to 1982, when the Federal Open Market Committee was most focused on monetary aggregates, policy makers were still concerned with interest rates in the setting of policy, and ultimate objectives for the output gap and inflation figured as criteria for policy decisions. See, for example, Taylor (1995, 1999), Clarida (1999), and Clarida, Galí, and Gertler (2000). In addition, Poole (1970) and Woodford (2003) are key references on the theoretical criticisms of monetary targeting.

POLICY RATE RULES

That vacuum, of course, was filled by John Taylor in his classic 1993 paper, "Discretion vs. Policy Rules in Practice." The average reader of this book need not be reminded of the enormous impact this single paper had not only on the field of monetary economics but also—and more important—on the practice of monetary policy. For our purposes today, I will note that the crucial insight of John's paper was that whereas a central bank could pick the "k" in a "k-percent" rule on its own, without any reference to the underlying parameters of the economy (including r^* and u^*), a well-designed rule for setting a short-term interest rate as a policy instrument should, John argued, respect several requirements.[5] First, the rule should anchor the nominal policy rate at a level equal to the sum of its estimate of the neutral real interest rate (r^*) and the inflation target. Second, to achieve this nominal anchor, the central bank should be prepared to raise the nominal policy rate by more than one-for-one when inflation exceeds target (the Taylor principle). And, third, the central bank should lean against the wind when output—or, via an Okun's law relationship, the unemployment rate—deviates from its estimate of potential (u^*).

In other words, whereas in Friedman's k-percent policy rule u^* and r^* are destinations irrelevant to the choice of k, in the Taylor rule—and most subsequent Taylor-type rules—u^* and r^* are necessary inputs. As Woodford (2003) demonstrates theoretically, the first two requirements for a Taylor-type rule are necessary for it to be consistent with the objective of price stability. The

---

5. On the specification and properties of the Taylor rule, see especially Taylor (1993, 1999), as well as Clarida, Galí, and Gertler (1999, 2000) and Woodford (2003). Another key study of simple interest rate rules was Henderson and McKibbin (1993). It should be noted that a Taylor-type rule is an *instrument* rule for achieving the inflation objective that enters the rule. In practice, it is one way to implement a flexible inflation targeting regime. See Bernanke et al. (1999) and Svensson (1997, 1999) for important contributions on the considerations involved in specifying an inflation-targeting monetary policy strategy.

third requirement—that monetary policy lean against the wind in response to an output or unemployment gap—not only contributes to the objective of price stability, but also is obviously desirable from the perspective of a central bank like the Fed that has a dual mandate.

The Taylor approach to instrument-rule specification has been found to produce good macroeconomic outcomes across a wide range of macroeconomic models. Moreover, in a broad class of both closed and open economy dynamic stochastic general equilibrium, or DSGE, models, Taylor-type rules can be shown to be optimal given the underlying micro foundations of these models.

In original formulations of Taylor-type rules, r^* was treated as constant and set equal to 2 percent, and potential output was set equal to the Congressional Budget Office (CBO) estimates of potential output, or, in specifications using the unemployment rate as the activity variable, u^* was set equal to the CBO's estimate of the natural unemployment rate. These assumptions were reasonable at the time, and in the years before the global financial crisis I myself wrote a number of papers with coauthors that incorporated them.[6]

A DIVE INTO DATA DEPENDENCE

Fast-forward to today. At each Federal Open Market Committee (FOMC) meeting, my colleagues and I consult potential policy rate paths implied by a number of policy rules, as we assess what adjustments, if any, may be required for the stance of monetary policy to achieve and maintain our dual-mandate objectives.[7] A presentation and discussion of several of these rules has been

---

6. See, for example, Clarida, Galí, and Gertler (1999, 2000).

7. For the FOMC's description of its mandate, see the FOMC's (2019) "Statement on Longer-Run Goals and Monetary Policy Strategy." The FOMC first adopted this statement in January 2012 and has reaffirmed the statement at the start of each subsequent year (including in 2019, when all seventeen FOMC participants supported it).

included in the semiannual *Monetary Policy Report* to Congress since July 2017.[8] One thing I have come to appreciate is that as I assess the benefits and costs of alternative policy scenarios based on a set of policy rules and economic projections, it is important to recognize up front that key inputs to this assessment, including u^* and r^*, are unobservable and must be inferred from data via models.[9] I would now like to discuss how I incorporate such considerations into thinking about how to choose among monetary policy alternatives.

A monetary policy strategy must find a way to combine incoming data and a model of the economy with a healthy dose of judgment—and humility!—to formulate, and then communicate, a path for the policy rate most consistent with the central bank's objectives. There are two distinct ways in which I think that the path for the federal funds rate should be data dependent.[10] Monetary policy should be data dependent in the sense that incoming data reveal at any point in time where the economy is relative to the ultimate objectives of price stability and maximum employment. This information on where the economy is relative to the goals of monetary policy is an important input into interest rate feedback rules—after all, they have to feed back on something. Data dependence in this sense is well understood, as it is of the type implied by a large family of policy rules, including Taylor-type

---

8. The box "Monetary Policy Rules and Systematic Monetary Policy" in the Board of Governors' February 2019 *Monetary Policy Report* (MPR) describes how simple policy rules are used in theory and in practical policy making. See Board of Governors (2019). The box "Complexities of Monetary Policy Rules" in the July 2018 MPR discusses how shifts in r^* complicate monetary policy decision making. See Board of Governors (2018). A note, titled "Policy Rules and How Policymakers Use Them," on the board's website covers similar ground and is available at https://www.federalreserve.gov/monetarypolicy/policy-rules-and-how-policymakers-use-them.htm.

9. As Friedman once put it, "I don't know what the natural rate is, neither do you, and neither does anyone else" (quoted in Bennett 1995).

10. See Clarida (2018a, 2018b).

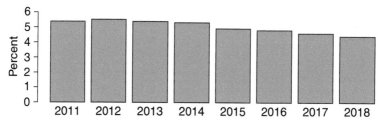

FIGURE 1.1. Assessments of the Longer-Run Normal Unemployment Rate from the Summary of Economic Projections

Source: Federal Reserve Board, Summary of Economic Projections for 2011 to 2013 (https://www.federalreserve.gov/monetarypolicy/fomc_historical.htm) and for 2014 to 2018 (https://www.federalreserve.gov/monetarypolicy/fomccalendars.htm).

Note: Calculated from the final Summary of Economic Projections in each calendar year (November for 2011; December for other years). The value shown is the median of the individual Federal Open Market Committee participant projections for the fourth quarter of each calendar year. (For 2014, the value is the midpoint of the central tendency, as the median is not publicly available.)

rules discussed earlier, in which the parameters of the economy needed to formulate such rules are taken as known.

But, of course, key parameters needed to formulate such rules, including u^* and r^*, are unknown. As a result, in the real world, monetary policy should be—and in the United States, I believe, is—data dependent in a second sense: policy makers should and do study incoming data and use models to extract signals that enable them to update and improve estimates of r^* and u^*. As indicated in the Summary of Economic Projections, FOMC participants have, over the past seven years, repeatedly revised down their estimates of both u^* and r^* as unemployment fell and real interest rates remained well below prior estimates of neutral without the rise in inflation those earlier estimates would have predicted (figures 1.1 and 1.2). And these revisions to u^* and r^* appeared to have had an important influence on the path for the policy rate actually implemented in recent years. One could interpret any changes in the conduct of policy as a shift in the central bank's reaction function. But in my view, when such changes result from revised estimates of u^* or r^*, they merely reflect an updating of an existing reaction function.

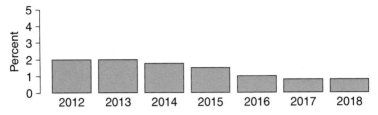

FIGURE 1.2. Assessments of the Longer-Run Inflation-Adjusted Federal Funds
Rate from the Summary of Economic Projections
Source: See the source note of figure 1.
Note: The value shown consists of the median of individual Federal Open Market Committee
(FOMC) participant assessments of the longer-run nominal federal funds rate or midpoint
of the target range, as given in the December Summary of Economic Projections for the indi-
cated year, minus the FOMC's inflation objective of 2 percent. (For each of the years shown,
FOMC participants' projections for the longer-run inflation rate also equaled 2 percent.)

In addition to u^* and r^*, another important input into any monetary policy assessment is the state of inflation expectations. Since
the late 1990s, inflation expectations appear to have been stable and
are often said to be "well anchored." However, inflation expectations
are not directly observable; they must be inferred from models, other
macroeconomic information, market prices, and surveys. Longer-
term inflation expectations that are anchored materially above or
below the 2 percent inflation objective present a risk to price stability.

For this reason, policy makers should and do study incoming
data to extract signals that can be used to update and improve estimates of expected inflation. In many theoretical rational expectations models, expected inflation is anchored at the target level by
assumption. From a risk-management perspective, it makes sense, I
believe, to regularly test this assumption against empirical evidence.

FINANCIAL MARKETS AND MONETARY
POLICY—EXTRACTING SIGNAL FROM NOISE

Because the true model of the economy is unknown, either because
the structure is unknown or because the parameters of a known

structure are evolving, I believe policy makers should consult a number and variety of sources of information about neutral real interest rates and expected inflation, to name just two key macroeconomic variables. Because macroeconomic models of r^* and long-term inflation expectations are potentially misspecified, seeking out other sources of information that are not derived from the same models can be especially useful. To be sure, financial market signals are inevitably noisy, and day-to-day movements in asset prices are unlikely to tell us much about the cyclical or structural position of the economy.[11] However, persistent shifts in financial market conditions can be informative, and signals derived from financial market data—along with surveys of households, firms, and market participants, data, as well as outside forecasts—can be an important complement to estimates obtained from historically estimated and calibrated macroeconomic models.[12]

Interest rate futures and interest rate swaps markets provide one source of high-frequency information about the path and destination for the federal funds rate expected by market participants (figure 1.3). Interest rate option markets, under certain assumptions,

---

11. Uncertainty regarding r^*, u^*, and long-term inflation expectations is not the only source of uncertainty that has implications for monetary policy. Edge, Laubach, and Williams (2005) show how the duration of a productivity shock can affect even the direction of the best monetary policy response. Erceg et al. (2018) find that even in conditions of substantial output gap uncertainty and uncertainty about the slope of the Phillips curve, a notable response to the estimated output gap in a Taylor-type rule is generally beneficial. And Eusepi and Preston (2018) show that replacing model-consistent expectations with forms of adaptive learning means that some, but not all, of the key results regarding best conduct in monetary policy under full information carry through.

12. Like many others, I believe that monetary policy should respond to financial market fluctuations when they have material implications for our outlook for employment and inflation, but monetary policy should not generally target asset prices themselves.

The Federal Reserve uses survey data and conducts surveys of its own on a range of macroeconomic and financial conditions. Among the surveys the Fed conducts are the Senior Loan Officer Opinion Survey on Bank Lending Practices and the Senior Credit Officer Opinion Survey on Dealer Financing Terms. In addition, the staff at the Federal Reserve Board uses disaggregated and high-frequency data to estimate the state of the economy in real time. Such data include disaggregated labor market data from ADP and data on expenditures from credit card transactions.

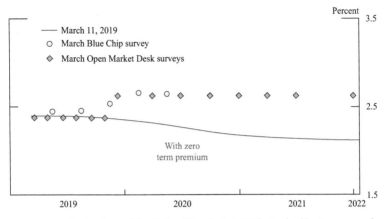

FIGURE 1.3. Projections of the Federal Funds Rate Path Implied by Surveys and Market Quotes

Source: Bloomberg Finance LP; Federal Reserve Board staff estimates; Wolters Kluwer, Blue Chip Financial Forecasts; Federal Reserve Bank of New York, Survey of Primary Dealers and Survey of Market Participants.

Note: The path with zero term premium is estimated using overnight index swap quotes with a spline approach and a term premium of 0 basis points.

can offer insights about the entire ex ante probability distribution of policy rate outcomes for calendar dates near or far into the future (figure 1.4). And, indeed, when one reads that a future policy decision by the Fed or any central bank is "fully priced in," this is usually based on a "straight read" of futures and options prices. But these signals from interest rate derivatives markets are only a pure measure of the expected policy rate path under the assumption of a zero risk premium. For this reason, it is useful to compare policy rate paths derived from market prices with the path obtained from surveys of market participants, which, while subject to measurement error, should not be contaminated with a term premium. Market- and survey-based estimates of the policy rate path are often highly correlated. But when there is a divergence between the path or destination for the policy rate implied by the surveys and a straight read of interest rate derivatives prices, I place at least as much weight on the survey evidence (e.g., derived from

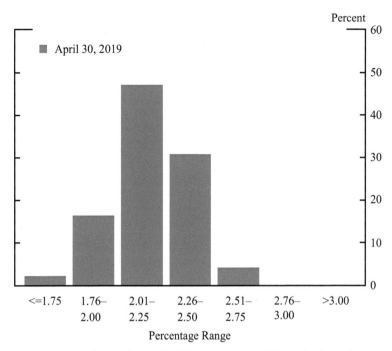

FIGURE 1.4. Market-Implied Probability Distribution of the Federal Funds Rate for Year-End 2019

Source: CME Group; Federal Reserve staff estimates.

Note: Estimated from federal funds futures options (not adjusted for risk premiums). Probabilities are zero for values above 2.75 percent.

the surveys of primary dealers and market participants conducted by the Federal Reserve Bank of New York) as I do on the estimates obtained from market prices (figure 1.3).

The Treasury yield curve can provide another source of information about the expected path and ultimate longer-run destination of the policy rate. But, again, the yield curve, like the interest rate futures strip, reflects not only expectations of the path of short-term interest rates but also liquidity and term premium factors. Thus, to extract signal about policy from noise in the yield curve, a term structure model is required. But different term structure models can and do produce different estimates of the expected path for policy and thus the term premium. Moreover, fluctuations in the term premium on US Treasury yields are driven in part by a significant "global" factor, which complicates efforts to treat the slope of the yield curve as a sufficient statistic for the expected path of US monetary policy (Clarida 2018c). Again, here, surveys of market participants can provide useful information—for example, about "the expected average federal funds rate over the next 10 years," which provides an alternative way to identify the term premium component in the US Treasury curve.

Quotes from the Treasury Inflation-Protected Securities (TIPS) market can provide valuable information about two key inputs to monetary policy analysis: long-run r^* and expected inflation.[13] Direct reads of TIPS spot rates and forward rates are signals of the levels of real interest rates that investors expect at various horizons, and they can be used to complement model-based estimates of r^*. In addition, TIPS market data, together with nominal Treasury yields, can be used to construct measures of "breakeven inflation" or inflation compensation that provide a noisy signal of market expectations of future inflation. But, again, a straight read of breakeven inflation needs to be augmented with a model to filter out the liquidity and risk premium components that place a wedge between inflation compensation and expected inflation.

As is the case with the yield curve and interest rate futures, it is useful to compare estimates of expected inflation derived from breakeven inflation data with estimates of expected inflation obtained from surveys—for example, the expected inflation over

---

13. Well before the launch of the TIPS market, Friedman (1984) stressed the benefits to monetary policy analysis that would arise from the availability of market-based estimates of longer-term inflation expectations, and he contrasted that situation with the one then prevailing, in which it was difficult to ascertain the real yields implied by the market's longer-term nominal yields. In a similar vein, Campbell and Clarida (1987, 105) observed—also in the pre-TIPS era—that "it is hard to measure expected long-term inflation rates."

FIGURE 1.5. Market- and Survey-Based Measures of Longer-Run Inflation Expectations

Note: Estimates based on smoothed nominal and inflation-indexed Treasury yield curves. Michigan survey expectations represent median responses. TIPS is Treasury Inflation-Protected Securities; CPI is consumer price index.

*Adjusted for lagged indexation of Treasury Inflation-Protected Securities (the carry effect).

Source: Federal Reserve Bank of New York; Federal Reserve Board staff calculations; Bloomberg Finance LP; University of Michigan, Surveys of Consumers, http://new.sca.isr.umich.edu.

the next five to ten years from the University of Michigan Surveys of Consumers (figure 1.5). Market- and survey-based estimates of expected inflation are correlated, but, again, when there is a divergence between the two, I place at least as much weight on the survey evidence as on the market-derived estimates.

The examples I have mentioned illustrate the important point that, in practice, there is not typically a clean distinction between "model-based" and "market-based" inference of key economic variables such as r^* and expected inflation. The reason is that market prices reflect not only market expectations but also risk and liquidity premiums that need to be filtered out to recover the object of interest—for example, expected inflation or long-run r^*. This filtering almost always requires a model of some sort, so even market-based estimates of key inputs to monetary policy are, to some extent, model dependent.

IMPLICATIONS FOR MONETARY POLICY

Let me now draw together some implications of the approach to models, markets, and monetary policy I have laid out in these remarks. Macroeconomic models are, of course, an essential tool for monetary policy analysis, but the structure of the economy evolves, and the policy framework must be—and I believe, at the Federal Reserve, is—nimble enough to respect this evolution. Although financial market signals can and sometimes do provide a reality check on the predictions of "a model gone astray," market prices are, at best, noisy signals of the macroeconomic variables of interest, and the process of filtering out the noise itself requires a model—and good judgment. Survey estimates of the long-run destination for key monetary policy inputs can—and, at the Fed, do—complement the predictions from macro models and market prices (figure 1.6).[14] Yes, the Fed's job would be (much) easier if the real world of 2019 satisfied the requirements to run Friedman's k-percent policy rule, but it does not and has not for at least fifty years, and our policy framework must and does reflect this reality.

This reality includes the fact that the US economy is in a very good place. The unemployment rate is at a fifty-year low, real wages are rising in line with productivity, inflationary pressures are muted, and expected inflation is stable. Moreover, the federal funds rate is now in the range of estimates of its longer-run neutral level, and the unemployment rate is not far below many estimates of u^*. Plugging these estimates into a 1993 Taylor rule produces a federal funds rate very close to our current target range for the policy rate.[15]

---

14. It is important to note that the range of model estimates that is shown in the shaded portion of figure 1.6 is not a confidence interval. If parameter uncertainty in the estimates was allowed for, the range would be wider still. Yield curve data can also be used to compute estimates of the neutral rate of interest, as in Bauer and Rudebusch (2019).

15. Figure 1.7 summarizes the overall pattern displayed over time of various model-based estimates of r^*. Recent r^* estimates from the models considered, as well as their confidence intervals, are shown in figure 1.8. The sources for both figures are given at the bottom of figure 1.8.

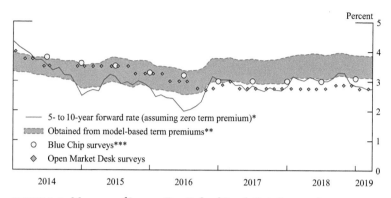

FIGURE 1.6. Measures of Longer-Run Federal Funds Rate Expectations

Source: Wolters Kluwer, Blue Chip Financial Forecasts; Federal Reserve Bank of New York, Survey of Primary Dealers and Survey of Market Participants; Federal Reserve Board staff estimates.

*Monthly average 5- to 10-year forward rate derived from prices of Treasury securities.

**Monthly average 5- to 10-year forward rate adjusted for three alternative model-based term premium estimates using Kim and Wright (2005), D'Amico, Kim, and Wei (2018), and Priebsch (2017).

***Most recent longer-run value is from the December 2018 Blue Chip survey.

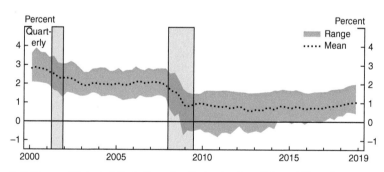

FIGURE 1.7. Historical Evolution of r^*: Estimates from Selected Time-Series Models

Source: Federal Reserve Board staff estimates of the r^* models in figure 8 below.

Note: The shaded bars indicate periods of business recession as defined by the National Bureau of Economic Research.

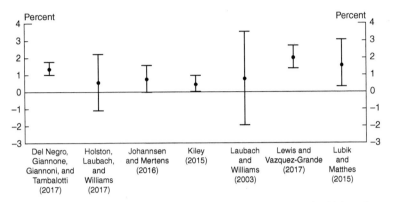

FIGURE 1.8. Uncertainty Bands around Recent Point Estimates of r^* (Selected Models)

Note: The circle gives the r^* estimate for the first quarter of 2019 from each model, while the bars indicate the 95 percent confidence interval for the estimate.

Source: Federal Reserve Board staff calculations, using the models indicated on the x-axis.

So with the economy operating at or very close to the Fed's dual-mandate objectives and with the policy rate in the range of FOMC participants' estimates of neutral, we can, I believe, afford to be data dependent—in both senses of the term as I have discussed—as we assess what, if any, further adjustments in our policy stance might be required to maintain our dual-mandate objectives of maximum employment and price stability.

References

Bauer, Michael D., and Glenn D. Rudebusch. 2018. "Interest Rates under Falling Stars." Federal Reserve Bank of San Francisco Working Paper 2017-16, revised January 2019.

Bennett, Amanda. 1995. "Inflation Calculus: Business and Academia Clash over a Concept: 'Natural' Jobless Rate." *Wall Street Journal*, January 24.

Bernanke, Ben S., Thomas Laubach, Frederic S. Mishkin, and Adam S. Posen. 1999. *Inflation Targeting: Lessons from the International Experience.* Princeton, NJ: Princeton University Press.

Board of Governors of the Federal Reserve System. 2018. *Monetary Policy Report,* July. Washington, DC: Board of Governors.

———. 2019. *Monetary Policy Report,* February. Washington, DC: Board of Governors.

Campbell, John Y., and Richard H. Clarida. 1987. "The Dollar and Real Interest Rates." *Carnegie-Rochester Conference Series on Public Policy* 27 (August): 103–39.

Clarida, Richard H. 1999. Comment on John B. Taylor, "A Historical Analysis of Monetary Policy Rules." In *Monetary Policy Rules,* edited by John B. Taylor, 341–44. Chicago: University of Chicago Press.

———. 2018a. "Outlook for the U.S. Economy and Monetary Policy." Speech given at the Peterson Institute for International Economics, Washington, DC, October 25.

———. 2018b. "Data Dependence and U.S. Monetary Policy." Speech at the Clearing House and the Bank Policy Institute Annual Conference, New York, November 27.

———. 2018c. "The Factor Content of Equilibrium Exchange Rates." NBER Working Paper Series 24735, June. Cambridge, MA: National Bureau of Economic Research.

Clarida, Richard, Jordi Galí, and Mark Gertler. 1999. "The Science of Monetary Policy: A New Keynesian Perspective." *Journal of Economic Literature* 37, no. 4 (December): 1661–707.

———. 2000. "Monetary Policy Rules and Macroeconomic Stability: Evidence and Some Theory." *Quarterly Journal of Economics* 115, no. 1 (February): 147–80.

D'Amico, Stefania, Don H. Kim, and Min Wei. 2018. "Tips from TIPS: The Informational Content of Treasury Inflation-Protected Security Prices." *Journal of Financial and Quantitative Analysis* 53, no. 1 (February): 395–436.

Del Negro, Marco, Domenico Giannone, Marc P. Giannoni, and Andrea Tambalotti. 2017. "Safety, Liquidity, and the Natural Rate of Interest." *Brookings Papers on Economic Activity* (Spring): 235–94.

Edge, Rochelle M., Thomas Laubach, and John C. Williams. 2005. "Monetary Policy and Shifts in Long-Run Productivity Growth." Unpublished paper, Board of Governors of Federal Reserve System, Division of Monetary Affairs, May.

Erceg, Christopher, James Hebden, Michael Kiley, David López-Salido, and Robert Tetlow. 2018. "Some Implications of Uncertainty and Misperception for Monetary Policy." Finance and Economics Discussion Series 2018-059, August. Washington, DC: Board of Governors of the Federal Reserve System.

Eusepi, Stefano, and Bruce Preston. 2018. "The Science of Monetary Policy: An Imperfect Knowledge Perspective." *Journal of Economic Literature* 56, no. 1 (March): 3–59.

Federal Open Market Committee. 2019. "Statement on Longer-Run Goals and
    Monetary Policy Strategy" (adopted effective January 24, 2012; amended
    as effective January 29, 2019). Washington, DC: Board of Governors of the
    Federal Reserve System https://www.federalreserve.gov/monetarypolicy/files
    /FOMC_LongerRunGoals.pdf.

Friedman, Milton. 1948. "A Monetary and Fiscal Framework for Economic
    Stability." *American Economic Review* 38, no. 3 (June): 245–64.

———. 1968. "The Role of Monetary Policy." *American Economic Review* 58, no. 1
    (March 1968): 1–17.

———. 1984. "Financial Futures Markets and Tabular Standards." *Journal of
    Political Economy* 92, no. 1 (February): 165–67.

Hall, Robert E., and Thomas J. Sargent. 2018. "Short-Run and Long-Run Effects
    of Milton Friedman's Presidential Address." *Journal of Economic Perspectives*
    32, no. 1 (Winter): 121–34.

Henderson, Dale W., and Warwick J. McKibbin. 1993. "A Comparison of Some
    Basic Monetary Policy Regimes for Open Economies: Implications of Different
    Degrees of Instrument Adjustment and Wage Persistence." *Carnegie-Rochester
    Conference Series on Public Policy* 39 (December): 221–317.

Holston, Kathryn, Thomas Laubach, and John C. Williams. 2017. "Measuring the
    Natural Rate of Interest: International Trends and Determinants." *Journal of
    International Economics* 108, no. S1 (May): S59–75.

Johannsen, Benjamin K., and Elmar Mertens. 2016. "A Time Series Model of
    Interest Rates with the Effective Lower Bound." Finance and Economics
    Discussion Series 2016-033, April. Washington, DC: Board of Governors of
    the Federal Reserve System.

Kiley, Michael T. 2015. "What Can the Data Tell Us about the Equilibrium Real
    Interest Rate?" Finance and Economics Discussion Series 2015-077, August.
    Washington, DC: Board of Governors of the Federal Reserve System.

Kim, Don H., and Jonathan H. Wright. 2005. "An Arbitrage-Free Three-Factor
    Term Structure Model and the Recent Behavior of Long-Term Yields and
    Distant-Horizon Forward Rates." Finance and Economics Discussion Series
    2005-33, August. Washington, DC: Board of Governors of the Federal Reserve
    System.

Laidler, David. 2018. "Why the Fuss? Friedman (1968) after Fifty Years." Department
    of Economics Research Report 2018-4, May. London, ON: Department of
    Economics, University of Western Ontario.

Laubach, Thomas, and John C. Williams. 2003. "Measuring the Natural Rate of
    Interest." *Review of Economics and Statistics* 85, no. 4 (November): 1063–70.

Lewis, Kurt F., and Francisco Vazquez-Grande. 2017. "Measuring the Natural Rate of Interest: Alternative Specifications." *Finance and Economics Discussion Series* 2017-059, February, revised May 2017. Washington, DC: Board of Governors of the Federal Reserve System.

Lubik, Thomas A., and Christian Matthes. 2015. "Time-Varying Parameter Vector Autoregressions: Specification, Estimation, and an Application." Federal Reserve Bank of Richmond, *Economic Quarterly* 101 (Fourth Quarter): 323–52.

Mankiw, N. Gregory, and Ricardo Reis. 2018. "Friedman's Presidential Address in the Evolution of Macroeconomic Thought." *Journal of Economic Perspectives* 32, no. 1 (Winter): 81–96.

Nelson, Edward. 2018. "Seven Fallacies concerning Milton Friedman's 'The Role of Monetary Policy.'" *Finance and Economics Discussion Series* 2018-013, February. Washington, DC: Board of Governors of the Federal Reserve System.

Phelps, Edmund S. 1967. "Phillips Curves, Expectations of Inflation and Optimal Unemployment over Time." *Economica* 34, no. 135 (August): 254–81.

Poole, William. 1970. "Optimal Choice of Monetary Policy Instruments in a Simple Stochastic Macro Model." *Quarterly Journal of Economics* 84, no. 2 (May): 197–216.

Priebsch, Marcel A. 2017. "A Shadow Rate Model of Intermediate-Term Policy Rate Expectations." *FEDS Notes*, October 4. Washington, DC: Board of Governors of the Federal Reserve System.

Svensson, Lars E. O. 1997. "Inflation Forecast Targeting: Implementing and Monitoring Inflation Targets." *European Economic Review* 41, no. 6 (June): 1111–46.

———. 1999. "Inflation Targeting as a Monetary Policy Rule." *Journal of Monetary Economics* 43, no. 3 (June): 607–54.

Taylor, John B. 1993. "Discretion versus Policy Rules in Practice." *Carnegie-Rochester Conference Series on Public Policy* 39 (December): 195–214.

———. 1995. "Changes in American Economic Policy in the 1980s: Watershed or Pendulum Swing?" *Journal of Economic Literature* 33, no. 2 (June): 777–84.

———. 1999. "A Historical Analysis of Monetary Policy Rules." In *Monetary Policy Rules,* edited by John B. Taylor, 319–41. Chicago: University of Chicago Press.

Woodford, Michael. 2003. *Interest and Prices: Foundations of a Theory of Monetary Policy.* Princeton. NJ: Princeton University Press.

GENERAL DISCUSSION

MICHAEL BORDO: My question is about the concept of data dependence. It seems pretty close to what Ben Bernanke and Rick Mishkin called "constrained discretion" a few years ago. So the question is, where do you draw the line between the constrained part, which could be what you call rule-like behavior, and discretion, which could be looking at everything, that is, fine-tuning. So the real question is how do you make that distinction?

RICHARD CLARIDA: It's a great point, and I agree it would be easier if u^* and r^* didn't move around. And so I agree with you. There needs to be a discipline there. And I think the ultimate discipline on the Fed or any central bank is whether or not we do achieve and maintain our objectives, so if the central bank consistently gets r^* and u^* wrong, and inflation moves up, as it did in the seventies, then discretion is not serving well. But I do believe that what focuses the Fed and other successful central banks is that they're being evaluated on achieving their objectives. And of course, not only actual but also expected inflation is a key element of this. So I think that in reality that is the check that we need to respect and we do respect.

JOHN TAYLOR: One of the things that I found very interesting about your remarks it that there's not only a strategy or rule, there's a way to determine the u^* or r^*. And I think sometimes one gets concerned that so much focus on u^* and r^* tends to dominate, and the fluctuations in those are bigger than any kind of rule. And I think you're trying to prevent that, but can you comment on that?

CLARIDA: You're right. And I think that was why I wanted to devote my remarks today to that, because I think the central issue that faces the Fed and other central banks is that it would be irresponsible to ignore the evolution of the economy. But also, you certainly need a check and a discipline and an approach to doing that, which is why I suggested in my talk, speaking for myself, I don't want to put all my eggs in the basket of either a theoretical model or market prices, so I'm constantly checking back and forth. And so, I think you need both. And as I mentioned in response to Mike's question, the ultimate discipline is the outcomes achieved, both in terms of inflation and in the case of the Fed as the dual mandate. And here, inflation expectations are also key.

So, John, when you and I began our careers in the seventies and eighties, if we'd had data on TIPS, I'm sure in the seventies they would have shown expected inflation was not 2, it was 14. I would have hoped that you and I would have paid attention to that then. So I think that's where the market pricing comes in as well.

CHRIS CROWE: You said that you saw the economy in a good place right now, and it's hard to disagree with that in the short term. But if you look historically, it's quite typical when the unemployment rate is this low that within a year or two the economy is in not such a good place, heading toward recession. Do you see any risks in that direction right now, and if not, what's different this time around?

CLARIDA: Obviously, policy needs to be forward looking. So, the decisions that a central bank makes today need to depend on the view that it has on the evolution of the economy, long and variable lags, as [Milton] Friedman taught us. And of course, at the Federal Reserve, we are very focused on looking at a wide range of indicators about trends in labor markets, in goods markets, and in financial market–based estimates of surveys. So, we do not see that evidence now. But in any economy that's evolving in a stochastic fashion, there are going to be upside and downside risks on that path. And central banks need to be vigilant and alert to both sides of those risks.

CHARLES PLOSSER: Thank you, Rich, for a great talk. I enjoyed it very
much. I want to follow up on Mike Bordo's question just a little
bit. I believe you're right, the ultimate test is, does the Fed meet
its mandated goals. That's one of the things that Milton would
have argued, I would think, with his *k*-percent rule, but it's more
than just meeting the goals. It's about the instability and uncertainty created in the economy. So you didn't mention that part
of it. And so, you can say, you might ask the question, well, is the
Fed meeting its goal? But at the same time, there's a question of
volatility or instability or uncertainty that can be created in the
policy reaction function, or the discretion that's being exercised.
So how do you balance that, because that's kind of like the counterfactual that, are you introducing more instability than might
be necessary by the discretionary part of your view?

CLARIDA: And I understand that, and indeed, I did make reference
in my prepared remarks to Friedman's case for the *k*-percent
rule, that it was sort of the Hippocratic Oath to do no harm.
And I certainly think my colleagues keep that in mind as well,
but again with the discipline that we have to deal and implement policy in the world as we find it, not as in the world that
Friedman assumed. That being said, certainly, none of us wants
to nor do we believe that we're a source of instability. But clearly,
that's an important discipline that we need to respect.

KRISHNA GUHA: Thank you. So, Rich, in your discussion you talked
about the importance of filtering for risk premia and so on
when we're extracting signals about expectations in financial
markets. But I wanted to ask you about risk premia themselves.
So, if we were to observe, which I think we have observed, that
persistent negative term premia, specifically persistent negative inflation risk premia, suggests that financial market participants see a need to ensure against the low-inflation state,
what would the implications for that be for policy? Would it
suggest the rule or framework needs to be reconsidered? Or

can you imagine that you were conducting policy appropriately, and the equilibrium condition was still a sizable negative inflation risk premium?

CLARIDA: I think there are several pieces to that Krishna. First, yes, we—and you—do consult those indicators of those tail risks. But as you can appreciate, those are all model specific, because, to get a little wonkish here, you have to specify the stochastic discount factor or risk-neutral pricing. So, yes. We are alert to that.

I think more generally, though, the way I think the essence of your question that's relevant for the Fed and other central banks is, because we're operating in a world of low riskless rates, a low r^* world, and it is a global phenomenon, and that's a factor that impinges on the United States, the fact that you have very, very low riskless rates in many other advanced countries, clearly a global capital market's going to have an influence here. And so, I do think that central banks need to be alert—that closer to the zero bound for any given probability of shocks, you're more likely to hit it. And that does need to factor into the way that we think about the evolution of policy, but I don't think in a mechanical way, as I'm sure you weren't suggesting.

SEBASTIAN EDWARDS: I want to follow up on what you just said right now. So those of us who follow the market and the macro picture will listen very carefully to what the chairman says, to what you say, to what your colleagues say. But we also listen to Mario Draghi and Mark Carney, and we look at the international picture. And until your answer to the previous question, you had sort of ignored that. And I know that you have done a lot of work on the subject. Is there information out there in the currency markets or in other nations? John Taylor mentioned your paper from a few years back, "Optimal Monetary Policy in Closed Versus Open Economies," but your talk from my perspective was very US centered, which is right for the vice chairman. But what about the signals that come from the open economy?

CLARIDA: A little self-promotion. So I gave a speech at the Banque de France conference about a month ago called "Global Considerations for US Monetary Policy." So I will send you that. There's an entire speech on that. And I did mention in my remarks, and certainly my professional career was devoted to this, there are a lot of US asset prices that have a substantial global component as predicted by both economic theory and empirical evidence. And so certainly, when I start talking about market prices, especially for bond yields, there's a very substantial global component that one needs to sort out. And it's just simply not the case that either the slope or the level of the US yield curve by itself is a sufficient statistic for the outlook for the United States. But that was another speech.

BRIAN SACK: So, long-term inflation expectations obviously are playing a key role in all of this framework discussion. And you can imagine that if you had a good measure of them, they would play a huge role in terms of measuring the accountability of the central bank and even as a variable that can enter into your reaction function. Now, as you noted, we don't have good measures of them. It's very complicated to extract signals from markets, to interpret surveys correctly, and to account for the whole set of information. But I wanted to ask, do you think we can do better than just saying, "Well, we don't measure them very well?" I mean, would there be an advantage to the Fed actually stating what its best reading is at any point in time of where long-term inflation expectations are, taking into account all these signals? Maybe that would deliver some accountability and a chance to actually be systematic in terms of how policy responds to them?

CLARIDA: I think it's an excellent point. What I would say, and I think Bob Rubin and Larry Summers deserve a lot of credit for actually introducing the TIPS market, because for all of its flaws and all of its problems, I think we're much better off as policy makers looking at those noisy signals than having zero signal.

So, my own sense is there's no unique signal of inflation expectations as there is for an absolute price index. So the reality is, you're going to always be comparing signals from different sources, you know? And whether or not one can come up with an ideal or index of weighting those is certainly something I haven't thought about but certainly something worth thinking about.

JOHN COCHRANE: Well, but you're willing to go on to ways we've learned beyond what Milton taught. It's not eternal verities. We're all data dependent in a way. And I liked the historical way you started. Which I put as: you know, once we went to the Taylor rule in the 1990s, u^* and r^* were sort of fixed numbers, and we've learned that they move over time. The Fed used to think everything was demand, and now gee, maybe what we can loosely call "supply" moves around. But there still seems to be an assumption that these things move very slowly through time. Whereas in fact, I think today's challenge is maybe u^*, r^*, and potential GDP move much more quickly than we thought. We have with us the father of real business cycle theory, Ed Prescott, in the room, who showed us that in fact a lot of variation can come from supply. And that's the Fed's central problem. Output goes up this quarter—was that demand that we need to offset, or was that supply?—which was just fine. And thinking about it, the Fed doesn't do much modeling of what is the changes of incentives in the tax code. What are the effects of deregulation? To what extent are we seeing high-frequency changes in supply? And it's the elephant in the room. Today's *Wall Street Journal* op-ed took the Fed to task for not thinking enough about whether even shorter-term fluctuations are supply-potential stars rather than signals of demand to be offset. So where do you think that's going? Should we be moving more in that direction, or is the current progress satisfactory?

CLARIDA: Well, I would not like to say to an academic audience that progress is satisfactory, so we can do better. But certainly, John, in my six or seven months as Fed vice chair, in a number of my public remarks I've tried to emphasize the supply side. And you just have to look at the data. Labor force participation is part of supply. Productivity is part of supply. And it's certainly something that we discuss extensively in our meeting. So I can assure you it's certainly not something that's ignored in the Eccles Building.

CHAPTER TWO

The Case for Implementing Effective Negative Interest Rate Policy

Andrew Lilley and Kenneth Rogoff

1. INTRODUCTION

This paper explores the case for gradually instituting the changes necessary to implement unconstrained negative interest rate policy as a long-term solution to the zero lower bound on interest rates (or more precisely the effective lower bound). To be clear, we distinguish between the very limited negative interest rate policy that has already been tried in Europe and Japan and the unconstrained negative interest rate policy we consider here. Effective unconstrained negative interest rate policy requires, at a minimum, that policy makers take administrative measures to forestall wholesale hoarding of physical currency by financial firms, insurance companies, and pension funds.[1] We shall argue that if unconstrained negative interest rate policy can be implemented, it would be by

---

1. A variety of approaches for implementing negative rates ranging from administrative measures to precluding large-scale hoarding to a dual electronic/physical currency system are discussed in Rogoff (2016, 2017). See Bordo and Levin (2019) for an approach that involves a combination of administrative measures and a digital retail currency. Agarwal and Kimball (2019) give a nuanced discussion of transition issues; see also Agarwal and Kimball (2015).

The authors are grateful to conference participants and especially Michael Bordo, Matthew Johnson, Andrew Levin, Edward Nelson, and John Taylor for helpful comments on an earlier draft for the May 2019 conference.

far the most elegant and stable long-term solution to the severe
limits on monetary tools that have emerged since the financial crisis. Admittedly, the question of how to resuscitate monetary policy
effectiveness is of more immediate relevance in Europe and Japan,
where interest rates remain at the effective lower bound (in many
cases mildly negative) more than a decade after the global financial
crisis and more than two decades after Japan's financial crisis. But
even the United States is likely to face severe constraints in the
event of another financial crisis, possibly even in a deep recession.

No one should expect the United States to be an early adopter
of unconstrained negative interest rate policy, especially given the
central role of the dollar in the global financial system. But we
would strongly disagree with those who say it is unthinkable and
will lead to widespread market dysfunction. As of October 2019,
over $15 trillion worth of bonds traded at negative interest rates
internationally, without market breakdown. On top of that, over
1 trillion euros worth of bank deposits carried negative rates in
the eurozone alone. There are ample historical precedents for cases
where monetary policy innovation was resisted on the grounds that
markets would collapse, including the move from fixed to floating
exchange rates in the 1970s. Perhaps the closest analogy is during
the 1951 episode when the Federal Reserve abandoned its bond
price pegging program. As Milton Friedman commented:

> Before the Federal Reserve gave up the pegging of the bond price, we
> heard all over the lot that a free market in bonds was going to be cha-
> otic, that the interest rate might go heaven-high or down, there might
> be capital losses, savings institutions might well be wiped out by their
> capital losses, and that we needed some basic peg price on which the
> market could form its anticipation. We abandoned the pegged price.
> None of these things happened. (Friedman and Roosa 1967, 173)

To be sure, implementing effective unconstrained negative
interest rate policy will require a host of legal, regulatory, and tax

changes, and not all of these can be instituted by the central bank alone.[2] The obstacles in different countries will vary. It is notable, however, that in countries that have implemented mild negative rate policy, none has tackled the main challenge, which is how to prevent paper currency hoarding and, as a corollary, how to protect bank profitability if rates go deeply negative. Of course, if one believes that it is impossible to have negative deposit rates, then the capacity for instituting negative rate policy is very limited. But in our view, once wholesale hoarding is dealt with (the vast majority of retail depositors can straightforwardly be exempted from negative rates [Rogoff 2016, 2017]), then the pass-through of negative rates to wholesale bank customers should be straightforward, just as the pass-through of negative policy rates has been to mortgages and other wholesale private debt obligations in many countries in Europe. In general, all of the various approaches to instituting unconstrained negative rate policy should be increasingly easy to navigate as paper currency becomes further marginalized in legal, tax-compliant transactions (outside low-value transactions) and as countries deal with financial inclusion.

So how might the monetary authorities discourage wholesale hoarding of currency in the event of deeply negative interest rates? There are a broad number of approaches that do not require going cashless. These include raising the cost of hoarding by phasing out large-denomination notes,[3] imposing fees on wholesale redeposits of currency at the central bank, and instituting regulatory limitations on legal hoarding facilities (Rogoff 2016, 2017). Bordo and Levin (2019) offer a more fully articulated administrative approach involving instituting a retail central bank digital currency.

It should be noted that there is a way to eliminate the hoarding problem without any change to the issuance or regulation of paper

---

2. Rogoff (2016) discusses a number of the issues, and Agarwal and Kimball (2019) provide an extremely useful handbook on transitioning to unconstrained negative rate policy.

3. Rogoff (1998) argues that phasing out large-denomination notes would be helpful in combatting tax evasion and crime, even independent of interest rate–setting issues.

currency. It involves taking steps so that electronic currency (currently bank reserves at the central bank) becomes the unit of account, and creating a crawling peg between electronic currency and paper currency (analogous to the proposal of Eisler 1933). Admittedly, there are complications to the Eisler plan having to do with the fact that paper currency and electronic currency are not perfect substitutes.

Until now, central banks up against the effective zero lower bound have been relying mainly on various forms of quasi-fiscal policy, but the weight of evidence suggests these are far less effective than normal interest rate policy. Often lost in the popular discussion, or at best hidden behind dubious political economy arguments, is the fact that central banks are wholly owned subsidiaries of the central government. For example, when central banks purchase long-term government bonds by issuing bank reserves that match the short-term Treasury bill rate, this amounts to no more than shortening the maturity structure of the consolidated government balance sheet. Treasuries do this routinely and are perfectly capable of handling it on their own and on scale. In general, the fiscal authorities have ample tools to accomplish (or undo) any quasi-fiscal actions that central banks might take. They have access to greater resources and certainly have greater political legitimacy. The quasi-fiscal powers of the central bank are essential only in crises where the ability to move quickly trumps other considerations.

Aside from quasi-fiscal policies, alternatives such as forward guidance have proved to be of very limited effectiveness as well. The main problem is that zero bound episodes last for years if not decades, making the credibility and commitment problems to promising elevated future inflation (after escape from the zero bound) exceedingly challenging. Raising inflation targets is a serious alternative to negative rate policy, but it, too, comes with severe limitations. A modest rise in the inflation target (including proposals on keeping 2 percent while adopting an inflation-averaging target) would not create the kind of policy space needed for dealing with deep recessions, much less systemic financial crises. A more significant rise in inflation targets, on top of greatly distorting relative prices even in normal times, would eventually lead to shorter nominal contract lengths and an increase in indexing. Both factors would limit the effectiveness of monetary policy, possibly even to the point of making an increase in the target inflation rate counterproductive. Another important drawback is that higher inflation targets would undermine central bank credibility after decades of committing to inflation targets of 2 percent or less. Last but by no means least, it is not clear how to make a higher target credible without having the tools (such as negative interest rate policy) to achieve it. The experience of Japan in raising its inflation target to 2 percent in 2013, accompanied by a large fiscal stimulus, and still failing to raise medium-term inflation expectations is emblematic.

In the first section of the paper, we discuss other options for dealing with monetary paralysis at the zero bound. The second part of the paper highlights the credibility struggles that major central banks have had in keeping inflation expectations at target over the medium term, arguably greatly exacerbated by investor skepticism that central banks have the tools to create inflation, even when the situation warrants it. This seems to be even more true today than during early rounds of quantitative easing when, as we show (following Lilley and Rogoff 2019), markets viewed there as being a small but measurable possibility that quantitative easing (QE) could lead to very high inflation for a decade. The third section of the paper discusses a range of issues related to implementing effective negative interest policy, including both economic and political economy problems. We conclude by arguing that the obstacles to unconstrained negative rate policy all seem fairly minor compared with some of the radical alternatives that have been proposed (e.g., the inherent difficulties implementing precisely calibrated, well-timed, and highly credible countercyclical fiscal policy on steroids). In a technical appendix, we show that even in the United States today, markets have at times attached a significant probability to having interest rates become at least mildly negative.

2. ALTERNATIVES TO NEGATIVE
INTEREST RATE POLICY

One has to acknowledge that invoking significant negative nominal interest rates (say, at least −2 to −3 percent) in a deep recession or a financial crisis would be, at this stage, an experimental policy. Even after making any necessary legal, tax, and regulatory modifications—above all having a mechanism for discouraging wholesale cash hoarding by financial institutions, pension funds, and insurance companies—there is always a possibility of unintended consequences. To put this risk in perspective, we first discuss in this section alternatives that have been proposed. We divide these into four broad classes: (1) "pure quantitative easing" policies that (we argue) do little more than change the maturity structure of government debt in a way the Treasury can do at least as effectively, (2) "fiscal quantitative easing" policies where the central bank buys private assets; the same equivalent policy can be achieved by having the Treasury trade government debt for private debt at face value, then having the central bank buy up the government debt via quantitative easing, (3) having the central bank engage in pure fiscal policy via (market interest-bearing) helicopter money, and (4) policies that genuinely relate to monetary policy, including forward guidance and changing the inflation target.[4]

2.1. Pure Quantitative Easing and Maturity Management of the Consolidated Government Balance Sheet

We begin with pure quantitative easing (pure QE), where the central bank issues bank reserves to purchase medium- and long-term debt. The degree of confusion surrounding these pure QE poli-

---

4. The discussion here is necessarily brief; for a more thorough discussion, see Rogoff (2016). For excellent recent discussions of how alternative monetary instruments have worked to date, see Bordo and Levin (2019) or Eberly et al. (2019).

cies is remarkable, in part because many overlook the equivalence between money and debt at the zero bound, and even more so because central banks have not wanted to acknowledge the inadequacy of their instruments. Point number one is that central banks do not have their own independent balance sheet. Any profits or losses the central bank earns pass through directly to the central government. (There is an important nuance in the case of the European Central Bank's balance sheet that we shall come to shortly.)

True, one way a central bank's independence can be compromised is if the market value of its assets has a negative net value. As is well known, this is somewhat meaningless since the central bank's monopoly over currency creation means it can never go bankrupt if its liabilities are in its own currency. The central bank can be reprimanded. It can be absorbed back into the Treasury it grew out of. But it cannot be disowned.

We now turn to the question of whether quantitative easing involves creating a new class of government liabilities that might fundamentally alter debt management. The short answer is a resounding no, as established by Greenwood et al. (2015a, 2015b, 2015c). Consider first the current situation in the United States (as of May 2019), where both required and excess bank reserves have a virtually identical yield to the one-week Treasury bill rate. Consider a quantitative easing exercise where the Treasury issues $100 billion in thirty-year debt, which the Fed soaks up by issuing $100 billion in bank reserves to buy up the debt. The net effect is that privately held floating rate debt has risen by $100 billion and privately held long-term debt has fallen by the same amount. The same could be achieved by having the Treasury just issue 100-billion-dollar debt at a one-week maturity (instead of long-term) and having the Fed do nothing.

Nor does the Fed have greater capacity to perform this maturity transformation. In any given year, the US Treasury typically has to roll over debt roughly equal to the Fed's $4 trillion postcrisis balance sheet, and should it desire to move faster, it buys up long-term debt before it matures, issuing very short-term debt to do so. The central bank is very much a junior partner when it comes to debt maturity management. Indeed, overreliance on quasi-fiscal policy deeply compromises central bank independence, since the fiscal authorities can undo all of the central bank's actions if they do not accord with the government's objectives. Whether inadvertently or not, the US Treasury's post-financial-crisis actions to extend the maturity structure of debt worked at cross-purposes with the central bank's quantitative easing policies to shorten maturity (Greenwood et al. 2015a).

Some may disagree and argue that changing the maturity structure of government debt on its own is enough, since the implementation of interest rate targeting has always involved the Fed purchasing securities, that is, merely changing the maturity structure of government debt. This critique overlooks the fundamental difference between reserves and government debt under conventional monetary policy. Away from the zero lower bound, swapping government securities for excess reserves (or the promise to) will serve to change the prevailing interest rate since banks would rather lend the excess reserves at a positive rate than hold them. It is only at the zero lower bound that swapping government debt for reserve balances is merely a maturity transformation.

A final question is whether maturity management is a substitute for monetary policy. Although early evidence suggested some effect from pure quantitative easing in the United States (again, this means central bank buying of government bonds), most recent academic authors have argued that the effects were extremely limited and in no way comparable to conventional interest rate policy (see Greenlaw et al. 2018; Chung et al. 2019). Eberly, Stock, and Wright (2019) are somewhat more positive and suggest that QE might have been more effective if the Fed had gone bigger and earlier. However, we argue here that one must also take into account that the first time around, markets expected much more of a long-run inflation effect than actually transpired. Specifically, in the third section, we show that while inflation expectations remained robust during QE1 and QE2, this was mostly attributable to a belief that inflation may accelerate to be well above target in the coming decade—a belief that rapidly disappeared after the Fed exited the zero lower bound without seeing a boom in money demand. This expectation of high inflation, or perhaps the misunderstanding of whether it is caused by pure quantitative easing, is unlikely to be repeated in any future iterations.

It must be noted that the European Central Bank is something of an exception, as there is no fiscal counterpart to its actions. In essence, when the European Central Bank (ECB) engages in QE, it is effectively issuing a short-term synthetic Eurobond to buy up the national debts of individual countries. There is no central government yet willing and able to perform the same function, and ECB quantitative easing certainly appears to have been very effective as a crisis management tool. That said, the difficulties that Europe has had in reaching its inflation target underscores that even in Europe, QE is no substitute for normal interest rate policy.

2.2 Fiscal Quantitative Easing

We next turn to fiscal quantitative easing, in which the central bank purchases private sector assets. There is no real debate about the fact that fiscal QE played a critical role during the financial crisis in preventing markets from freezing up and collapsing with potentially dire consequences. Nor should there be any debate that emergency credit policy is a perfectly valid function of the central bank; in a crisis, swift, effective action can sharply reduce costs to the real economy and (likely) the government balance sheet. Although this may involve having the central bank absorb a lot of junk debt on its balance sheet, in most countries the usual presumption is that within a relatively short period, the central government will create a special purpose vehicle to transfer the risk.

Outside of emergencies, fiscal QE can perfectly well be executed by the central government through a variety of mechanisms, most commonly by having the central government issue debt guarantees. Fiscal QE certainly has an effect, but outside of crises, it once again is much less powerful than normal interest rate policy, as the Bank of Japan's experience has clearly illustrated. On top of that, buying private debt in normal times involves picking winners and losers and is effectively a type of industrial or development policy. One can debate the extent to which the government should intervene directly into private credit markets. In principle, the real effects can be very large if the intervention is massive enough, but the distortions can be large too. In general, most advanced economies regard unelected central banker as ill suited to making these fundamentally political decisions. Regardless, the conclusion has to be that the fiscal QE is ill suited as a substitute for conventional monetary policy in normal times.

2.3. Helicopter Money, Debt Destruction, and Hyperactive Fiscal Policy

This takes us to helicopter money, where the central bank takes the lead in initiating fiscal transfers, which Buiter (2003), Turner (2015), and Bernanke (2016) have advocated, and which is enormously popular among the commentariat. In its crudest form, helicopter money involves having the central bank print money to issue pro-rata transfers to the public. This is, of course, equivalent to having the central government use debt finance to issue the same transfers to the public, then having the Federal Reserve engage in open market operations to buy up the debt. It is true that there is a strong theoretical presumption that temporary fiscal policy stimulus is more effective at the zero bound (mainly because the fiscal multiplier is not muted by a rise in interest rates). If executed forcefully enough, fiscal policy can lift the economy out of the liquidity trap (provided its temporary nature is credible; otherwise it is much less effective, as, for example, Christiano, Eichenbaum, and Rebelo [2011] show).

The issue is not whether well-calibrated debt-financed transfer policies can be an effective means of stimulus; this is always true whether monetary policy is allowed to fully operate or not. We need not get into the details of just how large the multiplier is.[5] (A growing body of evidence suggests that fiscal multipliers are lower at high levels of debt, partly through a Ricardian channel, partly through an interest rate channel; for a recent discussion, see Huidrom et al. 2019). The important question is what, if any, should be the role of the central bank in fiscal transfers? In our view, the argument for any variant of helicopter money in which the central bank plays an active role is weak. The case for having an independent central bank stems first and foremost from the need to keep down long-term inflation expectations by delegating money creation to an independent authority with a clear but narrowly defined remit to stabilize output and inflation (Rogoff 1985).[6] However, no central bank has been given the power to decide on either the level or the allocation of politically contentious direct transfers to the general public.

Even Bernanke's suggestion that the central bank might take the lead in determining the aggregate size of a transfer by funding a dedicated account that could be used at the government's discretion,

---

5. In her thorough survey of the academic literature, Ramey (2019) gives a more guarded estimate of fiscal multipliers that some advocates of fiscal stimulus would suggest, even at the zero bound.

6. Rogoff (1985) introduced the idea of having an independent central bank with a high weight on inflation stabilization (including through inflation targeting) and showed how this institutional device can substantially resolve the credibility problems first modeled by Kydland and Prescott (1977).

would be far beyond anything that the "unelected power" of the Fed was ever intended to do (in Tucker's 2018 terminology). One might perhaps rely on Congress and the public being fooled by the claim that when the Federal Reserve takes the lead, then what Bernanke terms a "money financed fiscal program" is perhaps a free lunch, relying on the public's ignorance. At the zero bound, a "money financed fiscal program" is no better or worse than "very short-term Treasury debt financed fiscal policy." That is because, at the zero bound, the Treasury can issue zero interest debt on its own. And as Bernanke recognizes, if the central bank does not change its inflation target, the public will expect the "money" to be soaked up as soon as interest rates start rising.

Equivalently, the central bank will have to start paying interest on reserves (as it is now doing), which is in essence equivalent to the Treasury issuing floating rate debt. Of course, the Fed can instead promise this injection to be a permanent increase in the money supply and reduce its own equity in the process. But for all intents and purposes, the Federal Reserve is still owned by the government—either it reduces its remittances to the Treasury in the future, it eventually receives an equity injection, or it operates with perpetually reduced equity. Both of the former two options are still increases in taxes, making the operation merely an opaque form of debt. One can go in circles on this, but it is unlikely that money-financed deficits are the panacea many would wish them to be. It is possible that in some unique circumstances, the central bank might choose to mortgage its credibility and independence, but surely it cannot be considered the best long-run solution.

There is, of course, an important literature on having an independent fiscal authority (see, for example, Halac and Yared 2018). A number of countries including the United Kingdom and Sweden have instituted fiscal councils, albeit with a limited remit. Creating a way to have stronger and more powerful fiscal institutions remains an important policy topic, but for now this remains a distant vision.

Helicopter money is at best a distraction from finding a serious solution to the zero bound, at worst a fast track to ending central bank independence.

Of course, one can argue that there is no reason for the central bank to do anything at the zero bound since fiscal policy becomes more potent, in theory at least. One only has to observe that in the United States, and in many other countries, neither the right nor the left has clear long-term control of power, and the different parties almost invariably have extremely different interpretations what "active" fiscal policy implies. In the United States, the Democrats might view active fiscal policy as running bigger deficits by increasing government spending toward its larger optimal size. For Republicans, on the other hand, active fiscal policy might entail running deficits by cutting taxes and constraining the long-run footprint of government to be smaller. Such conflict is hardly a recipe for creating a credible long-term path for government taxes and expenditures, underscoring why even if fiscal policy is to be used more in recessions, it is important to restore the efficacy of monetary policy.

2.4. Forward Guidance and Raising Inflation Targets

So far, we have considered only quasi-fiscal policies where the central bank is very much the junior partner in its relationships with the Treasury, outside of crises where the ability to act expeditiously is everything. We now turn to more policies that might more genuinely be thought of as monetary policy. One such policy is "forward guidance," à la Eggertsson and Woodford (2003), where the central bank recognizes that it is unable to lower the current interest rate (below zero), but by promising that when interest rate policy is restored, it will allow inflation to overshoot in the future. As Eggertsson and Woodford show, it is possible to achieve an equivalent optimal path for real interest rates, and thus the same effects on the real economy as if negative interest rate policy were possible. This is a completely reasonable idea from a theoretical perspective; Canzoneri et al. (1983) make a very closely related point, showing that if the central bank is unable to use the current interest rate to react, a lagged interest rate rule can have an exactly equivalent effect on the real interest rate through expected inflation.

However, in both cases, but particularly in the zero bound example, there is a severe credibility problem. The public needs to trust that the central bank will honor its promise to allow inflation to drift higher in the future. But the typical zero bound episode can last years (decades as in Japan and soon Europe), making it extremely difficult to trust commitments that are not time consistent, and will likely have to be honored by future policy makers backed by future politicians.[7] Forward guidance is an excellent idea but difficult to make credible, especially in deep recessions where the zero bound may be in place for a very long time, precisely the cases where having an effective monetary policy is most important.

This leaves only amending the path of the inflation target as a serious alternative. A number of alternative approaches have been proposed, from allowing a temporary overshoot after a period of low inflation (though this suffers some of the same credibility problems as forward guidance) to simply raising the inflation target, with the most common suggestion, originally analyzed by Fuhrer and Madigan (1997), being a rise in target inflation from 2 to 4 percent. Many others since, including Blanchard, have also suggested 4 percent. There are many possible objections, including (1) potential damage to the credibility of central banks that have long promised to target 2 percent, (2) the fact that higher inflation would lead to greater price dispersion in normal times if contracting frequency does not adjust, and (3) that if contracting frequency did eventually adjust (as theory would predict), monetary policy

---

7. Chung et al. (2019) emphasize this point; see also Rogoff (2016).

would be blunted (which could indeed imply that it would take larger policy rate changes to achieve the same stimulus, perhaps using up much of the extra 2 percent slack that higher inflation targets were supposed to buy); and (4) that absent a powerful instrument such a negative rate policy, markets might not take the new higher target as credible given the difficulties central banks have had with hitting a 2 percent target. One only has to look at the experience of the Bank of Japan, which set an inflation target of 2 percent in January 2013, constituting by any interpretation a hike in market perceptions of its inflation target, and yet long-term inflation expectation barely moved from its level of 0.5 percent.

Perhaps the biggest problem, though, is that even if raising the inflation target from 2 to 4 percent did help, it might not help nearly enough in the event of a sufficiently deep recession where the optimal interest rate change might still take interest rates well into negative territory if feasible.

Despite such reservations, Federal Reserve officials have still tried to reassure the public that the Fed's tools are sufficient (e.g., Yellen 2016). The fact that the top economics journals are replete with out-of-the-box alternatives to normal monetary policy at the zero bound is a testimony to general skepticism among economists. As we shall see in the next section, there is a serious skepticism in markets as well, with options pricing suggesting that markets seriously doubt the ability of even the US Fed to keep normal inflation rates at 2 percent. And of course, in the eurozone and Japan, there is really no one, even central bank officials, arguing that the existing tool kit is sufficient.

3. INFLATION EXPECTATIONS

The United States is not yet facing the paralysis of Japan, where the central bank has not been successful in pushing long-term inflation expectations up to 1 percent, much less 2 percent, or Europe, where inflation expectations have anchored below 2 percent since 2013. Nevertheless, there appears to have been a steady decline in long-term inflation expectations (at least as measured by the Treasury Inflation Protected Securities [TIPS] market).[8] The ten-year breakeven inflation rate in the United States has declined from around 2.4 percent before the crisis to 1.8 percent today. This decline cannot be dismissed as merely a reflection of the current state of the economy—breakevens that begin in ten years' time, looking beyond the contemporaneous cycle, have declined by a larger amount. Indeed, even the thirty-year breakeven inflation rate from TIPS has fallen from over 2.5 percent in 2011 to under 2 percent as of April 2019.

3.1. Are Long-Term Inflation Expectations of under 2 Percent Evidence of Strong Credibility or Lack of Confidence in Alternative Monetary Instruments?

Inflation-targeting evangelists might herald this decline in medium-term inflation expectations as a triumph of central bank policy and communications that proves the markets have great confidence in existing "alternative monetary instruments." However, this interpretation seems overly sanguine. If a central bank's 2 percent inflation target is to be viewed as the target in normal times, with an escape clause for fiscal emergencies, then the breakeven between real and nominal bonds should be distinctly higher than 2 percent, as it was in the early 2000s.[9]

---

8. Throughout this section we will treat inflation-linked bonds as risk-neutrally priced, such that the breakeven is an unbiased measure of inflation expectations. If the price level were expected to jump in very low consumption states, as documented by Barro and Ursua (2008), then inflation breakevens would be an upwardly biased measure of inflation expectations. Kitsul and Wright (2013) estimate that investors have high marginal utilities for both deflationary and high inflationary outcomes by comparing inflation option prices with model forecasts of inflation.

9. A secondary issue is that breakevens measure market expectations on inflation as measured by the Consumer Price Index (CPI), which is not the Fed's price target. The Fed's

TABLE 2.1. Market-Derived Inflation Expectations

Country	Market Inflation Expectation (average 10 yr)		Market Inflation Expectation (average 10 year, *starting in 10 years*)	
	2005–2007	2016–2019	2005–2007	2016–2019
United States	2.51%	1.81%	2.87%	1.92%
Europe	2.35%	1.43%	2.51%	2.02%
Japan	0.54%	0.39%	0.58%	0.58%

Note: Inflation expectations are calculated using the difference in yields of real and nominal Treasury bonds for the United States, with adjustments to estimate their yields for a constant maturity and without coupons. For Europe and Japan, inflation expectations are derived from zero coupon inflation swaps, due to the infrequent issuance of inflation-indexed bonds. Bond data are from Gürkaynak et al. (2007, 2010). Zero coupon swaps are from Bloomberg.

After all, on a time span of decades, the odds of a substantial fiscal shock at some point, sufficient to create strong pressures for inflation, are presumably nontrivial. Triggers could include an unprecedented catastrophic climate event, a cyberwar that spins out of control, a pandemic, a meltdown in the Chinese economy that leads to a deep global recession, or a new-age financial crisis, to name a few. These triggers are mainly abrupt events, but fiscal pressures to create higher inflation could also evolve very slowly over a long period of a decade or more. Although the United States may have ample fiscal space at present, excessive reliance on short-term debt to finance social programs, a greener society, or, for that matter, further tax cuts must ultimately have its limits. Another slow-moving fiscal shock would be a gradual reversal of the trend decline in global real interest rates that has allowed governments to manage high debt levels more easily than in the past. (Albeit it is still the case that countries with extremely high public debt levels such as Italy and Japan have also had very low growth.) While the risks may be small, it is naive to assert that no matter what the shock, the United

official target is the index of personal consumption expenditures, or PCE. The PCE includes a more comprehensive basket of goods and averages annual inflation, which is 30 basis points lower than the CPI (Bullard 2013).

States (or Europe or Japan) will simply be able to borrow as much as needed at ultra-low interest rates without a hiccup. Even if outright default (as with US abrogation of the gold clause in the 1930s) is unlikely, the duress could still be sufficient to create pressures for a sustained rise in inflation, say, to 4 percent or more for a decade.

Some have argued that even if fiscal pressures erupt, there will be no need for very high inflation because governments can simply resort to financial repression (as discussed in Reinhart and Rogoff 2009), using regulation and political pressure to force private agents to hold government debt at below-market interest rates. Financial repression can be useful in bringing down debt/GDP ratios gradually over time, but the process works much more quickly in an environment of moderate inflation. (Part of the reason Japan's debt/GDP ratio has continued to grow despite a moderate degree of financial repression is that inflation is so low, making it harder for growth in nominal GDP to outstrip the growth in debt.)

3.2. Measuring Inflation Expectations, Removing the Weight Coming from the Chance of Sustained High Inflation

It is possible that markets have bought into the view that advanced economies have such massive fiscal space going far into the future, that advanced country governments will be able to navigate any adverse scenario just by borrowing more without any consequence. To explore the tail risk of high sustained inflation in more detail, one can use a no-arbitrage argument to construct the price of a theoretical inflation-linked bond that features a cap, so that it provides insurance against moderate inflation but does not insure against a regime change that carries very high inflation.[10] Consider a ten-year real bond that would index to the Consumer Price Index (CPI) with a ceiling—if inflation averaged more than 3 percent for

---

10. Our analysis of tail inflation risks follows Lilley and Rogoff (2019).

ten years, it would only pay up to a ceiling of a cumulative 3 percent annual increase.[11] This bond would allow the Treasury to inflate debt away in an inflation-based default, but it would still provide for a complete inflation hedge if the government allowed the Fed to maintain its ordinary inflation-targeting mandate. In essence, part of the difference between a nominal bond and an inflation-linked bond is in default risk. A nominal bond has some default risk in real terms, while a real bond does not. By constructing this synthetic bond, we are making its inflation default risk equivalent to that of the nominal bond. (Note that if inflation temporarily strayed outside the band to a high level, say, 4 percent for a couple of years, it would not affect the cap—only a sustained deviation consistently over 3 percent would matter.) Such a bond would provide a better estimate of inflation expectations absent fiscal dominance.

If the Treasury were to offer such a bond, its payoff would be identical to an investor buying the ordinary inflation-linked bond but selling an inflation cap at a strike of 3 percent with the same principal as the inflation-linked bond. Under no-arbitrage, one can calculate the price paid for the theoretical bond in the time series by using the real bond price and the up-front payment received for selling this protection. We show the breakeven yield on this bond in figure 2.1. While the breakeven on the vanilla real bond has averaged 2.05 percent this decade, the breakeven on this synthetic bond has averaged only 1.81 percent. Notably, the difference between the ordinary and synthetic capped bond has shrunk in recent years, reflecting that markets appear to attach a much smaller probability to sustained inflation above 3 percent. In the first half of this decade, the breakeven inflation on this synthetic capped bond was 38 basis points (bps) lower than the actual TIPS breakeven inflation. Since the Fed's first hike in December 2015, the synthetic breakeven has averaged

---

11. It is worth noting that Treasury Indexed Bonds already include a floor of the opposite nature—if inflation is negative over the life of the bond, the principal indexation is capped at a cumulated 0 percent.

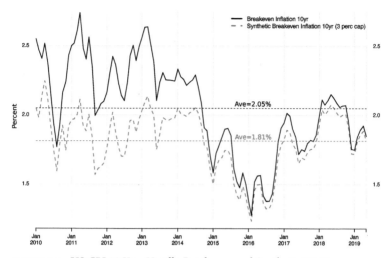

FIGURE 2.1. US CPI 10 Year Vanilla Breakeven and Synthetic 3% Cap Breakeven

Note: Breakeven Inflation 10 year is calculated using the difference in yields of real and nominal Treasury bonds for the United States, with adjustments to estimate their yields for a constant maturity and without coupons, using bond yield data from Gürkaynak et al. (2007, 2010). The synthetic ten-year breakeven is calculated with inflation option pricing from Bloomberg. To remove the impact of outliers, we use the median value within each month to construct each monthly observation. Further detail on the pricing of the synthetic inflation–linked bond is provided in the appendix.

only 7 bps lower than the actual. This vanishingly small premium must reflect evolving beliefs among market participants about the propensity for the Fed's enlarged balance sheet to create inflation.

3.3. Are Breakevens the Best Measure of Inflation Expectations?

A valid concern with measuring inflation expectations using breakevens is that the yield difference between nominal and real bonds may be changing due to other factors, which we would then comingle with changes in inflation expectations. Since we use the constructed yield curves of Gürkaynak et al. (2007, 2010), we do not need to be concerned with differences in coupons or maturities. The two most significant remaining factors are changes in inflation risk premia and liquidity risk premia. In particular, if inflation-linked bonds are less liquid than nominal bonds, the breakeven will be compressed due to the market premium required to hold inflation-linked bonds. While our synthetic bond construction above mitigates the impact of inflation risk premia by capping inflation payoffs below 0 percent and above 3 percent—precisely in the regions where investors pay a premium for inflation protection (Kitsul and Wright 2013)—it does not correct for liquidity premia.

The liquidity difference in our measure is abated by the fact that the yields we use exclude both on-the-run and first off-the-run nominal Treasury securities (which command a liquidity premium relative to most other bonds) but include the on-the-run Treasury indexed bonds, which are the most liquid of the curve (Andreasen et al. 2018). Daily trading volumes in on-the-run TIPS now average ~2 billion per security, whereas off-the-run nominal Treasury bonds average <1 billion (Brain et al. 2018). As such, it is unlikely that our measure of current inflation expectations is materially underestimated by the illiquidity of TIPS. We note that we may be *under*estimating the decline in inflation expectations, given the increased liquidity of inflation-indexed bonds, relative to nominal bonds. D'Amico et al. (2018) estimate breakevens underestimated inflation expectations by up to 100 bps in the early 2000s due to liquidity differences, though this premium had disappeared by 2012.

Zero coupon CPI swaps for the United States highlight a similar decline in market prices, though with a higher level (from an average 2.8 percent in 2005–2007 to an average 2.1 percent in 2016–2019). Inflation swaps are a much smaller market than TIPS and are likely consistently upwardly biased due to the prevalence of agents who are natural buyers of inflation protection derivatives (pension funds) and due to a paucity of natural sellers.

Survey measures provide an alternative benchmark to market pricing. Broadly, survey measures all show a material decline in inflation expectations across both households and professional

TABLE 2.2. Survey-Based Inflation Expectations

Country	Surveys of Professional Forecasters (Average Long Term)		Household forecast (Average Long Term)	
	2005–2007	2016–2019	2005–2007	2016–2019
United States	2.46%	2.22%	3.0%	2.5%
Europe	1.91%	1.83%	NA	NA
Japan	NA	NA	2.9%	2.0%

Note: For the United States, the long-term inflation forecast comes from the Survey of Professional Forecasters (Philadelphia Federal Reserve, March 22, 2019) for which we report the ten-year inflation forecast; household data are from the Michigan Survey of Consumer Finances (University of Michigan, April 12, 2019), for which we report the average five-year inflation forecast. For Europe, we use the Survey of Professional Forecasters (European Central Bank, April 11, 2019), for which we report the longer-term (five-year) forecast. Japanese household data are from the 77th Opinion Survey on the General Public's Views and Behavior (Bank of Japan, April 5, 2019), available from 2006, for which we use the median household's five-year inflation expectation.

forecasters, though not necessarily to below-target levels (table 2.2). Notwithstanding this, these surveys are consistently positively biased in levels.[12]

4. UNCONSTRAINED NEGATIVE RATE POLICY

We have argued previously (Rogoff 2015, 2016, 2017) that the elegant and effective tool to restore monetary policy effectiveness at the zero bound would be unconstrained negative interest rate policy, assuming all necessary legal, institutional, and regulatory changes were first instituted. Above all, this requires taking steps to preclude wholesale arbitrage into paper currency by insurance companies, pension funds, and financial firms. Preventing such

---

12. For the United States, the long-term surveys of professional and household inflation expectations were on average 0.25 percent and 0.75 percent higher respectively than realized outcomes since 1997. For Europe, the five-year ahead survey of professional forecasters' inflation expectations was on average 0.125 percent higher than realized since the survey began in 1997. For Japan, the median survey of five-year inflation expectations from surveyed households was on average 2.5 percent higher than the realized level since the survey began in 2006. All forecast errors are rounded to the nearest eighth of a percentage point.

arbitrage by no means requires changing the currency system, as we shall see. However, the more paper currency becomes marginalized in tax-compliant legal transactions, the more straightforward things become both institutionally and politically. Importantly from a political and perhaps equity perspective, it would not be difficult to shield small retail bank depositors from negative policy rates.[13]

4.1. Early Experience with Mildly Negative Rate Policy in Europe and Japan

The early experiences with very mild negative policy rates in Europe and Japan have been very helpful in revealing issues that need to be navigated, and by and large, this has proved straightforward (Dell'Ariccia et al. 2017). It is important to stress, however, that no country yet has taken the steps necessary to have the kind of deeply negative rates we are discussing here (say, minus 2 percent or more).

Much of the pushback on mildly negative rates has arisen from the claim that they strain bank profit margins, due to depositor resistance to negative rates. This leads a number of authors, including Brunnermeier and Koby (2017), as well as Eggertsson et al. (2019), to argue that in theory, negative interest rates (at least past a certain point) will not be expansionary because as bank capital is depleted, banks will contract lending. In practice, bank performance does not seem to have suffered except at small banks (Lopez et al. 2018). Many large banks actually benefit because a significant share of their borrowing comes from wholesale markets where interest rates have followed government rates into negative territory. Large banks have also been better positioned to mark up other services and bundle these with deposits. Switzerland and Japan have moved to protect bank profits by "layering" reserves so that legacy levels are shielded

---

13. See Rogoff (2016, 2017) and Agarwal and Kimball (2019) for discussions of how small deposits can be handled under this framework.

from negative rates; the ECB has recently adopted this approach. A drawback, though, is that layering considerably weakens the transmission mechanism to the real economy and, as rates go deeply negative, does nothing to prevent a run out of negative-interest-bearing debt, including both public and private.

In any event, as Altavilla et al. (2019) find, banks in the eurozone have indeed been passing on negative rates to larger depositors (with over 100,000 euros in deposits), with over 1 trillion euros worth of deposits now carrying negative rates. Our conjecture is that if cash hoarding is taken off the table (via any of the mechanisms Rogoff [2016] discusses and as we suggest here) and assuming necessary tax, legal, and regulatory changes are put in place, there is no reason to believe that bank profits would suffer excessively.

4.2. Implementing Negative Rate Policy in the Cashless Limit

Moving to a completely cashless system is neither necessary nor desirable into the foreseeable future. However, in thinking about negative rates, it is helpful to start with this case, in order to separate out issues that have only to do with cash. If there were no way to arbitrage into paper currency, of course, there would be nothing to stop investors from pulling out their savings to buy stocks, real estate, art, and gold coins. This is hardly an objection; the incentives go in the same direction whenever the central bank lowers interest rates. Indeed, since the main driver of these investments is changes in real interest rates, as opposed to nominal interest rates, there are already many examples of central banks implementing deep negative real interest rates, with short-term policy rates well below inflation. And it must be noted that a negative rate of 3 percent when inflation is zero is no more a tax on deposits in real terms than when the deposit rate is zero and the inflation rate is 3 percent.

What about bank profits? It is very hard to see why in a cashless world, banks could not easily pass on negative reserve charges to wholesale depositors. There would be nowhere to hide. Of course, deposits would fall as money flows into other assets (and into consumption); large banks could easily substitute by borrowing more in wholesale markets. All banks would benefit to the extent the economy is stimulated, thanks to greater demand for loans and a lower default rate. Discouraging cash hoarding would help free banks from finding indirect ways to charge depositors negative rates (as they do now) and thereby reduce distortions.

If we assume cash is dealt with (or that we are living in a cashless world), what other obstacles might have to be cleared to make negative interest rate policy as effective as normal interest rate cuts? What steps can be taken to reduce attendant financial risks?[14]

Although much further study is warranted (perhaps by an independent commission), for the most part all of the issues seem to involve relatively straightforward plumbing fixes and nothing on the order of the much more radical interventions that have been widely analyzed in major economic journals, ranging from engaging in fiscal policy on steroids to avoiding policies that might increase economic efficiency (thereby lowering prices and exacerbating deflation; see Eggertsson et al. [2014] or Eichengreen [2016] on how increased protectionism can fight deflation).

All the countries that introduced negative rates of 0.75 percent or less have managed to deal with financial plumbing fixes and in a reasonably short time period. For example, the idea that millionaires can arbitrage the system by overpaying estimated taxes and then claiming large refunds (thereby lending money to the government at a zero rate) is easily dealt with by paying a negative

---

14. These issues are detailed in Rogoff (2016), and Agarwal and Kimball (2019) have recently produced an extensive handbook.

interest rate on large overpayments.[15] One important point that must be emphasized is that many of the necessary plumbing fixes, while relatively minor, require the cooperation of the government and cannot be instituted by the central bank alone.

Many of the objections to negative nominal rates are mainly political or philosophical and similar to objections presented against moderate inflation. For example, some might argue that negative interest rates are an unfair tax on savers in much the same way as inflation. Averaged over the cycle, however, an inflation-targeting central will not have a first-order effect on the average value of real interest rates. As long as central banks are using negative rate policy to hit their inflation targets or, more generally, to implement Taylor rule–type monetary policies, there will be no effect on the average real tax rate paid over the cycle (when most of the time nominal rates will be above zero anyway). It must also be kept in mind that long-term nominal rates would likely rise, not fall, if the zero bound were fully eliminated, as Yellen (2016) has argued.

Savers would also benefit to the extent that negative rate policy boosts the value of real assets such as housing and equity. To shield small savers, governments can allow every citizen to register one debit (or savings) account as eligible for zero interest rate protection, with banks being subsidized accordingly. In today's digital world, such a system would be straightforward and inexpensive to implement; let's remember that the government would earn large profits on its short-term debt in a negative interest rate world; some countries such as Germany already do so today.

Perhaps the most fundamental objection to deep negative interest rate policy is that it has not been tried before, and there would be risks. We absolutely acknowledge this; there were similar objec-

---

15. See Rogoff (2016) and Agarwal and Kimball (2019) for further discussion of issues that would need to be addressed.

tions to the transition to floating exchange rates in the 1970s, but it had, at least, been tried before by a few countries on a limited basis. To some extent, this is how mild negative interest rate policy has evolved until now. It is a reasonable forecast that there will be experiments with open-ended negative rate policy in smaller countries before it is tried in larger countries, although Japan is still a very strong candidate for early adoption.

In any event, deep recessions and financial crises already entail large risks and considerable unknowns, and all directions that policy might take entail risks. The early experimentation with negative rates suggests that these risks are manageable. The experience will likely evolve in coming years as more and more countries experiment with deeper and deeper interest rates.

4.3. Approaches to Dealing with Legacy Paper Currency

So far we have set aside the elephant in the room, which is paper currency. Ample experience has shown that paper currency does not get in the way of mildly negative interest rates. It is by no means easy to store whole quantities of cash (billions of dollars). Any registered institution (bank, pension fund, insurance company) would need insurance costing at least 0.5 percent of stored funds, if available. There are large fixed costs to building storage vaults, which must include humidity and temperature controls. Yet there are no guarantees of how long negative interest rate policy will last, and therefore over what period the fixed costs may be amortized. Even porting the money from the central bank to the storage site (and eventually back) would be an expensive operation. Although it will differ by country, existing obstacles to physical currency transportation and storage likely are sufficient to allow central banks to take rates to −2 percent without having the economy crippled by runs into cash; again, it is simplest to think of small retail depositors as being excluded. If large bills (say, equivalent to $50 and above) were eliminated, the transportation and storage costs would be considerably amplified, most likely allowing negative policy rates of up to 2.5 to 3 percent without major cash runs. As Rogoff (1998) argues, getting rid of large-denomination notes likely makes sense anyway from a public finance perspective; it would take only a relatively small decrease in tax evasion and crime to more than pay back any lost seigniorage revenues. However, to allow the larger negative rates of 5 to 6 percent or more that might be needed in the event of a deep recession or a financial crisis, and to set aside bank concerns about pass-through of negative rates to large depositors, it is likely that administrative measures would also be needed, for example, taxing large redeposits of cash into the central bank and other regulatory impediments to cash hoarding (Rogoff 2016; see also Bordo and Levin 2019). Again, small depositors would be excluded, and the political economy of negative rates could be strengthened by providing universal basic debt accounts per Rogoff (2016), which might also in principle be at the central bank.

As noted in the introduction, there are approaches to placing a negative (or positive) interest rate on physical cash that are more nuanced. Setting aside impractical ideas such as a Gesselian stamp tax or Goodfriend's (2000) magnetic stripe in currencies, both of which are clever but flawed (mainly because cash becomes illiquid), by far the most important idea is the Eisler (1933) dual-currency system. Eisler's approach was first resuscitated in the modern context by Davies (2004, 2005) and Buiter (2005) and has been strongly advocated by economist Miles Kimball, including in Agarwal and Kimball (2019). Conceptually, the idea is to have a dual-currency system, where the central bank sets a moving exchange rate between paper and electronic currency. In the current regime, the exchange rate between electronic and paper currency is one. However, what the central bank can do when it wants to institute a negative rate on bank reserves is to announce that the exchange rate between paper currency and electronic currency will depreciate at the same negative rate being applied to electronic deposits. Concretely, if the central bank maintains a negative interest rate of 4 percent, then anyone turning in paper currency after three months will receive 99 cents, after six months 98 cents, after nine months 97 cents, and so on. Assuming that prices are set in electronic currency, then the zero bound will be eliminated, but there will be no run into paper currency.[16]

Formally, if $S(t)$ is the rate at which the central bank trades one dollar in paper currency for electronic currency (in dollars), and $-i(t)$ is the negative nominal interest rate at time t, then the central bank needs to set the rate of depreciation of electronic currency as

$$dS/dt = i(t)$$

The central bank would enforce this exchange change rate by setting it as the rate at which it redeemed paper money for electronic currency at its cash window. Eisler's ingenious device solves the problem of charging a negative rate on paper currency without making users carefully look at each bill to determine its exact value, and without any extra input or devices.

Unfortunately, the Eisler approach is not quite as neat as its advocates sometimes portray it. One problem is that paper currency and electronic currency are not actually perfect substitutes, which is, of course, why some central banks have been able to charge negative rates without first dealing with cash. Setting the rate of depreciation at the same level as the negative interest rate (as in the above formula) could set off a runout of cash (as opposed to into cash). Accelerating the move toward a "lower cash" society is a worthwhile goal for public finance and safety reasons. However, too abrupt a move, without dealing with financial inclusion or

---

16. As Buiter (2005) notes, there would still be a problem if prices continued to be set in paper currency, in which case the zero bound problem would persist, but the government can probably ensure that electronic prices are the focal point by setting taxes and all government contracts in electronic currency.

legacy payment systems, would not be desirable. Another tricky issue is that when the period of negative rates ends, the exchange rate between electronic and paper currency will be stuck at a non-unitary value, which could be an inconvenience in normal times. It is feasible to restore it as the central bank begins to pay a positive rate of interest on reserves by having the exchange rate appreciate instead of depreciating, though there can be some tricky expectations issues to navigate (e.g., if the public expects that the central bank will immediately restore paper currency to par as soon as the negative rate episode ends, it will defeat the effort to prevent hoarding).[17]

Another (less compelling) concern sometimes expressed is that if investors had to worry about negative interest rates, there would be "no safe asset." But government short- to medium-term government debt already pays negative rates in countries such as Germany and Japan, and it has not seemed to make investors regard them as any less safe. As already noted in the introduction, Friedman (Friedman and Roosa 1967) argues that fears of monetary Armageddon in the event of monetary regime changes have often been overblown in the past.

Indeed, far from impeding market clearing, allowing for negative policy interest rates arguably can preclude much more dangerous dynamics when price (the interest rate) is stuck at the effective zero lower bound and cannot clear the market for safe assets. For example, Caballero and Farhi (2018) argue that excess demand for safe assets can potentially induce a fall in real output to bring demand into line with supply. Allowing for negative interest rate policy allows the price of the bonds to clear the market, thereby preventing the distortion of the zero bound from creating new sources of monetary non-neutrality.

---

17. Agarwal and Kimball (2015, 2019).

Are negative rates "unfair" not only to depositors but to holders of currency? No more so than inflation, which is already a tax on paper currency. Indeed, proposals to raise the inflation target to 4 percent would be a significant increase in the tax on cash. Compared to negative rate policy that is likely to be mainly invoked in deep recessions, the tax from a higher inflation target would be in place all the time, not just in exceptional circumstances.

One of the reasons why, among large countries, Japan is a more obvious candidate as an early adapter of negative interest rates is that unlike the dollar, only a very small share of yen paper currency appears to be held outside Japan. Indeed, the issue of foreign currency holdings makes the United States quite distinct from any other country, albeit the eurozone and Switzerland face some of the same issues. Exactly how much of US currency is held abroad is a matter of considerable debate, as is the question of whether foreign use is a positive or negative externality to the rest of the world on net.[18] Independent of whether the externality is positive or negative, foreign use of the dollar is a profit center for the United States, though the benefits must be weighed against the fact that paper currency significantly facilitates tax evasion and crime in the United States, not just abroad. Rogoff (1998, 2016) argues that even assuming only a very modest effect on tax evasion and crime, the gains from (gradually) withdrawing large-denomination notes from circulation likely outweigh the benefits.

Another distinction between the United States and other advanced countries is that demographics are not yet quite so grim in the United States as they are in the eurozone and Japan, and overall growth is more dynamic. Again, this makes the case for Europe and Japan to

---

18. Rogoff (2016) argues that the negative externalities for the rest of the world are significant.

consider preparing for unconstrained negative interest rate policy much stronger than for the United States, but it hardly eliminates it from the United States. Kiley and Roberts (2017) find that the zero bound could be a problem for the United States by as much as 30 to 40 percent of the time (albeit Chung et al. [2019] argue that these estimates are likely high-side).

4.4. Financial Stability Concerns

Last but not least is the question of financial stability concerns. Dell'Ariccia et al. (2017) find that negative rate policy to date has not raised particularly acute financial stability concerns, but this is always a question whenever real interest rates are low. Dealing with financial stability is always an important issue, and it is not obvious that negative nominal rate policy would introduce substantially new concerns from those studies in the long history of negative real rate policy; this is certainly an issue meriting further study.

The financial stability argument can be flipped on its head. If central banks had been able to invoke effective negative nominal rate policy after the financial crisis, it is possible that the recovery period would have been much faster, and the period of ultra-low interest rates much much shorter, thereby reducing financial risks rather than exacerbating them. Being able to create moderate inflation in the aftermath of a financial crisis might actually be extremely helpful, letting the steam out of private debt problems (and in Europe, periphery country debt problems). Whether or not central banks wanted to elevate inflation, quantitative easing proved relatively ineffective. Unconstrained negative interest rate policy would have provided the tool needed if it had been available.

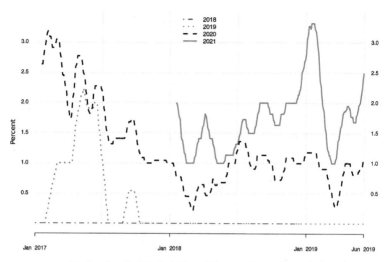

FIGURE 2.2. Market-Implied Probability of Negative Rates by End of Each Calendar Year

Note: Market-implied probabilities of three-month LIBOR (USD) rates setting below −0.25 percent at December 15 of 2018 through 2021. Market-implied probabilities are derived from options prices on the Eurodollar futures with strikes of 100.25 and 100.5, which correspond to LIBOR rates of −25 bps and −50 bps, respectively. Probabilities are lower bounds and are estimated assuming risk neutrality, averaged over the preceding month. Eurodollar option price data from Bloomberg. See appendix for details.

4.5. Expectations of Negative Rates Being Implemented in the Near Future

Though many may disagree with our prescriptions, it is worth noting that even in the United States, both market pricing and survey data attribute material probabilities to nominal interest rates moving into negative territory in the near future—and yet they hold these beliefs without an agreed framework for how they would be implemented.

First, we show that markets attribute a material probability to this event, using option prices. In figure 2.2, we show an estimate of the lower bound for the risk-neutral probability that markets ascribe to the short-term borrowing rates of high-credit banks (USD 3m LIBOR) being below −0.25 percent at the end of each calendar year. Markets have consistently assigned a positive probability that these borrowing rates will be materially below zero within the next three years, at times as high as 3 percent, implying Federal reserve rates that are even lower.

Surveys of the relevant parties yield similar conclusions. In the New York Fed's most recent market surveys, participants were asked for the percent chance that they attached to the target federal funds rate being in certain ranges by year-end 2021, conditional on moving to the zero lower bound at some point before this date. Primary dealers and investment managers assigned average probabilities of 12 percent and 17 percent, respectively, of ending 2021 with a negative target federal funds rate.

5. CONCLUSIONS

The strong case for having a rule-based international monetary system (Taylor 2016), implemented by independent central banks (Rogoff 1985), is well established. The quasi-fiscal tools presently available to monetary authorities at the zero bound make it difficult to conform to rules in part because they are of such limited and unpredictable effectiveness, and in part because they can just as easily be implemented—indeed even reversed—by the fiscal authorities. Other ideas such as forward guidance on interest rates do fall within the realm of monetary policy but during long zero bound episodes are extremely difficult to make credible. Modifying inflation targets is a plausible option but comes with many problems of its own, one of which is that it is difficult to make a higher inflation target credible when markets doubt that the central bank has the instrument to achieve it; the case of Japan well illustrates this point.

Borrowing the phrase of former US Treasury secretary Hank Paulson, the central bank needs a "bazooka" at the zero bound that makes credible its commitment to achieving its policy rule. Negative interest rate policy is precisely the requisite instrument and can be achieved by making the legal, tax, and regulatory changes needed to use unconstrained negative interest rate policy effectively in fighting a deep recession. Most of the necessary adaptations of the financial plumbing needed to make negative interest rate policy effective—potentially as effective as interest rate policy in positive territory—are straightforward. The most vexing issue is preventing large-scale cash hoarding by pension funds, insurance companies, and financial institutions (small depositors can easily be exempted). If hoarding is decisively dealt with (e.g., by allowing the trade-in value of paper currency at the central bank to depreciate over time during negative interest rate episodes à la Eisler [1933]), it should solve the problem of bank profitability (to the extent there is one) by making it straightforward to pass on negative interest rates on to large-scale depositors. This will ensure that the normal stimulus effects of lower interest rates on consumption and investment will transmit to the real economy. Of course, as is usually the case, lower interest rates will likely also push up the prices of housing, equities, and other assets, while at the same time pushing up nominal interest rates on longer-term bonds due to higher long-term expected inflation as well as stronger medium-term growth.

Monetary policy design should be forward looking and not backward looking. The increasing marginalization of cash (in legal, tax-compliant transactions) will make it ever easier to effectively implement negative interest rate policy in the coming years. The process could be constructively accelerated by phasing out large-denomination notes, which still play a significant role in tax evasion and crime but are largely vestigial in the legal economy. Indeed, thanks to the fact that hoarding cash is actually quite expensive for financial institutions, insurance companies, and pension funds, it is already possible to have mildly negative rates (perhaps as low as −2 percent) without any tax on cash, and eliminating large bills would likely increase the scope for negative rates somewhat further.

In any event, as cash steadily becomes marginalized in the legal economy, as countries take more steps to deal with financial inclusion, and assuming small depositors are excluded, political pushback on negative rate policy should evaporate, much as political pushback on flexible exchange rates evaporated over time.

The biggest drawback to unconstrained negative rate policy is that it has not really been tried anywhere, and unintended consequences are possible. But in a deep financial crisis, countries must often choose from a menu of difficult options, and a decade after the financial crisis, it is clear that none of the other options for restoring monetary policy effectiveness are particularly attractive or sustainable. As we have noted at the outset, the case for considering how to make unconstrained negative rate policy effective is stronger at present in Europe than in the United States, and stronger still in Japan. In our view, it is quite likely that in some advanced country central banks will experiment with unconstrained negative rate policy during a deep recession within the next decade. The United States is not the obvious first mover. However, given the steady downward drift in global real interest rates, the difficulties in raising expected inflation, the apparent ineffectiveness of quasi-fiscal instruments at the zero bound, and ultimately the importance to central bank independence of having an instrument that the Fed "owns," create a strong imperative for proactively preparing now for a negative interest rate world that is perhaps inevitable.

References

Agarwal, Ruchir, and Miles Kimball. 2015. "Breaking through the Zero Lower Bound." International Monetary Fund Working Paper 15-224.
———. 2019. "Enabling Deep Negative Rates: A Guide." International Monetary Fund Working Paper, April.
Altavilla, Carlo, Lorenzo Burlon, Mariassunta Giannetti, and Sarah Holton, 2019. "Is There a Zero Bound? The Effects of Negative Rates on Banks and Firm." Mimeo, European Central Bank, October.

Andreasen, Martin, Jens H. E. Christensen, and Simon Riddell. 2018. "The TIPS Liquidity Premium." Federal Reserve Bank of San Francisco Working Paper Series, March. https://doi.org/10.24148/wp2017-11.

Barro, Robert, and José Ursua. 2008. "Macroeconomic Crises since 1870." *Brookings Papers on Economic Activity* 2008, no. 1:255–335.

Bernanke, Ben. 2016. "What Tools Does the Fed Have Left? Part 3: Helicopter Money." Brookings Institution. https://www.brookings.edu/blog/ben-bernanke /2016/04/11/what-tools-does-the-fed-have-left-part-3-helicopter-money.

Bordo, Michael D., and Andrew T. Levin. 2019. "Digital Cash: Principles and Practical Steps." National Bureau of Economic Research Working Paper 24555, January.

Brain, Doug, Michiel De Pooter, Dobrislav Dobrev, Michael Fleming, Peter Johansson, Frank Keane, Michael Puglia, Tony Rodrigues, and Or Shachar. 2018. "Breaking Down TRACE Volumes Further." Federal Reserve Bank of New York, *Liberty Street Economics* (blog), November 29. https://liberty streeteconomics.newyorkfed.org/2018/11/breaking-down-trace-volumes -further.html.

Brunnermeier, Markus K., and Yann Koby. 2017. "The 'Reversal Interest Rate': An Effective Lower Bound on Monetary Policy." Princeton University, July.

Buiter, Willem H. 2003. "Helicopter Money: Irredeemable Fiat Money and the Liquidity Trap." National Bureau of Economic Research Working Paper 10163, December.

———. 2005. "Overcoming the Zero Bound: Gesell vs. Eisler." Mimeo, European Bank for Reconstruction and Development, London.

Bullard, James. 2013. "President's Message: CPI vs. PCE Inflation: Choosing a Standard Measure." Federal Reserve Bank of St. Louis, July 1. https://www .stlouisfed.org/publications/regional-economist/july-2013/cpi-vs-pce-inflation --choosing-a-standard-measure.

Caballero, Ricardo J., and Emmanuel Farhi. 2018. "The Safety Trap." *Review of Economic Studies* 85, no. 1 (January): 223–74.

Canzoneri, Matthew, Dale Henderson, and Kenneth Rogoff. 1983. "The Information Content of the Interest Rate and Optimal Monetary Policy." *Quarterly Journal of Economics* 98, no. 4 (November): 545–66.

Christiano, Lawrence J., Martin Eichenbaum, and Sergio Rebelo. 2011. "When Is the Government Spending Multiplier Large?" *Journal of Political Economy* 119, no. 1 (February): 78–121.

Chung, Hess, Etienne Gagnon, Taisuke Nakata, Matthias Paustian, Bernd Schlusche, James Trevino, Diego Vilán, and Wei Zheng. 2019. "Monetary Policy Options at the Effective Lower Bound: Assessing the Federal Reserve's Current Policy Toolkit." Finance and Economics Discussion Series 2019-003. Washington, DC: Board of Governors of the Federal Reserve System. https://doi.org/10 .17016/FEDS.2019.003.

D'Amico, Stefania, Don H. Kim, and Min Wei. 2018. "Tips from TIPS: The Informational Content of Treasury Inflation-Protected Security Prices." *Journal of Financial and Quantitative Analysis* 53, no. 1 (February): 395–436.

Davies, Stephen. 2004. "Comment on Buiter and Panigirtzoglou." Mimeo, Research Institute for Economics and Business Administration, Kobe, Japan.

———. 2005. "National Money of Account, with a Second National Money or Local Monies as Means of Payment: A Way of Finessing the Zero Interest Rate Bound." *Kobe Economic and Business Review* 49: 69–91.

Dell'Ariccia, Giovanni, Vikram Haksar, and Tommaso Mancini-Griffoli. 2017. *Negative Interest Rate Policies—Initial Experiences and Assessments.* Staff report, International Monetary Fund, August.

Eberly, Janice, James Stock, and Jonathan Wright. 2019. "Review of the Federal Reserve's Current Framework for Monetary Policy." Presented at the Conference on Monetary Strategy, Federal Reserve Bank of Chicago, June 4.

Eggertsson, Gauti, Andrea Ferrero, and Andrea Raffo. 2014. "Can Structural Reforms Help Europe?" *Journal of Monetary Economics* 61: 2–22.

Eggertsson, Gauti, Ragnar E. Juelsrod, Lawrence Summers, and Ella Getz Wold. 2019. "Negative Nominal Interest Rates and the Bank Lending Channel." National Bureau of Economic Research Working Paper 25416, January.

Eggertsson, Gauti B., and Michael Woodford. 2003. "The Zero Bound on Interest Rates and Optimal Monetary Policy." *Brookings Papers on Economic Activity* 2003, no. 1: 139–233.

Eichengreen, Barry. 2016. "What's the Problem with Protectionism?" *Project Syndicate,* July 13.

Eisler, Robert. 1933. *Stable Money: The Remedy for the Economic World Crisis: A Programme of Financial Reconstruction for the International Conference 1933; With a Preface by Vincent C. Vickers.* London: Search Publishing.

Friedman, Milton, and Robert V. Roosa. 1967. "The Balance of Payments: Free versus Fixed Exchange Rates." Washington, DC: American Enterprise Institute.

Fuhrer, Jeffrey, and Brian Madigan. 1997. "Monetary Policy When Interest Rates Are Bounded at Zero." *Review of Economics and Statistics* 79, no. 4 (November): 573–85. Earlier version published in 1994 as Federal Reserve Bank of San Francisco Working Paper in Applied Economic Theory 94-06.

Goodfriend, Marvin. 2000. "Overcoming the Zero Bound on Interest Rate Policy." *Journal of Money, Credit and Banking* 32, no. 4 (November): 1007–35.

Greenlaw, David, James D. Hamilton, Ethan Harris, and Kenneth D. West. 2018. "A Skeptical View of the Impact of the Fed's Balance Sheet." National Bureau of Economic Research working paper 24687, June.

Greenwood, Robin, Samuel G. Hanson, Joshua S. Rudolph, and Lawrence Summers. 2015a."Debt Management Conflicts between the U.S. Treasury and the Federal Reserve." In *The $13 Trillion Question: How America Manages Its Debt*, edited by David Wessel, 43–89. Washington, DC: Brookings Institution Press.

———. 2015b. "The Optimal Maturity of Government Debt." In *The $13 Trillion Question: How America Manages Its Debt*, edited by David Wessel, 1–41. Washington, DC: Brookings Institution Press.

Greenwood, Robin, Samuel G. Hanson, and Jeremy C. Stein. 2015c. "A Comparative-Advantage Approach to Government Debt Maturity." *Journal of Finance* 70, no. 4 (August): 1683–1722.

Gürkaynak, Refet S., Brian Sack, and Jonathan H. Wright. 2007. "The U.S. Treasury Yield Curve: 1961 to the Present." *Journal of Monetary Economics* 54, no. 8 (November): 2291–304.

———. 2010. "The TIPS Yield Curve and Inflation Compensation." *American Economic Journal: Macroeconomics* 2 no. 1 (January): 70–92.

Halac, Marina, and Pierre Yared. 2018. "Fiscal Rules and Discretion in the World Economy." *American Economic Review* 108, no. 8 (August): 2305–34.

Huidrom, Raju, Ayhan Kose, Jamus Lim, and Franziska Ohsorge. 2019. "Why Do Fiscal Multipliers Depend on Fiscal Positions?" *Journal of Monetary Economics* (forthcoming).

Kiley, Michael, and John Roberts. 2017. "Monetary Policy in a Low Interest Rate World." *Brooking Papers on Economic Activity* (Spring).

Kitsul, Yuri, and Jonathan H. Wright. 2013. "The Economics of Options-Implied Inflation Probability Density Functions." *Journal of Financial Economics* 110, no. 3 (December): 696–711.

Kydland, Finn, and Edward C. Prescott. 1977. "Rules Rather Than Discretion: The Inconsistency of Optimal Plans." *Journal of Political Economy* 85, no. 3 (June): 473–92.

Lilley, Andrew, and Kenneth Rogoff. 2019. "Unconventional Monetary Policy and Tail Inflation Risk." Mimeo, Harvard University, September.

Lopez, Jose A., Andrew K. Rose, and Mark M. Spiegel. 2018. "Why Have Negative Nominal Interest Rates Had Such a Small Effect on Bank Performance? Cross

Country Evidence." Federal Reserve Bank of San Francisco Working Paper Series 2018-7.

Ramey, Valerie. 2019. "Ten Years after the Financial Crisis: What Have We Learned from the Renaissance in Fiscal Research?" *Journal of Economic Perspective* 33, no. 2 (Spring): 89–114.

Reinhart, Carmen M., and Kenneth Rogoff. 2009. *This Time Is Different: Eight Centuries of Financial Folly.* Princeton, NJ: Princeton University Press.

Rogoff, Kenneth. 1985. "The Optimal Degree of Commitment to an Intermediate Monetary Target." *Quarterly Journal of Economics* 100, no. 4 (November): 1169–89.

———. 1998. "Blessing or Curse? Foreign and Underground Demand for Euro Notes." *Economic Policy* 13, no. 26 (April): 263–303.

———. 2015. "Costs and Benefits to Phasing Out Paper Currency." In *NBER Macroeconomics Annual 2014,* vol. 29, edited by Jonathan A. Parker and Michael Woodford, 445–56. Chicago: University of Chicago Press.

———. 2016. *The Curse of Cash.* Princeton, NJ: Princeton University Press.

———. 2017. "Dealing with Monetary Paralysis at the Zero Bound." *Journal of Economic Perspectives* 31, no. 3 (Summer): 47–66.

Taylor, John B. 2016. "A Rules-Based Cooperatively Managed International Monetary System for the Future." In *International Monetary Cooperation: Lessons from the Plaza Accord after Thirty Years,* edited by C. F. Bergsten and R. Green, 217–36. Washington, DC: Peterson Institute for International Economics.

Tucker, Paul. 2018. *Unelected Power: The Quest for Legitimacy in Central Banking and the Regulatory State.* Princeton, NJ: Princeton University Press.

Turner, Adair. 2015. *Between Debt and the Devil.* Princeton, NJ: Princeton University Press.

Yellen, Janet. 2016. "The Federal Reserve's Monetary Toolkit: Past, Present and Future." Paper presented at Federal Reserve Bank of Kansas City Economic Symposium, Jackson Hole, Wyoming, August 25–27. https://www.kansascityfed.org/~/media/files/publicat/sympos/2016/2016yellen.pdf?la=en.

APPENDIX: BOUNDING RISK-NEUTRAL
PROBABILITIES FROM THE MARKET PRICES
OF OPTIONS

We outline the process we use to infer risk-neutral probabilities from the market prices of various options. We first describe the process in general, since all probabilities in the paper are constructed in this manner. For parsimony, we assume a discount rate of zero in this explanation.

Consider the payoff of a call option over an asset with an underlying price of x, where the option has a strike of k. The payoff of the option at the exercise date has the following profile, where α is a general scaling parameter:

$$\Pi(x) = \alpha \cdot \begin{cases} x - k & \text{if } k < x \\ 0 & \text{if } x \le k \end{cases}$$

We can then construct a synthetic option that combines buying a call with a strike of k_2 and selling a call with a strike of k_1 on the same underlying asset, where $k_1 > k_2$. The payoff function of such a synthetic option follows:

$$\Pi(x) = \alpha(k_1 - k_2) \cdot \begin{cases} 1 & \text{if } k_1 \le x \\ \dfrac{x - k_2}{k_1 - k_2} & \text{if } k_2 < x < k_1 \\ 0 & \text{if } x \le k_2 \end{cases}$$

The risk-neutral valuation (V) of this synthetic option is therefore given by $V = \int pdf(x)\Pi(x)dx$. We do not observe the value of this synthetic option directly since it is not traded, but we can infer it from the market price of the call option with strike k_2 minus the price of the call option with strike k_1. We then use this valuation to provide a lower bound on the probability that $x > k_2$ under the assumption of risk neutrality.

$$V = \int pdf(x)\Pi(x)dx$$

$$= \int_{k_2}^{\infty} pdf(x)\Pi(x)dx$$

$$\leq \int_{k_2}^{\infty} pdf(x) \cdot \alpha(k_1 - k_2)dx$$

$$\rightarrow \frac{V}{\alpha(k_1 - k_2)} \leq \underbrace{\int_{k_2}^{\infty} pdf(x)dx}_{Pr(x>k_2)}$$

Therefore, we can use this general formula to provide a lower bound on the probability of interest rates being below −0.25%, so long as we can observe the market price of an option with a strike for the relevant event, and a second option that has a higher strike. The second option is necessary since there are an infinite number of combinations of outcomes and probabilities that would be consistent with one option price, but a second option price limits this space to at least a single lower bound.

Probability of negative rates: We provide a lower bound on the risk-neutral probability of three-month borrowing rates falling below −0.25% using Eurodollar call options. Eurodollar futures are cash-settled derivatives on the three-month LIBOR rate, the interest rate that a bank borrows at in US dollars for three months, subject to satisfying certain credit requirements. The price of these derivatives are quoted as 100 − r where r is in percentage points (e.g., for an interest rate of 0.5 percent the price of the derivative would settle at 99.50). A call option on Eurodollar futures with a strike of 100.25 entitles the buyer the right to enter into the long side of a Eurodollar future at the price of 100.25 with the option seller.

In this case, we construct the value of the synthetic option from the price of buying another Eurodollar call option with a strike of $k_2 = 100.25$ ($P_t^{C,K=100.25}$) and selling another with a strike of $k_1 = 100.5$($P_t^{C,K=100.5}$), yielding a lower bound for the risk-neutral probability that rates are below −0.25%.

$$Pr_t(r < -0.25) \geq \frac{P_t^{C,k=100.25} - P_t^{C,k=100.5}}{100 \cdot (100.5 - 100.25)}$$

Estimating a Synthetic Breakeven with a CPI Indexation Cap

Consider a ten-year real bond that would index to CPI with a ceiling on the indexation as follows. If inflation averaged more than 3 percent for ten years, it would only pay up to a ceiling of a cumulative 3 percent annual increase. The payoff profile of this bond is identical to a compound payoff profile, one where the investor buys the ordinary inflation-linked bond, but selling an inflation cap at a strike of 3 percent with the same principal as the inflation-linked bond. Under no-arbitrage, we can calculate the price paid for theoretical bond in the time series by using the real bond price and the up-front payment received for selling this protection.

To convert this up-front payment into the equivalent yield on the inflation-linked bond, we must adjust the yield according to the modified duration of the inflation-linked bond. Since the bond we are pricing has no coupons, the Macaulay duration is the years to maturity, and since its compounding is continuous, the modified duration is exactly the Macaulay duration:

$$r_t^{synthetic} = r_t - \frac{premium_t}{T}$$

The synthetic BEI is therefore the yield on the continuously compounding nominal bond minus the synthetic yield on the continuously compounding real bond.

DISCUSSANT REMARKS

Andrew Levin

This year's Monetary Policy Conference at the Hoover Institution was a particularly important occasion to reflect on monetary policy frameworks. May 2019 marked the tenth anniversary—within a month or so—of the date that the National Bureau of Economic Research (NBER) designated as the start of the recovery from the Great Recession. In retrospect, however, this recovery has clearly been the most protracted and painful since the Great Depression of the 1930s. Therefore, as policy makers proceed with their "Fed Listens" initiative, a key consideration should be that the current monetary policy framework has not provided satisfactory outcomes for ordinary American families. The ability of the Federal Open Market Committee (FOMC) to carry out its dual mandate has been substantially constrained by the effective lower bound (ELB) on nominal interest rates, and that constraint could become even more problematic in coming years. And in the context of a turbulent global economy, the challenge of strengthening the FOMC's policy toolbox has become increasingly urgent.

In light of these considerations, I am very glad to have this opportunity to discuss the work of Ken Rogoff and his colleague Andrew Lilley, who have presented a compelling case for expanding the Fed's capacity to push interest rates below zero in response to a severe adverse shock. I begin by highlighting some empirical findings from my forthcoming paper with Prakash Loungani, in which we document the limitations of quantitative easing (QE) as a tool for providing monetary stimulus.[19] And then I talk about how the introduction of digital cash can strengthen the Fed's ability to mitigate severe adverse shocks, drawing on my joint work with

---

19. See Levin and Loungani (2019).

Michael Bordo—including some highlights from the presentation that we gave at the Hoover conference two years ago as well as our recent Hoover working paper.[20] In particular, our analysis has demonstrated the merits of providing digital cash through a public-private partnership between the Federal Reserve and supervised financial institutions, and we've set forth design principles that would eliminate the effective lower bound while ensuring that ordinary households and small businesses are insulated from negative interest rates and are not burdened with any implicit taxes or fees.

ASSESSING THE ADEQUACY
OF THE ECONOMIC RECOVERY

In assessing the efficacy of the Fed's current monetary toolbox, it seems sensible to start by reviewing the experience of the past decade. As shown in the upper panel of figure 2.3, the US unemployment rate peaked at nearly 10 percent in autumn 2009 and declined at an agonizingly slow pace over subsequent years; indeed, it did not return to its prerecession level until 2017. That outcome may partly owe to policy makers' pessimism about the sustainable level of unemployment (u^*); as of 2015, the median estimate of FOMC participants was about 5.5 percent, suggesting that the labor market was already on the verge of overheating, whereas their latest estimates (as of June 2019) had a range of 3.6 to 4.4 percent.

However, the unemployment rate is not a satisfactory measure of labor market slack, especially in the context of a severe downturn and sluggish recovery—a point that I emphasized in my 2014 Hoover conference paper.[21] For example, the US unemployment rate began moving downward during 2010 and 2011, but that decline did not reflect unemployed workers taking jobs; instead,

---

20. See Bordo and Levin (2017, 2019).
21. See Erceg and Levin (2014) and Levin (2014).

Unemployment Rate

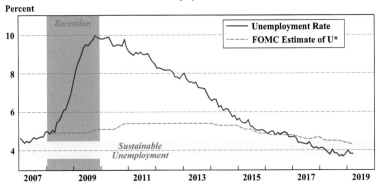

Labor Force Participation of Prime-Age Adults (Ages 25 to 54 Years)

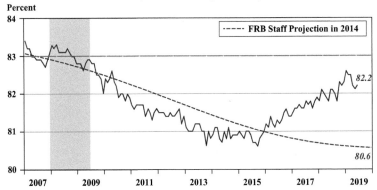

FIGURE 2.3. Characterizing the US Economic Recovery

Note: The unemployment rate and the prime-age labor force participation rate (LFPR) are published by the Bureau of Labor Statistics, and the recession dates are published by the National Bureau of Economic Research (NBER). The median projection by the Federal Open Market Committee (FOMC) of the longer-run normal unemployment rate (u^*) is published by the Federal Reserve Board. In the upper panel, the interval labeled "Sustainable Unemployment" denotes the range of FOMC participants' estimates of u^* as published in June 2019. In the lower panel, the short-dashed line denotes the projection of Aaronson et al. (2014), and the long-dashed line denotes the 2007 average.

discouraged individuals were simply giving up and exiting from the job market. As shown in the lower panel of figure 2.3, the labor force participation rate (LFPR) of prime-age adults declined markedly in the wake of the Great Recession. But the Federal Reserve Board's staff attributed that decline to structural factors as well as "permanent damage" from the recession, projecting in 2014 that prime-age LFPR would continue heading downward through the end of the decade. In effect, that projection characterized millions of people in their prime working years as permanently unemployable. Fortunately, it proved to be utterly mistaken: since 2015, the prime-age LFPR has moved back upward to just a bit below its prerecession average, suggesting that the US labor market still may not have fully recovered even a decade after the start of the recovery.

One clear implication is that the FOMC should start quantifying its "maximum employment" objective in terms of measures of employment, not merely the unemployment rate. For example, the FRB/US model was formulated in the early 1990s and continues to serve as the Fed's benchmark for conducting macroeconomic analysis, but that model gauges labor market slack solely in terms of unemployment gaps. Going forward, the Fed's analytical tools should explicitly incorporate cyclical movements in labor force participation and should assess resource slack in terms of the shortfall of employment from its maximum sustainable level.

REASSESSING THE FED'S MONETARY TOOLBOX

The painfully slow and protracted economic recovery has also highlighted the intrinsic limitations of the Fed's monetary toolbox. In particular, the Fed's open-ended asset purchase program, commonly referred to as QE3, was launched in fall 2012 with the aim of boosting the pace of the recovery by exerting downward pressure on term premiums and longer-term bond yields. Subsequent Fed analysis has continued to maintain that assumption about the transmission mechanism of QE; for example, a recent paper by Fed Board staff states that "the balance sheet expansion lowers the path of the term premium on 10-year Treasury yields."[22]

---

22. Chung et al. (2019, 27–28).

The assumed efficacy of QE has mainly rested on event studies of the Fed's initial round of asset purchases (QE1), which was initiated in late 2008 and expanded in March 2009.[23] Nonetheless, at the Jackson Hole conference in August 2012, Michael Woodford noted that such balance sheet actions might be very effective in the midst of a financial crisis but relatively ineffectual (except as a signaling device) once those financial strains had subsided. Thus, it seems sensible to revisit the QE3 program and examine its impact on term premiums as well as broader macroeconomic indicators.

The New York Fed's survey of primary dealers is helpful in disentangling the transmission mechanism of QE3. In particular, these surveys regularly elicited dealers' expectations regarding the likely timing of liftoff, that is, the first hike to the target federal funds rate. As of early September 2012, just prior to the launch of QE3, the median projection of the primary dealers was that liftoff would occur in the third quarter of 2015. And that interest rate outlook remained stable over the subsequent two-year period until the end of QE3 in September 2014.[24] One key implication is that QE3 did not shift investors' perceptions regarding the likely path of the target federal funds rate, that is, the QE3 program was *not* associated with any substantial signaling effects about the Fed's conventional monetary policy tool.

The FOMC's decision to launch QE3 was informed by Fed staff assessments of its efficacy. Fortunately, since FOMC materials are routinely released to the public after a five-year interval, we can now take a look at the staff analysis that was sent to the FOMC just a few weeks beforehand. That analysis assumes a direct relationship between the anticipated size of the asset purchase program and

23. Chung et al. (2011) gauged QE1 as having reduced the term premium by about 50bp, whereas the effects of QE2 were gauged at around 15bp.

24. The median projection for liftoff was 2015:Q3 in almost all of the surveys conducted over that two-year period, except for the surveys conducted in late June 2013 (median = 2015:Q2) and in December 2014 and January 2015 (median = 2015:Q4).

TABLE 2.3. Key Federal Open Market Committee (FOMC) Communications about QE3

Event	Dates of FRBNY Primary Dealer Surveys	Change in Expected Size of QE3 Program
Sept. 2012 FOMC Meeting (9/13/2012)	9/4/2012 & 9/19/2012	+$500 billion
Sept. 2012 FOMC Minutes (10/4/2012)	9/19/2012 & 10/15/2012	+$300 billion
Dec. 2012 FOMC Meeting (12/12/2012)	12/10/2012 & 12/17/2012	+$90 billion
May 2013 JEC Testimony (5/22/2013)	4/22/2013 & 6/10/2013	+$60 billion
June 2013 FOMC Meeting (6/19/2013)	6/10/2013 & 6/24/2013	−$80 billion

Source: Federal Reserve Bank of New York (FRBNY). Calculations are the author's.

the projected decline in the term premium: "The staff's analysis . . . indicates that [asset purchases] affect term premiums and thus longer-term interest rates primarily via their effect on the private sector's expectations of the future path of the stock of longer-term securities that will be held by the Federal Reserve."[25] This link was assumed to be approximately linear, and its proportionality factor was determined from event studies of QE1, which totaled about $1.7 trillion in asset purchases and reduced the ten-year term premium by about 50 basis points. Thus, in analyzing the prospective impact of QE3, Fed staff projected that the announcement of a $1 trillion program would cause the term premium to "fall immediately by about 35 basis points."

Thus, in assessing the actual efficacy of QE3, one key ingredient is to gauge the evolution of investors' expectations about its overall size. For this purpose, we can draw on the New York Fed's survey of primary dealers, which regularly elicited dealers' projections of the size and composition of the securities held in the Fed's System Open Market Account (SOMA). As shown in table 2.3, the regular

---

25. Laforte et al. (2012, 1).

survey was conducted a few days before the September 2012 FOMC meeting, and a special follow-up survey was performed a few days afterward, indicating that the FOMC's initial announcement of QE3 caused primary dealers to ramp up their expectations of the Fed's total security holdings by about $500 billion. The release of the FOMC minutes three weeks later evidently led dealers to mark up their projections by an additional $300 billion, which remained stable for the next couple of months and then increased somewhat further in conjunction with the December 2012 FOMC meeting. By contrast, their projections about QE3 barely changed at all during the so-called taper tantrum episode of late spring 2013, which was triggered by the Fed chair's testimony to the Joint Economic Committee (JEC) in late May and further magnified by the June FOMC meeting a few weeks later.

It should be noted that the actual term premium cannot be directly observed but can be inferred from the term structure of Treasury securities and the forward contracts on those securities. Thus, we use two distinct measures that are maintained and posted by Federal Reserve staff, namely, the series published by the Federal Reserve Board, which uses the methodology developed by Kim and Wright (2005), and the series published by the New York Fed, which uses the methodology of Adrian, Crump, and Moench (2013).

In gauging the impact of QE3 announcements, we follow the approach of Krishnamurthy and Jorgensen (2011) in analyzing the two-day change in the term premium (i.e., the day after the event minus the day before the event). In particular, for each of the FOMC communications that shifted investors' expectations about the size of QE3, we can use the Fed staff's framework to obtain the predicted impact on the ten-year term premium, and then we can compare that prediction with the actual two-day change in the term premium. This approach enables us to disentangle the effects of QE3 from other economic and financial developments outside each two-day window that may have influenced the overall level of the term premium.[26]

As shown in table 2.4, the Fed staff analysis implies that the initial announcement of QE3 in September 2012, which led investors to anticipate purchases of about $500 billion, should have reduced the term premium by about 17 basis points, whereas that announcement was actually associated with a substantial *increase* in the term premium. Similarly, the release of the September 2012 FOMC minutes should have reduced the term premium by an additional 11 basis points but instead generated a further *increase*. And the December 2012 FOMC meeting, which should have exerted downward pressure on the term premium, was also associated with an increase in the term premium. Evidently, the initial rollout of QE3 was not merely ineffectual but counterproductive, that is, each of these three FOMC announcements exerted upward pressure on the term premium.

Table 2.4 also documents the upward shifts in the term premium—totaling about 25 to 30 basis points—that were associated with the May 2013 JEC testimony and the June 2013 FOMC meeting. As noted above, investors' projections about the overall size of QE3 and the timing of liftoff hardly moved at all during this period. Rather, the surging term premium occurred in response to Fed communications about tapering the pace of asset purchases rather than simply ending the program. Such a taper was expected to have only minimal effects on the total amount of purchases, and hence the Fed staff's analytical framework indicated that it should not have substantial effects on the term premium. Thus, the Fed's leadership attributed the upward spike to transitory frictions and irrational market behavior, and hence this episode was labeled the "taper tantrum," analogous to the tantrum of an ill-tempered child.

---

26. Jim Hamilton's contribution to this volume also highlights the upward trajectory of the term premium following the launch of QE3.

TABLE 2.4. Was QE3 Helpful or Counterproductive?

| | Term Premium on Ten-Year Treasury Security (basis points) | | |
| | | Actual Two-Day Change | |
Event	Predicted Change	FRBOG Measure	FRBNY Measure
Sept. 2012 FOMC Meeting (9/13/2012)	−17	+6	+17
Sept. 2012 FOMC Minutes (10/4/2012)	−11	+8	+15
Dec. 2012 FOMC Meeting (12/12/2012)	−3	+7	+11
May 2013 JEC Testimony (5/22/2013)	−2	+8	+11
June 2013 FOMC Meeting (6/19/2013)	+3	+21	+14

Note: For each event, the second column indicates the predicted change in the term premium on a 10-year constant-maturity Treasury security, which is computed by applying the Federal Reserve Board staff's maintained assumption to the perceived shift in security holdings reported in table 2.3. The last two columns show the actual two-day change in the term premium for that event, as calculated by the Federal Reserve's Board of Governors (FRBOG) and by the Federal Reserve Bank of New York (FRBNY), respectively.

In retrospect, however, "taper tantrum" was an inapt characterization, because the upward shift in the term premium was not a transitory episode caused by market frictions but was in fact characteristic of the entire QE3 program. As shown in figure 2.4, the term premium started moving upward during the early stages of QE3, jumped 75 basis points in late spring 2013, and did not subside until QE3 ended in autumn 2014. Moreover, market participants specifically attributed these developments to the lack of clarity in FOMC communications. For example, the results of the New York Fed's June 2013 survey included the following summary: "Most primary dealers stated that a change in perception of or heightened uncertainty about the FOMC's view of appropriate monetary policy were key factors that generated the rise in the 10-Treasury yield."

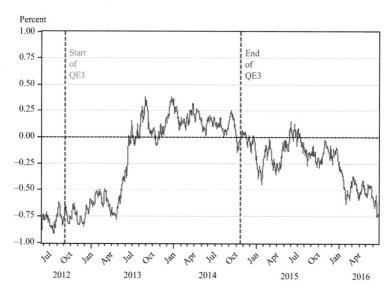

FIGURE 2.4.   QE3 and the Evolution of the Term Premium
Source: Federal Reserve Board.

Given that QE3 did not achieve its intended aim of reducing longer-term bond yields, it is not surprising that the program was ineffectual in spurring the US economic recovery. As shown in the upper panel of figure 2.5, QE3 had negligible effects on the growth of US real GDP, which fluctuated within a relatively narrow range in 2013 and 2014. Likewise, QE3 had no apparent impact on core PCE inflation (personal consumption expenditures, the Fed's preferred measure of underlying inflation), which averaged about 1.5 percent over this period, essentially the same as its average pace over preceding and subsequent years.[27]

The limited effectiveness of quantitative easing has also been underscored by the recent experiences of other major economies where conventional policy has been constrained by the ELB. For example, the Bank of Japan (BOJ) launched its quantitative

27. Levin and Loungani (2019) analyze a range of macroeconomic indicators and find no evidence of any statistically significant effects of QE3.

US Real GDP Growth

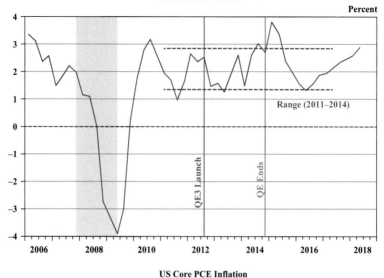

US Core PCE Inflation

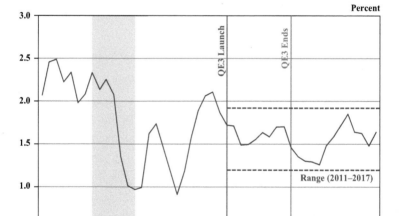

FIGURE 2.5. Did QE3 Affect the Economic Recovery?

Note: These two panels show the four-quarter average growth rates of real GDP and of the price index for personal consumption expenditures (PCE) excluding food and energy, as published by the Bureau of Economic Analysis, and the recession dates (shaded area) are determined by the National Bureau of Economic Research.

and qualitative easing program in April 2013 and initiated yield curve control in 2016, but Japanese core inflation (excluding food and energy prices) is still mired close to zero—far below the BOJ's 2 percent inflation target. Similarly, the European Central Bank (ECB) engaged in a large-scale asset purchase program from early 2015 through late 2018, but core consumer inflation (excluding food, energy, alcohol, and tobacco) edged upward only slightly and remains roughly a percentage point below the ECB's stated objective of keeping inflation "below but close to 2 percent over the medium run."

DESIGN PRINCIPLES FOR DIGITAL CASH

In my joint work with Michael Bordo, we have emphasized that digital cash can fulfill the three basic functions of money, serving as a practically costless medium of exchange, a secure store of value, and a stable unit of account.[28] While private forms of money can fulfill some aspects of these functions, there are intrinsic reasons why households and nonfinancial firms should also have access to a fiduciary form of money issued by the central bank. First, central bank money serves as a unit of measure—analogous to the inch or the meter—that facilitates the economic decisions and financial plans of ordinary consumers and small businesses. Second, in an efficient monetary system, the medium of exchange should also serve as a secure store of value that bears the same rate of return as other risk-free assets such as US Treasury bills; see Friedman (1960). By contrast, any purely private form of money (i.e., not backed by government authorities) is intrinsically subject to default risk and hence cannot serve as a reliable medium of exchange nor as a stable unit of account.

---

28. See Bordo and Levin (2017) for a comprehensive discussion of design principles for digital cash.

One conceivable approach to establishing digital cash might be for people to hold such accounts at the central bank itself. But it seems undesirable for the central bank to start competing directly with commercial banks in attracting deposits, especially in cases where the central bank also regulates and supervises those banks. Such an approach would also raise a host of concerns about privacy and bureaucratic inefficiencies and could pose risks to financial stability, for example, depositors shifting their funds from commercial banks to the central bank at the onset of a financial crisis.

Thus, our analysis indicates that digital cash should be provided through designated accounts held at supervised depository institutions, which would hold part or all of those funds in segregated reserve accounts at the central bank. This approach would foster competition among digital cash providers and protect the privacy of individual transactions while facilitating appropriate law enforcement. In effect, the provision of digital cash would be similar to that of many other public goods, such as water, electricity, and transportation.

Under this approach, payment transaction could be transmitted instantaneously and securely at practically zero cost, simply debiting the payer's digital cash account and crediting the payee's digital cash account. The scope and scale of fraudulent transactions could be mitigated by straightforward and convenient methods such as two-step identity verification.

Digital cash accounts could bear interest at essentially the same rate as Treasury bills, thereby serving as a secure store of value. This would tighten the link between the interest that banks earn on their reserves and the interest that they pay to ordinary depositors, thereby strengthening the monetary transmission mechanism. Moreover, such an arrangement would be a natural extension of the current monetary system, in which the Federal Reserve pays interest on the reserves of commercial banks, issues interest-bearing liabilities to a wider array of financial counterparties through its reverse repo facility, and maintains segregated accounts on behalf of the customers of systemically important financial market utilities.[29]

The interest rate on digital cash would serve as the FOMC's key monetary policy tool. During normal times, this interest rate would be positive. But in the face of a severe adverse shock, the FOMC would be able to cut the digital cash interest rate below zero to foster economic recovery and preserve price stability. As discussed below, such a system would appropriately insulate ordinary households and small businesses from incurring negative rates on their digital cash accounts.

In effect, the Federal Reserve would be able to provide an appropriate degree of monetary stimulus without resorting to QE, and hence its balance sheet would become very transparent. In particular, the Fed could simply hold short-term Treasuries in the same quantity as its liabilities of digital cash. The Fed's operating procedures would be correspondingly transparent: it would engage in purchases and sales of Treasury securities to adjust the supply of digital cash in line with movements in demand for digital cash.

MITIGATING THE ELB

Ken Rogoff's book was titled *The Curse of Cash,* and that theme is underscored in his latest paper with Andrew Lilley. Nonetheless, it would be inappropriate to abolish paper currency; rather, individuals and businesses should remain free to continue using it for the foreseeable future. As digital cash becomes ubiquitous, however, demand for paper cash is likely to diminish rapidly. After all, paper currency is inefficient and costly: sorting and cleaning it at

---

29. For example, segregated reserve accounts at the Federal Reserve Bank of Chicago have been created to hold the funds of customers of the Chicago Mercantile Exchange (http://www.cmegroup.com/notices/clearing/2017/03/Chadv17-107.html) and the initial margin accounts of customers of ICE Clear Credit (https://www.theice.com/publicdocs /clear_credit/circulars/Circular_2017_015_FINAL.pdf).

the bank, supplying it to ATMs, maintaining cash registers and safes at retail stores, using armored cars for transport, and ensuring that no cash is lost or stolen at any point in this cycle. In contrast, digital cash can be used instantly at practically no cost at all. Thus, as digital cash comes into widespread use, it seems reasonable to expect that paper currency will rapidly become obsolescent, just like typewriters and audiotapes.

But if paper cash is not abolished, then how would the Federal Reserve eliminate the ELB? Some analysts have proposed a time-varying exchange rate between paper currency and digital cash.[30] But such an approach would impose a severe burden on ordinary households and small businesses and would be fundamentally inconsistent with the notion that the Fed should provide a stable unit of account.

Thus, a far superior approach would be to eliminate the ELB by curtailing incentives for financial arbitrage between paper cash and digital cash, in effect introducing "sand in the wheels." In particular, the Fed could establish a graduated system of fees for transfers between paper cash and digital cash. Small transfers—say, up to $100 per week for an individual or $10,000 for a small business— would be completely exempt from such fees. Moderately larger transfers would be subject to a nominal fee (e.g., 2–3 percent), roughly similar to the size of withdrawal fees at many ATMs and cash service fees incurred by many small businesses. And the largest transfers (say, over $5,000) would be subject to an even larger fee (e.g., 5–10 percent). These arrangements would effectively eliminate the ELB while ordinary consumers and small businesses would remain free to use paper cash if so desired.

Finally, the Fed could insulate ordinary households and small businesses from incurring negative rates on moderate levels of digital cash balances. For example, an individual might hold funds in a single

---

30. See Agarwal and Kimball (2015).

digital cash account, and moderate balances in that account (e.g., up to $5,000) could be exempt from negative rates, while balances exceeding that limit would be subject to the negative interest rate.[31] Of course, individuals and businesses would also be free to hold multiple digital cash accounts at various financial institution banks; in such instances, one of those accounts would need to be designated as the user's "primary" digital cash account, and the exemption would apply only to the funds held in that particular account.

With this design, the Federal Reserve would be able to effectively foster economic recovery and price stability without imposing implicit taxes or fees on the digital cash balances held by ordinary households and small businesses. After all, the crux of the rationale for cutting the digital cash interest rate below zero is to influence the incentives of wealthy investors and large financial firms—not to penalize moderate account balances that facilitate day-to-day payment transactions.

FINANCIAL STABILITY

During a financial crisis, the central bank can expand the stock of digital cash as needed to provide emergency liquidity to supervised financial institutions. Alternatively, the central bank could extend such emergency safeguards to another public agency such as a bank regulator or the deposit insurance fund. Appropriate legal safeguards will be necessary to ensure that the lender of last-resort actions does not undermine the central bank's ability to carry out its commitment to price stability.

In the event of a financial crisis, the central bank would be able to reduce the digital cash interest rate below zero, thereby preventing runs from other financial assets into digital cash. In effect,

---

31. In effect, the yield on digital cash accounts would be analogous to that of US Treasury Inflation-Protected Securities (TIPS), which provide compensation for positive inflation but never shrink in nominal value.

a widening of risk spreads would be reflected by a corresponding drop in the risk-free interest rate, rather than a surge in private lending rates (which would remain close to normal levels).
Moreover, this policy strategy generates a steep yield curve that
facilitates the expansion of bank credit and fosters prudent risk taking—precisely the opposite of QE and "lower for longer" forward
guidance that encourage search-for-yield behavior. Thus, digital
cash would foster more rapid *V*-shaped recoveries instead of the
U-shaped recovery of the US economy over the past decade.

PRACTICAL STEPS

In light of these design principles, it's natural to ask whether digital
cash is truly feasible in the United States and, if so, over what time
frame? Rather than decades or centuries, our analysis indicates that
the Federal Reserve could take the essential steps by 2020, although
further refinements would surely take place in subsequent years.
In particular, the Federal Reserve should: (1) establish a real-time
clearing and settlement system that facilitates efficient payments
for consumers and businesses, and (2) facilitate the establishment
of safe and liquid bank accounts that accrue essentially the same
rate of return as Treasury bills.

As noted above, a key feature of digital cash is to serve as an *efficient medium of exchange*. Thus, a real-time clearing and settlement
system is crucial for facilitating secure payments and eliminating
counterparty risks by finalizing such transactions within minutes
rather than hours or days. The Federal Reserve should move forward expeditiously in establishing a secure and efficient real-time
payment system.

Another key design principle is that digital cash should serve
as a *secure store of value* that bears the same rate of return as other
risk-free assets, thereby eliminating the opportunity cost of holding money. In effect, consumers and businesses should be able to

receive essentially the same interest on checkable deposits and other current accounts that commercial banks receive on reserves held at the Federal Reserve, that is, the interest rate on reserves (IOR) less a very small margin to cover operating costs.

In a competitive banking system, it would be reasonable to expect that the interest rate on liquid deposits would roughly match or exceed the IOR. After all, commercial banks are required to hold only a small fraction of their liquid deposits as reserves at the Federal Reserve (which accrue the IOR), and they can earn a higher return by lending out the rest of those funds or investing in Treasury securities and other safe assets. In fact, however, most checkable deposits earn little or no interest, and even short-term savings accounts accrue interest at a rate far below that of IOR. In effect, a substantial portion of banks' current profit margin is being earned by paying noncompetitive rates on those deposit accounts.

One simple way for the Federal Reserve to foster a more competitive banking system would be to encourage the establishment of narrow banks. The business model of a narrow bank is remarkably simple and transparent, because such a bank would hold 100 percent of its deposits as reserves at the Federal Reserve. Thus, such deposits would accrue interest at essentially the same rate as IOR (less a small margin to cover the bank's operating costs). Narrow banks could significantly enhance the competitiveness of the banking system without displacing most conventional banks. After all, huge banks obtain the bulk of their funding from wholesale markets and earn profits from managing complex portfolios, while community banks specialize in "relationship banking" with small businesses and local residents. Finally, narrow banks would operate under the same legal arrangements as other commercial banks, namely, a charter from a state banking agency or the Treasury Department. But a narrow bank would have no need for FDIC insurance or access to the Fed's discount window, since its deposits would be inherently safe and liquid.

CONCLUSION

Although memories of the financial crisis are gradually receding, the global economy remains turbulent and unpredictable. Moreover, the "new normal" for the target federal funds rate is now expected to be around 3 percent—markedly lower than its level preceding that crisis—and hence the ELB is very likely to reemerge as a binding constraint on conventional monetary policy in coming years. And a clear lesson from recent experience is that QE and other unconventional monetary policy tools are complex, opaque, and ineffectual.

Therefore, an urgent priority for the Federal Reserve is to move ahead with the provision of digital cash as a means of mitigating the ELB. Digital cash should be provided to the public through accounts at supervised financial institutions, which hold part or all of those funds in segregated reserve accounts at the central bank. In the near term, the Federal Reserve can take practical steps in this direction by implementing a real-time payment system and by encouraging the establishment of narrow banks.

This approach will ensure that monetary policy will be systematic, transparent, and effective during normal times and in responding to severe adverse shocks.

References

Adrian, Tobias, Richard K. Crump, and Emanuel Moench. 2013. "Pricing the Term Structure with Linear Regressions." *Journal of Financial Economics* 110, no. 1 (October): 110–138.

Agarwal, Ruchir, and Miles Kimball. 2015. "Breaking through the Zero Lower Bound." International Monetary Fund Working Paper 15-224.

Bordo, Michael, and Andrew Levin. 2017. "Central Bank Digital Currency and the Future of Monetary Policy." NBER Working Paper 23711, National Bureau of Economic Research. Also published in *The Structural Foundations of Monetary Policy,* edited by Michael Bordo, John Cochrane, and Amit Seru. Stanford, CA: Hoover Institution Press, 2018

————. 2019. "U.S. Digital Cash: Principles & Practical Steps." Economics Working Paper 19101, Hoover Institution, January.

Cambron, Alyssa, Michelle Ezer, Andrew Figura, Joshua Frost, Jeff Huther, Jane Ihrig, John Kandrac, Don Kim, Beth Klee, Deborah Leonard, Dave Reifschneider, Julie Remache, John Roberts, Min Wei, and Nathaniel Wuerffel. 2012. "Options for Continuation of Open-Ended Asset Purchases in 2013." FOMC Memos, Federal Open Market Committee. https://www.federalreserve .gov/monetarypolicy/fomc-memos.htm.

Chung, Hess, Etienne Gagnon, Taisuke Nakata, Matthias Paustian, Bernd Schlusche, James Trevino, Diego Vilán, and Wei Zheng. 2019. "Monetary Policy Options at the Effective Lower Bound: Assessing the Federal Reserve's Current Policy Toolkit." Finance and Economics Discussion Series 2019-003. Washington, DC: Board of Governors of the Chung, Hess, Jean-Philippe Laforte, David Reifschneider, and John C. Williams. 2011. "Have We Underestimated the Likelihood and Severity of Zero Lower Bound Events?" Federal Reserve Bank of San Francisco Working Paper 2011-01, January. http://www.frbsf.org /publications/economics/papers/2011/wp11-01bk.pdf.

Erceg, Christopher, and Andrew Levin. 2014. "Labor Force Participation and Monetary Policy in the Wake of the Great Recession." *Journal of Money, Credit and Banking* 46: 3–49.

Friedman, Milton. 1960. *A Program for Monetary Stability.* New York: Fordham University Press.

Kim, Don H., and Jonathan H. Wright. 2005. "An Arbitrage-Free Three-Factor Term Structure Model and the Recent Behavior of Long-Term Yields and Distant-Horizon Forward Rates." Finance and Economics Discussion Series 2005-33, August. Washington, DC: Board of Governors of the Federal Reserve System.

Krishnamurthy, Arvind, and Annette Vissing-Jorgensen. 2011. "The Effects of Quantitative Easing on Interest Rates: Channels and Implications for Policy." *Brookings Papers on Economic Activity* (Fall): 215–65.

Laforte, Jean-Philippe, David López-Salido, Steve Meyer, Edward Nelson, and John Roberts. 2012. "Flow-Based Balance Sheet Policies: Communication Issues and Macroeconomic Effects." Staff memo sent to the FOMC on August 28, 2012, and released to the public in January 2018. https://www.federalreserve .gov/monetarypolicy/fomc-memos.htm#m2012.

Levin, Andrew. 2014. "The Design and Communication of Systematic Monetary Strategies." In "Frameworks for Central Banking in the Next Century." Special issue, *Journal of Economic Dynamics and Control* 49 (December): 52–69.

Levin, Andrew, and Prakash Loungani. 2019. "Reassessing the Efficacy and Costs of Quantitative Easing." Unpublished manuscript, Dartmouth College.

Woodford, Michael. 2012. "Methods of Policy Accommodation at the Interest-Rate Lower Bound." In *The Changing Policy Landscape: A Symposium Sponsored by The Federal Reserve Bank of Kansas City, Jackson Hole, Wyo.*, 185–288. Kansas City: Federal Reserve Bank of Kansas City.

GENERAL DISCUSSION

KENNETH ROGOFF: Well, thank you, Andrew, for those comments. I feel a little bit like we're in the fifties, and I have a design for an electric car and Andrew has a design for an electric car, but no one else wants to hear about electric cars. But I like their idea. I actually think it conforms very closely to my favorite idea in my book, which has the added element of encouraging the trend toward less use of cash. But my favored plan would have fees on large currency redeposits into the central bank under negative rates, would provide for financial inclusion, and would not necessarily require an explicit exchange rate between electronic and paper currency. Of course, before undertaking any approach, the first big step toward serious, negative, unconstrained monetary policy will be to put together a broad committee, one that has to have people from markets, etc., representation on the technical side and on the political side, etc. But I don't think the challenges are insurmountable. For most countries, when they went from a fixed exchange rate to a flexible exchange rate, critics made a very big deal about disastrous it would be. Yet after implementing negative rates, most of the countries found, "gosh, this works great." I, by the way, credit Marvin Goodfriend with emphasizing that point.

In practice, a lot of the pushback on negative rates has come from banks: "What about our profits?" This is particularly an issue at smaller banks. At many larger banks, which borrow extensively in wholesale markets at negative rates themselves, it has actually gone the other way. However, if you cushion small depositors, if you subsidize those accounts, then implementing effective negative rate policy will not be such a big deal for banks as they should be able to pass through negative rates to large depositors. Fundamentally, if you eliminate the cash arbitrage, the issue of bank profits should just go away.

PETER FISHER: I want to thank you both for a terrific summary of
all the reasons why QE, forward guidance, and lower for longer
didn't work very well, and certainly much less well than has been
asserted. And I think that's something that both the fourth estate
and the central bankers of the world might want to focus on.

But I'd love to ask each of you, Ken and Andy, to be a little
more precise about the transmission mechanism you expect
your version of negative rates to work. So if you're going to get
negative rates, it's going to incent the pension funds and the
insurance companies not to hoard cash, and they're going to do
something else. Well, what is that something else? You've also
said it will lead to faster rates of employment, and you've got a
little more of a burden to explain how that's going to work.

And Andy and Mike, could you think about the shape of the
yield curve, and it's not just bank profits you've got to worry
about, you've also got to worry about whether the banking system's balance sheet on the liability side starts to contract too
quickly. You may not get a lot of credit growth. I just want to
press you each to think a little—explain a little more, the particular transmission mechanism you think your version of negative rates is going to work through.

ROGOFF: It works exactly as monetary policy works (when rates are
positive). If you've taken care of the administrative, legal, and
regulatory issues, it's exactly symmetric. So, no, there would
be more consumption, more investment. The issues of credit
expansion having to do with bank profitability should substantially go away if people can't arbitrage into cash.

ANDY LEVIN: Peter and I have talked about this quite a bit, and I've
learned a lot from conversations with Peter Fisher. I think a
big reason for moving in the reason that Ken's recommended
and that Mike and I have been writing about is to get back to
V-shaped recoveries, instead of the kind of "lower for longer."
When we think about conventional monetary policy, like the

recovery in the early eighties, during '83 and '84, it was "happy days are here again." We had a V-shaped recovery. Well, that's because monetary policy had lots of room to cut as much as it needed low enough so you got a pretty fast recovery going, and then it pretty quickly normalized. And so, I think that if we can get into that world again, businesses, consumers, and families are all going to be very happy.

By the way, Ken is talking about this as decades away. I think this doesn't have to be decades away. It could be maybe a three- or four-year process to do this. But it doesn't have to be decades.

ROGOFF: I agree. The transition would be a three- or four-year process. But I think it's decades away, like my example of electric cars in the 1950s.

JOHN COCHRANE: I want to thank both of you. You gave a beautiful overview. The Treasury could issue overnight debt if it wanted to—fixed value, floating rate, electronically transferable, treasury debt, functionally the same as reserves. Why should the Treasury issue something else and then count on the Fed to transform it, in a form only accessible to banks? Let the Treasury issue it directly. It would solve most of the balance sheet problems.

I entirely agree with your main point: all the other proposals are ineffective or pie in the sky, exactly as you've said. I also agree: electronic interest–paying digital currency at low cost is a great thing. In fact, the Treasury could be doing that too. If attractive, it happens on its own, and it will happen on its own for other reasons, not to give us negative rates, and then by the way you get to have negative rates.

I want to express, though, a little skepticism that this will quickly produce V-shaped recoveries and it will be so powerful on its own. The premise is that the problem in a recession is a generic lack of 1930s Keynesian aggregate demand. It's a unidimensional view of our complex economy. Something goes wrong, and no matter what the source, the answer is more

stimulus. Where the stimulus comes from is as good as anywhere else. If the recession comes from somewhere outside the
Fed, then the Fed's job is to heroically step in and provide this
unidimensional aggregate demand.

In fact, lots of other views disagree with this simpleminded
Keynesian premise. The credit-constraint types think the problem is there's a bottleneck in credit markets, and no matter how
much aggregate demand, if the banks aren't open, you can't
get the economy going. That was Ben Bernanke's famous view.
The supply-side view that structural reform is the problem has
the same flavor. You can add the aggregate demand you want,
it's not going to help. Lots of countries have persistently high
unemployment, terrible labor markets, and there's nothing their
central banks can do about it. That may be the reason we had a
slow recovery.

The other view of the Fed is, channeling Milton Friedman,
that lots of recessions happened because the Fed screwed up,
made matters worse, told the banks to hold back, and that the
best thing for the Fed to do is simply not to screw up, as it did not
in 2008. It should make sure that the banks are open and working, and don't pretend that it can solve the structural reform
problem, especially in Europe and Japan.

ROGOFF: I certainly strongly agree with the point about Keynesianism
becoming sort of a secular religion in a lot of circles, and it's
missing a lot. And if one really looks across countries, there
are structural issues, not just differences in aggregate demand.
Someone asked me recently, why does Europe have worse performance than the United States? And I pointed them to Ed
Prescott's work on tax differences. I had a slide that I skipped
over emphasizing that monetary policy is not a panacea.

I did want to mention one interesting and important point
about digital currency. And that is that this is a game that the
Treasury can play. The United States actually has something

called TreasuryDirect. It takes about five minutes to set up. One can hold up to $20 million down to $100. You can make payments to other people on TreasuryDirect. In fact, a prototype digital savings account is already here. The Treasury doesn't advertise it much, perhaps because the banking system would go crazy if TreasuryDirect started accumulating too much money. By the way, TreasuryDirect charges no fees. So, that's proof of concept that this can be done and does not necessarily have to be done entirely by the Fed.

And one last point. There's a difference between the digital currency you want to use if you want to buy an apple, which is a high transaction cost, and a digital retail currency that can be used for larger payments. Cash is still very convenient for frequent small payments. But for large payments such as monthly rent, then the issues having to do with implementing a retail digital currency are very straightforward.

MICKEY LEVY: This is just a simple question following Peter's and John's point. If you hold retail accounts harmless, that is, keep the zero bound for consumers, then their incentive to save or invest is unchanged, and consumption will not be stimulated. That leaves the impact of expectations. Since consumption is 70 percent of GDP, how are you going to stimulate the economy if you don't impose negative rates on consumer accounts? Also, I worry about the transition from where we are to where you want to go, which may be tricky. The Fed now admits that its earlier assessments on the efficacy of QEII and QEIII overstated their stimulative impacts. How does the Fed transition to new regime and maintain credibility and build confidence in the business community?

LEVIN: So, Chris Erceg and I wrote a paper where we looked at disaggregated vector autoregressions to determine which components of consumption respond to a monetary policy shift. And what we found was the biggest shifts happen in consumer durables:

auto sales, refrigerators, and home construction. So, regarding Mickey's question about if it matters whether retail accounts have a zero or negative rate, I would say no, it doesn't matter. What matters to a household thinking about buying a car is: what's the car loan rate? When car loan rates were zero financing for five years, that made it much more appealing to buy a new car than when the rate was 2 or 3 percent or 4 percent. If the car loan rate went below zero, a family that's thinking about buying a new car would think, wow, that's really cool, they're going to pay us to take the new car. And so they might make the new purchase. The amount that they have on their thousand dollars in their checking account is not really material to those kinds of decisions.

ROGOFF: No, not at all. I agree with Andy that his major point is what are the interest rates that matter when a consumer is buying a car or consumer durable. Again, in my plan, small savers would be protected; they would be allowed an account of up to two or three thousand dollars where the interest rate would not go negative; the banks would be subsidized on those, when they're paying the negative interest rate on reserves. The Treasury and the Fed would be making a lot of money in negative interest rate environment, so providing such subsidies would not really be difficult to do.

You ask about the transition to negative rates, and of course that's a tricky question. I think the Fed is better positioned to carefully plan than is Europe or Japan, because they may need to make a transition more quickly. The Fed has a lot of time to sort of look at it in more of an abstract way, to have more distance. It's probably fair to say that almost everyone that thinks—I don't know if John does—that the Fed did a great job—I think you do say this—in 2008 and 2009. But after that, when the Fed was not in emergency mode anymore, it was trying hard to bolster public confidence by making big claims about the potency of its alternative monetary instruments. The Fed public relations machine was whirring. In retrospect it probably would have been better for the Fed to say "there's just not much we can do at this point unless we can do something very different" (like effective negative interest rate policy). If Congress wants to do more fiscal policy stimulus, we think that would be great. That, of course, is a very difficult position for the Fed to find itself in. It understandably wanted to encourage markets to think it's had everything under control, and obviously you don't want to come out and give a speech and say, "We're helpless." But I do think that thrust of more recent academic work is guiding them in that direction, and it will get easier and easier to say over time.

GEORGE SELGIN: This is for Andy, and it's a question related to the question about the credit channel and all that. It concerns the risk of having the Fed's involvement in retail payments become something that's not just a cyclical development but a secular one. I wonder if you could comment on that. How do you keep the Fed from competing with the commercial banks permanently once it gets into this retail trade? And if you can't do that, isn't there a concern about the allocation of credit in the economy and the Fed becoming even more important than it is now as an intermediary of credit?

LEVIN: So, Mike and I have a new Hoover working paper that we issued in January (which is coming out soon in the *Cato Journal*) where we talk about some of these practical issues. And we emphasize that establishing a public-private partnership is crucial to the design of digital cash. And this is a conversation I've been having with people in Europe and Japan as well. The World Bank gives advice to governments all over the world about how to provide electricity and telecommunications and other types of infrastructure. It's well understood now that this shouldn't be done solely by the government. After all, the government can be very bureaucratic and very inefficient and not very innovative. Public-private partnerships, especially where there's a bunch of private enterprises competing with each other, is the state-of-the-art approach for telecommunications and port facilities and so forth. And for the payment system, that's how it should be—there should be a partnership between the central bank and the supervised financial institutions that provides digital cash, ensuring that you have competition, that you can have privacy, that you can have innovation. If one bank comes up with a better smartphone app, and lots of digital cash holders start using that app, then other providers will have to improve their apps too. So, I don't see this as a static, stagnant initiative. It's going to be a dynamic process.

ROGOFF: I'd just say it's much more general than that, there are many ways to implement a digital government retail currency, and there are many ways the banking system can work together with it. We have very similar issues in the current system. Many countries have giant postal banks, gyro accounts, that soak up a lot of money that might go into the private sector banking system and that are incredibly inefficient. I've written about the analogies with the Chicago plan of the 1930s in my 2016 book. The problem is that digital currencies may be regarded by the public as a superior asset that will displace the banks. However, if one is looking over the next thirty or forty years, this may be coming regardless. If it isn't the government, it will be the tech industry. Banks are going to get disrupted one way or another, but the government doesn't have to be the one that supplants them.

UNKNOWN SPEAKER 1: Just a clarifying question. So, the point with introducing a negative interest rate policy is you want to prevent large players from storing large amounts of real value into hoarding cash. Is this correct?

ROGOFF: That's not the point of negative interest rates. What you have to stop is wholesale hoarding of paper currency.

UNKNOWN SPEAKER 2: Yeah, yeah. What you have to stop in order to implement this policy. So, what would prevent them from hoarding real amounts of real value into gold or diamonds? This would still put a lower bound?

ROGOFF: No, no. It's exactly the same as monetary policy today, when they cut the interest rate from 3 percent to 2 percent; this of course encourages people to shift funds into risky real assets, and that is part of the transmission mechanism of normal monetary policy. Very low rates are a fair part of the reason stock prices have gone up over the last decade, as well as housing prices.

LEVIN: I think this is why in our first Hoover paper, which is the one that's in the Hoover volume, Mike and I emphasize these basic principles of the monetary system, the most important of which is stable unit of account. Consumers and businesses need a stable currency to serve as a unit of measure, just like a meter or a yard or a liter bottle. They need to have a unit of account that they can use when making transactions. So the problem with these other commodities and real assets is they have a floating exchange rate against the unit of account. So you can go ahead and buy a house if you think it's going to appreciate in value. Or you can hold Bitcoin if you think it's going to appreciate in value. But there's no guarantee that it's going to have a stable unit of account. And I think this comes back to Milton Friedman. Richard Clarida emphasized at the beginning of his speech, Ken emphasized it, Mike and I have emphasized it too. The central bank's most important responsibility is to preserve the stability of the unit of account. When Milton Friedman said inflation's everywhere and always a monetary phenomenon, my understanding is that's fundamentally what he meant, namely, that monetary policy has to be able to commit and ensure that the unit of account remains stable over time. And if we think that the Fed and other central banks are running short of ammunition, and that the next time could be worse, we could be ending up in a situation, like in the Great Depression, where the price level dropped 30 percent, and it was catastrophic, because the Fed, constrained by the gold standard, was no longer able to carry out its commitment to maintain a stable price level. And so, there should be some sense of urgency here. We shouldn't just be thinking of ten- and twenty- and fifty-year horizons. We need to make sure that this problem gets solved soon enough so the Fed has the ammunition next time to carry out Milton Friedman's prescription.

ROGOFF: You stated that in a very precise way, and this conforms to the standard central bank answer for price stability, and it is a good one. But one has to remember that stuff happens. During World War I, central banks had little choice but to inflate; the seventies were a mistake. Right now, there are interesting ideas about making debt much, much, much larger and more short term, and having the Fed finance it. But of course there are risks. What if it turned out maybe not to work quite the way it was promised, and the federal government came under severe fiscal pressure from climate catastrophes, pandemics, cyberattacks, etc.? Do we really want to force the government to default rather than having the Fed inflate? And does the Fed have the tools to inflate at the moment. Another important issue is what to do if we have another financial crisis where the federal government still had good credit, but the private sector had huge debt problems, and you can't clean them up easily. Wouldn't it actually be good to have mild inflation to relieve private burdens? And how can this be done at present if interest rates are at the zero bound? I personally believe that having some inflation in the last crisis would have been great, perhaps 4 or 5 percent inflation for a few years, and I argued for that. Yes, that would be heterodox? But I'm not sure the Fed has the power to do that at the moment, anyway.

LEVIN: But this comes back again to ordinary consumers and small businesses. Because I think if you ask them. Ask them, not just the economic theories, ask those small businesses and ordinary consumers in vulnerable communities, would they have liked to have had 5 or 6 percent inflation in order to promote a faster recovery? They'd say, "Boy, I'm not ready for that." That's why people hated the 1970s, because it's really tough, if you can't hire a financial planner or portfolio manager, to deal with that sort of situation.

ROGOFF: But they don't have any money. They're gaining from the jobs . . .

LEVIN: In principle, we're on the same page here, because what you want is a V-shaped recovery, using the nominal interest rate as the standard tool of monetary policy, so you don't have to resort to unconventional and unreliable policy tools.

CHARLIE CALOMIRIS: Thanks very much for a great panel. But as long as we're getting futuristic, I wanted to point out, it seems like one of the assumptions in this discussion is that central banks will maintain their monopoly over the unit of account and the payment system. I don't think that's obvious. I think you could imagine stable-value cryptocurrencies that wouldn't even be using the dollar and that wouldn't have to be part of this, let's say, three or four decades from now. And I think you could imagine that if there were a protracted period of negative interest on the Fed payment system, that would actually hasten that.

ROGOFF: Well, we can take that up at the Hoover conference next year, but the last part of my book is about this. As far as there being other units of account, if you look at the history of currency, and I know you've thought about it a lot and Mike has, but I fundamentally say, the private sector can innovate, the private sector can do things for a while. But the central bank makes the rules of the game. In the long run, the government always wins.

UNKNOWN SPEAKER 2: You seem to make it a very smooth transition from traditional monetary policy to negative rates, and I'd like to push back on two buckets. You mentioned criticisms but then didn't dive into them. The one concern I have is on efficient capital allocation. I do have some questions on whether that is indeed happening and whether that happened after the financial crisis as well. You mentioned the survival of zombie companies or the creation of monopolies. But the question I'd like you to answer is the other bucket. You did mention fiscal policy would always be more efficient. Is there a point when monetary policy in your framework is really conducting fiscal policy, and if so, is there a limit as to how much monetary policy should be achieving? I guess it's more an ethical question than anything else, and a question also ultimately of independence. There are lots of arguments being raised. So in 2008 the government was ineffective; therefore, monetary policy had to step in. If that goes to an extreme with very negative rates, isn't there the theoretical solution of negative rates at risk because the government will intervene?

ROGOFF: You always want to use fiscal policy. The question is how nimble is fiscal policy. Did you watch the Kavanaugh hearings? Do you think this team is really going to be able to implement some highly refined technocratic policy to stimulate the economy and then turn off at exactly the right place? It's a joke. And I think you could say the same virtually about every country in the world. When it's a big crisis, fiscal policy acts, and it would be better if it acted more in some cases. It would be better if it acted more effectively. But I think to have monetary policy dead in the water, and Andrew and Mike said this very well in their paper also, is going to be a real problem when the next crisis happens. We'll get through it. We'll still be around. A lot of countries have not done as well as the United States, and they're still around. But it could be better.

CHAPTER THREE

Tying Down the Anchor: Monetary Policy Rules and the Lower Bound on Interest Rates

Thomas M. Mertens and John C. Williams

1. INTRODUCTION

The sizable decline in the natural rate of interest observed in many countries over the past quarter century implies that central banks are now likely to be constrained by the lower bound on nominal interest rates frequently, interfering with their ability to offset negative shocks to the economy (e.g., see, Laubach and Williams 2016 and Holston, Laubach, and Williams 2017). As a result, central banks face the challenge of inflation expectations potentially becoming anchored at too low a level, which further limits the policy space available to react to negative shocks to the economy.

This paper studies the effect of various monetary policy frameworks and associated rules on inflation expectations and

Mertens: Federal Reserve Bank of San Francisco, 101 Market Street, Mailstop 1130, San Francisco, CA 94105; Thomas.Mertens@sf.frb.org. Williams: Federal Reserve Bank of New York, 33 Liberty Street, New York, NY 10045; John.C.Williams@ny.frb.org. We thank Richard Clarida, Marc Giannoni, Krishna Guha, Monika Piazzesi, John Taylor, and audiences at the Federal Reserve Bank of Dallas, the University of Texas at Austin, and the Hoover Institution's Strategies for Monetary Policy conference for helpful discussions. Patrick Adams and Renuka Diwan provided outstanding research assistance. The views expressed in this paper are those of the authors and do not necessarily reflect the positions of the Federal Reserve Bank of San Francisco, the Federal Reserve Bank of New York, or the Federal Reserve System.

macroeconomic outcomes. It uses a standard New Keynesian model augmented with a lower bound on interest rates. An essential part of this setup is the forward-looking nature of economic decision making. Inflation is determined via a Phillips curve by which inflation increases with the output gap and expectations about future inflation. The output gap is linked to the real interest rate relative to the natural rate of interest as well as expectations of future output gaps. Both measures of economic activity—inflation and the output gap—are subject to uncertainty stemming from shocks on the supply and demand side. The supply shock enters the Phillips curve while the demand shock hits the investment/savings (IS) curve for the output gap. For analytical tractability, we assume that these shocks follow a uniform distribution and are independent and identically distributed (i.i.d.) over time.[1]

To close the model, a central bank sets the nominal interest rate. It chooses a monetary policy rule consistent with its assumed policy framework that dictates the path for the interest rate in every possible scenario, and evaluates the rule according to its social loss. Importantly, the central bank can credibly communicate its interest rate rule so that expectations about future economic activity can adjust. The social loss function penalizes deviations of the rate of inflation from its target as well as positive or negative output gaps. A parameter for the conservativeness of the central bank controls the relative weight that the central bank assigns to stabilizing output versus inflation. The choice of the policy rate is thereby constrained by a lower bound on interest rates. We focus our attention on the central bank's policy rule for the interest rate and abstract from unconventional monetary policy. As a result, the central bank is unable to stimulate the economy beyond cutting the nominal interest rate down to its lower bound. However, the monetary policy

---

1. Normally distributed shocks lead to a similar analysis, both qualitative and quantitative (see Mertens and Williams 2018).

framework can entail future policy responses to current economic conditions and therefore influence activity through the expectations channel, similar to forward guidance.

In the absence of a lower bound on interest rates, the central bank would find it desirable to fully offset demand shocks while partially, depending on its conservativeness, accommodating supply shocks. Under an optimal interest rate rule, there is a unique equilibrium in which optimal monetary policy features standard inflation targeting.[2]

When the central bank is constrained by a lower bound on interest rates, negative supply and demand shocks cannot be offset to the desired degree. As a result, optimal policy under discretion will result in occasional encounters with the lower bound that lead to below-target inflation and output gaps when the natural rate of interest is sufficiently low, as in Mertens and Williams (2019). Since the private sector will incorporate these scenarios into their forecasts, expectations of inflation and output gaps will be lower than they would be in the absence of a lower bound. The reduction in expectations, in turn, exacerbates the effects of the lower bound on the economy.[3]

We investigate three classes of monetary policy frameworks and their associated policy rules and compare them with our benchmark case of optimal policy under discretion. In the benchmark, policy can be implemented with an interest rate rule that is linear in the supply and demand shocks. Under this policy, occasional encounters with the lower bound on interest rates lead to suboptimally

---

2. There are multiple interest rate rules that can implement optimal policy.

3. A second equilibrium emerges due to the presence of a lower bound. This "liquidity trap" is characterized by lower expectations of inflation and output. Since lower expectations constrain the economy due to the forward-looking nature of the Phillips and IS curves, the probability of a binding lower bound increases. Resulting shortfalls in the output gap and the rate of inflation relative to target confirm expectations and an equilibrium emerges. For the purposes of this paper, we restrict our analysis to the target equilibrium and pay no attention to the liquidity trap. For an empirical investigation, see Mertens and Williams (2018).

low inflation expectations when the natural rate of interest is sufficiently low. The shortfall in expectations is due to the central bank's
inability to stimulate the economy any further when at the lower
bound and the lack of commitment to provide stimulus in periods
following the encounter with the lower bound on interest rates. In
all three classes of monetary policy frameworks, we give the central
bank the ability to commit to an interest rate rule. The first category
is standard inflation-targeting frameworks. Aside from the benchmark framework of optimal monetary policy under discretion, we
study dovish policies and the introduction of an upper bound on
interest rates in this category. An interest rate rule that limits the
responsiveness to supply and demand shocks leads to lower social
losses. The reason for improved outcomes is that a smaller response
to shocks reduces the chances of hitting the lower bound on interest rates. The resulting benefits do not arise from policy setting in
the current period but rather an increase in inflation expectations.
However, the benefits come at the cost of larger inflation and output variability.

The second category consists of average-inflation-targeting policies. First, we consider changes to the intercept in the interest rate
rule. Reducing the intercept in the rule is equivalent to targeting
a higher inflation rate each period. This in turn feeds back into
periods when the lower bound on interest rates is binding and mitigates its effects on the macroeconomy. As a result, higher inflation
during normal times spills over to all periods and lowers overall
social losses. Average-inflation-targeting practices thereby fare
better in terms of social losses than dovish policies. However, the
central bank can do even better by further raising expected inflation. Additional benefits from inflation expectations above target
arise due to the asymmetry of the inflation distribution. This distribution is negatively skewed because of the low-inflation scenarios
associated with the lower bound. We further show that it is suffi-

cient for the central bank to adjust the intercept of the rule relative to optimal monetary policy under discretion.

As an alternative to this rule, we study an interest rate rule that makes up for past missed stimulus due to the lower bound. Therefore, we allow the central bank to condition its interest rate, in addition to the previous components, on the sum of past shortfalls in interest rate cuts as in Reifschneider and Williams (2000). This dynamic rule leads the rate of inflation to be at target on average. However, because of its conditioning on past shortfalls in interest rate cuts, inflation expectations vary with the shortfall in stimulus and thus fluctuate over time. In particular, since the policy framework calls for more stimulus following episodes of binding lower bounds, that is, a "lower-for-longer policy," inflation expectations are already higher *during* a time when the central bank is constrained. As a result, inflation does not drop as far below target and the social loss is lower compared with when only the intercept gets adjusted.

The third class of policies are price-level targeting policies along with their variants. We consider price-level targeting within the framework of an interest rate rule that, compared with the rule under discretion, can additionally condition on a price level. Price-level targeting, just like the Reifschneider-Williams rule, leads inflation expectations to adjust dynamically with higher inflation expectations during economic downturns. We contrast price-level targeting with temporary price-level targeting as proposed by Evans (2010) and Bernanke (2017). For temporary price-level targeting, the price-level target enters the interest rate rule only following an encounter with the lower bound. As soon as the shortfall in inflation has been made up and the price level is back at target, the interest rate rule reverts to the static version. This framework has the advantage that it aims only to change inflation expectations when it is needed and works like standard inflation targeting otherwise.

A key conclusion from our analysis is that all of these policies work through affecting expectations. The monetary policy framework is only in effect during times when the central bank can set interest rates freely without being constrained by the lower bound. However, expectations of future policy already affect economic activity during encounters with the lower bound through the forward-looking nature of price setting and decision making.

A comparison among the frameworks shows that there is a ranking among the various policy options. Average-inflation-targeting practices fare better than dovish policies. And dynamic policies can improve on adjustments to the level of interest rates. Price-level targeting is known to get close to the first-best policy—even in the absence of a lower bound on interest rates. Particularly, in the presence of supply shocks, this policy framework works best among the alternatives. The Reifschneider-Williams rule has the advantage of addressing the shortfalls in stimulus through cuts in the interest rate directly and works about as well as price-level targeting when demand shocks are the driving factor behind economic fluctuations.

There are three strands of related literature. For each of those, we are able to cite only a few seminal papers due to space constraints. First, there is a literature on the model we use in this paper to perform the policy experiments. The basic framework is laid out in Clarida, Galí, and Gertler (1999) and Woodford (2003). Benhabib, Schmitt-Grohé, and Uribe (2001) demonstrate how the introduction of a lower bound can lead to two equilibria in a deterministic framework. Mendes (2011), Nakata and Schmidt (2016), and Mertens and Williams (2018) extend this analysis to stochastic environments.

Second, there is a literature on proposals for various policy frameworks. Bernanke and Mishkin (1997) discuss inflation-targeting practices by central banks. Svensson (1999) compares inflation targeting with price-level-targeting practices. Giannoni (2014) points out that price-level targeting can be robustly optimal and shows that price-level-targeting rules support determinacy of equilibria. Nominal GDP targeting, another proposal that we do not analyze here, is discussed in Taylor (1985) and Koenig (2013). Although these policy proposals were discussed mainly without regard to the lower bound on interest rates, several proposals specifically have been designed to deal with issues arising from a binding constraint on the central bank's actions.

A third strand of the literature compares the various policy options. This paper extends the work in Mertens and Williams (2019) to additional policy options and contains an analysis of a framework with demand shocks. An overview over various policy options can also be found in Svensson (2019). Harrison, Seneca, and Waldron (2019) study policy options when interest rates are low. Vestin (2006) shows that price-level targeting outperforms inflation targeting in a New Keynesian model without a lower bound on interest rates. Eggertsson and Woodford (2003) compute optimal monetary policy in the presence of a lower bound on interest rates. While our paper mainly focuses on the mechanism, Bernanke, Kiley, and Roberts (2019) compare the policy options within an estimated model for the US economy.

2. MACROECONOMIC MODEL

We use a standard New Keynesian model as, for example, described in Clarida, Galií, and Gertler (1999) and Woodford (2003) and modify it by incorporating a lower bound. Our focus is primarily on longer-term outcomes, and we thus abstract from some of the transition dynamics that would take place in richer models. Our simple model allows us to derive the mechanisms by which various policy frameworks and their associated interest rate rules affect the economy, and to evaluate them according to a social loss function.

The model describes the evolution of three endogenous variables: the rate of inflation π_t, the output gap x_t, and the short-term nominal interest rate i_t that is chosen by the central bank. Our starting point is the log-linearized version of the standard New Keynesian model that we simplify by assuming that shocks are i.i.d. This simplification allows us to derive analytical results and focus on the longer-term implications without having to track transition dynamics.

Inflation is governed by the forward-looking Phillips curve

$$\pi_t = \mu_t + \kappa x_t + \beta \mathbb{E}_t \pi_{t+1}, \quad \mu_t \sim iidU[-\hat{\mu},\hat{\mu}], \tag{1}$$

where $\mathbb{E}_t$ is the expectations operator conditional on time t information, μ_t a supply shock, $\beta \in (0,1)$ the agents' discount factor, and $\kappa > 0$. An IS curve, obtained by log-linearizing an Euler equation, determines the output gap

$$x_t = \epsilon_t - \alpha(i_t - \mathbb{E}_t \pi_{t+1} - r^*) + \mathbb{E}_t x_{t+1}, \quad \epsilon_t \sim iidU[-\hat{\epsilon},\hat{\epsilon}], \tag{2}$$

where $\alpha > 0$, r^* is the long-run neutral real rate of interest, and ϵ_t is a demand shock. Agents fully understand the model, including the distribution of the shock processes, and have full knowledge of all realized shocks up to the current period. For better exposition, we study the models with supply and demand shocks separately. To this end, we set the size of the support for the shocks that we want to disregard to zero.

The central bank chooses the short-term nominal interest rate i_t and has the ability to commit to a framework described by a policy rule. The choice of policy, however, is constrained by a lower bound on nominal interest rates, $i^{LB} < r^*$. It evaluates its policy framework according to a social loss function that favors inflation rates close to a target, normalized to zero, and output close to its potential:[4]

---

4. It is straightforward to generalize to a nonzero inflation target by interpreting πt as the gap between inflation and its target.

$$\mathcal{L} = (1-\beta)\mathbb{E}_0 \left[\sum_{t=0}^{\infty} \beta^t (\pi_t^2 + \lambda x_t^2) \right]$$

$$= (1-\beta)\sum_{t=0}^{\infty} \beta^t (\mathbb{E}_0[\pi_t]^2 + \mathrm{Var}_0[\pi_t] + \lambda(\mathbb{E}_0[x_t]^2 + \mathrm{Var}_0[x_t])). \quad (3)$$

The second part of the equation shows that the loss function is determined by the first two moments of inflation and the output gap. It is increasing in the variances and the average deviations of inflation or output from their desired levels.

The parameter $\lambda \geq 0$ specifies the central banker's preferences. For $\lambda = 0$, the central bank solely cares about stabilizing inflation, while larger values of λ introduce a preference for stabilizing the real side of the economy.

3. INFLATION-TARGETING FRAMEWORKS

In this section, we study various static monetary policy frameworks. We first solve for optimal monetary policy under discretion, which serves as a benchmark policy rule. From there, we start by exploring the benefits of an upper bound on interest rates and dovish policies.

3.1. Benchmark: Optimal Monetary Policy under Discretion

In the absence of a lower bound on nominal interest rates, the central bank can achieve optimal monetary policy under discretion by setting its interest rate depending on the current state of the economy, which can be fully described by the realization of the supply and demand shock as well as expectations about future inflation

$$i_t^{\mathrm{opt}} = \theta_0 + \theta_E \mathbb{E}_t \pi_{t+1} + \theta_\in \in_t + \theta_\mu \mu_t \quad (4)$$

where the intercept of the policy rule is $\theta_0 = r^*$, the coefficient on expectations is $\theta_E = 1 + \dfrac{1}{\alpha\kappa} - \dfrac{\lambda\beta}{\alpha\kappa(\kappa^2 + \lambda)}$, and the responses to supply and demand shocks are $\theta_\epsilon = \dfrac{1}{\alpha}$ and $\theta_\mu = \dfrac{\kappa}{\alpha(\kappa^2 + \lambda)}$, respectively.

The interest rate rule in equation (4) can be implemented with a Taylor rule (see Taylor 1993) of the form

$$i_t^{opt} = \phi_0 + \phi_E \mathbb{E}_t \pi_{t+1} + \phi_\pi \pi_t + \phi_x x_t. \tag{5}$$

Setting the coefficients to $\phi_0 = r^*$, $\phi_E = \dfrac{\kappa(-\alpha\theta_\epsilon - \beta\theta_\mu + \theta_E) + (1-\beta)\theta_\epsilon}{\kappa(1 - \alpha\theta_\epsilon)}$, $\phi_\pi = \dfrac{\theta_\mu}{1 - \alpha\theta_\epsilon}$, and $\phi_x = \dfrac{\theta_\epsilon - \kappa\theta_\mu}{1 - \alpha\theta_\epsilon}$ implements the interest rate rule in equation (4).[5]

Under this policy, the inflation process is given by

$$\pi_t = \alpha\kappa(r^* - \theta_0) + (1 - \alpha\kappa\theta_\mu)\mu_t + \kappa(1 - \alpha\theta_\epsilon)\epsilon_t \\ + (1 + \alpha\kappa - \alpha\kappa\theta_E)\mathbb{E}_t[\pi_{t+1}]. \tag{6}$$

The central bank thus finds it optimal to partially accommodate supply shocks unless its objective is purely to stabilize inflation, that is, $\lambda = 0$. Taking expectations at time $t - 1$ on both sides of the equation (6) shows that there is a unique steady-state level of expectations $\mathbb{E}_{t-1}\pi_t = \mathbb{E}\pi = 0$.

When incorporating a lower bound on interest rates, the policy rule that can implement optimal monetary policy under discretion is given by the optimal policy under discretion described above with the addition of the lower bound constraint

$$i_t = \max\{\theta_0 + \theta_E \mathbb{E}_t \pi_{t+1} + \theta_\epsilon \epsilon_t + \theta_\mu \mu_t, i^{LB}\} \tag{7}$$

---

5. To implement the interest rate rule with demand shocks, the coefficients on the output gap and inflation have to be infinite. This result can be seen by plugging the optimal coefficients for the interest rate rule in equation (4) into the coefficients for equation (5).

with the same values for the coefficients as in the unconstrained case of equation (4). Equation (7) can again be written in Taylor rule from $i_t = \max\{\phi_0 + \phi_E \mathbb{E}_t \pi_{t+1} + \phi_\pi \pi_t + \phi_x x_t, i^{LB}\}$. While all the rules for the different policies discussed below can be expressed in either form, we present them in terms of the underlying shocks. Under discretion, the lower bound on interest rate affects the interest rate rule only via inflation expectations when unconstrained and truncates the interest rate distribution on the downside.[6] As a result, the inflation process follows the same process as in equation (6) whenever the central bank is unconstrained in its policy action. At the constraint, however, the central bank sets an interest rate of i^{LB}, leading to an overall inflation process of

$$\pi_t = \begin{cases} \alpha\kappa(r^* - i^{LB}) + \mu_t + \kappa\epsilon_t + (1+\alpha\kappa)\mathbb{E}_t[\pi_{t+1}] & \text{constrained} \\ \alpha\kappa(r^* - \theta_0) + (1-\alpha\kappa\theta_\mu)\mu_t + \kappa(1-\alpha\theta_\epsilon)\epsilon_t \\ \quad + (1+\alpha\kappa - \alpha\kappa\theta_E)\mathbb{E}_t[\pi_{t+1}] & \text{otherwise.} \end{cases} \quad (8)$$

The central bank is thereby constrained whenever $\theta_\mu \mu_t + \theta_\epsilon \epsilon_t \le i^{LB} - r^* - \psi\mathbb{E}_t\pi_{t+1}$ where $\psi \equiv \left(1 + \frac{1}{\alpha\kappa} - \theta_E\right)$. With a sufficiently large support for the supply and demand shocks, the central bank finds itself either constrained in response to negative shocks or unconstrained after positive shocks. The lower bound will thus be binding occasionally. As a result, expected inflation can be computed from the process of inflation in (8), where we need to take the switching between equations into account depending on whether the lower bound is binding or not

$$\mathbb{E}\pi = \text{Prob}\left(i_t^{\text{opt}} < i^{LB}\right)\mathbb{E}\left[\pi_t^c \mid i_t^{\text{opt}} < i^{LB}\right] + \text{Prob}\left(i_t^{\text{opt}} \ge i^{LB}\right)\mathbb{E}\left[\pi_t^u \mid i_t^{\text{opt}} \ge i^{LB}\right]. \quad (9)$$

---

6. The optimality of this interest rate rule is derived in detail in Mertens and Williams (2018).

To illustrate the effects on the probability of a binding lower bound and inflation expectations, we turn to the model that features only supply shocks. There is a cutoff value for the supply shock $\bar{\mu} = \dfrac{1}{\theta_\mu}(i^{LB} - \theta_0 - \theta_E \mathbb{E}\pi_{t+1})$ such that interest rates are constrained by the lower bound whenever $\mu_t < \bar{\mu}$. Consequently, the constraint can be either always, never, or occasionally binding

$$\text{Prob}(i_t^{\text{opt}} < i^{LB}) = \begin{cases} 1 & \text{if} \quad -\bar{\mu} \leq -\hat{\mu} \\ \dfrac{1}{2\hat{\mu}}(\hat{\mu} + \bar{\mu}) & \text{if} \quad -\hat{\mu} < -\bar{\mu} < \hat{\mu} \\ 0 & \text{if} \quad -\bar{\mu} \geq \hat{\mu}. \end{cases}$$

As a result, inflation expectations are determined by

$$\mathbb{E}\pi_t = \begin{cases} -\alpha\kappa(i^{LB} - r^*) + (1 + \alpha\kappa)\mathbb{E}\pi_{t+1} & \text{if} \quad -\bar{\mu} \leq -\hat{\mu} \\ \begin{aligned} &-\dfrac{\alpha\kappa}{4\hat{\mu}}\theta_\mu(\bar{\mu} + \hat{\mu})^2 + (1 + \alpha\kappa(1 - \theta_E)) \\ &\mathbb{E}\pi_{t+1} - \alpha\kappa(\theta_0 - r^*) \end{aligned} & \text{if} \quad -\hat{\mu} < -\bar{\mu} < \hat{\mu} \\ -\alpha\kappa(\theta_0 - r^*) + (1 + \alpha\kappa)\mathbb{E}\pi_{t+1} & \text{if} \quad -\bar{\mu} \geq \hat{\mu}. \end{cases}$$

This expression shows that expected inflation in the current period is a piecewise quadratic function of expected inflation in the following period, as can be seen in figure 3.1. As a result, we can solve this equation for a steady state.

The lower bound on interest rates gives rise to a multiplicity of equilibria, as is known from Benhabib, Schmitt-Grohé, and Uribe (2001) for a deterministic economy and Mendes (2011), Nakata and Schmidt (2016), and Mertens and Williams (2018) for a stochastic economy. In particular, two levels of expected inflation are consistent with a steady state. Relatively benign expectations about inflation in the following period provide stimulus to the economy such that the central bank finds itself unconstrained most of the time. The resulting inflation stabilization confirms

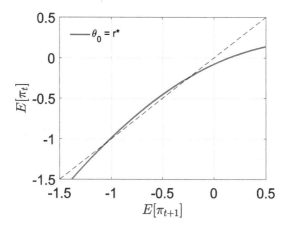

FIGURE 3.1. Expected inflation in the current period as a function of expected inflation in the following period. Parameter values are set to $\alpha = 1.25$, $\kappa = 0.8$, $\beta = 0.99$, $r^* = 1$, $\lambda = 0.25$, and $i^{LB} = 0.5$. The support for supply shocks is $\mu = 3.3$ and there are no demand shocks, that is, $\hat{\varepsilon} = 0$. Intersections with the dashed 45-degree line represent steady states. The coefficients in the policy rule are those of optimal monetary policy under discretion

the benign expectations we started out with. We refer to this scenario as the "target equilibrium." However, if, on the other hand, expected future inflation is low, the central bank needs to provide more stimulus and reaches the lower bound on interest rates more frequently. Constrained policy results in below-target inflation and thus confirms expectations. The economy is in a "liquidity trap." Throughout the paper, we assume that the economy is in the target equilibrium.[7]

As can be seen from figure 3.1, expected inflation runs below the target inflation rate. This shortfall in average inflation is due to inflation expectations taking into account scenarios both with and without binding lower bounds, as shown by equation (9). Although interest policy can offset supply and demand shocks to an optimal degree when unconstrained, a binding lower bound leads to below-target inflation. Taking all scenarios into consideration, average

---

7. For an empirical investigation lending support to the US economy being in the target equilibrium, see Mertens and Williams (2018).

inflation and thus inflation expectations are below target. Owing to the inability of the central bank to commit to future policy actions under this framework, average inflation runs at a level that is too low relative to the optimum. In the next sections, we show various policy frameworks that can bring about improvements relative to optimal monetary policy under discretion when the central bank can commit to an interest rate rule.

3.2. Static: An Upper Bound on Interest Rates

Since the root of undesirably low inflation expectations lies in the lower bound on interest rates, an upper bound on interest rates might help in anchoring inflation expectations at target. We therefore consider a modification to the interest rate policy under discretion in equation (7) that imposes an upper bound i^{UB}

$$i_t = \min\{\max\{\theta_0 + \theta_E \mathbb{E}_t \pi_{t+1} + \theta_\epsilon \epsilon_t + \theta_\mu \mu_t, i^{LB}\}, i^{UB}\}. \quad (10)$$

To compute inflation expectations, we now have to distinguish between six, instead of three, cases. Both the upper bound and the lower bound can be either always binding ("constrained"), never binding ("un-constrained"), or occasionally binding. We refer to these scenarios as $\mathbb{C}_u^{UB}$ for the upper bound to be never binding, $\mathbb{C}_c^{UB}$ for it to be always binding, and $\mathbb{C}_o^{UB}$ for an occasionally binding upper bound. The lower bound constraints are labeled analogously (see appendix A for the definitions of when the constraints are binding). The derivation of inflation expectations for the case where both a lower bound and an upper bound are present and only supply shocks hit the economy works analogously to the case of optimal monetary policy under discretion. Owing to the additional constraint, however, the list of distinct cases increases. With various conditions $\mathbb{C}^{LB}$ and $\mathbb{C}^{UB}$ on the lower and upper bounds, respectively, we distinguish the cases:

$$\mathbb{E}[\pi_t]=\begin{cases}
(1+\alpha\kappa)\,\mathbb{E}[\pi_{t+1}]-\alpha\kappa(i^{\mathrm{LB}}-r^*) & \text{if } \mathbb{C}_c^{\mathrm{LB}}\\[2ex]
\dfrac{\alpha\kappa}{4\theta_\mu\hat{\mu}}(i^{\mathrm{UB}}+i^{\mathrm{LB}}-2\theta_0-2\theta_E\mathbb{E}[\pi_{t+1}]) & \\
\quad((i^{\mathrm{UB}}-i^{\mathrm{LB}})-2\theta_\mu\hat{\mu})+(1+\alpha\kappa(1-\theta_E)) & \text{if } \mathbb{C}_o^{\mathrm{LB}} \text{ and } \mathbb{C}_o^{\mathrm{UB}}\\
\quad\mathbb{E}[\pi_{t+1}]+\alpha\kappa(r^*-\theta_0) & \\[2ex]
-\dfrac{\alpha\kappa\theta_\mu}{4\hat{\mu}}\left(\hat{\mu}+\dfrac{1}{\theta_\mu}(i^{\mathrm{LB}}-\theta_0-\theta_E\mathbb{E}[\pi_{t+1}])\right)^2+ & \text{if } \mathbb{C}_c^{\mathrm{UB}} \text{ and } \mathbb{C}_u^{\mathrm{UB}}\\
\quad+(1+\alpha\kappa(1-\theta_E))\,\mathbb{E}[\pi_{t+1}]+\alpha\kappa(r^*-\theta_0) & \\[2ex]
(1+\alpha\kappa)\,\mathbb{E}[\pi_{t+1}]-\alpha\kappa(i^{\mathrm{UB}}-r^*) & \text{if } \mathbb{C}_c^{\mathrm{UB}}\\[2ex]
\dfrac{\alpha\kappa\theta_\mu}{4\hat{\mu}}\left(\hat{\mu}-\dfrac{1}{\theta_\mu}(i^{\mathrm{UB}}-\theta_0-\theta_E\mathbb{E}[\pi_{t+1}])\right)^2+ & \text{if } \mathbb{C}_u^{\mathrm{LB}} \text{ and } \mathbb{C}_o^{\mathrm{UB}}\\
\quad+(1+\alpha\kappa(1-\theta_E))\mathbb{E}[\pi_{t+1}]+\alpha\kappa(r^*-\theta_0) & \\[2ex]
(1+\alpha\kappa(1-\theta_E))\mathbb{E}[\pi_{t+1}]+\alpha\kappa(r^*-\theta_0) & \text{if } \mathbb{C}_u^{\mathrm{LB}} \text{ and } \mathbb{C}_u^{\mathrm{UB}}
\end{cases}$$

As a result of the various conditions, a third equilibrium besides the target equilibrium and the liquidity trap emerges. This equilibrium is associated with the upper bound on nominal interest rates. That is, in the deterministic version of the model, the economy would face a binding upper bound on interest rates. But as in the case with only a lower bound, we restrict our analysis to the target equilibrium.

In the target equilibrium, the average rate of inflation varies with the level at which the upper bound on interest rates is set.

Lemma 1 (Inflation Expectations with Upper Bound)
If the upper bound on interest rates is set symmetrically to the lower bound around the neutral rate of interest r* *and the intercept of the policy rate is equal to* r*, *then inflation expectations are at target.*

Proof: Owing to the symmetry, it is easy to see that either both constraints are binding occasionally or none of the constraints are binding. Plugging $\theta_0 = r^*$ and $r^* = \frac{1}{2}(i^{\text{LB}} + i^{\text{UB}})$ into the above condition for inflation expectations delivers

$$\mathbb{E}[\pi] = \frac{\alpha\kappa}{4\theta_\mu\hat{\mu}}(-2\theta_E\,\mathbb{E}[\pi])((i^{\text{UB}} - i^{\text{LB}}) - 2\theta_\mu\hat{\mu}) + (1 + \alpha\kappa(1 - \theta_E))\mathbb{E}[\pi].$$

As a result, the equation is linear in inflation expectations, and inflation expectations of zero are the unique equilibrium. If none of the constraints is binding, inflation expectations are determined by

$$\mathbb{E}[\pi] = (1 + \alpha\kappa(1 - \theta_E))\mathbb{E}[\pi]$$

and, again, inflation expectations are at target. Appendix A shows the graph analogous to figure 3.1 for inflation expectations with an upper bound.

Weighing against the benefit of higher inflation expectations, the introduction of an upper bound on interest rates has the drawback of limiting the variance of interest rate policy. With an upper bound, the central bank finds itself constrained in stabilizing the effects of large positive supply and demand shocks. As a result, economic activity is more exposed to shocks and becomes more volatile. On net, the social loss is reduced relative to the case with discretion if the upper bound is set appropriately, as we discuss in more detail below.

3.3. Static: Dovish Policies

Optimal interest rate policy under discretion reacts to both supply and demand shocks. Because of occasional encounters with the lower bound, inflation expectations are below target. If the central bank responds less to shocks, it can reduce the probability of a binding lower bound. Specifically, the central bank lowers the response coefficients θ_μ and θ_ϵ while leaving all other parameters of the policy rule unchanged.

Smaller responses to shocks in the following period will result in, all else being equal, higher inflation expectations due to a smaller probability of reaching the lower bound. This benefit comes at the cost of suboptimally responding to shocks in the current period. Since the central bank aims to affect inflation expectations while reacting suboptimally in the current period, commitment is necessary to implement this policy rule. We investigate the effects of dovish policies on the social loss together with other static policies below.

4. AVERAGE-INFLATION TARGETING

This section consists of two parts. The first average-inflation-targeting framework is static in that it retains the feature that inflation expectations are constant over time. Then we discuss dynamic Reifschneider-Williams rules in which the central bank conditions on past misses in setting its interest rate relative to the benchmark rule.

4.1. Static Average-Inflation Targeting

For static average-inflation targeting, the central bank leaves the general form of its interest rate rule in (7) intact but adjusts the level θ_0, as, for example, discussed in Reifschneider and Williams (2000). By changing the level of interest rates, the central bank can bring average inflation to its target rate. In particular, if the central bank lowers the intercept of the policy rate to

$$\theta_0^* = r^* - \left(\sqrt{r^* - i^{LB}} - \sqrt{\theta_\mu \hat{\mu}}\right)^2 < r^*, \qquad (11)$$

inflation expectations are zero.[8] All other coefficients in the interest rate rule remain unchanged relative to optimal policy under discretion.

---

8. The intercept θ_0^* in equation (11) leads to zero average inflation whenever
$$0 < \theta_\mu < \frac{(r^* - i^{LB})(\kappa^2(1 + \alpha\kappa) + \lambda(1 - \beta + \alpha\kappa))^2}{\alpha^2\kappa^2(\kappa^2 + \lambda)^2 \bar{\mu}}.$$

As a result of this intervention, the central bank permanently provides more stimulus whenever it is unconstrained. It thus runs inflation above target whenever the lower bound permits, such that inflation is at target on balance. While inflation expectations rise in the target equilibrium due to the change in policy, they fall into the liquidity trap. Appendix B contains details.

Proposition 1 (Optimal Interest Rate Rule)

The optimal interest rate rule lowers the intercept θ_0 relative to the case under discretion such that average inflation is above target and leaves the responses to supply and demand shocks unchanged.

This proposition contains two important characterizations of the optimal rule. First, the central bank would want to lower the intercept of its policy rule whenever unconstrained to provide extra stimulus relative to optimal policy under discretion. Interestingly, the central bank finds it optimal to lower the intercept to a point where the average inflation rate is above target in order to compensate for the asymmetry of the inflation and output gap distributions, which have a larger tail toward the downside. Second, when the intercept of the rule is set optimally, the optimal response to shocks is the same as under discretionary policy. That is, there is no benefit from following a dovish policy response. As discussed earlier, dovish policies bring about welfare gains by raising inflation expectations. They achieve this outcome by lowering the probability of hitting the lower bound at the cost of insufficiently offsetting shocks today. If inflation expectations are already optimally set through the level of the interest rate rule, there is no need to incur the cost of allowing a greater pass-through of shocks in the current period.

These two predictions show that average-inflation targeting dominates dovish policies and brings about welfare gains. Since there is no need to engage in dovish policies for the optimally set level of the interest rate rule, we know that average-inflation targeting fares at least as well as dovish policies. In our further analysis, we focus on the case where the central bank aims for the average rate of inflation to be at target while keeping all other coefficients in the interest rate rule unchanged relative to the case under discretion.

4.2. Dynamic: Reifschneider-Williams

Reifschneider and Williams (2000) introduce the idea that the central bank keeps track of past misses in its desired interest rate relative to a benchmark rule due to the lower bound. A state variable z_t aggregates past deviations of the interest rate from a reference interest rate that, in the original form, was specified to be a Taylor rule (see Taylor 1993).

To implement this idea in the context of our setup, we specify the reference interest rate rule to take the same form as optimal monetary policy under discretion in equation (7). The sum of past misses z_t follows the law of motion

$$z_t = \rho z_{t-1} + i_{t-1}^{\text{ref}} - i_{t-1}, \tag{12}$$

where i_t is the actual policy rate and i_t^{ref} is the reference rate. We augment the interest rate rule in equation (7) such that it can condition on past policy discrepancies

$$i_t = \max\left\{\theta_0 + \theta_E E_t[\pi_{t+1}] + \theta_\mu \mu_t + \theta_\epsilon \epsilon_t + \theta_z z_t, i^{\text{LB}}\right\}. \tag{13}$$

The reference rate is defined as the rule with the same coefficients but absent the lower bound on interest rates and the conditioning on past misses. We leave all coefficients of the interest rate rule unchanged relative to optimal policy under discretion.

Two special cases are of interest. First, if the coefficient θ_z is zero, the rule coincides with that of equation (7) and optimal policy under discretion emerges. Second, if $\theta_z = \rho = 1$, which is our main specification of the model, past misses are made up within one period whenever possible.[9] A persistence of $\rho = 1$ implies that all interest rate misses will have to be fully made up for. And we can interpret the coefficient θ_z as the fraction of past misses that are made up for each time the central bank is not constrained by the lower bound.

The interest rate rule in equation (13) operates by keeping rates "lower for longer" following periods of binding lower bounds. To see this, note that the only deviation of the interest rate rule from the benchmark rate can arise from a previous encounter with the lower bound. The accumulated shortfall z_t lowers the nominal interest rate and supports, on average, above-target inflation.

With this interest rate rule in place, inflation expectations adjust dynamically. Since inflation will, on average, be higher following periods when the lower bound is binding, inflation expectations are higher *during* encounters with the lower bound. That is, the dynamic adjustment of the interest rate rule helps provide stimulus through higher inflation expectations precisely at a time when the central bank cannot provide any further stimulus through concurrent interest rate policy.

Lemma 2 (Average Rate of Inflation under Reifschneider-Williams)
When $\theta_z = \rho = 1$, the Reifschneider-Williams policy rule leads to an average rate of inflation equal to the target rate.

Appendix C contains a proof. The reason for the result in Lemma 2 is that missed interest rate cuts, and thus shortfalls in inflation, due to the lower bound are made up one-for-one in the future. The interest rate is thus, by design, set at the same average level as it would be under optimal monetary policy under discretion in the absence of a lower bound, a case where inflation expectations are at target.

---

9. In a numerical analysis, $\theta_z = 1$ turns out to be close to optimal.

Note that under the Reifschneider-Williams rules, past misses in inflation do not have to be made up for unless they arose from the inability to cut the policy rate. A negative supply shock will partially pass through to inflation but does not alter the future stance of monetary policy unless it causes the policy rate to be cut to the lower bound.

5. PRICE-LEVEL TARGETING FRAMEWORKS

In this section, we evaluate policies that aim to stabilize a price level. The main difference between the price-level targeting frameworks and the average-inflation-targeting policies of the previous section lies in the fact that price-level targeting makes up for past below-target inflation. Hence it does not treat bygones as bygones. We consider two alternatives. First, standard price-level targeting has been discussed as a policy framework within a New Keynesian model. It has been found to provide, under certain conditions, first-best macroeconomic outcomes (e.g., see Vestin 2006). Second, we consider temporary price-level targeting that specifically addresses the issue of a binding lower bound on interest rates (for the proposals, see Evans 2010 and Bernanke 2017).

5.1. Dynamic: Price-Level Targeting

Price-level targeting aims to achieve a stable path for a price. Whenever the price level falls below its target level, the central bank would keep rates lower than it otherwise would in order to bring about higher inflation temporarily until the shortfall is corrected. For a price level above target, the central bank would engage in contractionary monetary policy until the price level is back at target.

To formalize the policy framework, we introduce a price level whose logarithm p_t evolves according to $p_t = p_{t-1} + \pi_t$.[10] We augment the interest rate rule in equation (7) with the log of the price level

$$i_t = \max\{\theta_0 + \theta_E \mathbb{E}_t \pi_{t+1} + \theta_\epsilon \epsilon_t + \theta_\mu \mu_t + \theta_p p_t, i^{LB}\}. \qquad (14)$$

We implement this policy rule by keeping all the coefficients at the same level as in optimal monetary policy under discretion in equation (7) and varying the level of θ_p.

As a result of this adjustment to the policy rule, inflation expectations become a function of the price level. Appendix D contains details on the algorithm and computation of the expectations function. It shows that inflation expectations are an increasing function of the log price level if θ_p is positive.

The mechanism by which inflation expectations vary with the price level can best be seen when considering a situation where the price is initially at its target level. Suppose that there is a shortfall in inflation relative to target due to, say, a very negative supply shock that pushes the nominal interest rate to the lower bound in the current period. As a result, the price level will fall below its target level and, because of its influence on the policy rate, will induce nominal interest rates to remain low in the following period. The anticipation of low rates in the following periods, and the accompanying higher inflation rates, will result in higher inflation expectations already in the current period. Through the forward-looking Phillips curve, higher inflation expectations have an accommodating effect on the economy in the current period. As a result, higher inflation expectations mitigate the deleterious effects of negative supply shocks and encounters with the lower bound.

---

10. In practice, the central bank would keep track of the difference between the log price level and a reference level, for example, a price level that grows at the target inflation rate. In our setup, the reference price level is normalized to 1 such that its logarithm and associated inflation vanish from the equations.

Price-level targeting operates even when the lower bound on interest rates is not binding. When the price level is at target and a positive supply shock hits the economy, the central bank optimally allows the supply shock to partially pass through to inflation. As a result, however, the price level rises faster than its target value, prompting future contractionary policy. The policy does not treat bygones as bygones and makes up for all past misses of inflation from their target value. Through this mechanism, price-level targeting has been shown to mitigate the effects of supply shocks even in the absence of a lower bound on interest rates.

The nature of shocks is critical since optimal monetary policy under discretion already offsets demand shocks fully if the central bank is constrained in its policy setting. Supply shocks, however, affect the rate of inflation under optimal policy if the central banker puts weights on both inflation and real activity in its loss function, that is, $\lambda > 0$.

5.2. Temporary Price-Level Targeting

As discussed earlier, price-level targeting changes interest rate setting by the central bank even in the absence of a lower bound on interest rates. Therefore, changing to price-level targeting is a substantial shift in policy relative to standard inflation targeting.

State-dependent price-level targeting can specifically address the effects of the lower bound on interest rates. Under this policy, the central bank follows standard inflation-targeting practices during normal times. An encounter with the lower bound would trigger an episode of temporary price-level targeting. The central bank would keep rates at the lower bound until the price level is back at target.

We implement this idea in a slightly generalized form. Policy is conducted according to the following interest rate rule:

$$i_t = \begin{cases} \max\{\theta_0 + \theta_\mu \mu_t + \theta_\epsilon \epsilon_t + \theta_E \mathbb{E}(\pi_{t+1} \mid \hat{p}_t = 0), i^{\text{LB}}\} & \text{if } p_{t-1} = 0 \\ \max\{\theta_0 + \theta_\mu \mu_t + \theta_\epsilon \epsilon_t + \theta_E \mathbb{E}(\pi_{t+1} \mid \hat{p}_t) + \theta_p \hat{p}_t, i^{\text{LB}}\} & \text{if } \hat{p}_{t-1} < 0. \end{cases} \tag{15}$$

We again use the same coefficients that we obtained for optimal monetary policy under discretion. We can adjust how much the interest rate responds to the deviations of the log price level from its targeting by varying the coefficient θ_p.

If the value of the supply shock is below $\mu^c = \dfrac{i^{\text{LB}} - \theta_0 - \theta_E \mathbb{E}[\pi_{t+1} \mid \hat{p}_t] - \theta_p \hat{p}_t}{\theta_\mu}$, the lower bound on interest rates binds. The (temporary) price level evolves according to:

$$\hat{p}_t = \begin{cases} 0 & \text{if } i_t > i^{\text{LB}} \text{ and } \hat{p}_{t-1} = 0 \\ \min\{\hat{p}_{t-1} + \pi_t, 0\} & \text{if } i_t = i^{\text{LB}} \text{ or } \hat{p}_{t-1} < 0. \end{cases} \tag{16}$$

This rule states that a temporary price-level-targeting episode will be triggered by the policy rate hitting the lower bound on interest rates. During that episode, the interest rate rule conditions on a price-level target. The episode ends as soon as the price level is back at its target value. Similar to price-level targeting, inflation expectations become a function of the price level during temporary price-level-targeting episodes. Appendix E describes the numerical algorithm to compute the expectation functions.

The specification in equation (15) generalizes the original proposals in the following way. If the responsiveness of interest rates to the price level, θ_p, is infinite, interest rates will be at the lower bound whenever a temporary price-level episode has been triggered. If $\theta_p = 0$, the policy is exactly the one described in standard inflation targeting.

The mechanism is similar to price-level targeting in that encounters with the lower bound are followed by periods of lower interest rates to make up for the shortfall in the price level. Contrary to price-level targeting, however, its temporary counterpart reacts only to shortfalls in inflation due to the lower bound and does not correct for periods of high inflation.

As a result, the unconditional distributions of inflation and the output gap are asymmetric. Following an encounter with the lower bound on interest rates, temporary price-level targeting makes up for any change in inflation until the price level is back at its target value. The same inflation rate would not trigger a policy response outside of the price-level targeting regime. Owing to this asymmetry, the average rate of inflation can differ from the target rate.

6. COMPARISON OF MONETARY POLICY FRAMEWORKS

This section compares the various monetary policy frameworks and explains how they affect inflation expectations and macroeconomic outcomes. We start by discussing the baseline calibration of the model that underlies the graphs we show. We split the discussions of static and dynamic frameworks since they have different effects on inflation expectations.

6.1. Parameterization

The goal of the calibration is to illustrate the key mechanisms with a set of paths for inflation and output gaps and compute social losses for the monetary policy frameworks. The main emphasis is on qualitative results, and the model simulations are thus best thought of as an illustration of the model behavior.

We choose a baseline annual calibration with a parameterization of $\beta = 0.99$ for the time preference factor, $\alpha = 1.25$ for the coefficient on interest rates in the IS curve, and $\kappa = 0.8$ for the slope of the

Phillips curve.[11] The natural rate of interest is set to $r^* = 1$ such that all results are to be interpreted as percentage points. We choose a lower bound on interest rates of $i^{LB} = -0.5$. In the baseline specification, the central bank puts a weight of $\lambda = 0.25$ on stabilizing the output gap. We choose $\hat{\mu} = 3.3$ for the model with supply shocks and $\hat{\epsilon} = 3$ for the model with demand shocks. The volatility of supply shocks implies roughly a 25 percent chance of reaching the lower bound on interest rates when policy is conducted optimally under discretion.

Finally, for the Reifschneider-Williams rule, we choose a persistence of $\rho_z = 1$ such that all misses of the interest rate rule have to be made up for. The corresponding interest rate rule has a coefficient of $\theta_z = 1$ such that the central bank makes up for past misses within one period if the lower bound on interest rates permits.

6.2. Comparison of Static Frameworks

We compare all of the three static frameworks—the upper bound on interest rates, dovish policies, and static average-inflation targeting—to optimal monetary policy under discretion. Therefore, we choose a setting where only supply shocks hit the economy. Figure 3.2 shows inflation expectations and social losses for the three policy frameworks.

The dashed black vertical line in figure 3.2 shows the benchmark case of optimal policy under discretion, a special case for all of the three frameworks. Moving to the left varies the parameters for the different frameworks. For example, following the purple line in the upper panel to the left shows how inflation expectations rise when the central bank lowers the intercept of the policy rule. The changes in parameters for the three frameworks are normalized

---

11. A different calibration might help in understanding the quantitative aspects of the model, but that is not the focus of this paper. In particular, a flatter Phillips curve might lead to smaller effects on inflation.

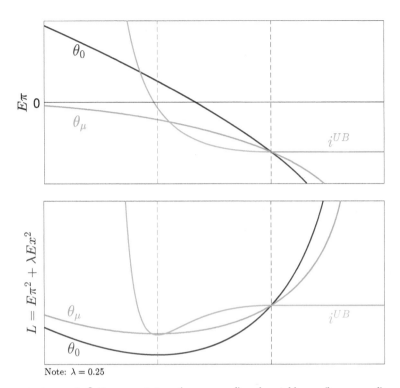

FIGURE 3.2. Inflation expectations (upper panel) and social losses (lower panel) under an upper bound on interest rates (light blue line), dovish policies (green line), and different intercepts for the policy rule (purple line) for changes in the corresponding parameter. The graphs are computed under the baseline specification with supply shocks only.

such that the minimal social loss occurs at the dashed red vertical line.

Figure 3.2 shows that static average-inflation targeting (SAIT) dominates both an optimally set upper bound on interest rates and an optimal dovish policy. The social loss is lower than for the other frameworks supported by inflation expectations running above target—even on average and not just whenever unconstrained. The reason is the asymmetry of the inflation distribution that prevails under average-inflation targeting. Note that inflation expectations

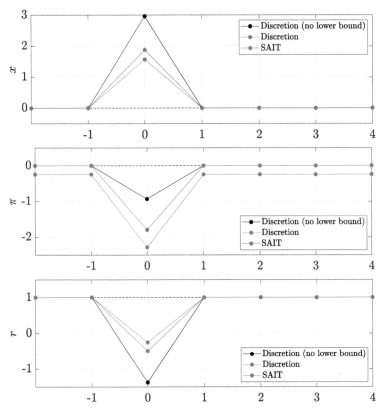

FIGURE 3.3. Impulse response functions under different policies in response to a negative supply shock $\mu_0 = -\hat{\mu}$ at time zero for the output gap (upper panel), the rate of inflation (middle panel), and the real interest rate (lower panel). We used the benchmark calibration with $\lambda = 0.25$.

are positive at the optimal intercept for the policy rule, denoted by the vertical red dashed line.

To see the mechanics of the static average-inflation framework, figure 3.3 plots impulse response functions under this policy and compares it with optimal monetary policy under discretion in both the absence and the presence of a lower bound on interest rates. For all of these paths, a large negative supply shock of $\mu_0 = -\hat{\mu}$ hits the economy at time zero, whereas the economy follows its average behavior at all other times. We therefore simulate the economy, impose the negative shock at time zero for each simulation, and average across all paths.

There are two differences in the economy's response to a negative supply shock under the different frameworks. First, the immediate impact varies under different policies. When there is no lower bound that can constrain the central bank, the central bank can offset the shock optimally by lowering the real interest rate. As a result, the output gap becomes positive while inflation is below target. Because of the i.i.d. nature of the shocks, the effects are purely temporary. Second, average inflation differs across the policies. While average-inflation targeting and optimal policy in the absence of a lower bound both keep inflation at target on average, optimal policy in the presence of a lower bound runs inflation expectations below target as discussed above. As a result of this lower level of inflation expectations, the impact on inflation is more severe.

Figure 3.4 shows that the ranking among the policy options is the same when there are only demand shocks. Again, all of the policy rules lead to reductions in social losses. Average-inflation targeting thereby dominates an upper bound on interest rates and dovish policies.

To see the mechanics of the policy frameworks with demand shocks, figure 3.5 shows these impulse response functions for a negative demand shock at time 0. Optimal policy under discretion in the absence of a lower bound calls for complete stabilization of the demand shock. It neutralizes the impact of the shock on inflation and the output gap by sharply reducing the real interest rate.

Whenever the central bank is constrained by the lower bound on interest rates, it cannot reduce real interest rates sufficiently to offset the shock. As a result, inflation falls below target on impact and the output gap is negative. However, owing to higher inflation expectations under static average-inflation targeting, the contraction in inflation and real activity is less pronounced compared with optimal policy under discretion.

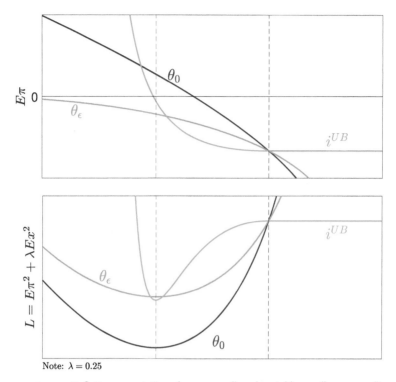

Note: $\lambda = 0.25$

FIGURE 3.4. Inflation expectations (upper panel) and social losses (lower panel) under an upper bound on interest rates (light blue line), dovish policies (green line), and different intercepts for the policy rule (purple line) for changes in the corresponding parameter. The graphs are computed under the baseline specification with demand shocks only.

6.3. The Mechanics of the Dynamic Policy Frameworks

To illustrate and compare the different frameworks, we show the average paths for inflation, the price level, the output gap, and the real interest rate within the context of a model that features only supply shocks. Therefore, we simulate the model under the benchmark calibration and show average paths following a given shock realization. In this experiment, we show the mean of the unconditional distribution in period −1 and pick a shock realization in

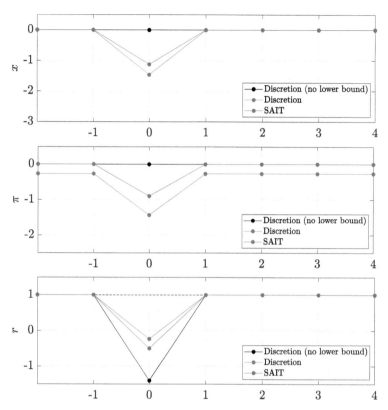

FIGURE 3.5. Impulse response functions under different policies in response to a negative demand shock $\epsilon_0 = -\hat{\epsilon}$ at time zero for the output gap (upper panel), the rate of inflation (middle panel), and the real interest rate (lower panel). We used the benchmark calibration without supply shocks to parameterize the model.

period 0. In all future periods, we average the responses across all simulated economies.

First, we show the response to a positive supply shock where $\mu_0 = \hat{\mu}$. Since supply shocks are only partially offset by the central bank, they spill over to inflation and thus affect the price level. As shown in figure 3.6, there are a number of differences among the various policies.

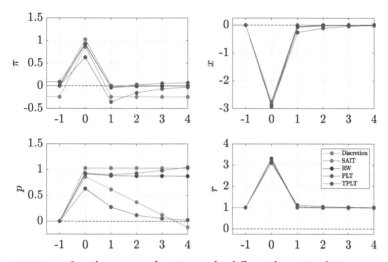

FIGURE 3.6. Impulse response functions under different dynamic policies in response to a positive supply shock at time 0, $\mu_0 = \hat{\mu}$ for inflation (upper left-hand panel), the price level (lower left-hand panel), the output gap (upper right-hand panel), and the real interest rate (lower right-hand panel). We used the benchmark calibration with supply shocks to parameterize the model.

Period −1 shows that average inflation is negative when interest rates are set optimally under discretion. By design, inflation is at target for average-inflation targeting and the Reifschneider-Williams (RW) rule. Temporary price-level targeting (TPLT) features above-target inflation that leads to a positive drift in the price level (see lower left panel of figure 3.6). The average rate of inflation under price-level targeting (PLT) is very close to target.

In response to the positive supply shock in period 0, inflation rises under all policy frameworks. The main differences across the various policies are visible from period 1 on. Price-level targeting stands out in its policy response in that the central bank makes up for the high inflation with future below-target inflation in order to bring the price level back to its target. As shown in the lower left-hand panel, the price level reverts back to target while the shock is treated as a bygone under all other frameworks. Since we start from

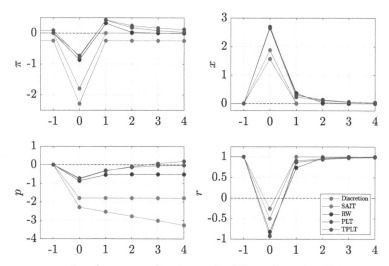

FIGURE 3.7. Impulse response functions under different dynamic policies in response to a negative supply shock at time 0, $\mu_0 = \dot{\mu}$ for inflation (upper left-hand panel), the price level (lower left-hand panel), the output gap (upper right-hand panel), and the real interest rate (lower right-hand panel). We used the benchmark calibration without supply shocks to parameterize the model.

"normal" times where no temporary price-level episode has been triggered, the inflation path under temporary price-level targeting also displays only a temporary upswing in inflation.

Next we investigate the response to a single large negative supply shock in period zero that sends the policy rate to the lower bound. All further realizations of supply shocks are at their average values. There are significant differences in the response to this shock among the various policy frameworks, as figure 3.7 demonstrates. For average-inflation targeting, the episode of the lower bound is purely temporary and does not affect inflation in subsequent periods. The path under the Reifschneider-Williams rule looks very different. Inflation falls significantly less due to higher inflation expectations. These inflation expectations have to be justified by higher inflation in the subsequent period. By that time, the shortfall in the interest rate cut due to the lower bound has been made

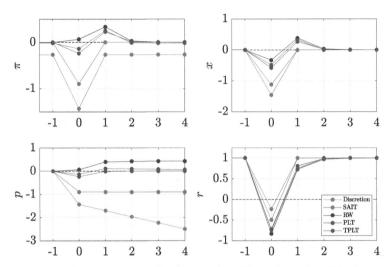

FIGURE 3.8. Impulse response functions under different dynamic policies in response to a negative demand shock at time 0, $\epsilon_0 = -\hat{\epsilon}$ for inflation (upper left-hand panel), the price level (lower left-hand panel), the output gap (upper right-hand panel), and the real interest rate (lower right-hand panel). We used the benchmark calibration without supply shocks to parameterize the model.

up for and inflation from period two on is at target. Under (temporary) price-level targeting, encounters with the lower bound have a longer-lasting impact. While higher inflation expectations reduce the impact of a negative shock, inflation remains above target for several periods thereafter.

Figure 3.8 shows the responses to a negative demand shock that would be fully offset by optimal policy absent a lower bound on interest rates. When the central bank has to obey a lower bound on interest rates, a negative demand shock spills over to inflation and the output gap. Importantly, all dynamic policies achieve a rate of inflation close to the target rate. Small discrepancies for the temporary price-level-targeting rules are due to the asymmetry of the unconditional distribution we discussed earlier. Appendix F contains a list of moments for the unconditional distributions under

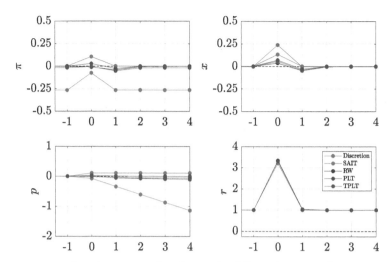

FIGURE 3.9. Impulse response functions under different dynamic policies in response to a positive demand shock at time 0, $\epsilon_0 = \hat{\epsilon}$ for inflation (upper left-hand panel), the price level (lower left-hand panel), the output gap (upper right-hand panel), and the real interest rate (lower right-hand panel). We used the benchmark calibration without supply shocks to parameterize the model.

various policy rules. The policies differ in the way they anchor inflation. While static and dynamic average-inflation-targeting policies treat the shock to inflation and thus the price level as temporary, price-level-targeting rules make up for past shortfalls.

Figure 3.9 shows the responses to a positive demand shock. Here, we start with the average of the unconditional distribution in period −1 and force a shock realization of $\epsilon_0 = \hat{\epsilon}$ in period 0 for all simulated economies. As a result, inflation is higher for optimal policy under discretion and average-inflation targeting. This result emerges because inflation is above average during normal times. Reifschneider-Williams, on the other hand, can stabilize inflation during normal times just as an optimal rule would demand. The price-level targeting practices achieve almost full stabilization.

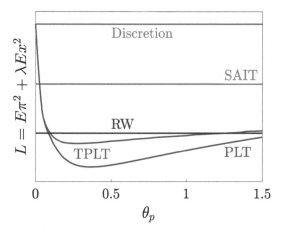

FIGURE 3.10. Social losses for different monetary policy frameworks as a function of the responsiveness of the interest rate rule to the price level. The economy is hit only by supply shocks.

6.4. Outcomes under Different Policy Frameworks

In this section, we investigate the effect of the various policy frameworks on social losses. Therefore, we first use the baseline model with supply shocks. For the Reifschneider-Williams rule, we compute the social loss under the parameterization $\rho_z = \theta_z = 1$ such that all interest rate misses will be made up for in one period whenever feasible. And last, for price-level targeting, we compute the social loss as a function of the coefficient on the price-level using the same benchmark parameterization.

Figure 3.10 shows social losses for the different policies. Because only the price-level targeting and temporary price-level targeting frameworks are influenced by the parameter θ_p, the lines for all other policies are flat. While the magnitude of the differences between the social losses varies with the parameterization, the ordering should be stable across a wide range of parameters.

Optimal monetary policy under discretion serves as our bench-mark policy. Since this policy suffers from inefficiently low infla-tion expectations, average-inflation targeting can improve on social welfare. Because of the dynamic nature of policy adjustments, Reifschneider-Williams rules lower social losses further by raising inflation expectations at a time when they are needed the most. Optimally parameterized price-level targeting dominates the other policy proposals in the case of supply shocks. As discussed before, this improvement in terms of social outcomes is due to the policy framework reacting more strongly to deviations of inflation from target irrespective of whether the nominal interest rate is at the lower bound or not. Temporary price-level targeting slightly dominates Reifschneider-Williams due to its ability to make up for shocks during temporary price-level targeting episodes, as we show below. In that sense, price-level targeting frameworks are a more fundamental departure from inflation targeting than the alterna-tives we discuss.

We contrast the findings for the model with supply shocks with the analogous results for a model with demand shocks in figure 3.11. The mechanics for demand shocks are different since, even under optimal policy under discretion, demand shocks are fully offset unless the lower bound on interest rates becomes a binding constraint. In that sense, demand shocks give us a way to assess the influence of the lower bound on interest rates directly.

The ranking among the policy options is still the same for the static monetary policy frameworks. The bias in inflation expec-tations is directly related to the probability of hitting the lower bound. The mechanism behind the static policies is thus the same for supply and demand shocks.

The difference comes in for dynamic policies. The various opti-mized dynamic policies all yield the same loss in the case of demand shocks. Price-level targeting and temporary price-level targeting

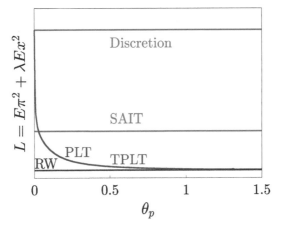

FIGURE 3.11. Social losses for different monetary policy frameworks as a function of the responsiveness of the interest rate rule to the price level. The economy is hit only by demand shocks.

lead to virtually identical social losses since makeup strategies are in effect only after negative shocks when the temporary price-level target is triggered whereas positive shocks are fully offset through higher interest rates. Both policies lose some of the advantages they had in the presence of supply shocks relative to the Reifschneider-Williams framework. Reifschneider-Williams is specifically designed to deal with issues associated with the lower bound on interest rates while (temporary) price-level targeting deals with these issues indirectly through a commitment to make up for the larger shortfalls in inflation cause by the lower bound. The results instead suggest that the additional gains under (temporary) price-level targeting for the case of supply shocks were, to a large extent, derived from policy commitments away from the lower bound.

7. CONCLUSION

This paper analyzes various monetary policy frameworks and associated policy rules within a simple New Keynesian model with a lower bound on interest rates. We use the model to discuss both the mechanics of the policies and their implementation. We compare three broad classes of policy frameworks. Inflation expectations are the key vehicle through which the policy frameworks affect price setting and the macroeconomy. Dovish policies dampen the reaction to shocks and thereby bring about welfare gains.

Static average-inflation targeting eliminates the downward bias in inflation expectations. Once the level of the interest rate rule is set optimally, no further adjustment needs to be made to the responsiveness to shocks relative to optimal policy under discretion. Therefore, static average-inflation targeting dominates dovish policies.

Dynamic policy frameworks fare best. Reifschneider-Williams rules lead to an average inflation rate equal to target. Under this policy, the central bank promises to keep rates "lower for longer" and thus stimulates the economy precisely at a time when the central bank is constrained.

Particularly in the presence of supply shocks, price-level targeting rules lead to the lowest social losses. Because the difference with other frameworks is stronger in the presence of supply rather than demand shocks, we infer that some of these welfare benefits stem from policy commitments away from the lower bound.

While the focus of this paper is on the mechanisms of the various policies, further work is needed to evaluate their robustness by analyzing them within different economic models. Furthermore, a quantitative assessment of the policy frameworks within an estimated larger-scale DSGE model would be informative about the magnitude of the welfare gains under the various rules.

References

Benhabib, Jess, Stephanie Schmitt-Grohé, and Martín Uribe. 2001. "The Perils of Taylor Rules." *Journal of Economic Theory* 96, nos. 1–2 (January): 40–69.

Bernanke, Ben S. 2017. "Monetary Policy in a New Era." Paper presented at Rethinking Macroeconomic Policy conference, Peterson Institute for International Economics, October 12–13.

Bernanke, Ben S., Michael T. Kiley, and John M. Roberts. 2019. "Monetary Policy Strategies for a Low-Rate Environment." *American Economic Review, Papers and Proceedings* 109 (May): 421–26.

Bernanke, Ben S., and Frederic S. Mishkin. 1997. "Inflation Targeting: A New Framework for Monetary Policy?" *Journal of Economic Perspectives* 11, no. 2 (Spring): 97–116.

Clarida, Richard, Jordi Galí, and Mark Gertler. 1999. "The Science of Monetary Policy: A New Keynesian Perspective." *Journal of Economic Literature* 37, no. 4 (December): 1661–707.

Eggertsson, Gauti B., and Michael Woodford. 2003. "The Zero Bound on Interest Rates and Optimal Monetary Policy." *Brookings Papers on Economic Activity* 2003, no. 1: 139–233.

Evans, Charles L. 2010. "Monetary Policy in a Low-Inflation Environment: Developing a State-Contingent Price-Level Target." Speech at the Federal Reserve Bank of Boston's 55th Economic Conference, Revisiting Monetary Policy in a Low Inflation Environment, Boston, October 16.

Giannoni, Marc P. 2014. "Optimal Interest-Rate Rules and Inflation Stabilization versus Price-Level Stabilization." *Journal of Economic Dynamics and Control* 41 (April): 110–129.

Harrison, Richard, Martin Seneca, and Matt Waldron. 2019. "Monetary Policy Options in a 'Low for Long' Era." Mimeo, Bank of England.

Holston, Kathryn, Thomas Laubach, and John C. Williams. 2017. "Measuring the Natural Rate of Interest: International Trends and Determinants." *Journal of International Economics* 108, no. S1 (May): S59–75.

Koenig, Evan F. 2013. "Like a Good Neighbor: Monetary Policy, Financial Stability, and the Distribution of Risk." *International Journal of Central Banking* 9, no. 2 (June): 57–82.

Laubach, Thomas, and John C. Williams. 2016. "Measuring the Natural Rate of Interest Redux." *Business Economics* 51, no. 2 (July): 57–67.

Mendes, Rhys R. 2011. "Uncertainty and the Zero Lower Bound: A Theoretical Analysis." Bank of Canada.

Mertens, Thomas M., and John C. Williams. 2018. "What to Expect from the Lower Bound on Interest Rates: Evidence from Derivatives Prices." Federal Reserve Bank of San Francisco, Working Paper 2018-03, August.

———. 2019. "Monetary Policy Frameworks and the Effective Lower Bound on Interest Rates." *American Economic Review, Papers and Proceedings* 109 (May): 427–32.

Nakata, Taisuke, and Sebastian Schmidt. 2019. "Gradualism and Liquidity Traps." *Review of Economic Dynamics 31* (January): 182–99.

Reifschneider, David L., and John C. Williams. 2000. "Three Lessons for Monetary Policy in a Low-Inflation Era." *Journal of Money, Credit and Banking* 32, no. 4 (November): 936–66.

Svensson, Lars E. O. 1999. "Price Level Targeting vs. Inflation Targeting: A Free Lunch?" *Journal of Money, Credit and Banking* 31, no. 3 (August): 277–95.

———. 2019. "Monetary Policy Strategies for the Federal Reserve." Mimeo, Stockholm School of Economics

Taylor, John B. 1985. "What Would Nominal GDP Targeting Do to the Business Cycle?" In *Carnegie-Rochester Conference Series on Public Policy* 22: 61–84.

———. 1993. "Discretion versus Policy Rules in Practice." *Carnegie-Rochester Conference Series on Public Policy* 39 (December): 195–214

Vestin, David. 2006. "Price-Level versus Inflation Targeting." *Journal of Monetary Economics* 53, no. 7 (October): 1361–76.

Woodford, Michael. 2003. *Interest and Prices: Foundations of a Theory of Monetary Policy.* Princeton. NJ: Princeton University Press.

APPENDIX A: UPPER BOUND

The various conditions determine whether a constraint never binds, $\mathbb{C}_u$; occasionally binds, $\mathbb{C}_o$; or always binds, $\mathbb{C}_c$. The specific conditions on the lower bound are

$$\mathbb{C}_u^{\mathrm{LB}} = \left\{ \frac{1}{\theta_\mu}(i^{LB} - \theta_0 - \theta_E\, \mathbb{E}[\pi_{t+1}]) < -\hat{\mu} \right\}$$

for the lower bound to never bind,

$$\mathbb{C}_o^{\mathrm{LB}} = \left\{ -\hat{\mu} \leq \frac{1}{\theta_\mu}(i^{LB} - \theta_0 - \theta_E\, \mathbb{E}[\pi_{t+1}]) \leq \hat{\mu} \right\}$$

for the lower bound to occasionally bind, and

$$\mathbb{C}_c^{\mathrm{LB}} = \left\{ \frac{1}{\theta_\mu} (i^{LB} - \theta_0 - \theta_E \, \mathbb{E}[\pi_{t+1}]) > \hat{\mu} \right\}$$

for the lower bound to always bind.

For the upper bound, the conditions are

$$\mathbb{C}_u^{\mathrm{UB}} = \left\{ \frac{1}{\theta_\mu} (i^{UB} - \theta_0 - \theta_E \, \mathbb{E}[\pi_{t+1}]) > \hat{\mu} \right\}$$

for the upper to never bind,

$$\mathbb{C}_o^{\mathrm{UB}} = \left\{ -\hat{\mu} \le \frac{1}{\theta_\mu} (i^{UB} - \theta_0 - \theta_E \, \mathbb{E}[\pi_{t+1}]) \le \hat{\mu} \right\}$$

for the upper bound to occasionally bind, and

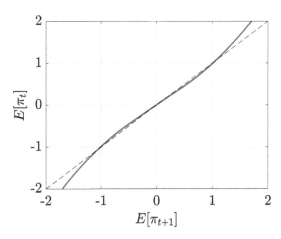

FIGURE 3.12. Expected inflation in the current period as a function of expected inflation in the following period. Parameter values are set to $\alpha = 1.25$, $\kappa = 0.8$, $\beta = 0.99$, $r^* = 1$, $\lambda = 0.25$, $i^{LB} = 0.5$, and $i^{UB} = 2.5$. The support for supply shocks is $\hat{\mu} = 3.3$ and there are no demand shocks, that is, $\hat{e} = 0$. Intersections with the dashed 45-degree line represent steady states. The coefficients in the policy rule are those of optimal monetary policy under discretion.

$$\mathbb{C}_c^{UB} = \left\{ \frac{1}{\theta_\mu}(i^{UB} - \theta_0 - \theta_E\,\mathbb{E}[\pi_{t+1}]) < -\hat\mu \right\}$$

for the upper bound to always bind.

Computing inflation expectations under the various scenarios delivers the graph of expected inflation as a function of expected inflation in the subsequent period shown in figure 3.12.

APPENDIX B: STATIC AVERAGE-INFLATION TARGETING

When adjusting the level of interest rates such that average inflation is at target, inflation expectations fall into the liquidity trap equilibrium. Figure 3.13 shows the mapping from next period's expected inflation to the current period's expected inflation.

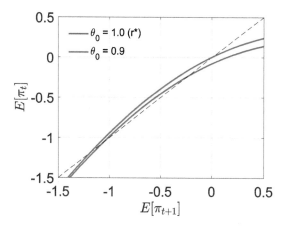

FIGURE 3.13. Expected inflation in the current period as a function of expected inflation in the following period. Parameter values are set to $\alpha = 1.25$, $\kappa = 0.8$, $\beta = 0.99$, $r^* = 1$, $\lambda = 0.25$, and $i^{LB} = 0.5$. The support for supply shocks is $\hat\mu = 3.3$ and there are no demand shocks, that is, $\hat{e} = 0$. Intersections with the dashed 45-degree line represent steady states. The coefficients in the policy rule are those of optimal monetary policy under discretion, except θ_0, which is set according to equation (11).

APPENDIX C: REIFSCHNEIDER-WILLIAMS RULE

C.1. Proof of Lemma 2

Proof: Iterating the IS curve in equation (2) forward results in

$$x_t = \varepsilon_t - \alpha \sum_{s=t}^{\infty} \mathbb{E}_t[i_s - \mathbb{E}_s \pi_{s+1} - r^*].$$

Taking unconditional expectations on both sides delivers

$$\mathbb{E}x_t = -\alpha \sum_{s=t}^{\infty} \mathbb{E}[i_s - \mathbb{E}_s \pi_{s+1} - r^*].$$

By design, the Reifschneider-Williams rule delivers an average nominal interest rate equal to r^*. This result derives from the fact that the reference nominal interest rate i_t^{ref} in equation (13) has r^* as its intercept and all shortfalls in interest rate cuts are made up for by design. Plugging in $\mathbb{E}[i_s] = \mathbb{E}[i_s^{\text{ref}}] = r^*$ in the previous equation shows that the output gap is given by

$$\mathbb{E}x_t = \alpha \sum_{s=t}^{\infty} \mathbb{E}[\pi_{s+1}].$$

The only nonexplosive solution has an average inflation rate at target, that is, $\mathbb{E}[\pi_s] = 0$.   ∎

C.2. Algorithm for Reifschneider-Williams Rules

We show the algorithm for the case of supply shocks in this section and the case of demand shocks works analogously. The model with supply shocks only for the Reifschneider-Williams rule can be summarized by the following equations:

$$x_t = -\alpha(i_t - \mathbb{E}_t(\pi_{t+1}) - r^*) + \mathbb{E}_t(x_{t+1})$$
$$\pi_t = \beta \mathbb{E}_t(\pi_{t+1}) + \kappa x_t + \mu_t$$
$$i_t^{\text{ref}} = \theta_0 + \theta_\mu \mu_t + \theta_E \mathbb{E}_t(\pi_{t+1})$$

$$i_t = \max(i_t^{\mathrm{ref}} + \theta_z z_t, i^{\mathrm{LB}})$$

$$\tilde{i}_t = i_t^{\mathrm{ref}} - i_t$$

$$z_{t+1} = z_t + \tilde{i}_t$$

The algorithm approximates and stores the following objects:

- One-period-ahead expected inflation: $g_\pi(z) = \mathbb{E}[\pi_{t+1} | z_{t+1} = z]$
- One-period-ahead expected output gap: $g_x(z) = \mathbb{E}[x_{t+1} | z_{t+1} = z]$
- Realized Taylor rule deviation: $f_{\tilde{i}}(\mu, z) = \tilde{i}_t | \mu_t = \mu, z_t = z$
- Realized inflation: $f_\pi(\mu, z) = \pi_t | \mu_t = \mu, z_t = z$
- Realized output gap: $f_x(\mu, z) = x_t | \mu_t = \mu, z_t = z$

To solve the model, we approximate these functions using linear interpolation and use the following iterative algorithm to solve for the functions' values at points along the following grids for z and μ (respectively):

- $\mathcal{Z}$: 101 equally spaced points between -10 and 0.
- $\mathcal{M}$: 201 equally spaced points between $-\hat{\mu}$ and $\hat{\mu}$.

Algorithm

1. Initialize inflation expectations
2. Given the approximation of one-period-ahead inflation expectations $\left(g_\pi^{(j-1)}(z) | z \in \mathcal{Z}\right)$ from the previous iteration, solve the following fixed-point problem at each pair of gridpoint values $\{(\mu, z) | \mu \in \mathcal{M}, z \in \mathcal{Z}\}$ in order to update the approximation of the realized Taylor rule deviation $f_{\tilde{i}}^{(j)}(\mu, z)$:

$$f_{\tilde{i}}^{(j)}(\mu, z) = \left(\theta_0 + \theta_\mu \mu + \theta_E g_\pi^{(j-1)}(z + f_{\tilde{i}}^{(j)}(\mu, z))\right)$$
$$- \max\left(\theta_0 + \theta_\mu \mu + \theta_E g_\pi^{(j-1)}(z + f_{\tilde{i}}^{(j)}(\mu, z)) + \theta_z z, i^{LB}\right).$$

$$(17)$$

3. Given approximations for the realized Taylor rule deviation $\{f_i^{(j)}(\mu,z)|\mu\in\mathcal{M},z\in\mathcal{Z}\}$ and expectations $\{g_\pi^{(j-1)}(z)|z\in\mathcal{Z}\}$, $\{g_x^{(j-1)}(z)|z\in\mathcal{Z}\}$ from the previous iteration, at each pair of gridpoint values $\{(\mu,z)|\mu\in\mathcal{M},z\in\mathcal{Z}\}$ update the following approximations:

$$f_i^{(j)}(\mu,z):=\max(\theta_0+\theta_\mu\mu+\theta_E g_\pi^{(j-1)}(z+f_i^{(j)}(\mu,z))+\theta_z z,i^{LB}) \quad (18)$$

$$\begin{aligned} f_x^{(j)}(\mu,z):=&-\alpha(f_i^{(j)}(\mu,z)-g_\pi^{(j-1)}(z+f_i^{(j)}(\mu,z))-r^*) \\ &+g_x^{(j-1)}(z+f_i^{(j)}(\mu,z)) \end{aligned} \quad (19)$$

$$f_\pi^{(j)}(\mu,z):=\beta g_\pi^{(j-1)}(z+f_i^{(j)}(\mu,z))+\kappa f_x^{(j)}(\mu,z)+\mu \quad (20)$$

4. Update approximations for one-period-ahead expectations $\{g_\pi^{(j)}(z)|z\in\mathcal{Z}\}$ for all $z\in\mathcal{Z}$, using the following discrete sum approximation for integration over μ:

$$g_\pi^{(j)}(z)=\sum_{\mu\in\mathcal{M}}f_\pi^{(j)}(\mu,z) \quad (21)$$

$$g_x^{(j)}(z)=\sum_{\mu\in\mathcal{M}}f_x^{(j)}(\mu,z). \quad (22)$$

5. Iterate steps 2–4 until all of the approximations have converged.

The Reifschneider-Williams rule results in inflation expectations as a function of the cumulative shortfall in interest rate cuts.

APPENDIX D: ALGORITHM FOR PRICE-LEVEL TARGETING

For price-level targeting, we again present the algorithm for the case of supply shocks only. The algorithm for the case of demand shocks works analogously. Therefore, we use the following set of equations for the model:

$$x_t = -\alpha(i_t - \mathbb{E}_t[\pi_{t+1}] - r^*) + \mathbb{E}_t[x_{t+1}]$$
$$\pi_t = \beta E_t(\pi_{t+1}) + \kappa x_t + \mu_t$$
$$i_t = \max\{\theta_0 + \theta_\mu \mu_t + \theta_E \mathbb{E}_t[\pi_{t+1}] + \theta_p p_t, i^{LB}\}$$
$$p_t = p_{t-1} + \pi_t.$$

The numerical procedure approximates and stores the following objects:

- One-period-ahead expected inflation: $g_\pi(p) = \mathbb{E}[\pi_{t+1} | p_t = p]$
- One-period-ahead expected output gap: $g_x(p) = \mathbb{E}[x_{t+1} | p_t = p]$
- Realized inflation: $f_\pi(\mu, p) = \pi_t | \mu_t = \mu, p_{t-1} = p$
- Realized output gap: $f_x(\mu, p) = x_t | \mu_t = \mu, p_{t-1} = p$

To solve the model, we approximate these functions using interpolation and use the following iterative algorithm to solve for the functions' values at points along the following grids for p and μ (respectively):

- $\mathcal{P}$: the union of the following evenly spaced grids (intended to give a high density of gridpoints around $p = 0$):
  1. $\{-70, -65, \ldots, 65, 70\}$
  2. $\{-20, -19, \ldots, 19, 20\}$
  3. $\{-5, -4.75, \ldots, 4.75, 5\}$
  4. $\{-1, -0.9, \ldots, 0.9, 1\}$
- $\mathcal{M}$: 201 equally spaced points between $-\hat{\mu}$ and $\hat{\mu}$

Algorithm
1. Initialize inflation expectations $g_\pi^{(0)}(p) := 0$ for all $p \in \mathcal{P}$.
2. Given the approximations of one-period-ahead expectations for inflation $\{g_\pi^{(j-1)}(p) | p \in \mathcal{P}\}$ and the output gap $\{g_x^{(j-1)}(p) | p \in \mathcal{P}\}$ from the previous iteration, solve the following fixed-point problem at each pair of gridpoint values

$\{(\mu, p)|\mu \in \mathcal{M}, p \in \mathcal{P}\}$ in order to update the approximation of realized inflation $f_\pi^{(j)}(\mu, p)$:[12]

$$f_\pi^{(j)}(\mu, p) = \kappa(-\alpha(\max(\theta_0 + \theta_\mu \mu_t + \theta_E g_\pi^{(j-1)}(p + f_\pi^{(j)}(\mu, p))$$
$$+ \theta_p p, i^{LB}) - r^*) + g_x^{(j-1)}(p + f_\pi^{(j)}(\mu, p)))$$
$$+ (\alpha\kappa + \beta)g_\pi^{(j-1)}(p + f_\pi^{(j)}(\mu, p)) + \mu. \tag{23}$$

3. Given approximations to realized inflation $\{f_i^{(j)}(\mu, p)|\mu \in \mathcal{M}, p \in \mathcal{P}\}$ and expectations $\{g_\pi^{(j-1)}(p)|p \in \mathcal{P}\}$, $\{g_x^{(j-1)}(p)|p \in \mathcal{P}\}$ from the previous iteration, at each pair of gridpoint values $\{(\mu, p)|\mu \in \mathcal{M}, p \in \mathcal{P}\}$ update the approximation for the realized output gap $f_x^{(j)}(\mu, p)$:

$$f_x^{(j)}(\mu, p) := -\alpha(\max(\theta_0 + \theta_\mu \mu_t + \theta_E g_\pi^{(j-1)}(p + f_\pi^{(j)}(\mu, p))$$
$$+ \theta_p p, i^{LB}) - g_\pi^{(j-1)}(p + f_\pi^{(j)}(\mu, p)) - r^*)$$
$$+ g_x^{(j-1)}(p + f_\pi^{(j)}(\mu, p)) \tag{24}$$

4. Update approximations for one-period-ahead expectations $\{g_\pi^{(j)}(p)|p \in \mathcal{P}\}$ for all $p \in \mathcal{P}$, using the following discrete sum approximation for integration over μ:

$$g_\pi^{(j)}(p) = \sum_{\mu \in \mathcal{M}} f_\pi^{(j)}(\mu, p) \tag{25}$$

$$g_x^{(j)}(p) = \sum_{\mu \in \mathcal{M}} f_x^{(j)}(\mu, p). \tag{26}$$

5. Iterate steps 2–4 until all of the approximations have converged.

---

12. Note that the equations determining the nominal interest rate and output gap have been substituted into the equation determining inflation, so that realized inflation is the only endogenous time t-variable that appears in the expression.

APPENDIX E: TEMPORARY
PRICE-LEVEL TARGETING

As in the other cases, we focus on the case of supply shocks only. The algorithm for the case with demand shocks works in the same way.

Policy is conducted according to the following interest rate rule:

$$
i_t = \begin{cases} \theta_0 + \theta_\mu \mu_t + \theta_E \, \mathbb{E}[\pi_{t+1} \,|\, p_t = 0] & \text{if } \mu_t > \mu^c \text{ and } p_{t-1} = 0 \\ i^{LB} & \text{if } \mu_t \le \mu^c \text{ or } p_{t-1} < 0. \end{cases} \tag{27}
$$

The "cutoff" supply shock value is defined as $\mu^c \equiv \dfrac{i^{LB} - \theta_0 - \theta_E \mathbb{E}[\pi_{t+1} \,|\, p_t = 0]}{\theta_\mu}$. The (temporary) price level evolves according to:

$$
p_t = \begin{cases} 0 & \text{if } \mu_t > \mu^c \text{ and } p_{t-1} = 0 \\ \min(p_{t-1} + \pi_t, 0) & \text{if } \mu_t \le \mu^c \text{ or } p_{t-1} < 0. \end{cases} \tag{28}
$$

In words: when $\mu_t \le \mu^c$, the nominal interest rate will surely be constrained if PLT is not initiated; when a negative shock of this magnitude occurs, the policy maker fixes $i_t = i^{LB}$ and initiates PLT, keeping the interest rate at the lower bound until the price level returns to its level in the period before the shock (i.e., until $p_t = 0$).

This rule induces discontinuities in both realized and expected inflation. In particular, when $p_{t-1} = 0$ (PLT has not already been initiated), π_t is higher when $\mu_t = \mu^c - \epsilon$ than when $\mu_t = \mu^c + \epsilon$, since the former shock is just big enough to trigger a TPLT "episode" and deliver stimulus through a guarantee of low future interest rates. Similarly, $\mathbb{E}_t[\pi_{t+1} \,|\, p_t = -\epsilon]$ is much larger than $\mathbb{E}_t[\pi_{t+1} \,|\, p_t = 0]$ since a TPLT "episode" is initiated only in the former case.

The following page displays plots of the solutions for expected and realized inflation, as well as sample paths for inflation, the nominal interest rate, the temporary price level, and the shocks μ.

The horizontal lines in the interest rate and shock charts below denote i^{LB} and μ^c, respectively. Yellow dots in the interest rate chart denote periods where $i_t = i^{LB}$, while red dots denote periods where $p_t < 0$.

APPENDIX F: THE UNCONDITIONAL DISTRIBUTION OF INFLATION AND THE OUTPUT GAP

This section presents a list of moments for the unconditional distributions of inflation and the output gap under various policy rules. Table 3.1 contains a list of moments for the model with supply shocks, while table 3.2 shows the analogous statistics for the model with demand shocks.

TABLE 3.1. Moments of the unconditional distribution under various policy rules. We use the benchmark calibration for each policy framework in the model with supply shocks

	Discretion (no lower bound)	Discretion	SAIT ($E\pi=0$)	RW	PLT	TPLT
$\mathbb{E}(\pi_t)$	0.000	−0.244	0.000	0.000	0.002	0.083
$\mathbb{V}(\pi_t)$	0.287	0.675	0.501	0.282	0.191	0.239
$\mathbb{E}(x_t)$	0.000	−0.003	0.000	−0.002	−0.001	0.000
$\mathbb{V}(x_t)$	2.934	2.053	2.381	2.757	2.780	2.787
$\mathbb{E}(\pi_t^2)+\lambda\mathbb{E}(x_t^2)$	1.020	1.248	1.096	0.973	0.887	0.946
$\mathbb{P}(i_t=i^{LB})$	0.000	0.273	0.205	0.202	0.076	0.088
$\mathbb{E}(\pi_t\,\vert\,i_t=i^{LB})$	—	−1.389	−1.124	−0.701	−0.650	−0.650
$\mathbb{E}(\pi_t\,\vert\,i_t>i^{LB})$	0.000	0.185	0.290	0.178	0.056	0.154
$\mathbb{E}(x_t\,\vert\,i_t=i^{LB})$	—	1.567	1.875	2.225	2.561	2.503
$\mathbb{E}(x_t\,\vert\,i_t>i^{LB})$	0.000	−0.591	−0.484	−0.566	−0.213	−0.242
θ_o	1.000	1.000	0.900	1.000	1.000	1.000
θ_μ	0.719	0.719	0.719	0.719	0.719	0.719
θ_ε	1.722	1.722	1.722	1.722	1.722	1.722
$\theta_p,\ \theta_z$	0.000	0.000	0.000	1.000	0.360	0.280

TABLE 3.2. Moments of the unconditional distribution under various policy rules. We use the benchmark calibration for each policy framework in the model with demand shocks

	Discretion (no lower bound)	Discretion	SAIT ($E\pi = 0$)	RW	PLT	TPLT
$\mathbb{E}(\pi_t)$	0.000	-0.266	0.000	-0.001	0.000	-0.017
$\mathbb{V}(\pi_t)$	0.000	0.137	0.060	0.009	0.007	0.007
$\mathbb{E}(x_t)$	0.000	-0.003	0.000	0.000	0.001	-0.002
$\mathbb{V}(x_t)$	0.000	0.215	0.093	0.019	0.029	0.027
$\mathbb{E}(\pi_t^2) + \lambda\mathbb{E}(x_t^2)$	0.000	0.262	0.083	0.014	0.014	0.014
$\mathbb{P}(i_t = i^{LB})$	0.000	0.283	0.209	0.207	0.206	0.196
$\mathbb{E}(\pi_t \,|\, i_t = i^{LB})$	—	-0.753	-0.397	0.037	-0.086	-0.063
$\mathbb{E}(\pi_t \,|\, i_t > i^{LB})$	0.000	-0.074	0.105	-0.010	0.023	-0.006
$\mathbb{E}(x_t \,|\, i_t = i^{LB})$	—	-0.612	-0.497	-0.139	-0.233	-0.223
$\mathbb{E}(x_t \,|\, i_t = i^{LB})$	0.000	0.237	0.132	0.037	0.062	0.052
θ_o	1.000	1.000	0.895	1.000	1.000	1.000
θ_η	0.800	0.800	0.800	0.800	0.800	0.800
θ_E	1.722	1.722	1.722	1.722	1.722	1.722
θ_p, θ_z	0.000	0.000	0.000	1.000	1.500	2.290

DISCUSSANT REMARKS

Monika Piazzesi

The organizers of this conference gave me a great paper to read and think about. First, let me say that I am excited and grateful that my policy maker—John Williams, president of the New York Federal Reserve and vice chair of the Federal Open Market Committee, which decides on monetary policy—took the time to provide a detailed explanation of how he thinks about policy in the current environment with low interest rates. An added bonus is that the explanation comes in the form of elegant formulas that nicely illustrate how optimal policy looks like in this environment.

An important question for policy is, what should we do if interest rates continue to stay low? To address this question, the paper uses a standard New Keynesian model for inflation, π_t, and the output gap, x_t. The model consists of two equations, a Phillips curve and an Euler equation:

$$\pi_t = \mu_t + \kappa x_t + \beta E_t \pi_{t+1}$$
$$x_t = \epsilon_t - \alpha(i_t - E_t \pi_{t+1} - r^*) + E_t x_{t+1},$$

Here, i_t is the short-term nominal interest rate, r^* is the real rate in the long run, μ_t is a supply shock, and ϵ_t is a demand shock.

How should monetary policy be conducted in this model if we continue to stay in a low-interest-rate environment? Suppose there is a lower bound on the short-term nominal interest rate, i_t. Imagine that the rate i_t cannot be negative, so it has to stay positive or at zero. This idea is captured with a constraint $i_t \geq 0$. How should monetary policy be conducted in the presence of this constraint? What policy rule should the central bank use to determine i_t?

The answer is that the central bank should commit to rules that raise inflation expectations, broadly speaking. In the zero-lower-bound environment, such a policy prevents the central bank from cutting rates in response to bad shocks, because there will be times where it would have to cut below zero. With discretion, policy leads to lower inflation expectations. By committing to a policy rule, the central bank can then increase these inflation expectations.

The paper describes a number of interest-rate rules that would increase inflation expectations. The paper finds that many different rules can do the job. If we start from an optimal discretionary rule, we will find there are dovish policies that just respond less to shocks. An alternative rule is static average inflation targeting, which translates in this world to simply using a lower intercept in the Taylor rule. The Reifschneider-Williams rule is another alternative, which responds to past deviation from the inflation target and is therefore a dynamic rule. Price-level targeting is yet another alternative, which seems to work out best in this particular model. But all these rules achieve the same goal of lowering policy rates for a longer time, especially after bad shocks, and thereby raising inflation expectations.

Why do we believe that the short-term nominal rate has a lower bound? The typical argument for why there is a lower bound is cash arbitrage. In a New Keynesian model, the nominal short rate is the interest rate on savings. The government also provides cash, which pays zero interest. If the savings rate drops below zero, households will go to the bank, withdraw their savings, and start holding cash. This cash-arbitrage argument implies that the central bank cannot lower rates below zero.

However, in modern economies, the lion's share of payments is not made with cash. Instead, payments are made electronically, either with deposits or with short credit (e.g., households use credit cards to pay for goods and services, and firms use credit lines to pay their workers). These electronic payments are handled by banks that provide the payment instruments. Banks manage these payments by paying reserves to one another. Banks have reserve accounts at the central bank. In all modern economies, banks pay these reserves to one another using a gross settlement system provided by the government. The central bank decides whether or not to pay interest on these reserve accounts. If banks receive interest on reserve holdings, the production of payment instruments becomes cheaper. In such a world, the question is, can the government pay negative rates on reserves? Moreover, do banks pass these negative rates on to households and firms?

The recent experience in Europe provides some information about the answers to these questions. And so, I thought I was going to show some evidence from Europe. Heider, Saidi, and Schepens (2019) illustrate what happened in Europe to the various interest rates.[13] The interest rate that the European Central Bank (ECB) pays on reserves went negative in 2014. Other rates also became negative, like the three-month Euribor rate, which is a rate that banks pay to one another. Importantly, banks are able to handle negative rates.

Heider, Saidi, and Schepens (2019) also answer the question of whether banks pass the negative rates on to households or firms.[14] The upper chart in their figure shows that the distribution of rates that households receive on their deposit accounts does not include negative rates. In other words, banks tend to spare small deposits from negative rates. The lower chart in their figure shows that large deposits by nonfinancial corporations are being paid negative rates. In other words, banks do pass negative rates on to their large depositors.

In sum, is there a zero lower bound for the nominal short-term interest rate? For Europe, central banks in many countries have

13. See figure 1 in Heider, Saidi, and Schepens (2019).
14. See figure 2 in Heider, Saidi, and Schepens (2019).

been paying negative rates on reserves. Not just the ECB—that was the evidence in the figures by Heider et al.—but also Norway, Denmark, Sweden, Switzerland, and Japan have all used negative rates on reserves. Moreover, the evidence from Europe suggests that banks will pass negative rates on to their larger depositors. These facts raise the question of why banks pass negative rates on to some of their customers. The paper by Mertens and Williams addresses the question of optimal monetary policy in an environment where a constraint prevents rates from going negative. What is the reason for this constraint? What is the microfoundation for this constraint? To address the question of optimal monetary policy in a low-interest-rate environment, it would be important for future research to answer the question of whether a lower bound for interest rates exists, whether the lower bound is zero, and what the economic rationale for the lower bound is.

As interest rates stay low and we are thinking about optimal policy in this environment, we should also reopen the question on whether the central bank should be paying positive interest on reserves at all. In the United States, the Fed started to pay positive interest on reserves in 2008. Before then, the Fed did not pay any interest on reserves. Is it optimal for the Fed to pay interest on reserves? The answer to this question is far from clear. A higher reserve rate redistributes wealth from taxpayers to shareholders of banks, as interest on reserves subsidizes the business of banks.

The United States switched from a system without such subsidies to a system with subsidies in 2008. Soon after, the amount of reserves in the banking system exploded after quantitative easing. Figure 3.14 shows the evolution of reserve balances and their increase to trillions of dollars since the financial crisis. Any small basis point of an interest rate on trillions of dollars is a large subsidy. I understand that it is difficult in these circumstances to reduce the reserve rate back to zero without seriously damaging the banking system. However, we should talk about whether reserves should be

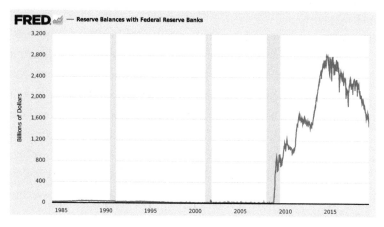

FIGURE 3.14. Reserve Balances with Federal Reserve Banks in Billions of
Dollars.
Source: FRED, Federal Reserve Bank of St. Louis.

reduced to a lower level, such as those we had in the environment
before the financial crisis. With a lower amount of reserves, the
government could think about reducing the interest on reserves
more easily, without causing serious damage to banks.

The question about the optimality of interest on reserves is
beyond the focus of this paper, of course. This paper focuses on
interest rate policy in the presence of a constraint that prevents
interest rates from being negative. However, the size of the Fed balance sheet is another policy instrument. We should debate the optimal size of this balance sheet in a low-interest-rate environment
in the future. The current size is large, and a small interest rate on
reserves involves large payments that benefit banks. Moreover, we
should consider policies that involve negative interest on reserves.

The idea of negative rates on reserves is intriguing, but what will
happen in the long run if such a policy is adopted? The European
experience is relatively short. Europe started adopting negative
rates only in 2014. If reserve rates stay negative over a long period
of time, it is plausible that banks will start thinking about whether

they can adopt a different system to pay one another, and thereby circumvent the gross settlement system provided by the government. Banks might design alternative systems that help minimize the use of reserves. Banks will probably try to net more during the day and maybe use more cash deliveries, if that is a cheaper way of running their business. Any policy that plans to set negative reserve rates over extended periods of time has to face the possibility that banks will innovate and think about how best to pay each other. Will this innovation support bank lending and lead to financial stability? These are the questions we will have to address over the next months.

Reference

Heider, Florian, Farzad Saidi, and Glenn Schepens. 2019. "Life below Zero: Bank Lending under Negative Policy Rates." *Review of Financial Studies* 32, no. 10 (October): 3728–61.

GENERAL DISCUSSION

KEVIN WARSH (INTRODUCTION): One can view the proximity of the current Fed policy stance to the zero lower bound as an accident of history, or a wise choice. So, too, the grand scale and scope of the Fed's balance sheet. No matter one's judgment, the Fed finds itself with less conventional and unconventional ammunition.

With ammunition low, Fed credibility—to act independently, get policy right, and explain well the rationale for its actions—is at a premium. Fed cred will be relied on most when the economy slows or confronts a shock. So it's encouraging that Fed is open to considering reforms in the conduct of monetary policy.

Most of our students on campus know well the financial crisis of 2008–2009. But it's no more resonant than, say, the Great Depression. Big and consequential. An important chapter of our American history. But the panic of the period is not something they experienced. Many students of the financial crisis are neither scared nor scarred. Some of us who served view their innocence with equal parts envy and concern. The past isn't even past.

The regime change of the economy in the last decade—from "crisis" to "recovery" to "sustained expansion"—did not correspond to a significant change in the profile or practice of the modern central banker. The Federal Reserve neither exited the front stage nor fell off the front page.

Some view monetary dominance over the last decade with grave concern, if not suspicion. Others, attuned to the polarization of our politics, are relieved that the Fed sees fit to be a steadying force. And in the high-minded spirit of a modern Wilsonian, they see a cadre of policy professionals compensating for the failings of much of the rest of government.

The Fed's actions—and preeminence—continue to leave a heavy mark on the economy, banking system, and financial markets. And with its elevated status, the Fed finds itself considerably more exposed to the broader body politic. The central bank's prominence has caused its policy choices to be scrutinized through a different lens and its independence to be tested. The Fed has long been powerful. Setting interest rates matters to households and businesses and governments. In the period between the Treasury-Fed Accord of 1951 and the financial crisis of 2008, the Fed's monetary powers were thought to be limited, well circumscribed. Monetary and fiscal policy were clearly delineated. And the distinction came with a difference: the conduct of monetary policy alone was largely accorded the benefit of central bank independence.

To what do we owe the heightened scrutiny of the Fed in recent years? It is fashionable—and true—to talk about the hyper-partisanship of our time. And of the divisions in our country. It is less fashionable—but no less true—to believe that the financial crisis is a piece of the polarization. One observes the casting of prospective nominees to our central bank in the last decade as either "with us" or "against us." This is a troubling development.

Until the last couple of years, it's also true that growth in real economic output and median take-home pay were modest and well below consensus forecasts. Blame is assigned for the economic shortfall. And the Fed—at center stage—serves a useful, if sometimes undeserved, target. The central bank has no shortage of good intentions. But the Fed is not an altogether unwitting victim of the political scrum.

When monetary policy makers herald their record of job creation, they risk their institutional prerogatives. Policy pros can rarely force-rank the individual efficacy of monetary, fiscal, trade, and regulatory policy. Moreover, economic expansions often owe more to the resilient, micro-foundations of the economy than macroeconomic fine-tuning. Even if the Fed merits special commendation, bowing at center stage is incompatible with safeguarding independence.

For most of the postcrisis period, the Fed grew the size and scope of its balance sheet in order to provide greater monetary accommodation. In recent months, the Fed announced another big shift in its balance sheet plans. It would maintain a large balance sheet on a seemingly permanent basis. But no longer was monetary policy the rationale. The Fed justified its new policy stance on regulatory and operational grounds: the big banks need high-quality, Fed-provided reserves.

But what happens when the bright line between monetary and regulatory policy fades? And when the line between monetary policy and fiscal policy blurs? Line-crossing poses real risks.

This is not about party or president. If Congress does not have the votes for an extension of the debt limit, why not get emergency relief from the Fed. If the appropriations process is deadlocked, call on the Fed to fund a government agency directly. If housing prices are falling, push the Fed to buy four mortgages. If Congress and the administration cannot agree on new fiscal policy, pressure the Fed to provide more stimulus.

Demanding central bank independence in the conduct of quasi-fiscal and quasi-regulatory policy is a break with historic norms. By custom, the Fed is granted carefully circumscribed authority to conduct monetary policy independently. Not fiscal policy, which is the province of Congress. And not regulatory policy, which is to be executed under the rules that govern many other government agencies.

If the Fed becomes a general-purpose agency of economic policy, it will lose its special monetary prerogatives. And the printing press it keeps will be a temptation for mischief. Modern monetary theory (MMT) is the new name for an old temptation to conflate monetary and fiscal policy. The Fed's monetary independence arises not by constitutional sanction but from something more subtle, a norm. Independence requires constant vigilance by all parties, not least the central bank itself. Independence, however, is not the objective of sound monetary policy. Instead, it's a time-tested, effective means to get policy right. But that's not all.

Like sound legal opinions from the high court, monetary policy decisions are more important for the reasons they give, not the results they announce. The Fed's real institutional power comes not from its ability to pronounce but its ability to persuade. A policy decision that gets the reasons wrong gets a lot wrong.

The Fed is right to change its judgment when circumstances dictate, but its rationale must be comprehensive and compelling. Recitation of the Fed's latest quarterly dot-plot forecast—inspired by the Fed's workhorse models—is not sufficient to justify a policy stance. Nor is reference to an ostensibly settled monetary policy rule.

In my view, the scale and scope of monetary policy makers' ambitions have expanded over the past decade. Yet its policy choices are narrower, and more difficult.

KRISHNA GUHA: So, [John Williams], you presented sort of a hierarchy of effectiveness in the model. You also, early on, made the point that in a sense the challenges regarding credibility and commitment also escalate in the same order. My own view, just based on speaking to lots of market participants, is that a framework review conclusion that promised to behave differently and contingently in the future would be regarded as having relatively little credibility today in financial markets relative to changes that involved you actually changing your real-time observable behaviors today. So, what I wanted to ask is, first, how do you think about evaluating that trade-off that you presented between the efficacy in the model and what you're asking by way of central banks' credibility and forward-looking inflation expectations formation process. How are you going to evaluate that? And should we think of it as an either-or, or could we think of a situation in which behaving somewhat differently in the present could enhance the credibility of promises to take firmer commitments in the future contingency lower bound events?

JOHN WILLIAMS: On your question of how will we evaluate these trade-offs, my answer is: carefully and thoughtfully, and deliberately. It is the Federal Reserve. So, you know, I agree with your point. It's easier to teach people what your reaction function is every day when you conduct yourself consistent with that reaction function. I think that's one of the strengths of being consistent and coherent in your strategy. And when we think about these contingent strategies—for example, the temporary price-level targeting policy proposed by Charlie Evans and Ben Bernanke, or the Reifschneider-Williams policy, or some variation of that—they only get used following lower bound episodes. The challenge with these approaches is that you're saying, "Hey, seven or eight years in the future, or whenever, this is what we'll do." The way I think about your question—again, I'm speaking for myself—and this is really more conceptually rather than what the answer ultimately will be, is first you want to be very clear on setting out the goals of your framework and your strategy, and what you're trying to achieve, how you understand that, and communicate that to the public.

From that follows the operational issues and implementation. Thomas Mertens and I described average inflation targeting in our paper as either static or dynamic. I view the Reifschneider-Williams policy as being a version of average inflation targeting. So the strategy might be, for example, hypothetically to say we want the average inflation rate over the longer run to be 2 percent. That means that in periods when we're away from the lower bound, we would expect inflation to be somewhat above our

2 percent goal. And then there might be the execution issue as well: how exactly would you carry that out? It could be described in terms of a policy reaction function, something along the lines of one of the variations on these rules. So, I think there's a way to get from a strategy framework to a desired outcome to a "well, now we're going to talk about the nitty-gritty of what does the policy reaction function look like." But I agree with the premise that some of these are easier to do successfully when people have a lot of muscle memory around them. You know, the more that we do consistent monetary policy—I'm not just talking about today—I think the more that just becomes ingrained in people's expectations and behavior, the more likely we will succeed.

JOHN COCHRANE: As much as I am a fan of price-level targeting, as you are, the models that you're using have the unsettling property that promises further in the future have bigger effects today. I tried this out last week. I asked my wife, if I promise to clean the dishes five years from now, will you cook dinner for a month? She said no.

As you know, there's an industry now trying to repair that feature of the model. So I would suggest at least considering toning that feature down if possible. And it may lead to the conclusion that the Friedman rule isn't so bad after all. Zero percent interest rates and slight deflation—what is so terribly wrong with that? The economies that are sitting at the bound have in fact had less output and inflation volatility than the ones where the central banks are moving interest rates all the time. Maybe we didn't get any shocks, but maybe that situation isn't so bad after all.

VOLKER WIELAND: Just one quick comment for John and one for Monika. John, first, I think it is a fascinating paper. It is also particularly neat how you derive this adjustment with the r^* and intercept. Very nice. One thing—this was all derived under the assumptions of rational expectations and commitment. And this reminds me—other people have been mentioning their own papers—of a short note in the AER [*American Economic Review*] Papers and Proceedings issue joint with Günter Coenen in May 2004, where we looked at exit strategies from the zero bound. We evaluated price-level targeting. Mike Woodford was pushing for that. We looked at Lars Svensson's proposal to fix the exchange rate and at quantitative easing, which Orphanides and I had been writing about. Once we introduced a lack of credibility involving learning about the inflation objective or the price-level objective of the central bank, the benefits of commitment to price-level targeting disappeared, while strategies that require doing something right away, such as quantitative easing or setting the exchange rate, allow the central bank to prove its commitment to the public. Thus, credibility may be key to your results.

You mentioned there was a big change with forward guidance. If I look at the European case, we had forward guidance resulting because the ECB [European Central Bank] said, "Look, we've got to keep buying assets. And eventually we keep buying less and less before we raise the policy rate." Thus, the actions of quantitative easing reinforced the forward guidance on rates. So in terms of the strategies you propose, how do you convince markets of what you announce you will do in the future?

And quickly on the European experience with negative rates, I think there are two things to consider. One is that there are legal constraints in terms of the contract underlying the regular bank account that prevent negative rates. Then, the banks try to hit the households indirectly with fees. However, in case of clients with large deposits, including pension funds or investment funds, banks negotiate to pass on the negative rate.

MONIKA PIAZZESI: So, I think whatever it is that gives rise to the zero deposit rates the banks pay, we need to understand what they are to think about optimal monetary policy, because in designing optimal monetary policy it's going to be important what the constraint is. And if it's legal, it's interesting. If legal restrictions restrict deposit rates on small accounts, let's say, and not on large accounts, that's interesting, and that will affect the design of monetary policy. In thinking about what's optimal, that's certainly going to matter for that.

WILLIAMS: So, first, I want to connect Krishna's comments and Volker's comments, which I think are very much on point. What we've learned is John should do the dishes every day, and if he does them every day, then his commitment to do them in five years will be more credible. I think that what we're trying to do in this paper, by the way, is not to sell price-level targeting but rather show the mechanisms by which it works. There are two points I'd like to make on that. The first is that it has effects on positive as well as negative inflation shocks and acts to reverse both. And some people think that's a positive or a negative attribute, but that is a part of the how this policy works, so it's good to point that out. But I will say that one of the advantages of the Reifschneider-Williams policy, and here I'm leaning to my own papers, is that the commitment is not a commitment to reverse price movements in all situations. The way this policy works, and this is true of other papers that have studied it, is that after a lower bound period, you keep interest rates lower longer for, you know, a matter of quarters or a few years, until you've spent that buildup of missed policy actions due to the lower bound, and then you're back to normal. So, it's not working the way that some of these forward-guidance puzzles work, which you're promising things way, way off in the future. The promises are more immediate, but they still are promises.

ROBERT WENZEL: It's a two-part question. The first part is in Paul Volcker's memoir, he wrote: "I puzzle about the rationale. A 2 percent target or limit was not in my textbook years ago. I know of no theoretical justification. It's difficult to be both a target and a limit at the same time. And a 2 percent inflation rate successfully maintained will mean the price level doubles in little more than a generation." Would you comment on that? The second part of my question is, how high above the 2 percent target would you be comfortable with given current economic data?

GEORGE SELGIN: My question is related to John Cochrane's. I think I may just be putting a similar point as he did but in a different way. It begins with the observation that your framework makes the lower bound problem seem a greater problem than it might actually be, and by doing that it also misrepresents the virtue of some of the different policies. I specifically refer to your objective function that makes a constant inflation rate ideal.

To make this concrete, let's suppose you're right at the lower bound, and it's not binding yet, and you have a positive supply shock. Now, that's a problem in your model, because it's not possible to lower the policy rate, so you're going to have lower inflation, because more goods are being produced. Well, so? If in fact you discard the assumption of ideal zero volatility in the inflation rate for one that calls only for a constant long-run inflation rate, then you can just say, well, goods get cheaper because there are more of them, and bygones are bygones, and we're done. And that is in fact what an NGDP [nominal GDP] target would do. It wouldn't say you have to make up for it later on. It would just say, if you have a negative supply shock, then you would have to let the price level rise. That's a different result, though, from the optimal result than you would get in your model, because your model simply assumes that a constant inflation rate is best. I wonder if you could comment on this observation, because it's related to John's. I don't think it's quite the same, but you could get a Friedman rule out of it if you pushed it into growth rate space.

WILLIAMS: So, first, the 2 percent target just wasn't pulled out of the air. Clearly, part of the discussion in both the United States and central banking across the world was a recognition of lower bound issues, measurement issues, where "true" inflation is likely to be well below the measured value, and trying to get a good point trading off these issues with the desire to have very low inflation. In terms of our model, and you look at the work by Bernanke, Kiley, and Roberts and the work that Dave Reifschneider and I have done, you don't overshoot inflation by that much during the good times. It depends on the model and everything about it. But because you're trying to get the mean inflation at two, you're basically going to overshoot by a few tenths, not percentage points. And so, I think that some of the worries around average inflation targeting are you going to aim for 3 or 4 percent during good times. In fact, at least, based on the historical experience, you're talking about a just a few tenths. Let me give you a concrete example. Last ten years, core inflation in the United States has been running about 1.6 percent on average despite the worst recession of our lifetimes. That gives you an idea that even with inflation, the miss isn't that huge, even in that example.

THOMAS MERTENS: Let me briefly add to that. What the dynamic rules show is that you do not need to run inflation much above target during normal times. The key factor is that you increase inflation expectations during the time when the lower bound binds to prevent a larger drop in inflation. Dynamic rules achieve that by having higher inflation right after the end of the lower bound period. As a result, inflation can be close to target during normal times.

JIM BULLARD: On changing the inflation target, I like John's comment about how it has become an international standard. I think for the United States to move off that international standard would set off a global race and it would be a bad thing. That's one of the biggest arguments for sticking with the 2 percent target.

And then on Volker Wieland's comment and for researchers in the room, there'd be a lot more to do here. If the central bank really wanted to do this, you'd want to know what the transition to the new regime looks like. There might be things happening during the transition that we don't like or don't understand at this point. You could analyze that either under rational expectations or under some kind of learning assumption. That would be interesting, I think.

My final comment is, what about nominal GDP targeting? This is a full model that has an output gap. Are there interpretations as nominal GDP targeting? Are you just not calling it nominal GDP targeting? What is your view on that?

WILLIAMS: You have to understand that my opening remarks should have said, "Thank you, Thomas, for doing all the work, and I should be blamed for any mistakes in the presentation." So, nominal GDP targeting is literally an extension of the model that we're working on now.

I think on the price-level aspect, many of the results we found will carry over to nominal GDP targeting. But there are, as was pointed out, some differences. That's part of the agenda. It's a little bit more complicated, so we're working on it.

WARSH: We enjoy eavesdropping on the FOMC discussion, but let me push you a little bit on Jim's comment about the regime change. So, let's say that the Fed adopts a new inflation regime. How do you assure yourself that that future regime doesn't find its way immediately into changing expectations for markets, households, and businesses? Might the regime shifting be tumultuous?

WILLIAMS: Well, luckily, we've got Rich Clarida in the room, who's running this project. I think these are relevant concerns. First, what should the decision be? Does the current regime work well? What modifications are appropriate or not? How do we communicate that? How would we the transition work, etc.? I think these are all relevant concerns, and obviously we know at the Fed that markets are very sensitive to this issue. This is something that we hear a lot about. I do go back to something that both Andy [Lilley] and Ken [Rogoff] said earlier. And I'm not talking about negative interest rates. But if you really believe that the neutral real interest rate is something like half a percent, not only in the United States but in Europe and Japan and many other countries. If you assume that the lower bound, at least for now, until we figure out maybe other solutions, is a binding constraint on central banks, then you need to figure out a good strategy—a framework, a strategy, and an implementation for this, during these times when the economy is in a relatively benign place. We need to prepare, make the transition, and get all of that done, so that we're in a better position when the next recession or a negative shock hits, so that we can effectively achieve our dual-mandate goals. It really gets back to making sure that monetary policy can be as effective as possible at achieving our goals in a future situation. And what exactly that entails, we're going to be discussing over the next year, and then we're obviously going to have to work very hard on explaining and communicating anything that may or may not come out of that.

CHAPTER FOUR

Perspectives on US Monetary Policy Tools and Instruments

James D. Hamilton

1. INTRODUCTION

This paper discusses the policy instruments that the central bank uses in pursuit of its broader strategic objectives of influencing variables like inflation and output. For many decades, the primary instrument of US monetary policy was the federal funds rate, which is an interest rate on overnight loans of Federal Reserve deposits between depository institutions. When this rate fell essentially to zero in 2009, the Fed implemented massive purchases of Treasury securities and mortgage-backed securities as an alternative policy instrument with which it hoped to influence longer-term interest rates. Although the fed funds rate is no longer at the effective lower bound, today the Fed continues to treat both the fed funds rate and its holdings of securities as policy instruments.

I review the current operating procedures and conclude that neither instrument is well suited for achieving the Fed's broader strategic objectives. The fed funds rate has become a largely administered rate that is heavily influenced by regulatory arbitrage and divorced from its traditional role as a signal of liquidity in the banking system. To the extent that the size of the Fed's balance sheet matters today, it is primarily from the liabilities rather than the asset side

I thank Peter Ireland, Andrew Levin, and John Taylor for helpful suggestions.

of the balance sheet, with the size of the balance sheet at best a very blunt tool for influencing interest rates. I discuss alternative possible operating procedures such as a corridor system based on repurchase agreements.

Section 2 reviews the effects of the Fed's asset holdings on long-term interest rates over 2009 to 2019. I conclude that this instrument has less influence on interest rates than is sometimes believed. Section 3 describes a traditional corridor system such as that used by the European Central Bank. Sections 4 and 5 discuss the discount rate and interest on excess reserves, respectively, tools that could in principle operate like the ceiling and floor of a corridor system but in US practice have not. Section 6 discusses the reverse repo rate and argues that this policy rate is the true floor on short-term interest rates in the current system. Section 7 notes how the operation of the system changed in 2018. Section 8 concludes with some thoughts on how the United States could transition to a system that would give the Federal Reserve more accurate tools with which to influence inflation and output.

2. THE EFFECTS OF LARGE-SCALE ASSET PURCHASES

Figure 4.1 displays the Fed's holdings of Treasury and mortgage-backed securities. These rose from $500 billion at the start of 2009 to $4.5 trillion by 2017. These purchases are sometimes described as "quantitative easing" and were implemented in three phases popularly referred to as QE1, QE2, and QE3. In November of 2017, the Fed stopped some of its purchases of new securities, allowing its holdings of securities to gradually decline to a level of $3.8 trillion as of May 2019.

In many standard macroeconomic and finance models, if the nominal interest rate is zero, purchases of securities by the central bank would have no effects on any real or nominal variable of inter-

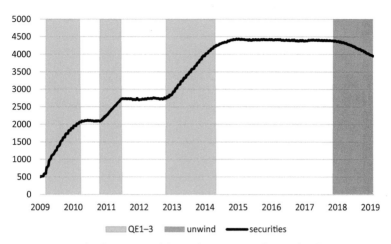

FIGURE 4.1. Federal Reserve Holdings of Securities, Billions of Dollars. Weekly Fed holdings of Treasury securities, mortgage-backed securities, and agency debt, plus unamortized premiums minus unamorized discounts, Wednesday values, January 7, 2009, to February 6, 2019

Source: Federal Reserve H.4.1 release. Shading dates for QE1: March 18, 2009, to March 24, 2010; QE2: November 3, 2010, to June 22, 2011; QE3: November 7, 2012, to April 30, 2014 (halfway through taper); unwind: November 22, 2017, to present.

est; see, for example, Eggertsson and Woodford (2003). As discussed by Hamilton (2018), adding various financial frictions to the models can change that prediction; see among others Cúrdia and Woodford (2011), Gertler and Karadi, (2011), Chen, Cúrdia, and Ferrero (2012), Hamilton and Wu (2012), Woodford (2012), Greenwood and Vayanos (2014), Eggertsson and Proulx (2016), and Caballero and Farhi (2018). However, it is not clear from theory how large the potential stimulus arising from these channels could be.

A number of empirical studies concluded that QE1–3 were successful in their goal of bringing down long-term interest rates; for surveys of this literature, see Williams (2014), Borio and Zabai (2018), and Swanson (2018). It is useful to put these claims in perspective. Figure 4.2, updated from Woodford (2012), plots the interest rate on 10-year Treasury bonds over this period. On net, this rate rose during QE1 when the Fed was trying to bring it down, fell when QE1 ended,

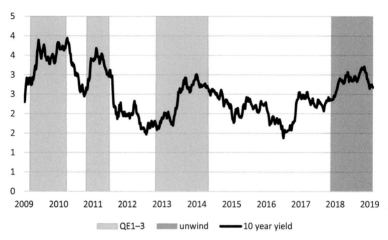

FIGURE 4.2. Interest Rate on 10-Year Treasury Bond
Source: FRED Economic Data, Federal Reserve Bank of St. Louis.

rose in QE2 when the Fed again resumed its efforts to lower long-term rates, and dropped after QE2 was halted, only to rise again in QE3. One can of course claim that if the Fed had not been purchasing bonds, the rate would have risen even more than it did during the QE1–3 episodes. But at a minimum, we are forced to conclude that Fed purchases were only one of many factors influencing bond yields during these episodes, and certainly not the most important factor.

One way we might try to isolate the effects of Fed actions is to focus only on the particular days when the Federal Open Market Committee (FOMC) issued a statement or released its minutes, or when the Fed chair gave a speech on the economy or monetary policy. Figure 4.3, adapted from Greenlaw et al. (2018), shows the cumulative change in the 10-year yield that occurred on those days alone. Figure 4.3 turns out to show the same broad pattern as figure 4.2—yields on average rose, not fell, during QE1–3, even if we focus on just days in which the Fed made an announcement.

Many researchers have conducted event studies using a subset of days on which there were particularly important announcements of the Fed's intentions to implement additional large-scale

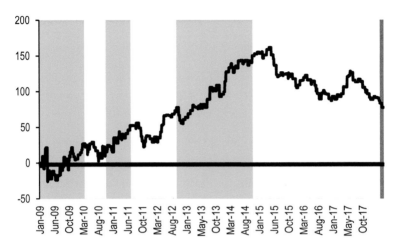

FIGURE 4.3. Cumulative Change in 10-Year Yield on Fed Days. Cumulative change in interest rate on 10-year Treasury bond on FOMC meeting days, days when FOMC minutes were released, or days with speech by Fed chair on economy or monetary policy, January 1, 2009, to December 29, 2017
Source: Adapted from David Greenlaw et al. (2018).

asset purchases. But the analysis of some of these days by Thornton (2017), Hamilton (2018), and Levin and Loungani (2019) suggests that previous studies may have overestimated the role of the purchases in moving interest rates. One key question is the extent to which interest rates were responding to the Fed's assessment of the economic situation rather than to the purchases themselves. See Melosi (2016), Nakamura and Steinsson (2018), and Miranda-Agrippino and Ricco (2018) for more discussion of this issue.

Regardless of one's position on whether large-scale asset purchases are an important tool when the traditional instrument of controlling the fed funds rate is unavailable, the case for its importance in 2019 when short rates are significantly above zero is far from compelling. I conclude below that the primary relevance of the size of the Fed's balance sheet today for the conduct of monetary policy comes from the liabilities side rather than any tangible consequences of its asset holdings for long-term interest rates. But before returning to that issue, I first discuss alternative monetary procedures for controlling the short-term interest rate.

3. THE CORRIDOR SYSTEM FOR CONTROLLING SHORT-TERM INTEREST RATES

The European Central Bank (ECB) is one of many central banks that use a corridor system for controlling interest rates. The ECB stands ready to lend to banks as much as they want at a particular rate i_L that is set by policy. This sets a ceiling on short-term loans between banks. Why should I pay more than i_L to borrow from another bank when I can get all I want from the ECB at i_L? The ECB sets another rate i_D on funds that are left on deposit with the ECB. One can think of these as short-term loans from private banks to the ECB. The rate i_D sets a floor on the interest rate on interbank loans. Why should I lend to another bank for less than i_D when I can earn i_D risk free just by leaving my funds with the ECB? The policy instruments are the ECB's choices for i_L and i_D, which define a corridor within which the interbank loan rate trades, as seen in figure 4.4. Since June 2014 the ECB has charged a fee rather than pay interest on deposits (essentially a negative value for i_D) and has used the fee to cause interest rates to become negative.

It's worth remembering that the core power that gives the central bank the ability to specify i_L and i_D as instruments of policy is its ability to create new deposits of private banks with the ECB. This is what enables the central bank to satisfy all demand for borrowing at the chosen i_L. By choosing particular values for i_L and i_D, the ECB is implicitly committing to a level and growth rate of the monetary base that may or may not be consistent with its broader strategic inflation objective. Indeed, one could think of monetary policy equivalently either as a decision for i_L and i_D or as a decision about monetary aggregates. Modern economic theory (e.g., Woodford 2003) and central bank practice usually adopt the for-

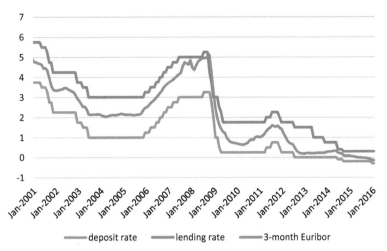

FIGURE 4.4. Corridor System for Controlling Interest Rates Used by the
European Central Bank. End-of-month values for ECB marginal lending rate
(orange) and deposit facility (blue) along with monthly average 3-month
Euribor rate (gray), January 2001 to January 2016
Source: European Central Bank.

mer perspective, essentially for reasons described by Poole (1970):
the demand for monetary aggregates can be very volatile, making
targeting interest rates a more reliable tool than targeting monetary
aggregates for purposes of stabilizing inflation and real activity.

4. THE FEDERAL RESERVE'S DISCOUNT WINDOW

Like the ECB, the US Federal Reserve historically offered to lend
to banks at a policy-determined rate i_L through its discount window. Figure 4.5 compares the fed funds rate with the discount rate.
Over most of the last half century, the fed funds rate was above the
discount rate. In the United States, i_L served as a floor, not a ceiling,
for the fed funds rate!

Why would I pay another bank an interest rate higher than i_L to
borrow funds? The answer is that US banks traditionally imputed

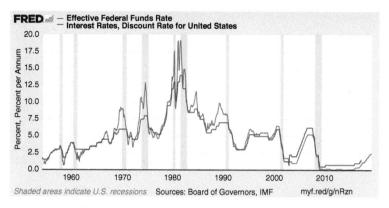

FIGURE 4.5. Fed Funds Rate and Discount Rate. Monthly average effective fed funds rate, April 1954 to April 2019 (blue) and discount rate, April 1954 to April 2017 (red)

Source: FRED Economic Data, Federal Reserve Bank of St. Louis.

some nonpecuniary costs to borrowing at the discount window. Although the identities of banks that borrowed at the discount window were not publicly released, other banks could usually find out who had borrowed, and borrowing from the discount window was associated with a certain stigma. Banks wanted to borrow at the discount window only if they had trouble borrowing fed funds from other banks, which could be a sign of weakness.

Banks differed in their perceived nonpecuniary costs and would turn to the discount window when the marginal nonpecuniary cost was less than the spread between the fed funds rate and the discount rate. Figure 4.6, adapted from Goodfriend and Whelpley (1986), illustrates how the fed funds rate was determined in this system. The Fed's open-market operations resulted in a certain level of nonborrowed reserves, which are deposits with the Fed that banks would have even if they do no borrowing at the discount window. As the fed funds rate rises above the discount rate, more banks would be willing to borrow at the discount window, thereby increasing the total supply of nonborrowed plus borrowed reserves until supply equals demand.

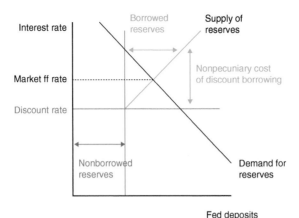

FIGURE 4.6. Determination of Fed Funds Rate in Historical US System
Source: Adapted from Goodfriend and Whelpley (1986).

Figure 4.7 compares the gap between the fed funds rate and the discount rate (top panel) with the total volume of discount window borrowing (bottom panel), showing how the system worked in practice. A higher value for the fed funds rate relative to the discount rate was associated with a higher volume of borrowing. Indeed, some observers at the time thought of the operating system as one of borrowed reserves targeting rather than fed funds rate targeting.

5. INTEREST ON EXCESS RESERVES

Beginning in October 2008, the Federal Reserve began paying an interest rate on excess reserves (IOER), akin to the interest rate i_D in a corridor system. Figure 4.8 shows the recent relation between the fed funds rate and IOER. Whereas i_D acts as a floor in the traditional corridor system, until very recently IOER seemed to be a ceiling on the fed funds rate! Indeed, at times IOER looked like a deterministic ceiling. On most days, the average effective fed funds

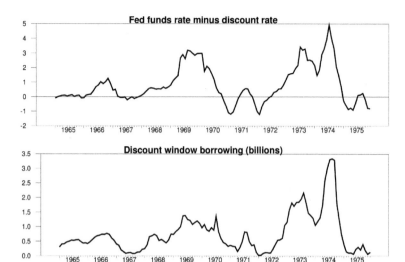

FIGURE 4.7. Volume of Borrowed Reserves and Gap between Fed Funds Rate and Discount Rate. The top panel shows monthly average effective fed funds rate minus discount rate, January 1965 to December 1975. The bottom panel shows discount window borrowings of depository institutions from the Federal Reserve, billions of dollars

Source: FRED Economic Data, Federal Reserve Bank of St. Louis.

rate would be exactly nine basis points below the interest on excess reserves, though it would drop significantly below on the last day of the month.

Why would anyone offer to lend at a fed funds rate below IOER if they could earn IOER just by parking the funds with the Fed? The answer is that not all depository institutions can earn IOER. Federal Home Loan Banks (FHLBs) have deposits with the Fed but are not paid IOER, so they have an incentive to lend to banks that can earn IOER. But why wouldn't banks that can earn IOER bid up the fed funds rate so as to earn the risk-free arbitrage from borrowing at the fed funds rate and earning IOER? Part of the answer is on the supply side; individual FHLBs set limits on to whom and how much they lend. Afonso, Armenter, and Lester (2019) modeled these frictions using a search and matching model for the fed

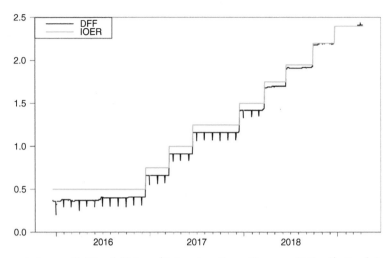

FIGURE 4.8. Fed Funds Rate and Interest on Excess Reserves. Daily effective fed funds rate (black) and interest on excess reserves (green), December 17, 2015, to April 10, 2019

Source: FRED Economic Data, Federal Reserve Bank of St. Louis.

funds market. Another factor is nonpecuniary costs on the demand side, as discussed by Klee, Senyuz, and Yoldas (2016), Banegas and Tase (2017), and Anbil and Senyuz (2018). If a bank tries to arbitrage by borrowing fed funds and holding fed deposits to earn IOER, it expands its balance sheet. A larger level of assets exposes US banks to higher fees from the Federal Deposit Insurance Corporation. For this reason, foreign banks are a more natural counterparty than domestic banks to borrow the fed funds from the FHLB. In addition, both domestic and foreign banks are subject to complicated capital requirements, another source of nonpecuniary costs associated with borrowing fed funds. A larger balance sheet may require the bank to make other adjustments to meet capital requirements, which imposes another nonpecuniary cost on arbitraging the IOER–fed funds spread. For European banks, the capital requirements are primarily based on end-of-month assets. This explains why before 2018 there was usually a sharp spike in the gap between IOER and the fed funds rate on

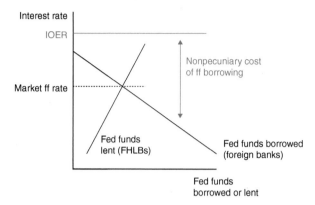

FIGURE 4.9. Determination of the Fed Funds Rate in 2017

the last day of a month; this was the one day those banks didn't want to borrow fed funds.

One can think about the determination of the fed funds rate in this setting as in figure 4.9. Banks differ in their marginal nonpecuniary costs of borrowing fed funds and would be willing to borrow more the bigger the gap between IOER and fed funds. The apparent deterministic nature of the IOER–fed funds gap in early 2017 arose from the fact that, on days other than the last day of the month, and over the range of volume traded at that time, there was a sufficient volume of borrowers with fixed nonpecuniary costs of nine basis points. In other words, the demand curve was flat over that range, resulting in essentially a constant gap between IOER and the fed funds rate.

6. REVERSE REPO RATE

The true floor in the current operating system comes not from IOER but instead from a different facility. The Fed offers to conduct reverse repurchase (RR) agreements with a broader group of financial institutions that includes money market funds. These are essentially short-term loans from the institution to the Fed at a

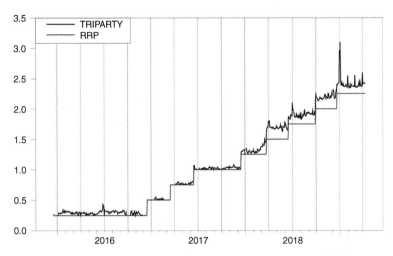

FIGURE 4.10. Tri-Party Repo Rate and Interest on Excess Reserves. Daily interest rate on tri-party repurchase agreements based on Treasury securities (black) and Fed reverse repo rate (blue), December 17, 2015, to April 10, 2019. Vertical lines denote last day of a quarter

Source: Tri-party repo rates from Bank of New York Mellon (https://repoindex.bnymellon .com/repoindex).

policy-determined rate RR. Figure 4.10 compares RR with the tri-party Treasury repo rate. In a typical tri-party repo transaction, a money market fund would lend overnight to a primary security dealer (one of the large financial institutions authorized to be a counterparty to transactions with the trading desk of the Federal Reserve Bank of New York). The agreement is settled through one of the large clearing banks (Bank of New York Mellon or JPMorgan Chase), with the security dealer temporarily delivering Treasury securities to the clearing bank, essentially as collateral for the loan. Unlike the fed funds rate, the tri-party repo rate is a true market rate that varies daily with market conditions. But RR puts a floor under the tri-party repo rate for the same reason that i_D functions as a floor in a traditional corridor system. Why should a money-market fund lend to a private counterparty at the private repo rate when it can earn RR risk-free from the Fed?

7. CHANGES IN 2018

But while RR puts a floor under the tri-party repo rate, as seen in figure 4.11, IOER does not set a ceiling. Up until the end of 2017, the tri-party repo always traded in between RR and IOER. This fact could give the impression that the system was functioning something like a corridor system. But there's nothing that prevented the private repo rate from going above IOER, and indeed throughout 2018 it often did.

Figure 4.11 also plots another market-determined short-term interest rate, the Treasury general collateralized finance rate (GCF). These are also repurchase agreements collateralized with Treasury securities that are cleared through a third party, in this case the Fixed Income Clearing Corporation.[1] A typical transaction here would be a loan from a primary security dealer to a nonprimary security dealer, again collateralized by Treasuries, with the primary dealer often rehypothecating the Treasury securities for purposes of its own borrowing through tri-party repos. The GCF rate is generally above the tri-party repo rate. It's interesting to compare the 2018 portion of figure 4.11 with figure 4.8. GCF started to trade consistently above IOER at the same time that IOER stopped being the de facto ceiling on the fed funds rate.

What changed in 2018? The elimination of the gap between IOER and fed funds could have come either from a rightward shift of the demand curve in figure 4.9—the nonpecuniary costs of borrowing fed funds decreased, leading borrowing banks to bid up the cost of fed funds—or from a leftward shift of the supply curve—FHLBs are less willing to lend fed funds. If the first explanation was correct, we would expect to see an increase in the volume of fed funds lending, whereas if the second was correct, we would expect to see a decrease. Figure 4.12 plots the effective fed funds rate together

---

1. For more details on GCF, see Agueci et al. (2014).

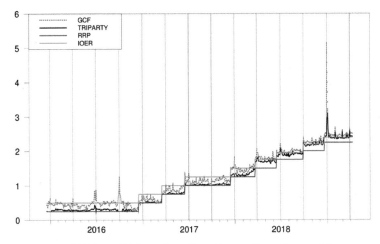

FIGURE 4.11. GCF Rate, Tri-Party Repo Rate, Reverse Repo Rate, and Interest on Excess Reserves. Daily general collateralized finance rate for repurchase agreements based on Treasury securities (dashed red), rate on tri-party repurchase agreements based on Treasury securities (black), interest on excess reserves (green), and Fed reverse repo rate (blue), December 17, 2015, to April 10, 2019

Source: GCF data from DTCC (http://www.dtcc.com/charts/dtcc-gcf-repo-index#download).

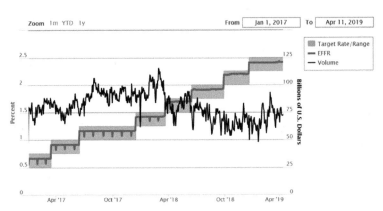

FIGURE 4.12. Daily Effective Fed Funds Rate and Volume of Fed Funds Lending

Source: Federal Reserve Bank of New York (https://apps.newyorkfed.org/markets/autorates/fed%20funds).

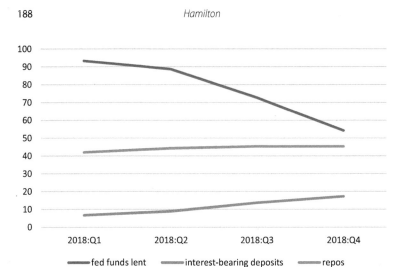

FIGURE 4.13. Selected End-of-Quarter Assets of Federal Home Loan Banks (billions of dollars)

Source: FHLB end-of-quarter financial reports (http://www.fhlb-of.com/ofweb_userWeb /pageBuilder/fhlbank-financial-data-36).

with the volume of borrowing. It shows that the disappearing gap between IOER and fed funds coincided with a decreased volume of fed lending, favoring the second explanation based on the supply side. Figure 4.13 plots selected assets held by the FHLB. It paints a picture of the FHLB turning from lending fed funds to alternative ways of investing short-term funds that presumably provide a higher yield.

8. PERSPECTIVES ON THE CURRENT AND POTENTIAL FUTURE OPERATING SYSTEMS

I've described the current operating system as one with a floor but no ceiling. What then is holding rates down? I think the answer is twofold. First, there has been weak demand for investment both in the United States and around the world for some time. Second, there remains a huge volume of reserves in the system. Figure 4.14 summarizes the implications of the Fed's balance sheet from the

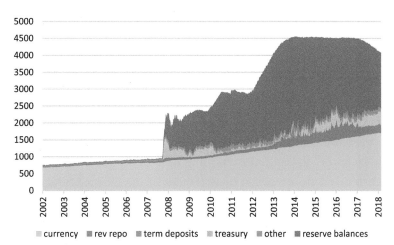

FIGURE 4.14. Weekly Federal Reserve Liabilities (billions of dollars)
Wednesday values, December 18, 2002, to February 6, 2019. Currency: currency
in circulation; rev repo: reverse repurchase agreements; treasury: US Treasury
general account plus supplementary financing account; reserve balances: reserve
balances with Federal Reserve Banks
Source: Federal Reserve H.4.1 release.

perspective of its liabilities. The large security purchases of figure 4.1 were primarily financed by an expansion of bank deposits
with the Fed. Banks so far have been willing to hold these reserves
as a result of IOER. As the Fed's balance sheet contracted (and as
demand for cash gradually climbed), excess reserves have slowly
been coming down.

Another important development in 2018 was increasing demand
for borrowed funds, in part arising from an elevated level of borrowing by the US Treasury to finance the federal government budget deficit. This could be one of the factors that has driven GCF up
in 2018 and that pulled lending away from the fed funds market.
As we look ahead, we should expect demand for loans to continue
to change. The Fed will want some more accurate policy tools to
respond to these changes.

One option would be to allow reserves to shrink until we are
back in something like the historical system in figure 4.6. That

system worked when fluctuations in the Treasury's balance with the Fed (which are a choice of the Treasury, not the Fed) were on the order of a few billion dollars. But one sees in figure 4.14 that fluctuations today are in the hundreds of billions. It's also far from clear how we would make a smooth transition from the current operating system to something like figure 4.6.

A more natural transition from the current system would begin by acknowledging that something like the tri-party repo rate is currently a more relevant market measure than the fed funds rate. The Fed could introduce an open repo facility from which the same institutions that currently use the reverse repo facility could also use direct repos to borrow all the funds they usually wanted at a chosen policy rate. This would establish a corridor system for controlling the private repo rate. I specify "usually" here because it would not be necessary, or even desirable, to fully smooth out the "window dressing" that one sees in the end-of-quarter spike in private repo rates. The end-of-quarter spikes arise because some institutions do not want to acknowledge the extent of their exposure to private counterparty repos in their publicly available statements, which are based only on assets as of the last day of a quarter. There's no compelling policy reason why the Fed should accommodate that seasonal demand. Indeed, historically a specified fed funds target was viewed as perfectly consistent with end-of-month spikes in the effective fed funds rate above the target arising from such forces.

The drawback of such a system would be that it puts the Fed in the position of effectively insuring a broader set of institutions than those over which it has regulatory authority. The longer-run goal should therefore be to return both the ceiling and the floor for the policy rate to offers to lend or borrow from only regulated institutions. The Fed could initially implement a repo corridor system with a broad range of counterparties at the same time that it continues to reduce the volume of excess reserves. As we reach a level when banks are more actively managing their reserve balances, the Fed could restrict access to both repo facilities to regulated institutions. This could be a practical path toward the goal of replacing the discount window with a stigma-free facility.

References

Afonso, Gara, Roc Armenter, and Benjamin Lester. 2019. "A Model of the Federal Funds Market: Yesterday, Today, and Tomorrow." Working paper, Federal Reserve Bank of Philadelphia.

Agueci, Paul, Leyla Alkan, Adam Copeland, Isaac Davis, Antoine Martin, Kate Pingitore, Caroline Prugar, and Tyisha Riva. 2014. "A Primer on the GCF Repo® Service." Staff report no. 671, Federal Reserve Bank of New York.

Anbil, Sriya, and Zeynep Senyuz. 2018. "Window-Dressing and the Fed's RRP Facility in the Repo Market." Finance and Economics Discussion Paper Series 2018-027. Washington Board of Governors of the Federal Reserve System.

Banegas, Ayelen, and Manjola Tase. 2017. "Reserve Balances, the Federal Funds Market and Arbitrage in the New Regulatory Framework." October 18. Available at SSRN 3055299.

Borio, Claudio, and Anna Zabai. 2018. "Unconventional Monetary Policies: A Re-appraisal." In *Research Handbook on Central Banking,* edited by Peter Conti-Brown and Rosa Maria Lastra, 398–444. Cheltenham: Edward Elgar Publishing.

Caballero, Ricardo J., and Emmanuel Farhi. 2018. "The Safety Trap." *Review of Economic Studies* 85, no. 1 (January): 223–74.

Chen, Han, Vasco Cúrdia, and Andrea Ferrero. 2012. "The Macroeconomic Effects of Large-Scale Asset Purchase Programmes." *Economic Journal* 122, no. 564 (November): F289–F315.

Cúrdia, Vasco, and Michael Woodford. 2011. "The Central-Bank Balance Sheet as an Instrument of Monetary Policy." *Journal of Monetary Economics* 58, no. 1 (January): 54–79.

Eggertsson, Gauti B., and Kevin Proulx. 2016. "Bernanke's No-Arbitrage Argument Revisited: Can Open Market Operations in Real Assets Eliminate the Liquidity Trap?" National Bureau of Economic Research working paper 22243.

Eggertsson, Gauti B., and Michael Woodford. 2003. "The Zero Bound on Interest Rates and Optimal Monetary Policy." *Brookings Papers on Economic Activity* 2003, no. 1: 139–233.

Gertler, Mark, and Peter Karadi. 2011. "A Model of Unconventional Monetary Policy." *Journal of Monetary Economics* 58, no. 1 (January): 17–34.

Goodfriend, Marvin, and William Whelpley. 1986. "Federal Funds: Instrument of Federal Reserve Policy." *Federal Reserve Bank of Richmond Economic Review* 72, no. 5 (September/October): 3–11.

Greenlaw, David, James D. Hamilton, Ethan Harris, and Kenneth D. West. 2018. "A Skeptical View of the Impact of the Fed's Balance Sheet." National Bureau of Economic Research working paper 24687, June.

Greenwood, Robin, and Dimitri Vayanos. 2014. "Bond Supply and Excess Bond Returns." *Review of Financial Studies* 27, no. 3 (March): 663–713.

Hamilton, James D. 2018. "The Efficacy of Large-Scale Asset Purchases When the Short-Term Interest Rate Is at Its Effective Lower Bound." *Brookings Papers on Economic Activity* (Fall): 543–54.

Hamilton, James D., and Jing Cynthia Wu. 2012. "The Effectiveness of Alternative Monetary Policy Tools in a Zero Lower Bound Environment." *Journal of Money, Credit and Banking* 44 (February): 3–46.

Klee, Elizabeth, Zeynep Senyuz, and Emre Yoldas. 2016. "Effects of Changing Monetary and Regulatory Policy on Overnight Money Markets." Working paper, Federal Reserve Board.

Levin, Andrew, and Prakash Loungani. 2019. "Reassessing the Efficacy and Costs of Quantitative Easing." Unpublished manuscript, Dartmouth College.

Melosi, Leonardo. 2016. "Signaling Effects of Monetary Policy." *Review of Economic Studies* 84, no. 2 (September): 853–84.

Miranda-Agrippino, Silvia, and Giovanni Ricco. 2018. "The Transmission of Monetary Policy Shocks." Working paper, Bank of England.

Nakamura, Emi, and Jón Steinsson. 2018. "High Frequency Identification of Monetary Non-neutrality: The Information Effect." *Quarterly Journal of Economics* 133, no. 3 (August): 1283–1330.

Poole, William. 1970. "Optimal Choice of Monetary Policy Instruments in a Simple Stochastic Macro Model." *Quarterly Journal of Economics* 84, no. 2 (May): 197–216.

Swanson, Eric. 2018. "The Federal Reserve Is Not Very Constrained by the Lower Bound on Nominal Interest Rates." *Brookings Papers on Economic Activity* (Fall): 555–572.

Thornton, Daniel L. 2017. "Effectiveness of QE: An Assessment of Event-Study Evidence." *Journal of Macroeconomics* 52 (June): 56–74.

Williams, John C. 2014. "Monetary Policy at the Zero Lower Bound: Putting Theory into Practice." Brookings Institution.

Woodford, Michael. 2003. *Interest and Prices: Foundations of a Theory of Monetary Policy*. Princeton. NJ: Princeton University Press.

———. 2012. "Methods of Policy Accommodation at the Interest-Rate Lower Bound." In *The Changing Policy Landscape: A Symposium Sponsored by The Federal Reserve Bank of Kansas City, Jackson Hole, Wyo.*, 185–288. Kansas City: Federal Reserve Bank of Kansas City.

DISCUSSANT REMARKS

Peter N. Ireland

Monetary Policy Implementation: Macro and Micro Questions

James Hamilton's conference paper does an excellent job of describing how the Federal Reserve currently implements its federal funds rate–targeting strategy by manipulating the interest rate it pays on its own liabilities—reserves issued to banks and reverse repurchase agreements with nonbank financial institutions—as well as the size of its balance sheet. His paper usefully compares the implementation procedures used today with those employed in the past and proposes changes to make the new procedures more effective in the future.

Since the paper's descriptions of the Fed's operating procedures and their effects on financial markets are so clear and informative, they require few additions or improvements. Thus, these comments are directed instead at answering three broader questions that the paper's analysis raises. First, at the macroeconomic level, what do the details of the Fed's current implementation procedures have to do with monetary policy? Very little, it turns out. Instead, these procedures appear to be directed more specifically at eliminating high-frequency volatility in short-term nominal interest rates, that is, at interest-rate smoothing.

Answering this first question therefore leads to two more. What macroeconomic or microeconomic concerns make it desirable for the Fed to smooth interest rates in this way? And what microeconomic modifications to the current operating procedures would allow the Fed to smooth interest rates more efficiently in the future?

WHAT IS "MONETARY POLICY"?

Monetary policy can be defined most clearly with reference to two basic macroeconomic principles: the classical dichotomy, which draws the distinction between real and nominal variables; and the doctrine of long-run monetary neutrality, which assigns to monetary policy the principal task of determining the behavior of the aggregate nominal price level.

In a capitalist system, prices play a key role in allocating scarce resources. Specifically, prices adjust to keep in balance the supply of and demand for individual goods and services, thereby allowing real variables—physical quantities of those same goods and services— to respond efficiently to all kinds of shocks.

The prices that play this resource-allocating role, however, are relative prices. Therefore, some additional institutional arrangement must be imposed to pin down the absolute level of prices and to determine, by extension, the behavior of nominal variables: those denominated in the economy's unit of account.

Under our fiat money system, this institutional arrangement is embodied by the Federal Reserve. It is up to the Fed to conduct monetary policy in a way that pins down the aggregate nominal price level. The Fed achieves this goal by exercising its monopoly control over the supply of base money: currency plus bank reserves.

Today, as before the crisis, the Fed implements monetary policy by targeting the federal funds rate. The federal funds rate, however, is a market rate of interest, charged by one bank to another on a very short-term loan of reserves. The Fed does not set the funds rate directly. Instead, the Fed's operating procedures must link the federal funds rate, which the Fed can only influence, to the monetary base, which the Fed can precisely control.

Before the financial crisis of 2007–2008, the link between the funds rate and the supply of base money was more immediate and therefore more obvious. Whenever the Fed wanted to lower its target for the funds rate, it conducted an open market purchase, buying US Treasury securities to inject new reserves into the banking system. The increased supply of bank reserves put downward pressure on the equilibrium funds rate, moving it lower in line with the new target. Conversely, whenever the Fed wanted to raise its target for the funds rate, it conducted an open market sale of US Treasury securities to drain reserves from the banking system and put upward pressure on the funds rate.

Since December 2015, however, the Fed has gradually lifted its federal funds rate target off its zero lower bound using a floor system. Under this floor system, the Fed uses its newly granted ability to pay interest on reserves to manipulate the federal funds rate, without having to conduct open market operations right away. By raising the interest rates paid to banks on reserves and nonbank financial intermediaries on reserve repurchase agreements, the Fed has successfully moved the federal funds rate up in lockstep. And, presumably, when the next easing cycle begins, the Fed will lower the interest rates on reserves and reverse repurchase agreements to bring the federal funds rate back down.

Even under a floor system, however, all monetary policy actions taken to influence the trajectory for the aggregate nominal price level must be supported, sooner or later, by open market operations that change the supply of base money. Although the floor system relieves the trading desk at the Federal Reserve Bank of New York from having to actively manage the supply of reserves on a day-to-day basis, it still implies that the Fed accomplishes its principal macroeconomic function—pinning down the aggregate nominal price level—by exercising its control over the supply of base money.

A simple thought experiment illustrates why this must be true.[2] Suppose, first, that the market for reserves begins in a long-run

---

2. Ireland (2014, 2017, 2019a) presents richer and more realistic examples of how, even under a floor system, the Fed must continue using open market operations to bring about

equilibrium, in which the Fed is satisfied with the dollar volume of reserves it has supplied to the banking system and banks, in turn, are happy to hold the same dollar volume of reserves supplied. Suppose, next, that starting from this initial equilibrium, nominal GDP grows at an average annual rate of 5 percent.

Looking ahead, five years beyond the initial equilibrium point, 5 percent annual growth translates, after allowing for compounding, into an increase in the level of nominal GDP of more than 25 percent. Thus, if the Fed uses a floor system to target the federal funds rate over this five-year period without ever conducting an open market operation, it is easy to see that the initial equilibrium will be severely disturbed. Banks will not want to hold the same dollar volume of reserves when the nominal size of the economy is more than 25 percent larger! This thought experiment confirms that, indeed, over the five-year period, the Fed will still have to conduct open market operations to allow the monetary base to grow at approximately the same 5 percent annual rate as nominal GDP.

Many economists would prefer to describe the chain of events that unfold in this story in a different way. They would point to the Federal Open Market Committee's (FOMC 2019a, 2019b) own policy statements to reemphasize that the Fed now uses a floor system to target the funds rate, and that the Fed's monetary policy strategy is to target the funds rate in order to achieve its statutory dual mandate for price stability and maximum sustainable employment. From this more popular perspective, the open market operations that appear in the thought experiment appear as technical details, necessary only to accommodate the increased demand for currency and bank reserves that reflects the slow but steady growth of the US economy as a whole.

---

changes in the supply of base money that support desired changes in the aggregate nominal price level.

This popular view of the Fed's operation procedures and policy strategies is not inaccurate or incorrect. But it remains incomplete in one key respect and, as a consequence, risks confusing cause and effect. This is because it fails to explain why nominal GDP would be growing at a 5 percent annual rate in the first place. It totally ignores the fact that nominal GDP is growing because everyone expects the Fed to conduct monetary policy in a way that allows for the same slow but steady growth in the stock of base money!

From the viewpoint of macroeconomic theory, therefore, open market operations remain a critical part of the Fed's implementation procedures. Managing the monetary base to determine the behavior of the aggregate nominal price level still constitutes the clearest and most accurate description of the Fed's monetary policy strategy. From this perspective, it is the floor system that appears as the set of technical details, intended to accomplish something else: to clamp down on what would otherwise be high-frequency fluctuations in short-term nominal interest rates. This raises the next question: why would the Fed want to smooth interest rates in this way?

WHY SMOOTH INTEREST RATES?

There are, in fact, both macroeconomic and microeconomic reasons why the Fed might wish to adopt operating procedures that minimize short-term fluctuations in interest rates even as it also manages the monetary base to ensure price-level stability in the long run.

From a macroeconomic perspective, Poole (1970) shows that in a Keynesian model, which describes events over a time frame short enough to take the aggregate nominal price level as fixed, nominal interest rate instability may create real instability. To assess the relevance of this result to issues relating to the design of the Fed's floor system, however, one must decide first on an interpretation of "the interest rate" in Poole's model. Does Poole's result imply only that the Fed should aim to stabilize the federal funds rate, on average, around a constant target over each six-week period between Federal Open Committee Meetings? Or does his result also mean that the Fed should strive to eliminate even daily fluctuations in the funds rate? Only in the latter case would the Fed's new floor system offer advantages over the more traditional procedures used before the financial crisis.

Microeconomic arguments, therefore, provide more compelling support for interest rate smoothing of the kind the Fed wishes to pursue. Under our fiat money system, liquidity can be created by the Fed at constant, zero marginal cost. Therefore, economic efficiency dictates that the opportunity cost that households, businesses, and financial institutions incur when they hold stocks of liquid assets should remain low and stable as well. This can be accomplished partly by paying interest on bank reserves as advocated by Tolley (1957) and Friedman (1960) but also by keeping market rates of interest rates low and stable, as prescribed by Friedman (1969).[3]

Professional funds managers, in particular, should be directing the bulk of their time and effort toward identifying the most productive investment projects that provide the highest private and social rates of return, not gambling on day-by-day movements in money market rates. Thus, these microeconomic efficiency arguments provide good reason for the Fed to smooth interest rates, even at very high frequencies.

---

3. Plosser (2018) describes how interest on reserves, as used by the Federal Reserve to maintain an exceptionally large balance sheet even after the financial crisis and Great Recession of 2007–2009, exposes the Fed to a myriad of economic and political risks. For many of the same reasons cited by Plosser, Ireland (2019b) argues that microeconomic efficiency in the markets for currency, bank reserves, and other liquid assets would be maintained better through Friedman's (1969) proposal for low and stable market rates of interest than through Friedman's (1960) proposal for paying interest on reserves.

HOW TO SMOOTH INTEREST RATES
MORE EFFICIENTLY?

In theory, the idealized corridor or floor systems described in Hamilton's paper should make it easy for the Fed to do all three of these things at once: manage the stock of base money to stabilize the aggregate nominal price level, target the federal funds rate so as to achieve the Fed's stabilization objectives for the real economy, and eliminate high-frequency interest rate volatility that leads to socially wasteful but privately lucrative trading activity in the money markets. Moreover, these systems have the advantage of using market mechanisms to achieve automatic smoothing of short-term interest rates without daily intervention from the trading desk.

In a corridor system, the Fed's discount rate, at which it stands ready to lend reserves to the banking system, sets a ceiling above which the federal funds rate will not rise. This is because if, to the contrary, the funds rate was to exceed the discount rate, any bank could borrow at the discount window, lend the funds out in the interbank market, and thereby book instantaneous profits. Excess supply of loans in the interbank market would then push the funds rate back below the discount rate.

Similarly, in either a corridor or a floor system, the interest rate that the Fed pays on bank reserves sets the floor below which the federal funds rate will not fall. If, to the contrary, the funds rate was to drop below the interest rate on reserves, then any bank could borrow funds in the interbank market, deposit the funds in its account at the Fed, and again book instantaneous profits. Excess demand for loans in the interbank market would then drive the funds rate back above the interest rate on reserves.

Hamilton's paper usefully notes, however, that historically, the discount rate hasn't always set a ceiling for the federal rate and, more recently, the interest rate on reserves has not set the floor. As his paper explains, regulatory and institutional constraints have often prevented banks and other financial institutions from exploiting the arbitrage opportunities as required to make the system work. Again, microeconomic concerns loom largest. Unexploited arbitrage opportunities—just a fancy term describing specific deviations from what more generally would be called "the law of one price"— are almost always a sign of microeconomic inefficiency. They mean that different economic agents face budget constraints with different slopes. Marginal rates of substitution and transformation will then differ across agents as well, implying that there are gains from trade that would make everyone better off but have gone unrealized.

The most useful and important message of Hamilton's paper is exactly this. If Federal Reserve policy makers really wish to smooth interest rates, they should clean up their floor system. Less encumbered by formal and informal regulatory constraints and institutional complications, an ideal corridor or floor system lets freely functioning financial markets automatically smooth out high-frequency movements in short-term interest rates. Relieved from the task of intervening daily in those financial markets, Federal Reserve officials can then focus on their more basic macroeconomic objective of creating and maintaining an environment of aggregate price stability. Within this most favorable monetary environment, our capitalist system can do what it does best: delivering robust and sustainable long-run growth in real incomes and jobs for all Americans.

References

FOMC (Federal Open Market Committee). 2019a. "Statement on Longer-Run Goals and Monetary Policy Strategy" (adopted effective January 24, 2012; amended as effective January 29, 2019). Washington, DC: Board of Governors of the Federal Reserve System. https://www.federalreserve.gov/monetarypolicy/files/FOMC_LongerRunGoals.pdf.

———. 2019b. "Statement Regarding Monetary Policy Implementation and Balance Sheet Normalization." January 30. https://www.federalreserve.gov/news events/pressreleases/monetary20190130c.htm.

Friedman, Milton. 1960. *A Program for Monetary Stability*. New York: Fordham University Press.

———. 1969. "The Optimum Quantity of Money." In *The Optimum Quantity of Money and Other Essays*. Chicago: Aldine Publishing.

Ireland, Peter N. 2014. "The Macroeconomic Effects of Interest on Reserves." *Macroeconomic Dynamics* 18 (September): 1271–1312.

———. 2017. "A Monetarist View of Policy Normalization." Position Paper. New York: Shadow Open Market Committee, September 15. https://www.shadowfed.org/wp-content/uploads/2017/09/IrelandSOMC_September2017.pdf.

———. 2019a. "Monetary Policy Implementation: Making Better and More Consistent Use of the Federal Reserve's Balance Sheet." Position paper. New York: Shadow Open Market Committee, March 29. https://www.shadowfed.org/wp-content/uploads/2019/03/IrelandSOMC-March2019.pdf.

——— 2019b. "Interest on Reserves: History and Rationale, Complications and Risks." *Cato Journal* 39 (Spring/Summer): 327–37.

Plosser, Charles I. 2018. "The Risks of a Fed Balance Sheet Unconstrained by Monetary Policy." In *The Structural Foundations of Monetary Policy*, edited by Michael D. Bordo, John H. Cochrane, and Amit Seru. Stanford, CA: Hoover Institution Press.

Poole, William. 1970. "Optimal Choice of Monetary Policy Instruments in a Simple Stochastic Macro Model." *Quarterly Journal of Economics* 84, no. 2 (May): 197–216.

Tolley, George S. 1957. "Providing for Growth of the Money Supply." *Journal of Political Economy* 65 (December): 465–85.

GENERAL DISCUSSION

JAMES HAMILTON: Thanks a lot, Peter. Of course, you're right. At a deeper philosophical level, the ultimate power of the central bank comes from it being the monopoly supplier of base money. But the reason you can run a corridor system, a traditional corridor system, the only way you can offer to lend as much as anybody wants at a fixed rate is if you have the power to create those funds. Without that power, you can't do it. So, yeah, that's behind the traditional system, absolutely.

Now, as far as the demand for base money, the game we've been playing is if we've been paying interest on reserves, maybe there's an essentially infinite demand. I mean, we go from one trillion to two trillion to whatever. And my point is, well, that worked for a while. That worked in a certain environment when there really aren't other opportunities. But it's not fundamentally a system for controlling the interest rate. And so, that's why my conclusion is we do need the discount window, something as a real corridor system, and we might be thinking about it that way. But actually, thank you for pointing out the value of the market allocation. The point is when the fed funds rate is the set interest rate minus 9 basis points every day, this is not a market allocation of anything. It's sort of a crazy system to be thinking that was our target for influencing the price level or economic activity.

JOHN TAYLOR: So, neither of you referred too much to how it worked before 2008. The Fed set a federal funds rate. They voted on it. They adjusted the supply of reserves so it would come in to meet pretty close to the target. Peter Fisher ran the desk pretty well at that time. It seemed to work. So why not just go back to that? It worked. Policy was good. We had good economic performance. I think in a way it was more market determined. You didn't have an administered rate, right? You had the market. And the market

allocated capital to different banks. And you also had a connection between the monetary aggregates and the banks, which has
disappeared at this point. So it seems to me that's a possible way
to go. I don't know if we're going to get back to that, but why not
consider that?

HAMILTON: That system we were talking about, $5 billion was sort
of the level of reserves. So now we're talking about $2 trillion.
There's a big gap between those. A big gap before you get back to
the point where reserves are so precious that you get to balance
supply and demand based on changing the volume. One technical issue is how do you deal with the other sources of volatility?
The Treasury balance, for example, used to just vary by a billion
from one day to the next, and now we're talking about hundreds
of billions of dollars over the course of a few months there. So,
there would be technical issues with that. We definitely have to
get away from the reverse repo on demand, because that puts
huge volatility into the level of reserves. So, I think that's a harder
place to get to from where we are now, relative to just saying,
okay, a corridor system.

PETER IRELAND: Right. My answer to your question, John, would say:
that simply rephrases my first point, which is that I think a lot of
this doesn't have to do with monetary policy at all. If you want
to join me in thinking about policy as controlling the base to
stabilize the price level, that's fine. If you want to think about it as
following a Taylor rule in order to stabilize nominal spending, or
some other linear combination of output growth and inflation,
to achieve the dual mandate, basically, that's fine too. There's
nothing about the new system that says we have to have it and
can't go back to the old way. But conditional on having a giant
balance sheet, conditional on the New York Fed saying we don't
want to have to play the game of estimating the demand for
reserves on a day-to-day basis, and conditional on saying that
you're going to continue targeting the federal funds rate with a

floor system, my response would be: okay, if that's where you're at, then why not run a better version of what you have now that lets markets do most the work for you. By that I mean a floor or corridor system held together based on arbitrage opportunities. Why should we be stuck with a flawed system where the floor isn't the floor and there is no ceiling?

JEFF LACKER: It seems simpler than you make it sound, Jim. In the period before the crisis that you explained with such clarity, the RP rate varied significantly from the funds rate target, at times 10, 20 basis points below, at times 10, 20 basis points above, and in fact was pretty volatile day-to-day, week-to-week, month-to-month. Now, we seem to care about the gap between the RP [repurchase] rate and the funds rate or whatever the interest rate on excess reserves, and I never heard at the FOMC [Federal Open Market Committee] a coherent reason why. The federal funds rate used to be our target. Now we set an interest rate on excess reserves. And as you rightly point out, the federal funds rate is sort of a niche market, an anachronistic appendage in some sense. So, from my point of view, interest rate control seems simple. The Fed controls the interest rate on excess reserves, period. And the spreads between the interest rate and excess reserves and other rates are determined by the vagaries of the various regulatory constraints on various classes of participants in financial markets, and we let that do what it does for various reasons, as you illustrated with the federal funds rate. But equally cogent regulatory constraints, as you pointed out, affect the RP rate on a day-to-day, week-to-week, month-to-month basis. So, why don't we just set the interest rate on excess reserves and go home? Now, there is a coherent reason, and that has to do with Fed governance. The law that gave the Federal Reserve the authority to set interest on reserves gave that authority to a subset of the Federal Open Market Committee, the Board of Governors. And setting the federal funds rate target has always been the purview of the Federal Open Market Committee. So, in some sense, targeting the federal funds rate is really window dressing around this inconvenient governance arrangement around the interest rate on excess reserves. The obvious solutions would be a very simple, one-line bill that reassigns authority to the Federal Open Market Committee rather than the board.

HAMILTON: So, I was using an RP rate not so much because I was wanting to say that's what the target should be, but because that's a true market rate, unlike the fed funds rate, which is kind of a meaningless signal here. But I think ultimately, the issue is what we care about are things like the three-month commercial paper rate. That's what ultimately is going to influence economic activity. If you have a tight link between your policy rule and that, then you have an ability to get the price level and economic activity where you want. I'm not sure I see how just a pure interest on reserves, with no upper bound, would really give the Fed the ability to hit its target. So your answer is, if they've set the interest on reserves, and we see commercial paper too much above that, we'd just flood more and more reserves out there until it comes down? Is that it?

LACKER: Well, we never in the past, I think, at the Fed, engaged in some feedback from the CP [commercial paper] rate. I mean, it was looking at the entire macroeconomy. Commercial paper rate would vary. But setting the funds rate is equivalent to now setting the interest rate on reserves. Why don't we just say we've set the interest rate on reserves. We don't need the RRP [reverse repurchase] facility. And we could back away from the funds market as a target. In the end, it's about the banks' indifference about keeping money as reserves or in other investments or about lending and the funds market, as it was under the other system.

JOHN COCHRANE: I'd like to ask the opposite of John Taylor's question, in part because this is one issue on which we disagree, and in part because it's the elephant in the room. It's a central issue for the Fed's strategy question. We've learned in the last ten years that you can pay interest on reserves, and the economy can be satiated in reserves, and guess what? That doesn't cause inflation. Second, the Fed targets interest rates. If you want to target the price of tomatoes, you have to say, "Tomatoes are three bucks a pound, come and get them." Offer to buy and sell infinite amounts. But, somehow, the Fed wants to target an interest rate and also target the quantity.

Why not have a narrow corridor, with a flat supply curve? Bring us your treasuries, we'll give you as many reserves as you want. Conversely, we'll lend you as many reserves as you want. If you want to target an interest rate, that's what you've got to do. It seems like the logical conclusion to all of these problems is just to target the rates. Don't, as Jim said later, limit the RP project. Let anyone who wants have to them at the same rate as anyone else. Given that we're trying to target interest rates, why bother controlling the level of reserves at all?

Leaving aside political considerations, why limit the size of the balance sheet? There's some sort of vague memory of $MV = PY$ and so forth. But that has disappeared from our models and experience. The Fed has just been targeting interest rates. So, why limit the size of the balance sheet at all? That seems to me the elephant in the room.

HAMILTON: I think that was the point I was trying to make in response to Peter, that you are committed. If you have the upper and lower bound, lend to all the people you want. You are committing to a quantity from that. You can't choose the two things separately.

And then the question is what's the interest rate and implicit quantity that's consistent with price stability. So, that's where it all comes down. But just in terms of the mechanical question of how do you do it, I think what you do is announce "come and get it," and make sure the price you've announced is one that's consistent with everything else you want to see happen.

IRELAND: Right. Remember, the one added degree of freedom that the Fed has received since 2008 is the ability to pay interest on reserves. So now, you've got the overall level of nominal interest rates economy wide, which we think through some Keynesian interest rate channel on aggregate demand is what really matters for monetary policy. And then, as you say, either you can decide how much reserves you want in the banking system and peg the spread, the opportunity cost to banks of holding reserves, or you can peg the spread and you accept the dollar volume of reserves. But let me say that even under that system, here's what I was trying to get at: as a logical matter, no one should care whether we're measuring reserves in dollars or cents. What we're talking about with reserves demand is a real demand for reserves. So in a macroeconomic model, if you have a dynamic stochastic general equilibrium with a steady-state growth path for nominal variables where they grow at 2 percent per year, my point is that after the transition is done, you've either set the spread and accepted the real quantity or set the real quantity and accepted what the spread has to be. From that moment forward, it is still true that the monetary base is going to grow, is going to have to grow, at a rate proportional to the price level. The only reason why I bring this up again is that it's an element of incompleteness that runs the risk of letting the system that you say works well unravel completely. This is what you hear from central bankers during a hyperinflation. They'll say, "But we have to keep printing money to keep up with the demand, because the price level is rising so fast." I'm uneasy about an intellectual framework that appears to suggest, in exactly the same way, that an expansion in a nominal magnitude is just done exclusively to accommodate demand.

SEBASTIAN EDWARDS: Should we be worried about the cost of paying for the very large excess reserves? I think it's about $2 trillion now? At 2.5 percent, it's nontrivial. My region of interest has been Latin America, where central banks basically have to be bailed out every four years. Is this something we should worry about?

IRELAND: I think we should, and to support that view I would just refer you to Charlie Plosser's article from this conference, I guess it was two years ago. If I was deciding, I would say, as Charlie did, there are just so many economic and political costs and complications of working with a big balance sheet. There's the direct cost, and there's also the political cost, because the Fed is seen as an institution that can issue interest-earning liabilities and use the proceeds to purchase interest-earning assets. That starts to make the Fed look less and less like a central bank and more and more like a commercial bank. And you mentioned MMT, which feeds into that entire mentality. So, from a long-run perspective, I'd rather just work the balance sheet back down and do it, as John Taylor said, in the old way. But just to go back to what Jim said earlier, given that the balance sheet is so big at this moment, and given that the consensus seems to be the adjustment has to take place over time, you have to pay interest on reserves for now. Otherwise, you'll get inflation right away.

HAMILTON: Let me just add, if you're asking should we be worried that the Fed's going to make a loss, the answer to that on average is clearly no. The Fed is borrowing short and lending long at a higher rate. They're raking in money with this carry trade. On average. Now, it's not always that way, and you can imagine a situation where they have a pretty big loss, and there's a political economy question of does the Treasury actually bail them out? How mechanically do you run the loss? And there are the various issues that Peter raises. But there's no doubt, currently, it's very profitable for the Fed to have this huge volume of short-term borrowing that it essentially does with interest on reserves and then earning a higher rate on their portfolio.

EDWARDS: Unless it gets inverted.

HAMILTON: Unless it gets inverted, yeah. So on average, it isn't.

ANDY LEVIN: Yeah, it's a really great panel. I wanted to follow up on Jeff Lacker's question. So, you want to have a simple corridor system. You need to use a large, liquid market, which the fed funds market is not anymore. What about using the repo market? So the floor would be the reverse repo offer rate, which they already have, and you'd have a ceiling of a repo offer rate, which I think they're contemplating. And then you'd shoot for a midpoint. But ECB [European Central Bank] and other central banks do this. They call it fine-tuning operations. So, sometimes you hit the floor. Sometimes you hit the ceiling. You adjust the reserves. You can do it once a week or once a month. It's not a big deal even if you're running at the ceiling or the floor, if the floor and the ceiling aren't too far apart. And this would become an FOMC decision, because historically open-market operations are set by the FOMC. And so the FOMC could set the repo offer rate and the reverse repo offer rate and avoid the governance problems that have been mentioned. The setting of IOER [interest rate on excess reserves] would be pushed much further into the background. And a lot of the Fed's liabilities and the assets would become repos and reverse repos. Maybe bank reserves would also shrink a lot. I'm just wondering, would that be a direction that's worth considering?

IRELAND: Yes. Very much.

UNIDENTIFIED SPEAKER 1: Jim, I had a quick comment on something you said, because I think it's a bit of an urban myth. It's actually a New York myth. You said that the volatility of the TGA [treasury general account] makes it hard to go back to a corridor. But that's not the right story. When they went to a floor system, the TGA, the Treasury understood that it didn't have to worry about smoothing the TGA account. It stopped using the TT&L [Treasury and Tax Loan Program] accounts. So this is a perfect example of where Lucas's critique applies. The Treasury balance is volatile because they've gone to a floor system. It would be less so if the Treasury had an incentive to manage the TGA as it used to when it was necessary to help a corridor system or corridor-type system work. So, I don't think that should be treated as a deep parameter.

HAMILTON: Yeah, as we were discussing last night, I think there is definitely something to that. But I think there's also the political factors with the debt ceiling and so on that are also playing a role in those very huge buildups of the Treasury account that we see.

UNIDENTIFIED SPEAKER 2: Let's say for the sake of argument that despite the Fed's best efforts, nothing comes out of this year's review. So, they're the same tools, the same framework, and we go into a recession. It seems likely QE [quantitative easing] is going to be an important tool. We're going to see the balance sheet expand even more, because we have low interest rates. So this is going to be an increasingly important issue; the size of the balance sheet is going to get larger and larger. And to me, this is consequential, because it gets into the question of how big of a footprint do you want the Fed to have? Do you want to crowd out the money markets? I think that's the first question. The second one would be, do you want the Fed to get into the role of public debt management? I mean, by taking treasury securities out and putting reserves onto the market, you're substituting one form of government liability for the other, and reserves aren't as fungible as treasuries. And I think that's a question that needs to be wrestled with as an implication of sticking with a large balance sheet.

IRELAND: That was a statement, not a question. But I agree with it.

UNIDENTIFIED SPEAKER 3: Jim, you talked a lot about the corridor. But how would you feel about shrinking the size of the corridor until it becomes a line? And at that point the Fed just borrows and lends at one rate?

HAMILTON: Well, as Peter was saying, I think it's very helpful to the Fed to have a real market signal of something. And so, we've got a range, and we see it's bumping against the top of that range, and that tells us something. And also I want to underscore what Peter was saying. There is a long-run equilibrium, what this volume of reserves ought to be and how it ought to grow over time. And watching that feedback is the essence of what monetary policy has to be. So, I'm in favor of a range. I'm in favor of a real market signal within that range, giving the Fed guidance as to whether their plans are consistent with where they want to take the economy.

UNIDENTIFIED SPEAKER 3: I think you'd have more of a signal and less noise with a line, because then—

HAMILTON: Will you get your line back, when you get a line?

UNIDENTIFIED SPEAKER 3: —because then you would observe the quantity, and that would tell you just how much the reserves demand curve had moved horizontally. So instead of getting a mixed signal, that would be a clean one.

HAMILTON: Well, that gets us back to the whole Friedman debate. Are the quantities the more useful signal or the interest rates? I think interest rates are pretty useful signals.

UNIDENTIFIED SPEAKER 4: I just want to follow up on John Taylor's comment earlier. It may seem because of the current size of the fed funds market that it's irrelevant and that it can't be used as a tool. But that's very much a consequence of policy decisions. So, let me remind you how you could bring back the fed funds market.

So, first, it wouldn't be too hard to raise required reserves on large banks with little consequence, because currently they face under the Basel requirements very high liquid asset requirements. So you could soak up a lot of the excess reserves by just making required reserves for banks bigger. You could avoid your micro problem, Peter, by paying interest on required reserves only, like fed funds less 10 basis points. And then you could pay zero interest on excess reserves. And then it would also be helpful to shut the GSEs [government-sponsored enterprises] out of the fed funds market. So if you did those things, it wouldn't be too hard to go back to the world of pre-2008. Now I understand that some people have other worlds in mind. But I think it's an attractive world in a lot of ways. And I think we got away from that world because of, in my view, political reasons and that the Fed wanted to use adjustments to monetary policy that didn't cause their balance sheet to change size. So reverse repos are an obvious example of a way that you can shrink and contract your monetary policy without actually reducing your reported size and having the accounting consequences of capital losses that go along with that.

So, I think the political consequences are more of a driver than maybe our discussion is indicating. And I think returning to the pre-2008 environment is not so inconceivable if we had the will to do that.

ANDY FILARDO: We haven't yet talked about the LCR [liquidity coverage ratio] requirement and its implications for the monetary policy operating system. To satisfy the LCR regulatory requirement, banks are currently free to choose to hold US treasuries, reserves, or a mix of the two. This makes me wonder if such uncertainty about the demand for reserves may be one of the reasons why a floor system appears to be more attractive to some than a traditional corridor system. One popular approach proposed to resolve this uncertainty is to ask banks for their demand for reserves. But we may never be able to elicit how much banks truly need. There is an incentive for banks to inflate their estimates because reserves that are remunerated at or close to the policy rate implicitly provide subsidized liquidity insurance relative to treasuries. To reduce the avoidable uncertainty, should the Fed specify the amount of the LCR requirement banks can fulfill by using reserves? If so, might this approach strengthen the case for a corridor system or for a return to something akin to the pre-2008 operating regime?

HAMILTON: Well, my point was not so much the uncertainty about it but the deterministic nature of it, at least at these volumes. Rather than an equilibrium marginal regulatory cost, it was just essentially some fixed number for quite a while. And the key aspect of that was that the fed funds signal is nothing other than that input you put in through the interest on excess reserves. So, I was talking about it from a more mechanical point of view. Now, there are other questions. I mean, this whole idea of you're only going to worry about your capital requirements the last day of the month is very strange to me. And that's introducing all kinds of volatility daily in these interest rates.

JAMES BULLARD: I want to push back a little bit on the idea of returning to the 2008, or earlier, operating procedure. First, it's not at all clear to me that that's the optimal way to do things. It's not like it's a holy grail. The size of the balance sheet is going to be much bigger. Currency is much bigger today: it's about $1.7 trillion. The Treasury general account used to be $5 billion, now it is $250 billion. That's a decision of the US Treasury, not of the Fed. I guess that's something we've just got to take on board. You also have the regulatory environment changing with Dodd-Frank: the emphasis on high-quality liquid assets has driven the demand for reserves from $30 billion or $40 billion up to a trillion dollars or more. I guess you could push back against that, but the Milton Friedman side of me says, well, if the world needs liquidity, supply the liquidity. That's going to put you up at $3 trillion or more right off the bat, and you're not going to go back to that earlier size of the balance sheet. When I look at central banks around the world, they've got corridor systems, just like Jim [Hamilton] was talking about. By putting in a repo program to complement the reverse repo program, you would meet an international standard, which seems to work well for other central banks. We get rid of our kind of jerry-rigged system that we had before the crisis. So all of this seems OK to me, even if you're a Chicago monetarist. I don't think evil things are happening, except that I do buy the political critique that there's room for more mischief.

IRELAND: But that was my message to the Fed, which you seem to have fully absorbed. I mean, if that's what you want to do, run with the big balance sheet and smooth out interest rates, then the corridor system makes a lot of sense, because it lets the market do it for you. So yes, why not work toward a system that is unencumbered by all of these institutional and regulatory constraints? Workarounds like targeting the GCF [General Collateral Finance]/RP rate instead of the federal funds rate as Jim suggested, and introducing a replacement for the discount window without stigma, like what David Andolfatto and Jane Ihrig have proposed, that would harness market forces to do exactly what you want to do.

CHAPTER FIVE

Evaluating Rules in the Fed's Report and Measuring Discretion

John H. Cochrane, John B. Taylor, and Volker Wieland

1. INTRODUCTION

How would the economy have behaved, and how will the economy behave, if one or another monetary policy rule is followed? In particular, what are the effects of the various rules that the Federal Reserve considers in setting policy and has listed in its *Monetary Policy Report*? (Federal Reserve Board 2019). These counterfactual questions must be answered with models. We examine the rules in the Fed's report, and a few others, in a battery of models. We evaluate the means and variances of inflation and output, as predicted by the models with varying rules. Each model generates an optimal set of rules, optimal combinations of interest rate responses to output and inflation. We summarize model-specific optimal rules by a trade-off curve of output versus inflation volatility. A good simple rule should not produce results too far from a model-specific optimum but should be robust across models.

Many central banks deviate from rules at certain times. Central bankers often defend this practice as a response to other events. What are the benefits and costs of such discretion? True, in any model the fully optimal policy responds to all variables and all shocks of the model. But can a real-world central bank implement

We thank Livio Cuzzi Maya, Lazar Milivojevic, and Balint Tatar for research assistance. The research was supported by the Alfred P. Sloan Foundation grant G-2016-7176.

such an optimal-control response? If it could, would the complexity and obscurity of such policy suffer because it is non-transparent, is hard to communicate, and hence leads to uncertain expectations? The Board of Governors and the Federal Open Market Committee (FOMC) have formally discussed interest rate rules since the 1990s, according to the record documented by Kahn (2012). FOMC chairs Greenspan, Bernanke, Yellen, and Powell have all referred to interest rate rules in explaining FOMC decisions. Since 2017, the prescriptions of selected rules for the federal funds rate have been shown in the Board of Governors' semiannual *Monetary Policy Report,* and they have been published on the Fed's Monetary Policy Principles and Practices web page. These rules include the Taylor (1993a) rule, a so-called balanced-approach rule, and a difference rule. Additionally, there are two rules that take particular account of periods with near-zero federal funds rates and implement a forward-guidance promise to make up for zero bound periods with looser subsequent policy, the adjusted Taylor (1993a) rule and the price-level rule.

First, we take the policy rules to the data. We calculate the prescriptions of the rules given the data, and we calculate the deviations from each rule. We find that one period of large deviations from the rules reported by the Fed occurred in the 1970s, a period of poor macroeconomic performance. We also find that the measure of discretion with all the rules reported by the Fed was small in most of the 1980s and 1990s, a period of relatively good macroeconomic performance. We find that the measure of discretion began to grow again in the early 2000s, though not as large as in the 1970s, and note that this occurred prior to the Great Recession.

Next, we consider a range of macroeconomic models that are available in the Macroeconomic Model Data Base (Wieland, Afanasyeva, Kuete, and Yoo 2016). These models include a simple New Keynesian model using the approach of Rotemberg and Woodford (1999), a simple Old Keynesian model using the approach of Ball (1999) and Rudebusch and Svensson (1999), a medium-size policy model using the approach of Christiano, Eichenbaum, and Evans (2005) and Smets-Wouters (2007), and a few larger-scale macroeconomic models that include, among other ingredients, exports, imports, exchange rates, the term structure of interest rates, additional financial frictions, and other behavioral assumptions.

Next, we evaluate each rule in each model. What is the volatility of output and inflation in each model, if the Fed follows each of the rules? We find that the rules in the Fed's report work well, though some are not very robust. In particular, the first difference rule, described below, does very well in forward-looking New Keynesian models but leads to infinite output and inflation volatility in backward-looking Old Keynesian models.

Finally, we calculate for each model the optimal rules for varying weights on inflation and output, generating a frontier of the best attainable inflation versus output volatility under that model. We compare the Fed's simple rules to those optimal rules. We find that many of the Fed's reported rules are close to the inflation-output volatility curve of optimal rules.

2. SOME LITERATURE ON DISTINGUISHING RULES AND DISCRETION IN PRACTICE

Many economists have endeavored to test whether economic performance is better with a rules-based monetary policy than with a discretionary policy. A common approach is to look at actual economic performance during periods when policy rules were in place and compare that with performance when there was more discretion. Indeed, there are periods when policy seems to have been close to prescriptions from rules and other periods with large deviations. However, distinguishing between rules and discretion in practice is difficult with much disagreement and debate, as discussed by McCallum (1999). Moreover, often it is said that particular developments and risks called for discretionary decision making, and that such deviations have led to better economic performance.

Friedman (1982) and later Meltzer (2012) and Taylor (2012) use a broad historical approach to distinguish rules from discretion. This approach did not require specifying that rules-based policy was predicated on a specific algebraic formula. Rather, policy was deemed rules based if it was predictable and strategic, while policy was discretionary if it is was mostly tactical with few strategic elements. Using this approach, Meltzer (2012) and Taylor (2012) find that the period from 1985 to 2003 in the United States was rulelike while the years before and after that interval were discretionary, and they noted that economic performance was better in the 1985–2003 period.

Nikolsko-Rzhevskyy, Papell, and Prodan (2014) use a more specific statistical procedure. They define rules-based policy as a specific policy rule for the interest rate, and discretion as deviations of the actual interest rate from that policy rule, as we do. They employ real-time data and three rules of the form

$$i_t = \varphi_\pi \pi_t + \varphi_y y_t + \mu \qquad (1)$$

with $\varphi_y = .5$, $\varphi_\pi = 1.5$ (as in Taylor 1993a), $\varphi_y = 1.0$, $\varphi_\pi = 1.5$, and φ_y and φ_π estimated. π denotes the four-quarter inflation rate (change from a year ago of the GDP deflator) and y the output gap. The latter is the difference between the log of actual and potential GDP. The constant, $\mu = r^* - (\varphi_\pi - 1) \pi^*$. The inflation objective is given by π^*, while r^* is the long-run equilibrium real interest rate. Discretion is defined as deviations of the actual interest rate from equation (1).

They find that economic performance in the United States was worse in periods of discretion relative to each of those rules. For example, using a quadratic loss function with equal weights on inflation and output, they find that the *loss ratio*—the ratio of the average loss during discretionary periods to the average loss during more rules-based periods—was 3.17, 1.85, and 1.70 for the three rules, respectively. Teryoshin (2017) obtains similar results for other countries. Nikolsko-Rzhevskyy, Papell, and Prodan (2018) perform similar calculations for four hundred rules of this form, with the coefficients φ_y and φ_π each taking twenty different values ranging from 0.1 to 2.0. They find with very few exceptions that the loss ratio is greater than one. They find that "inflation-tilting" rules, that is, rules with a higher response coefficient concerning inflation, result in better performance, and they thus conclude that the set of rules that the Fed publishes regularly in its *Monetary Policy Report* should be extended to include an inflation-tilting rule.

Another approach is to use economic models to evaluate rules versus discretion. This is the approach taken in Taylor (1979), where the output-inflation variance trade-off curve from an optimal money growth rule for a specific model is compared with the variances of output and inflation with actual policy and with suboptimal rules. An advantage of this approach is that it brings more economic theory into the calculation. A disadvantage is that it is model specific, but by doing the calculation with many different models, one can reduce this disadvantage (Levin, Wieland, and Williams 2003; Taylor and Wieland 2012).

Nikolsko-Rzhevskyy, Papell, and Prodan (2018) (NPP 2018 in the following) also report some model-based calculations with the Smets-Wouters (2007) model drawn from the Macroeconomic Model Data Base[1] and with the FRB-US model as described in Tetlow (2015). They simulate policy rules of the above form using one hundred different values of the φ_y and φ_π parameters, each taking ten different values from 0.1 to 1.0. The results are completely opposite in the two models: For the Smets-Wouters model, the

---

1. See www.macromodelbase.com for further details on the database and models as well as Wieland et al. (2016).

rule with the lowest loss (not loss ratio) has $\varphi_y = 0.3$ and $\varphi_\pi = 1.0$. For the FRB-US model, the rule with the lowest loss is at the other end of the range: $\varphi_y = 1.0$ and $\varphi_\pi = 0.1$. This result is suggestive of an underappreciated large difference between models used for policy making.

3. THE RULES IN THE FED'S REPORT

As stated, for example, in the most recent report by the Fed, "The prescriptions for the policy interest rate from these rules can provide helpful guidance to the FOMC" (Federal Reserve Board 2019). Accordingly, one guiding principle is that monetary policy should respond in a predictable manner to changes in economic conditions. Its effectiveness is higher, if it is well understood by the public. Another key principle emphasized by the Fed's report is that policy should be accommodative when inflation is below its longer-run objective and employment is below its maximum sustainable level, and vice versa. Yet another key principle in the report "is that, to stabilize inflation, the policy rate should be adjusted by more than one-for-one in response to persistent increases or decreases in inflation."

The specific interest rate rules considered by the Fed define systematic responses to the four-quarter rate of inflation and the unemployment gap. The five rules are summarized in table 5.1.

The Taylor (1993a) rule and many other rules are typically expressed in terms of the deviation of real GDP from potential GDP. The FRB report version of the Taylor (1993a) rule uses an Okun's law relationship with a factor of 2 to translate the output gap into an unemployment gap. We translate the rules back into a version with the output gap. Many of our models do not include the unemployment rate. The Taylor (1993a) rule and the so-called balanced-approach rule then correspond to the specifications of equation (1) with $\varphi_y = 0.5$, $\varphi_\pi = 1.5$ and $\varphi_y = 1.0$, $\varphi_\pi = 1.5$, respec-

TABLE 5.1. The Rules in the *Monetary Policy Report*

Taylor (1993a) rule: *T93*	$i_t^{T93} = \pi_t + 0.5(\pi_t - \pi^*) + (u_t^* - u_t) + r_t^*$
Balanced-approach rule (BA)	$i_t^{BA} = \pi_t + 0.5(\pi_t - \pi^*) + 2(u_t^* - u_t) + r_t^*$
First-difference rule (FD)	$i_t^{FD} = i_{t-1} + 0.5(\pi_t - \pi^*) + (u_t^* - u_t) - (u_{t-4}^* - u_{t-4})$
Taylor (1993a) adjusted (T93adj)	$i_t^{T93adj} = \max\{i_t^{T93} - Z_t, 0\}$
Price-level rule (PL)	$i_t^{PL} = \max\{\pi_t + 0.5(PLgap_t) + (u_t^* - u_t) + r_t^*, 0\}$

Note: i_t is the nominal federal funds rate; π_t is the inflation rate, for which the Fed uses core PCE inflation; u_t is the unemployment rate; π^* is the Fed's longer-run inflation objective of 2%; r_t^* is an estimate of the level of the neutral real federal funds rate in the longer run derived from long-run Blue Chip forecasts; similarly u_t^* is an estimate of the rate of unemployment in the longer run derived from long-run Blue Chip forecasts. Z_t is the cumulative sum of past deviations from the Taylor rule forced by the zero bound, and $PLgap_t$ is the price-level gap, defined as the percent deviation of the actual level of prices from a price level that rises 2 percent per year from its level in a specified starting period.

tively, abstracting from a possibly time-varying equilibrium real interest rate.

However, Okun's law does not hold perfectly in the models or the data, and this translation leaves out the important problem of defining the time-varying natural rate of unemployment, leaving in its place the equally important problem of defining and measuring potential GDP. The numerical comparisons may well be affected by this substitution, and rules that respond to the unemployment rate and capture the Fed's difficult job of estimating changes in the natural rate may perform differently.

With regard to inflation, the FRB report uses the PCE deflator excluding food and energy prices. Instead, we will use the GDP deflator, because the models we consider do not include core PCE inflation, and most of them also do not include the overall PCE deflator.

NPP (2018) as well as Papell (see Discussant Remarks following this chapter) refer to the Taylor (1993a) rule as a balanced rule, because it has the property that the same change in the inflation gap and the output gap implies the same effect on the real interest rate. Accordingly, they call rules of the type of the Fed's "balanced-approach" rule as output gap–tilting rule. Such rules imply

a stronger response of the real rate to the output gap than to the inflation gap. We agree with the interpretation of NPP and Papell. For this
reason, we put the term "balanced-approach" in quotation marks.

A major question of implementation haunts the first-difference
FD rule. As defined in the Fed's report, the FD rule is the "rule
suggested by Orphanides (2003)," and it is also the rule considered
in robustness studies such as those in the volume summarized by
Taylor (1999). The rules as presented in the Fed report (table 5. 1)
do not include any residuals, deviations, or errors. In the data, of
course, actual interest rates persistently deviate from the rule. The
first-difference FD rule as stated in the Fed's report and in these earlier studies makes the previous period's actual interest rate, including its deviation, instantly part of the rule! A rule "I won't eat any
more donuts than I ate yesterday" means that one donut turns into a
permanent part of what will turn out not to be a very successful diet.

With this issue in mind, we explore a different type of first-
difference rule,

$$i_t^{FD} = i_{t-1}^{FD} + 0.5(\pi_t - \pi^*) + (u_t^* - u_t) - (u_{t-4}^* - u_{t-4})$$

$$i_t = i_t^{FD} + v_t \qquad (2)$$

Here, v_t is a serially correlated disturbance, which can be interpreted as the discretionary component of the rule. We refer to this
rule as the "dynamic first-difference" rule, FDdyn.

The Fed's recent *Monetary Policy Report* includes rules in part
to request comment on the rules, and our first major comment
is that the Fed should consider the alternative FD rule in equation (2). It makes a very large difference to the interpretation of
the data—what is a rule, and what is deviation or discretion—and
it makes a potentially large difference to economic performance
under the rule.

The adjusted Taylor (1993a) rule and the price-level rule are
meant to account for periods when policy is constrained at the

zero lower bound on nominal interest rates. They also include a forward-guidance promise to keep policy looser than it would otherwise be in the wake of a zero bound event. The adjusted Taylor (1993a) rule makes up for periods when the rule prescribes a negative federal funds rate, but the actual rate is constrained at zero. The rule keeps the funds rate lower for longer once the Taylor rule again prescribes a positive policy interest rate. The adjustment factor Z_t is the cumulative sum of such past deviations. The price-level rule makes up for a period of below-target inflation by a period of above-target inflation in order to catch up with a price-level target that steadily increases with the target inflation rate. In some models promises of future looser-than-usual policy can stimulate output during the period of the zero bound.

Our second major comment is to take up a suggestion from NPP (2018) to include an inflation-tilting rule in the list of rules examined in the report, that is, a rule with a higher response coefficient concerning inflation than the Taylor (1993a) rule. Specifically, they propose a rule that is nested in equation (1) with $\varphi_y = 0.5$, $\varphi_\pi = 2$. We call this the NPP rule.

4. RULES AND DEVIATIONS: MEASURING DISCRETION

In this section, we compare the rules with actual policy, which is characterized by more discretion, and compute deviations. This comparison leads to a natural definition of discretion in the form of deviations from a particular rule.

4.1. Real-Time Measures of Discretion: NPP

Nikolsko-Rzhevskyy, Papell, and Prodan (2018) contrast actual interest rate policy with the Taylor rule. Figure 5.1 shows the interest rate setting according to the Taylor rule (T93) along with the

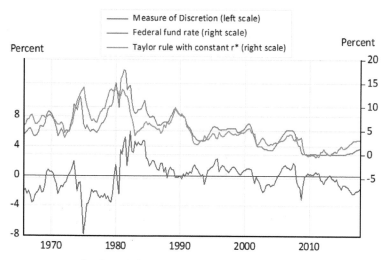

FIGURE 5.1. Federal Funds Rate, Taylor rule and Deviations
Source: Nikolosko-Rzhevskyy, Papell, and Prodan (2018) and the authors' own calculations.

actual interest rate. Nikolsko-Rzhevskyy, Papell, and Prodan (2018) use real-time data available to Fed decision makers at the time to construct the Taylor rule. The chart uses the actual federal funds rate for the interest rate throughout the sample period rather than a "shadow interest rate" during the 2009–2015 period as in Nikolsko-Rzhevskyy, Papell, and Prodan (2018).

The difference between the actual rate and the rule is plotted below the interest rate paths in figure 5.1. This deviation can be considered a measure of discretion. Discretion so defined captures any deviation from the posited rule, including different rules, time-varying rules, rules that respond to additional variables and shocks, perhaps in a time-varying way. The line between such generalized "rule" and discretion seems blurry, but the main point of rules is that people know them, expect them, and understand them, and a complex time-varying rule is indistinguishable from seat-of-the-pants discretion to observers, so it is likely uninformative for us.

The measure of discretion in figure 5.1 is large and negative in the 1970s, especially in the late 1970s. Inflation was high and variable, and output fluctuations were large during this period of generally poor economic performance.

Policy then changed. A positive deviation in the early 1980s was just as large as the negative deviation in the 1970s. We interpret this period as a transition to a new policy with less discretion. During the transition—a period of disinflation—the interest rate went above the rule as the Fed brought inflation down and established credibility.

Following this transition, there were nearly two decades during which there was virtually no discretion—from about 1985 to 2002— by this measure. Economic performance was very good during this period, which is frequently called the great moderation or the long boom.

However, one can see another bout of discretion during the 2003–2005 period. According to figure 5.1, this was not as large as the deviation in the 1970s, but it did suggestively precede the terrible performance during the Great Recession. To see what happened in recent years, we update the measures and include other policy rules in the next section.

4.2. Deviations from Rules in the Fed's Report

We do the same calculations as in figure 5.1 using current data (rather than real-time data) for all of the policy rules considered by the Fed's report. Additionally, we include the inflation-tilting rule with coefficients $\varphi_y = 0.5$, $\varphi_\pi = 2$, which we call the NPP rule. Since the numbers for r_t^* used by the Fed are not made available in the *Monetary Policy Report,* we use a constant equilibrium interest rate of $r^* = 2\%$ together with an inflation target of $\pi^* = 2\%$, and the measure of potential GDP from the Congressional Budget Office (CBO). Figure 5.2 shows the actual interest rate and the monetary policy rules T93, BA, FD, and

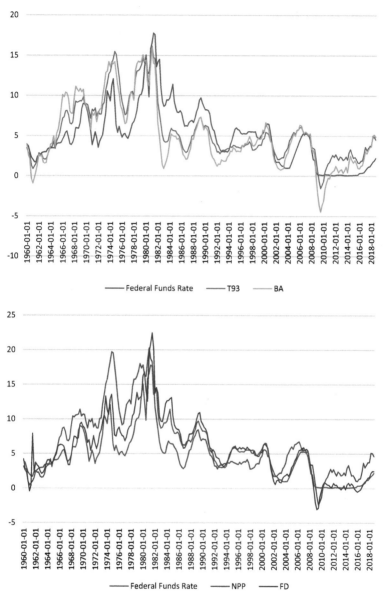

FIGURE 5.2. Federal Funds Rate and Rules: T93 and BA, NPP and FD

Note: We use current data and not the real-time data that were available to Fed decision makers when they set the federal funds rate. Nikolsko-Rzhevskyy, Papell, and Prodan (2018) use the real-time data for their analysis. On the basis of current data, we produce "ex-post" measures of discretion derived from the rules from the Fed's report.

NPP. Figure 5.3 shows the *difference* between the actual interest rate and these rules, which again is our measure of discretion.

Figures 5.2 and 5.3 show that the T93, BA, and NPP rules all display patterns of discretion similar to those in figure 5.1 for T93 with real-time data. There is a big deviation in the 1970s, a transition period, a period of less discretion, and a period of increased discretion. The deviations—especially in 1970s—suggest that policy could have improved outcomes substantially by more closely following the rules. The difference between the calculations in figure 5.1 and those in figure 5.2 may be due to the use of real-time data in figure 5.1 compared with current data in the figure 5.2.

The deviations from the FD rule suggest a much smaller degree of discretion. There is no noticeable deviation for the whole period, except possibly a small negative deviation in the 1970s. For the full sample period in figure 5.3, the standard deviation of the differences between the federal funds rate and first difference rule is $SD(i\text{-}i^{FD}) = 1.34$, while for the other three rules the standard deviations are $SD(i\text{-}i^{T93}) = 2.54$, $SD(i\text{-}i^{BA}) = 3.02$, and $SD(i\text{-}i^{NPP}) = 3.06$.

The adjusted Taylor (1993a) (T93adj) rule and the price-level (PL) rule are meant to account for periods when policy is constrained at the zero lower bound on nominal interest rates. Hence we follow the Fed's report and compute these rules for the recent period since the year 2000. The results are shown in figure 5.4.

Of course, the T93 rule and the T93adj rule result in the same interest rate prescriptions, unless the T93 rule calls for a negative setting. It turns out that the T93 rule only implies four quarters of negative rates, namely, 2009:Q2 to 2010:Q1. The T93adj rule makes up for the constrained period by keeping the policy rate at zero a bit longer, that is, until the first quarter of 2011.

The price-level target used by the PL rule has to be initiated in a particular period. From that period onward, it grows with a fixed rate of 2 percent. We follow the Fed's report and set the initial period for the price-level target in 1998:Q1. If the rate of inflation subsequently exceeds 2 percent, there will have to be a period

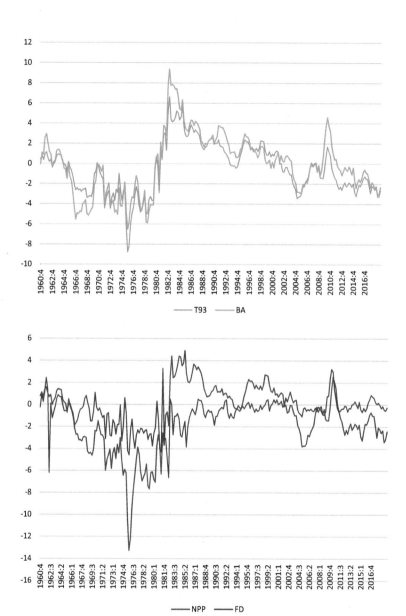

FIGURE 5.3. Measure of Discretion, T93 and BA, NPP and FD

Note: We use current data and not the real-time data that were available to Fed decision makers when they set the federal funds rate. Nikolsko-Rzhevskyy, Papell, and Prodan (2018) use the real-time data for their analysis. On the basis of current data, we produce "ex-post" measures of discretion derived from the rules from the Fed's report.

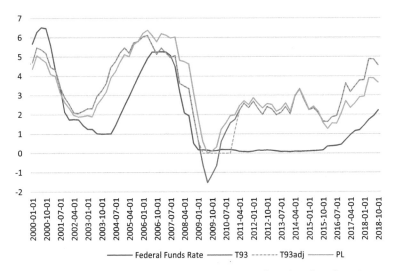

FIGURE 5.4. Federal Funds Rate and Rules: T93, T93adj, and PL based on GDP Deflator. We use current data and not the real-time data that were available to Fed decision makers when they set the federal funds rate. On the basis of current data, we produce "ex-post" measures of discretion derived from the rules from the Fed's report.

with inflation below 2 percent to bring the price level back to the price-level target path consistent with 2 percent growth. Similarly, if the rate of inflation falls short of 2 percent, there will have to be a period with inflation above 2 percent in order to bring the price level back to the price-level target path. It is this latter effect that helps push inflation expectations up during periods when the central bank is constrained at the zero bound. As shown in figure 5.4, the PL rule touches zero only in the second quarter of 2009.

It is remarkable that the interest rate under the PL rule is so close to the various Taylor rules. One would expect the cumulative inflation rate to drift away from 2 percent price-level growth. Apparently, over long time periods, the long periods of inflation below target have been just matched by equally long periods of above-target inflation. Yet there is nothing in an inflation-based policy rule to produce this outcome.

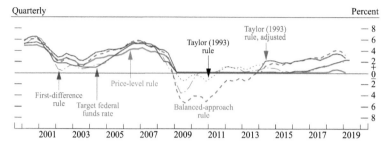

FIGURE 5.5. Historical Federal Funds Rate Prescriptions from Simple Policy
Rules

Source: Federal Reserve Bank of Philadelphia, Wolters Kluwer, Blue Chip Economic
Indicators, Federal Reserve Board Staff estimates.

Note: The rules use historical values of inflation, the federal funds rate, and the unemployment rate. Inflation is measured as the 4-quarter percent change in the price index for personal consumption expenditures (PCE) excluding food and energy. Quarterly projections of
long-run values for the federal funds rate and the unemployment rate are derived through
interpolations of biannual projections from Blue Chip Economic Indicators. The long-run
value for inflation is taken as 2 percent. The target value of the price level is the average level
of the price index for PCE excluding food and energy in 1998 extrapolated at 2 percent per
year. The target federal funds rate data extend through 2019:Q2.

Actual fed funds rates stayed near zero for a much longer period,
that is, from December 2008 until December 2015. Interestingly,
the T93adj rule and the PL rules shown in the Fed's *Monetary Policy
Report* also imply fairly long periods of prescriptions near zero. As
shown in figure 5.5, taken directly from the 2019 report, the Taylor
(1993a) rule in the Fed's report prescribes a near-zero fed funds rate
for about five years. The PL rule prescribes a funds rate of (near)
zero for about nine years.

There are several potential sources of the differences between
figure 5.4 and figure 5.5:

(i)   We use the GDP deflator (because it is the inflation variable in
      our models), while the Fed chart uses the PCE deflator excluding
      food and energy.

(ii) We use the CBO output gap, while the Fed uses an unemploy-
      ment gap.

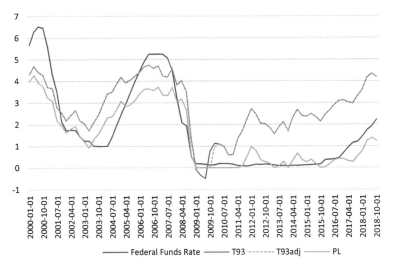

FIGURE 5.6.   Federal Funds Rate and Rules: T93, T93adj, and PL based on PCE Deflator

Note: We use current data and not the real-time data that were available to Fed decision makers when they set the federal funds rate. On the basis of current data, we produce "ex-post" measures of discretion derived from the rules from the Fed's report.

(iii) We use a long-run equilibrium real rate (r^*) of 2 percent, while the Fed uses a variable r^* that is derived by interpolating biannual projections from Blue Chip Economic Indicators. Similarly, the natural unemployment rate, u^*, that underlies the unemployment gap used in the Fed's report is derived by interpolating biannual projections from the Blue Chip Economic Indicators. Unfortunately, the values of r^* and u^* are not made available by the Fed.

Figure 5.6 shows the T93, T93adj, and the PL rules using the core PCE deflator rather than the GDP deflator. In this case, the PL rule provides much lower fed funds rate prescriptions. It stays near zero till 2011 and returns to zero several times afterward. The PCE deflator excluding food and energy increased less than the GDP deflator in recent years. As a result, its level falls behind the 2 percent price-level target more and more. Yet, the effect is still not as strong as in the rules chart reported in the Fed's report. As for the T93 and T93adj rules, they do not imply substantially longer periods near zero in figure 5.6, which uses the PCE deflator as measure of inflation than in figure 5.4, which uses the GDP deflator instead.

Thus, the use of the unemployment gap instead of the CBO output gap and the particular series for the long-run real interest rate, r^*, in the Fed's report must also be important factors pushing down the fed funds rate prescriptions. Unfortunately, we cannot check this as the Fed does not make the values it uses available. Moreover, time variation in r^* has only really achieved such prominence in the Fed's deliberations in recent years.

Finally, all of the rules other than the FD rule show persistent, highly serially correlated deviations. By putting the lagged interest rate in the rule (see table 5. 1), the first-difference rule counts yesterday's "deviation" as today's "rule," so the "deviations" are no longer persistent. The dynamic first-difference rule, FDdyn, interprets the lagged interest rate as the lagged rule, not the lagged actual rate. As a reminder, this rule is defined by equation (2).

We implement this rule by dynamic simulation from a specific starting point. As in the case of the PL rule, we choose 1998:Q1 to initialize the rule. The resulting interest prescriptions are shown as FDdyn in figure 5.7.

The dynamic simulation of the FDdyn rule uses actual historical inflation and output data but does not reset to the actual lagged interested rate every period. As a result, it deviates much further from the actual federal funds rate path than the FD rule. It suggests that the small amount of discretion relative to the FD rule indicated in figure 5.3 is misleading. This interpretation of the FD rule, which we think is more sensible, also indicates substantial deviations over time.

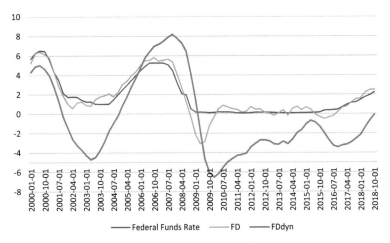

FIGURE 5.7. Federal Funds Rate and Rules: FD, FDdyn

Note: the dynamic simulation of the rule, FDdyn, is initialized in 1998:Q1. We use current data and not the real-time data that were available to Fed decision makers when they set the federal funds rate. On the basis of current data, we produce "ex-post" measures of discretion derived from the rules from the Fed's report.

5. EVALUATING THE FED'S RULES IN MACROECONOMIC MODELS

To make further progress on these questions, we simulate the different policy rules in macroeconomic models, which account for the endogenous response of output and inflation to the choice of policy rule.

We consider the T93, BA, FD, and NPP rules. These rules are nested by this extended four-parameter version of equation (1):

$$i_t = \varphi_\pi \pi_t + \varphi_y y_t + \varphi_{yl} y_{t-4} + \varphi_i i_{t-1} \tag{3}$$

This equation does not have an error term. Thus, in the model simulations the actual interest rate always corresponds exactly to the proposed policy rule. Thus, in the model simulations we conduct here, the FD and FDdyn rules are identical.

We do not include the adjusted Taylor (1993a) rule and the price-level rule in the model comparison because we abstract for now from a zero bound or effective lower bound constraint. The separate and nonlinear effects of the zero bound limit, and the forward guidance promise, are important questions and likely to differ greatly across models. Based on whether dominant eigenvalues are above or below one, some models have dramatic effects of zero bound episodes and forward-guidance promises, and some have very slight effects. (See Cochrane 2017.) We leave these important questions for another day, and our calculations apply for "normal times" when the interest rate is above zero.

To start, we consider two small models. While less realistic, they illustrate some lessons of the larger models. The first model is a version of the small New Keynesian model of Rotemberg and Woodford (1997) and Goodfriend and King (1997). It consists of purely forward-looking Phillips and IS curves. The dynamic behavior therefore is driven by serially correlated shocks. There are technology, government spending, and cost-push shocks. We use the empirical specification of this model from Levin, Wieland, and Williams (2003).

Small New Keynesian Model (NK):

$$y_t = E_t y_{t+1} - 1.59(i_t - E_t \pi_{t+1} - r_t^*)$$

$$r_t^* = 0.35 r_{t-1}^* + \eta_t$$

$$\pi_t = .99 E_t \pi_{t+1} + .096 y_t + \varepsilon_t$$

Here r_t^* is the natural real interest rate. It follows a serially correlated process. The innovations η_t are independent and identically distributed with a standard deviation of 3.72. ε_t is a cost-push shock, which is independent and identically distributed with standard deviation of 2.25.[2]

---

2. Levin, Wieland, and Williams (2003) set the parameters of the aggregate demand equation and the inflation equation based on Woodford (2003) and calibrate the standard

The second model is a simple traditional Keynesian model with backward-looking dynamics. This model is similar to Ball (1999), Orphanides and Wieland (2000), and Rudebusch and Svensson (1999). We refer to it as the small Old Keynesian model. We use the empirical specification of Rudebusch and Svensson (1999). They show that the models with lagged dependent variables can explain US inflation and output dynamics quite well without taking recourse to serially correlated errors.[3]

Small Old Keynesian Model (OK):

$$y_t = 1.16 y_{t-1} - .25 y_{t-2} - .1(i_{t-1}^{4q} - \pi_{t-1}) + \eta_t$$

$$\pi_t^q = .7\pi_{t-1}^q - .1\pi_{t-2}^q + .28\pi_{t-3}^q + .12\pi_{t-4}^q - .14 y_{t-1} + \varepsilon_t$$

The superscript ^{4q} denotes the four-quarter average of the federal funds rate and the superscript ^{q} denotes the quarterly inflation rate. The disturbances η_t and ε_t are independent and identically distributed (i.i.d.) with zero mean and standard deviations of 0.89 and 1.009, respectively.

Medium-Scale Policy Model (SW):
We consider a medium-scale dynamic stochastic general equilibrium model using the approach of Christiano, Eichenbaum, and Evans (2005) as extended and estimated in Smets and Wouters (2007). The model contains a greater number of equations and

---

deviation of the independent and identically distributed (i.i.d.) cost-push shock so that the unconditional variance of inflation under their benchmark estimated policy rule matches the sample variance of US quarterly inflation over the period 1983:1–1999:4. The model is available for download at www.macromodelbase.com.

3. Rudebusch and Svensson (1999) estimate these two equations with ordinary-least squares for data from 1961:1–96:2. They report that almost identical estimates were obtained with seemingly unrelated regressions and system maximum likelihood methods. The hypothesis that the sum of the lag coefficients of inflation is equal to unity had a *p*-value of 0.42 and was imposed in estimation. Estimation errors were serially uncorrelated. They also conducted subsample stability tests that did not uncover a lack of stability. The model is available for download at www.macromodelbase.com.

macroeconomic shocks than the above small-scale models. It aims to explain more variation in key variables, and to also include other variables and to match data dynamics. The model is estimated with Bayesian methods that allow—and require, as some model parameters are poorly identified—priors on model parameters.

In the long run, the medium-scale model is consistent with a balanced steady-state growth path driven by labor-augmenting technological progress. The model assumes that firms index wages to a weighted average of lagged and steady-state inflation. It does not impose a delayed effect of monetary policy on other variables, and there is no so-called cost channel in the model. In the following, we use the specification of the model from Smets and Wouters (2007) and thus label this model SW, though it can be also traced to research by Christiano, Eichenbaum, and Evans (2005).[4]

To obtain measures of performance, we replace the model's specified policy rule with one of the alternative rules, and we assume there are no monetary policy shocks. We then compute the steady-state or unconditional distribution of the endogenous variables and report the standard deviations of the four-quarter inflation rate (growth in GDP deflator from prior year) and the quarterly output gap.

The steady-state distribution for any particular model depends on the parameters of that model, the policy rule, and the covariance matrix of the structural shocks of that model. The models are linear, or linear approximation of originally nonlinear models. Thus, we can calculate unconditional variances and covariances analytically, as in Levin, Wieland, and Williams (2003) and Taylor and Wieland (2012).

---

4. For more detail on the derivation of the model and model equations, the reader is referred to Smets and Wouters (2007). Model equations, parameters, and shock covariances are implemented for use with the Macroeconomic Model Database and available for download from www.macromodelbase.com. The website also provides a replication package that reproduces the original analysis by Smets and Wouters.

5.1. Performance of the Four Rules

Table 5.2 reports standard deviations of inflation and the output gap in the NK, OK, and SW models for the four different rules: T93, BA, NPP, and FD. When we have the model's estimated rule and the process and covariance matrix of its residuals, we use these to generate the model's variance of inflation and output.

The standard deviations of inflation and the output gap differ across models in table 5.2 for a number of reasons. First, of course, the models are different. Second, the data samples and estimation periods of the OK and SW models are quite different, and the NK model is calibrated and not estimated. Third, the output gap concepts are different: in the SW model the gap is between actual GDP and the modeled flexible-price level of GDP that varies with a number of economic shocks.

These differences enable us to examine the robustness of the different rules to alternative assumptions. A robust rule performs reasonably well across all models that would be considered as relevant for evaluating policy.

There are some obvious findings in terms of variation across rules within any given model. First, consider the interest rate–level rules: T93, BA, and NPP. The BA rule has the same response coefficient on inflation as T93, but it has twice as large a coefficient on the output gap (1 instead of 0.5). In all three models, the standard deviation of the output gap is smaller under the BA rule than under the T93 rule. The standard deviation of inflation is greater under BA than under T93, but except for the SW model the increase is small.

The NPP rule has a greater coefficient on inflation than the T93 rule, 2 instead of 1.5, but the same output gap coefficient. It tilts toward inflation relative to T93, while BA tilts toward output compared to T93. In all three models, the standard deviation of inflation under the NPP rule is smaller than under the T93 and BA rule,

TABLE 5.2. Steady-State Standard Deviation of Inflation and Output Gap in the Models

Rules/ Models	OK Inflation	OK Output Gap	NK Inflation	NK Output Gap	SW Inflation	SW Output Gap
T93	3.45	2.27	0.90	4.24	4.50	4.27
BA	3.49	1.99	0.96	2.83	6.87	3.56
NPP	2.65	2.59	0.84	4.38	2.83	4.74
FD	∞	∞	0.88	3.12	1.39	4.62
E	2.33	2.80	0.86	2.78	2.22	4.61

Note: The models are the small Old Keynesian (OK), small New Keynesian (NK), and the medium-size policy model (SW). The rules are the Taylor (1993) rule (T93), the so-called balanced-approach rule (BA), the inflation-tilting rule proposed by Nikolsko-Rzhevskyy, Papell, and Prodan rule (NPP), and the first-difference rule (FD). E refers to the outcome under the model's estimated rule with its residuals, when that rule and residual covariance matrix is available, or to sample standard deviations when not available.†

† OK model: Rudebusch and Svensson did not provide an estimated rule, but they report sample standard errors for 1961 to 1996 that are reported here. NK model: Levin, Wieland, and Williams (2003) estimated a benchmark interest rate rule and calibrated the standard deviation of the cost-push shock such that it replicates the unconditional variance of inflation in their sample under this benchmark rule. SW model: Smets and Wouters (2007) estimated a policy rule along with the model. The unconditional variance reported accounts for the standard error of serially correlated policy shocks.

while the standard deviation of the output gap is greater than under these two other level rules.

The first-difference rule, FD, delivers quite different outcomes. First, in the OK model it is dynamically unstable, so it produces infinite output and inflation variation. This is denoted by the ∞ symbol in the table. Ideally, the central bank should avoid pursuing a policy that is dynamically unstable! In the small NK model and in the SW model, however, the FD rule performs quite well. In the small NK model, it achieves the second-lowest standard deviations of inflation and the output gap among the four rules considered. In the SW model it achieves by the far the lowest standard deviation of inflation, but the second-highest standard deviation of the output gap.

The FD rule seems to be optimized to forward-looking models but performs poorly in a backward-looking economy. The Taylor rule achieves robustness across the two classes of models in a straightforward way. Old Keynesian models are unstable under an interest rate peg. The Taylor rule with an inflation coefficient greater than one renders those models stable. New Keynesian models are already stable under an interest rate peg but indeterminate; there are multiple equilibria. The Taylor rule renders them determinate, eliminating multiple equilibrium indeterminacy. The same rule has a different but beneficial effect in two quite different classes of models. As a result it is "robust." The FD rule does not have this property, as it does not cure the instability of Old Keynesian models under an interest rate peg.

Overall, therefore, the FD rule is not as robust as the other rules. The FD rule may also be geared to avoid having to account for a slowly time-varying natural rate that the central bank cannot observe. Our models do not include this feature.

5.2. More Models

In addition to the three models (NK, OK, and SW) considered in table 5. 2, we consider four more models:

- TMCM: A multi-country model due to Taylor (1993b), which is a first-generation New Keynesian model. It is a model with rational expectations, nominal rigidities based on staggered contracts, and an interest-rate policy rule.
- CCTW10: A model due to Cogan, Cwik, Taylor, and Wieland (2010), which extends the SW model. It includes Keynesian rule-of-thumb consumers. This modification affects, for example, the size of the fiscal multipliers and improves fit a little bit.
- CMR14: A model due to Christiano, Motto, and Rostagno (2014), which adds financial frictions and considers postcrisis data.
- IN10: A model of Iacoviello and Neri (2010), which adds a housing market as well as financial frictions.

Cochrane, Taylor, and Wieland

Descriptions of these models and the equations that define the models can be found on the Macro Model Data Base web page.

We report the *relative* standard deviations of inflation and the output gap for the rules compared with the T93 rule. For each of the seven models, we divide outcomes under BA, NPP, and FD with the outcome under the T93 rule. A value of 1, for example, for the standard deviation of inflation indicates that inflation volatility is the same as under the T93 rule. A value above (below) 1 indicates that it performs worse (better) along that dimension than the T93 rule. We make this comparison because the raw standard deviations reflect different standard deviations of shocks as well as different performance. We do not want to say that model A produces smaller inflation variation simply because that model has smaller shocks, for example, if it was fit to a quieter data set.

The results are shown graphically in figure 5.8 for the seven models: NK, OK, SW, TMCM, CCTW10, CMR14, and IN10. We find that the BA rule reduces output gap variability relative to the T93 and the NPP rule in all seven models. In two models, inflation variability under BA is significantly higher than under the T93 and NPP rules. NPP, on the other hand, always reduces inflation variability relative to T93 and BA.

The FD rule delivers the lowest degree of inflation variability in the four additional models, and the lowest output gap volatility in two of them. For the forward-looking models, the unit root in the FD rule seems to be a positive feature, though it causes dynamic instability in the models of the type of the OK model.[5] This lack of robustness illustrates the important and strong differences between new and Old Keynesian models.

The results seem to be consistent with earlier model comparison studies. For example, in a review of one model comparison with

---

5. In figure 8, a value of 2 is chosen to indicate the case of dynamic instability in the OK model.

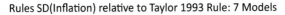

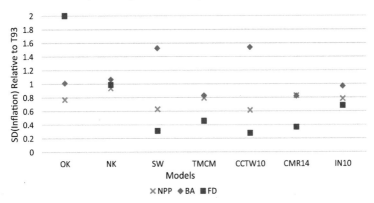

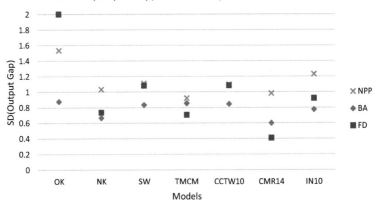

FIGURE 5.8. Standard Deviation of Inflation and Output Gap

Note: The figure shows the standard deviations of inflation and the output gap of each of the rules relative to the Taylor 1993 rule in seven different models. The rules shown are the c rule (BA), the first-difference rule (FD), and the inflation-tilting rule (NPP). The models are as follows: (1) OK model, specification from Rudebusch and Svensson (1999), (2) NK model, specification from Levin, Wieland, and Williams (2003), (3) SW model from Smets and Wouters (2007), (4) TMCM model from Taylor (1993a), (5) CCTW10 model from Cogan, Cwik, Taylor, and Wieland (2010), (6) CMR14 model from Christiano, Motto, and Rostagno (2014), and (7) IN10 model from Iacoviello and Neri (2010).

four rules and eight models, Taylor (1999) reported that rules with lagged dependent variables, such as first difference rules, resulted in large—even infinite—variances as in table 5. 2. The models that performed worse with the first-difference rules were the backward-looking models, again as in table 5. 2.

5.3. Comparison with Optimal Rules in Macroeconomic Models

How good are the four rules considered above relative to an optimal rule within a given model? By "optimal" we mean the best among rules that respond to inflation and output and the lagged interest rate, not to other variables including observable shocks. Specifically, we consider two classes of rules: (1) 2-parameter rules that respond to four-quarter inflation and the output gap, and (2) 4-parameter rules that also include the lagged interest rate and the lag of the output gap similar to the FD rule.

We find optimal response coefficients φ for these rules that solve in each model

$$\underset{\{\varphi\}}{Min} \; Var(\pi) + \lambda Var(y) + Var(\Delta i)$$

$$s.t. \quad i_t = \varphi_\pi \pi_t + \varphi_y y_t + \varphi_{yl} y_{t-1} + \varphi_i i_{t-1}$$

We include the variance of interest rate changes in the objective. Without it, coefficients on inflation and output and the variance of the interest rate become unreasonably large. For a description of the methodology for minimizing the loss function of the variances, see, for example, Levin, Wieland, and Williams (1999).

We solve this problem for different values of the weight λ on the output gap. As a result, we obtain an output-inflation variability trade-off curve as computed in Taylor (1979). We focus on two of the models considered so far, the OK model and the SW model. These two models deliver quite different policy implications, in particular concerning the possible benefits or costs of a first-difference rule relative to a level rule. Furthermore, both models have been estimated and include a full set of shocks.

Figure 5.9 shows the output-inflation variability curves for the OK (upper panel) and SW (lower panel) models. The vertical axis

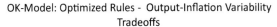

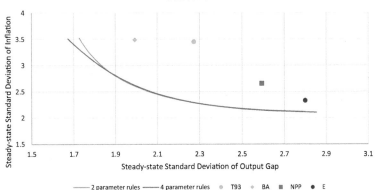

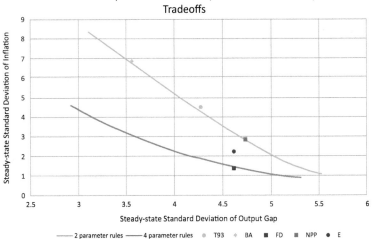

FIGURE 5.9. Output-Inflation Variability Trade-offs

Notes: The curves show the outcomes for the standard deviation of inflation and the output gap for rules, for which the response parameters have been optimized with respect to loss functions with different weights on output and inflation variability. The symbols report outcomes for particular rules such as the T93, BA, FD, NPP rules and estimated rules (E).

denotes the standard deviation of inflation, the horizontal axis the standard deviation of the model-consistent output gap. The trade-off curves are downward sloping through the relevant range. The panels also include outcomes for the standard deviation of inflation and the standard deviation of the output gap for the rules discussed in the previous section.

Figure 5.10 shows the optimal coefficients in the rule for different values of the output variance. For example, in all four panels, as the coefficient on the output gap in the rule goes down the variance of the output gap goes up.

In the OK model, the trade-off curves for 2-parameter and 4-parameter rules are almost identical except for very large weights λ on output gap variance in the loss function. Even then, there is little to be gained from including the lag of the interest rate or the lag of the output gap in the rule. The optimal coefficient on the lagged interest rate is close to zero, as can be seen in the top right-hand-side panel in figure 5.10.

As the weight λ on the variance of the output gap in the loss function is increased, the optimal coefficient on inflation declines and the optimal coefficient on output increases, and consequently, the resulting standard deviation of the output gap (inflation) declines (increases) (see figure 5.10 top left-hand-side panel).

In the SW model, however, the trade-off curve for 4-parameter rules is a good bit closer to the origin than the trade-off curve for 2-parameter rules. Thus, including the lagged interest rate and the fourth lag of the output gap significantly improves outcomes for any weight λ on output gap variability. As shown in figure 5.10, lower right panel, the optimal coefficient on the lagged interest rate is slightly *above* unity for any choice of weight λ.

The outcome under the FD rule lies almost on the 4-parameter trade-off curve or frontier. Similarly, the three level rules, that is, T93, BA, and NPP, are close to the 2-parameter frontier. This means that there is some value of λ for which any of these rules are near optimal within their specific class of rules. By contrast, the OK model indicates that outcomes could be improved substantially by changing the policy coefficients. In particular, it calls

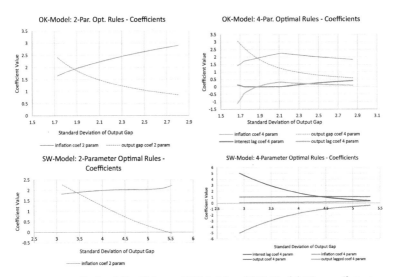

FIGURE 5.10. Optimal Coefficients: OK Model and SW Model. The coefficients shown are the response parameters in the respective rules that have been optimized with respect to loss functions with different weights on output and inflation variability. They correspond to the outcomes for the standard deviations of inflation and the output gap shown in figure 5.9

for higher coefficients on inflation and the output gap. Possibly, a higher weight on interest rate variability would shift the frontier out toward the three rules. The FD rule is not shown because the variance grows without bounds due to dynamic instability.

Given that the optimal coefficient on the lagged interest rate in the SW model is slightly above unity, these optimized rules would all generate dynamic instability in the OK model. Thus, they are not robust as discussed previously.

6. CONCLUSION

To sum up, the purpose of this paper is to examine the policy rules that the Fed has begun to regularly publish in its semiannual *Monetary Policy Reports* during of 2017, 2018, and 2019, as well as on Fed's web page. We address two main questions: Using each rule, how do we interpret the history of rules versus. deviations or discretion? Which rules produce better economic outcomes? For the latter question, we use seven different models: a simple New Keynesian model, a simple Old Keynesian model, a medium-sized policy model, and four models that are part of the Macroeconomic Model Data Base. We compare the policy rules in the Fed's report, plus one more, to each other, to optimal rules from those models, and to actual policy. We thereby create a measure of discretion.

The results show that most of the rules in the Fed's report would have worked well and roughly similarly. The results also show that the rules reported by the Fed are close to the optimal rules within a certain class. The first difference rule is an outlier. The Fed needs to clarify if indeed it means to accept yesterday's actual interest rate as today's "rule." The first difference rule also works very well but only in forward-looking models. It is disastrous in models with backward-looking expectations. We note that most policy discussion reflects such models, in which inflation stability rather than indeterminacy is the main concern of monetary policy.

The deviations from the rules show that there was much discretion in the 1970s. These discretionary actions coincided with poor economic performance. In contrast, the measures of discretion with all the rules reported by the Fed were small in most of the 1980s and 1990s, a period of relatively good macroeconomic performance. The measures of discretion began to grow again in the early 2000s, though they did not get as large as in the 1970s, and we noted that this occurred just prior to the Great Recession.

We close with a question that we are pursuing in follow-up research. Central bankers defend discretion, or adjusting interest rates in response to variables and shocks not included in these simple rules, as stabilizing. By responding to other events, they can, in principle, deliver lower output and inflation variance than these simple rules produce. If they are able to do so in practice, however, output and inflation volatility should be *lower* if one *includes* monetary policy disturbances than if one leaves them out. The observed monetary policy disturbances should, in effect, be negatively correlated with right-hand variables, in such a way as to produce less variance. The relative variation of output and inflation when residuals are included or excluded therefore can provide a measure of the benefits of discretion.

One can check this by computing perfect tracking residuals: Find the time-series of shocks that makes a model, with a given policy rule, exactly account for the data. Then, turn off the monetary policy shocks, simulate the model with the remaining historical shocks, and see if predicted inflation and output turn out to be less variable in this simulation than they were in history. Future research could also use the methods in this paper to evaluate policy rules in other countries that have been presented and discussed by other central banks.

References

Ball, Lawrence. 1999. "Efficient Rules for Monetary Policy." *International Finance* 2, no.1 (April): 63–83.

Board of Governors of the Federal Reserve System. 2019. *Monetary Policy Report,* February 22. Washington, DC: Board of Governors. https://www.federalreserve .gov/monetarypolicy/files/20190222_mprfullreport.pdf.

Christiano, Lawrence, Martin Eichenbaum, and Charles Evans. 2005. "Nominal Rigidities and the Dynamic Effects of a Shock to Monetary Policy." *Journal of Political Economy* 113, no. 1 (February): 1–45.

Christiano, Lawrence, Roberto Motto, and Massimo Rostagno. 2014. "Risk Shocks." *American Economic Review* 104, no. 1 (January): 27–65.

Cochrane, John H. 2011a. "Determinacy and Identification with Taylor Rules." *Journal of Political Economy* 119, no. 3 (June): 565–615.

———. 2011b. Appendix to "Determinacy and Identification with Taylor Rules." https://faculty.chicagobooth.edu/john.cochrane/research/papers/taylor_rule _jpe_final.pdf.

———. 2017. "The New-Keynesian Liquidity Trap." *Journal of Monetary Economics* 92 (December): 47–63.

Cogan, John, Tobias Cwik, John B. Taylor, and Volker Wieland. 2010. "New Keynesian versus Old Keynesian Government Spending Multipliers." *Journal of Economic Dynamics and Control* 34, no. 3 (March): 281–95.

Friedman, Milton. 1982. "Monetary Policy: Theory and Practice." *Journal of Money, Credit and Banking* 14, no. 1 (February): 98–118.

Goodfriend, Marvin, and Robert King. 1997. "The New Neoclassical Synthesis and the Role of Monetary Policy." *NBER Macroeconomics Annual*, vol. 12, edited by Ben S. Bernanke and Julio Rotemberg, 231–96. Cambridge, MA: MIT Press.

Iacoviello, M., and S. Neri. 2010. "Housing Market Spillovers: Evidence from an Estimated DSGE Model." *American Economic Journal: Macroeconomics* 2, no. 2 (April): 125–64.

Kahn, George A. 2012. "The Taylor Rule and the Practice of Central Banking." In *The Taylor Rule and the Transformation of Monetary Policy*, edited by Evan F. Koenig, Robert Leeson, and George A. Kahn, 63–102. Stanford, CA: Hoover Institution Press.

Levin, Andrew, Volker Wieland, and John C. Williams. 2003. "The Performance of Forecast-Based Monetary Policy Rules under Model Uncertainty." *American Economic Review* 93, no. 3 (June): 622–45.

McCallum, Bennett. 1999. "Issues in the Design of Monetary Policy Rules." In *Handbook of Macroeconomics*, volume 1C, edited by John B. Taylor and Michael Woodford, 1483–530. Amsterdam: Elsevier.

Meltzer, Allan. 2012. "Federal Reserve Policy in the Great Recession." *Cato Journal* 32, no. 2 (Spring/Summer): 255–63.

Nikolsko-Rzhevskyy, Alex, David H. Papell, and Ruxandra Prodan. 2014. "Deviations from Rules-Based Policy and Their Effects." *Journal of Economic Dynamics and Control* 49 (December): 4–17.

———. 2018. "Policy Rules and Economic Performance," Unpublished working paper, University of Houston, December 11.

Orphanides, Athanasios, and Volker Wieland. 2000. "Inflation Zone Targeting." *European Economic Review* 44, no. 7 (June): 1351–87.

———. 2003. "Historical Monetary Policy Analysis and the Taylor Rule." *Journal of Monetary Economics* 50, no. 5 (July): 983–1022.

Rotemberg, Julio J., and Michael Woodford. 1997. "An Optimization-Based Econometric Framework for the Evaluation of Monetary Policy." In *NBER Macroeconomics Annual*, vol. 12, edited by Ben S. Bernanke and Julio Rotemberg, 297–361. Cambridge, MA: MIT Press.

———. 1999. "Interest Rate Rules in an Estimated Sticky Price Model." In *Monetary Policy Rules,* edited by John B. Taylor, 57–126. Chicago: University of Chicago Press.

Rudebusch, Glenn, and Lars E. O. Svensson. 1999. "Policy Rules for Inflation Targeting." In *Monetary Policy Rules,* edited by John B. Taylor, 203–62. Chicago: University of Chicago Press.

Smets, Frank, and Rafael Wouters. 2007. "Shocks and Frictions in U.S. Business Cycles: A Bayesian DSGE Approach." *American Economic Review* 97, no. 3 (June): 586–606.

Taylor, John B. 1979. "Estimation and Control of a Macroeconomic Model with Rational Expectations." *Econometrica* 47, no. 5 (September): 1267–86.

———. 1993a. "Discretion versus Policy Rules in Practice." *Carnegie-Rochester Conference Series on Public Policy* 39 (December): 195–214.

———. 1993b. *Macroeconomic Policy in a World Economy: From Econometric Design to Practical Operation.* New York: W. W. Norton.

———. 1999. "Introductory Remarks on Monetary Policy Rules." In *Monetary Policy Rules,* edited by John B. Taylor, 1–14. Chicago: University of Chicago Press.

———. 2012. "Monetary Policy Rules Work and Discretion Doesn't: A Tale of Two Eras." *Journal of Money, Credit and Banking* 44, no. 6 (September): 1017–32.

Taylor, John B., and Volker Wieland. 2012. "Surprising Comparative Properties of Monetary Models: Results from a New Model Database." *Review of Economics and Statistics* 94, no. 3 (August): 800–816.

Tetlow, Robert. 2015. "Real-Time Model Uncertainty in the United States: 'Robust' Policies Put to the Test." *International Journal of Central Banking* 11, no. 2 (March), 113–55.

Teryoshin, Yevgeniy. 2017. "Historical Performance of Rule-Like Monetary Policy." Working Paper No. 17-005, Stanford Institute for Economic Policy Research, February.

Wieland, Volker. 2019. Macro Model Data Base. www.macromodelbase.com.

Wieland, Volker, Elena Afanasyeva, Meguy Kuete, and Jinhyuk Yoo. 2016. "New Methods for Macro-Financial Model Comparison and Policy Analysis." In *Handbook of Macroeconomics,* vol. 2, edited by John Taylor and Harald Uhlig, 1241–319. Amsterdam: Elsevier.

Woodford, Michael. 2003. *Interest and Prices: Foundations of a Theory of Monetary Policy.* Princeton. NJ: Princeton University Press.

DISCUSSANT REMARKS

David Papell

The paper by Cochrane, Taylor, and Wieland (which I will subsequently refer to as CTW) is about two subjects, evaluating rules in
the Fed's *Monetary Policy Report* and measuring discretion. I will
first discuss the two subjects and then combine the two by talking
about evaluating rules by measuring policy rule deviations.

Figure 5.11 is a picture of a universe of policy rules of the form
introduced by Taylor (1993a),

$$i_t = \pi_t + \alpha(\pi_t - \pi^*) + \gamma y_t + R^* \tag{1}$$

where i_t is the target level of the federal funds rate, π_t is the inflation
rate, π^* is the target level of inflation, y_t is the output gap, the percent deviation of actual real GDP from an estimate of its potential
level, and R^* is the neutral real interest rate that is consistent with
output equal to potential output and inflation equal to the target
level of inflation.

The inflation gap, the difference between inflation and target inflation, is on the vertical axis and the output gap is on the horizontal
axis. The coefficients on the two gaps are between 0.1 and 1.0 with
increments of 0.1, so the figure depicts one hundred rules. The coefficients on inflation are greater than one, so they satisfy the Taylor
principle and provide a stable inflation target. The coefficients on the
output gap are also positive, so they satisfy the dual mandate.

CTW analyze three of these rules in seven well-known macroeconomic models. (They also analyze a first-difference rule.) The
rules are highlighted in figure 5.11. Two of the rules are in the

---

This paper is based on joint work with my two coauthors, Alex Nikolsko-Rzhevskyy and
Ruxandra Prodan.

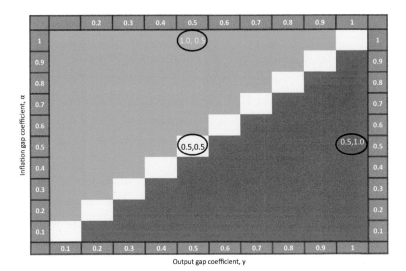

FIGURE 5.11. Policy Rules. The cells in the figure represent balanced policy rules on the 45-degree line as in Taylor (1993a), output gap–tilting rules below the 45-degree line as in Yellen (2012), and inflation gap–tilting rules above the 45-degree line as in Nikolsko-Rzhevskyy, Papell, and Prodan (2019).

Monetary Policy Report. The first rule is the Taylor (1993a) rule with $\alpha = \gamma = 0.5$. We call this a balanced rule because it has the same coefficients on the inflation gap and the output gap and, maybe more important, it has the property that the same change in the inflation gap and the output gap produces the same effect on the real interest rate. It is not the only balanced rule, as all of the rules on the upward-sloping 45-degree line have the same coefficients on the two gaps.

The second rule in the *Monetary Policy Report* analyzed by CTW has $\alpha = 0.5$ and $\gamma = 1.0$. This is an example of an output gap–tilting rule because it has a higher coefficient on the output gap than on the inflation gap. Yellen (2012) called this rule the "balanced-approach rule," and that is the terminology used in the *Monetary Policy Report.* I think this is a brilliant marketing strategy, because what's the opposite of a balanced-approach rule? An unbalanced-approach rule, and we wouldn't want an unbalanced rule. It is not the only output gap–tilting rule, as all of the rules below and to the right of the 45-degree line have higher coefficients on the output gap than the inflation gap. CTW also analyze a rule with $\alpha = 1.0$ and $\gamma = 0.5$, which is not in the *Monetary Policy Report*. They call it the NPP rule following Nikolsko-Rzhevskyy, Papell, and Prodan (2019). It is an example of an inflation gap–tilting rule because the coefficients are above and to the left of the 45-degree line.

The first part of the CTW paper involves evaluating policy rules. They compute optimal policies and inflation-output variance trade-off curves and compare economic performance under model-specific optimal policies with performance under the four policy rules. As in Taylor and Wieland (2012), there is a lot of robustness across the models except for the first-difference rule.

Smets and Wouters (2007) present one of the models analyzed by CTW. Using this model, we ask the following question. Out of the one hundred rules, which are the twenty best, the next twenty, and so on? The answer is provided in figure 5.12. Inflation gap–tilting rules are clearly the best, followed by balanced and output gap–tilting rules. Among the three rules considered by CTW, the NPP (2019) rule is in the first (best) quintile, the Taylor (1993a) rule is in the third (middle) quintile, and the Yellen (2012) rule is in the fourth (second from worst) quintile. Similar results are found using the Christiano, Eichenbaum, and Evans (2005) and Taylor (1993b) models.

We then ask the same question using the Federal Reserve Board—United States (FRB-US) model, which is not analyzed by CTW. The results are shown in figure 5.13, and they are completely opposite from those using the Smets and Wouters (2007) model. The output gap–tilting rules are clearly the best, followed by the balanced and the inflation gap–tilting rules. Among the three rules considered by CTW, the Yellen (2012) rule is in the first quintile, the Taylor (1993a) rule is in the third quintile, and the NPP (2019) rule is in the fourth quintile.

	0.1	0.2	0.3	0.4	0.5	0.6	0.7	0.8	0.9	1	
1	29.97	29.45	29.40	29.76	(30.46)	31.45	32.69	34.15	35.80	37.61	1
0.9	29.94	29.48	29.58	30.14	31.08	32.36	33.91	35.70	37.68	39.84	0.9
0.8	29.95	29.60	29.89	30.72	32.00	33.64	35.59	37.79	40.20	42.78	0.8
0.7	30.03	29.83	30.41	31.62	33.34	35.47	37.94	40.67	43.62	46.73	0.7
0.6	30.23	30.27	31.28	33.02	35.36	38.16	41.31	44.74	48.38	52.18	0.6
0.5	30.62	31.07	32.72	35.27	(38.49)	42.22	46.32	50.68	55.23	(59.90)	0.5
0.4	31.38	32.56	35.26	39.05	43.59	48.66	54.07	59.69	65.44	71.23	0.4
0.3	32.95	35.51	40.06	45.87	52.45	59.49	66.76	74.10	81.41	88.62	0.3
0.2	36.69	42.21	50.23	59.51	69.35	79.32	89.17	98.76	107.99	116.84	0.2
0.1	48.82	61.39	76.24	91.45	106.16	120.02	132.92	144.85	155.85	165.99	0.1
	0.1	0.2	0.3	0.4	0.5	0.6	0.7	0.8	0.9	1	

Inflation gap coefficient, α (vertical axis label)

Output gap coefficient, γ

FIGURE 5.12. Smets and Wouters (2007) Model. The cells in the figure depict quadratic loss functions for each policy rule with lower values preferred to higher values

Let's look at this more generally. Take the best twenty rules from the first quintile of the Smets and Wouters (2007) model and put them in the FRB-US model. Fifteen of the rules are in the fifth quintile while five are in the fourth quintile. Now take the best twenty rules from the first quintile of the FRB-US model and put them in the Smets and Wouters (2007) model. Sixteen of the rules are in the fifth quintile while four are in the fourth quintile. The message in CTW is one of robustness across models. Including the FRB-US model, which is very different from those considered by CTW, you end up with much less robustness. I think this should give you pause about making definitive conclusions from any one model, or even a class of models if it's not a wide enough class.

The second part of the paper involves measuring discretion by calculating deviations from the Taylor (1993a) rule with data that, except for using the actual federal funds rate instead of a shadow federal funds rate during the 2009–2015 period, are identical to the data in NPP (2019). The authors depict the well-known pattern of

α \ y	0.1	0.2	0.3	0.4	0.5	0.6	0.7	0.8	0.9	1
1	70.54	68.39	66.60	65.14	(63.97)	63.05	62.36	61.88	61.57	61.44
0.9	70.04	67.86	66.05	64.58	63.40	62.49	61.80	61.33	61.04	60.92
0.8	69.57	67.36	65.52	64.04	62.85	61.95	61.27	60.81	60.53	60.42
0.7	69.13	66.88	65.02	63.52	62.33	61.43	60.76	60.31	60.04	59.95
0.6	68.72	66.42	64.53	63.02	61.83	60.93	60.28	59.83	59.58	59.50
0.5	68.34	65.99	64.08	62.55	(61.36)	60.46	59.82	59.39	59.15	(59.09)
0.4	67.99	65.59	63.65	62.10	60.91	60.02	59.39	58.97	58.75	58.70
0.3	67.67	65.22	63.25	61.69	60.50	59.61	58.98	58.58	58.37	58.33
0.2	67.39	64.88	62.88	61.31	60.11	59.23	58.61	58.22	58.02	58.00
0.1	67.14	64.58	62.54	60.96	59.76	58.88	58.27	57.89	57.71	57.69

Inflation gap coefficient, α (vertical axis)

Output gap coefficient, y (horizontal axis)

FIGURE 5.13. FRB-US Model. The cells in the figure depict quadratic loss functions for each policy rule with lower values preferred to higher values

high deviations in the 1970s and early eighties, low deviations in the Great Moderation period, and an increase in deviations during the 2003–2005 period. Their visual evidence is supported by structural change tests on the absolute value of the deviations, as in Nikolsko-Rzhevskyy, Papell, and Prodan (2014). The deviations are very large in the Great Inflation and Volcker Disinflation periods, are very low during the Great Moderation, and increase starting in 2001, although not to the levels before 1985.

I will conclude by discussing evaluating policy rules by measuring deviations. In NPP (2019), we calculate deviations from the one hundred policy rules discussed above with coefficients on the inflation and output gaps from 0.1 to 1.0 and divide the sample into high- and low-deviations periods. We then evaluate the rules by calculating quadratic loss ratios with the two gaps for the high- and low-deviations periods, with a "good" rule having worse performance during high-deviations periods than during low-deviations periods so that the quadratic loss ratio is greater than one. The central results of the paper are (1) economic performance is better

	0.1	0.2	0.3	0.4	0.5	0.6	0.7	0.8	0.9	1.0	
1.0	3.29	3.17	3.33	3.46	3.44	3.87	3.84	4.33	5.59	4.79	**1.0**
0.9	3.04	3.11	3.11	3.30	3.29	2.96	3.39	3.33	3.63	3.50	**0.9**
0.8	2.53	2.54	2.63	2.76	3.16	3.10	3.10	3.31	4.12	3.46	**0.8**
0.7	2.54	2.56	2.67	2.92	3.10	3.27	3.54	2.93	3.06	2.62	**0.7**
0.6	2.27	2.37	2.54	2.73	3.03	3.06	3.12	2.76	2.25	2.06	**0.6**
0.5	1.93	2.00	2.07	2.56	2.82	2.93	3.01	2.39	2.15	1.82	**0.5**
0.4	1.88	2.08	2.11	2.36	2.47	2.40	2.36	2.26	2.23	1.85	**0.4**
0.3	1.98	1.87	1.82	1.96	1.99	1.97	2.09	1.99	1.95	1.48	**0.3**
0.2	1.65	1.74	1.75	1.83	1.79	1.80	1.67	1.80	1.75	1.43	**0.2**
0.1	1.13	1.21	1.26	1.26	1.39	1.38	1.28	1.37	1.58	1.31	**0.1**
0.0	0.1	0.2	0.3	0.4	0.5	0.6	0.7	0.8	0.9	1.0	**0.0**

Inflation gap coefficient, α (vertical axis)

Output gap coefficient, γ

FIGURE 5.14. Quadratic Loss Ratios. The cells in the figure depict quadratic loss ratios, the loss in high deviations periods divided by the loss in low deviations periods, for each policy rule. Higher values are preferred to lower values

in low-deviations periods than in high-deviations periods for the vast majority of rules and (2) inflation gap–tilting rules are preferred to output gap–tilting rules. This is illustrated in figure 5.14. Among the three rules considered by CTW, the NPP rule is in the first quintile, the Taylor (1993a) rule is in the second quintile, and the Yellen (2012) rule is in the fourth quintile. The policy recommendation from the paper is to put what CTW call the NPP rule in the Fed's *Monetary Policy Report* in addition to the Taylor (1993a) and Yellen (2012) rules.

References

Christiano, Lawrence, Martin Eichenbaum, and Charles Evans. 2005. "Nominal Rigidities and the Dynamic Effects of a Shock to Monetary Policy." *Journal of Political Economy* 113, no. 1 (February): 1–45.

Nikolsko-Rzhevskyy, Alex, David H. Papell, and Ruxandra Prodan. 2014. "Deviations from Rules-Based Policy and Their Effects." *Journal of Economic Dynamics and Control* 49 (December): 4–17.

———— [NPP]. 2019. "Policy Rules and Economic Performance." Unpublished manuscript, University of Houston.

Smets, Frank, and Rafael Wouters. 2007. "Shocks and Frictions in U.S. Business Cycles: A Bayesian DSGE Approach." *American Economic Review* 97, no. 3 (June): 586–606.

Taylor, John B. 1993a. "Discretion versus Policy Rules in Practice." *Carnegie-Rochester Conference Series on Public Policy* 39 (December): 195–214.

————. 1993b. *Macroeconomic Policy in a World Economy: From Econometric Design to Practical Operation.* New York: W. W. Norton.

Taylor, John B., and Volker Wieland. 2012. "Surprising Comparative Properties of Monetary Models: Results from a New Model Database." *Review of Economics and Statistics* 94, no. 3 (August): 800–816.

Yellen, Janet. 2012. "Perspectives on Monetary Policy." Speech at the Boston Economic Club Dinner, June 6.

SYMPOSIUM
"The Interaction of Markets
and Policy"

Introduction

George P. Shultz

This discussion of the interaction of markets and policy contributes to the Fed's review of its strategies and its communication policy. But here are some comments that I offer for the Fed. First, when I was secretary of the Treasury, I appointed a little committee to advise, and I persuaded my friend Bill Martin, former chairman of the Fed, to become a member of it. After I left office, I also became a member. We were sitting and having a discussion, and Bill Miller, who then was chairman of the Fed, came to see us. He was for some reason getting worried about foreign exchange problems and he was worried about the dollar. He said, "I've said *this* about the dollar, I've said *this* about the dollar. What should I say about the dollar?" And there was a sort of dead silence. Then Bill Martin's squeaky voice came, "You should say *less.*" There's a point there.

Then there's another suggestion. You remember the great slugger Ted Williams from the Red Sox? He was the last major leaguer to hit .400. He never said much, and some reporter yelled to him once, "Hey, Ted. Why aren't you talking?" He said, "I let my bat do the talking." The Fed has a big bat, and of course it can say something. But I think it should take the advice of Bill Martin and Ted Williams, because sometimes the talk is confusing. And the more you talk, the more you get drawn into politics, almost inevitably. It's better off to stay out of it.

My second point is a little different. And it is my worry in particular, not with the Fed so much as, generally, that people forget that classical, orthodox Milton Friedman–like policies have worked. When you analyze things and say, "Oh my gosh, everything's different, so we'll have to have new policies," watch out, because classical, orthodox policies work.

Here's an example. In the Kennedy administration, they wanted to get the economy moving again. They worried about inflation, so the Council of Economic Advisers put out a view in favor of what were called "guidelines" for wage and price changes, guidelines to steer companies and others on what they should do. I read this and I worried a little, because it's the conceptual underpinning of wage and price controls. So, I had a conference at the University of Chicago, where I was teaching on the subject, and Milton Friedman came and gave a terrific talk. Bob Solow came and talked about the case; its title was "The Case against the Case against the Guidelines." It was a very lively discussion, and then we published a book on it, so the subject was on my mind.

Then I was appointed secretary of labor under Richard Nixon, and that was a different atmosphere. I was worried about interfering in large labor disputes and discrimination in the workplace, and was working with Pat Moynihan on welfare reform and other things. And all of a sudden, I became the first director of the Office of Management and Budget. I found out that the chairman of the Fed, Arthur Burns, saw that a big financial company named Penn Central had mismanaged its affairs and was about to go bankrupt. He thought that would have a terrible impact on the financial markets and was considering a government bailout. I observed that Helmut Schmidt, former minister of finance and chancellor of Germany, thought Arthur was the "pope of economics." He called him infallible, but I thought he was wrong. So I found myself arguing with Burns in the Oval Office, with half of me saying, "What am I doing, arguing with Arthur Burns about financial markets?"

In walked a guy named Bryce Harlow, who was a smart political adviser. He said, "Mr. President, in its infinite wisdom, the Penn Central has just hired your old law firm to represent them in this matter. Under the circumstances, you can't touch this with a ten-foot pole." So there was no bailout. And guess what? The financial markets were strengthened, because people saw that and avoided the bailout mentality, which is: we can get away with anything and they'll bail us out. So, I thought, you know, Arthur could be fallible. He did one good thing: he flooded the market with liquidity, which is, it seems to me, what the Fed's role should be. See that there's plenty of liquidity, but don't intervene.

Later, we were worried about inflation. As I said, I had the guidelines experience, so I could somehow smell wage and price controls coming, and I gave a speech called "Steady As You Go." The argument was: we had the budget under control, we had sensible monetary policies, and if we were willing to stick with it, then inflation would come under control—steady as you go. Well, I lost, and wage and price controls were put into effect. I knew that Burns was in favor of them, but not too long ago I discovered in the Hoover archives a letter from Arthur Burns, chairman of the Fed, to President Richard Nixon. The argument of the letter was as follows: The economy has changed, and it's much more rigid than it was before, partly due to trade unions; therefore, classical monetary policy won't work. So what do you have to do? Wage and price controls.

I realized then why I lost so definitively. But what was produced was a failure of the US economy, a miserable decade, thanks, in part, to the chairman of the Fed. I resigned as secretary of the Treasury when Nixon reimposed the controls over my objections.

When I came back with Ronald Reagan in 1980, inflation was in the teens and the economy was going nowhere. That's what this innovative policy had produced. Paul Volcker was at the Fed at the time. He'd been my under secretary when I was secretary of the Treasury, and I knew him well. We talked, and I could see he was doing what needed to be done at that time. People kept running into the Oval Office saying, "Mr. President, Mr. President, it's going to cause a recession. We're going to lose seats in the midterm election." Reagan knew that we had to get rid of inflation if we were going to have a decent economy and that Paul Volcker was doing the right thing, so he basically put a political umbrella over him. Paul told me that he noticed on many occasions that the press would float up a question to the president, inviting him to take on the Fed, but the president always brushed off those questions.

By the time 1982 came to an end, we did have a recession and we did lose seats. But by that time, inflation was clearly under control, and it was obvious that it was going to stay that way. The tax changes that had been put into effect and the regulatory withdrawal kicked in, and the economy took off like a bird. So the lesson is that thinking you should have an unorthodox policy because everything has changed did not work. Paul Volcker proved that, despite Arthur's analysis, classical policy *did* work. So that's my message: be careful when you stray too far away from policies that work.

CHAPTER SIX

THE INTERACTION OF MARKETS AND POLICY: A CORPORATE FINANCE PERSPECTIVE

Laurie Simon Hodrick

Our panel has been asked to consider the interaction of markets and policy. In my remarks today, I will specifically consider the interaction between the stock market and the monetary policy of the Federal Reserve, which is set to foster economic conditions that achieve the dual-mandate objectives of maximal employment and price stability (targeted as a 2 percent inflation rate). I want to reconcile seemingly conflicting evidence when we interpret the stock market in its aggregate and when we consider an individual firm that trades in the market.

As we consider stocks in the market, there are important differences between common, or correlated, risks and idiosyncratic, or independent, risks. When we combine many stocks into a portfolio, firm-specific risks diversify away, while systematic risks remain. This important insight is helpful in understanding the drivers by which Fed policy does and does not affect valuations, at both the firm and aggregate levels.

Let's look first at the firm level. Although we know that firm-specific risk diversifies in the aggregate, this does not reduce the importance of idiosyncratic factors to a particular firm. Hence, while all corporations monitor, evaluate, and forecast the macroeconomic environment, and thus implicitly engage in a degree of Fed watching, firms and the investors who value them are also intensely concerned about that firm's own microeconomic prospects, not only in the short term but also in the medium and longer terms. Let me develop this logic through the lens of corporate finance.

When we value a firm in corporate finance, one common approach is to use the discounted free cash flow model. We calculate the present value of the expected stream of future free cash flows that the firm will have available to pay its investors:

$$\text{Firm Value} = \text{PV(Future Free Cash Flows)} = \sum_{t=1}^{\infty} \frac{FCF_t}{(1+r)^t}$$

In the next few minutes I will identify the key drivers of this valuation, with the goal of identifying where Fed policy does, and does not, have a first-order effect on the value of a specific firm.

Let's start with the discount rate, r, which is the cost of capital used to take the present value of the forecasted future free cash flows:

$$r = WACC = \frac{E}{(D+E)} r_e^L + \frac{D}{(E+D)} (1 - \tau_C) r_D$$

For unit consistency between the cash flows and their discount rate, we use firm enterprise-level values after corporate taxation, typically in nominal terms. Here the firm's WACC is its weighted average cost of capital, the effective after-tax cost of capital to the firm. Since WACC equals the weighted average of the cost of equity and the after-tax cost of debt, its three critical components are the cost of equity, r_e^L, the after-tax cost of debt, $(1 - \tau_C) r_D$, and the weights that reflect the firm's leverage ratio, $\dfrac{D}{(E+D)}$. Using Capital Asset Pricing Model (CAPM) methodology, for example, this entails a nominal risk-free rate, the expected market risk premium, the company's equity beta, the company's debt beta, the marginal corporate tax rate, and a market measure of the proportion of debt to firm value.[1]

Which of these key drivers are and are not affected by Fed policy? Since all firms' costs of capital are derived similarly, firms are commonly affected through the risk-free rate, the equity risk premium, and the tax code, and individually affected through their beta units of priced risk and their leverage. Monetary policy affects the risk-free rate through the rate the Fed sets, and uncertainty about future policy affects the risk premia. It is the firm's asset risk and debt capacity, though, which are unaffected by monetary policy, that uniquely define their cost of capital.

Let's next consider the free cash flows, which each year equal the earnings generated from both core and new investments:

$$FCF_t = NOPLAT_t - Net\ Investment_t$$

To capture cash flows from current investments, we measure $NOPLAT_t$, net operating profit less adjusted taxes. To capture cash flows from investment in new capital, we measure $Net\ Investment_t$. Firms decide how to deploy and allocate their capital, choosing between investments and payments to claimants. A firm's net investment creates value when it is positive net present value, that is, when it earns a risk-adjusted rate of return above the firm's WACC. Said differently, because investment reduces free cash flows in the short run, to be warranted an investment must generate sufficiently larger free cash flows in the future.

Which of these key drivers are or are not affected by Fed policy? Since all firms' free cash flows are derived similarly, firms are commonly affected through aggregate business cycles and aggregate

---

1. Although here the notation for the discount rate is not maturity dependent, if there is a slope to the term structure, then discount rates will be different for different maturities.

long-term growth rates, including long-term inflation, and individually affected through their specific business conditions and investment opportunities. Monetary policy clearly affects inflation and may affect aggregate cyclical conditions. It is the firm's current competitive advantage and longer-term real growth opportunities, though, which are unaffected by monetary policy, that uniquely define their free cash flows.

Collectively, therefore, monetary policy can affect the risk-free rate and inflation, the risk premium, and the business cycle. It does not, however, affect a firm's asset risk, specific debt capacity, or idiosyncratic business conditions and investment opportunities that generate long-term real growth.

At the firm level, vector autoregressions allow us to decompose innovations in stock returns into news about cash flows and news about discount rates. At the firm level, news about expected future cash flows is an important determinant of firm stock returns. Vuolteenaho (2002), for example, shows that for stock returns at the firm level, the variance of news about cash flows is twice that of the variance of news about discount rates. This suggests a limited role for monetary policy's impact on individual stock returns. As an example of the extremely idiosyncratic nature of firm valuations, *The Economist* analyzed a set of twelve former and current internet-focused unicorns to better understand their current valuations.[2] To justify their current valuations, these twelve firms each must be expected to increase their sales by a compound annual rate of 49 percent for ten years. That expectation equals the actual realization of the extraordinary growth enjoyed by Amazon, Alphabet, and Facebook in the decade after their IPOs.

---

2. Unicorns are private companies each with a valuation of at least one billion dollars, and these twelve companies have a combined value in excess of a third of a trillion dollars. Currently, there are 344 unicorns worldwide, and *The Economist*'s set of twelve includes Uber, which went public on May 10, 2019. "Herd Instincts" (2019).

How does this firm-level analysis map to the aggregate stock market? Since much of the cash flow news is idiosyncratic, it can be diversified away, while since much of the discount rate news is correlated across firms, it cannot be diversified away. At the aggregate level, Campbell (1991, 1996, and subsequent research) finds that news about future cash flows accounts for much less of the variance of unexpected stock returns than does news about future discount rates. As highlighted earlier, only a subset of the innovations of the discount rate is driven by Fed policy, limiting the Fed's impact. As Cochrane (2008) notes in his chapter in the *Handbook of the Equity Risk Premium*, "almost all stock price movements are due to changing expected excess returns . . . meaning that we have to tie the stock market movements to the macroeconomy entirely through harder to measure time-varying risk premia."

What is the role of the Fed in affecting risk premia? By conducting monetary policy that predictably follows well-understood rules, the Fed can minimize its contribution to aggregate uncertainty, and thus reduce its impact on time-varying risk premia. This is consistent with the model in Pastor and Veronesi (2012) wherein policy changes increase volatility, risk premia, and correlations among stocks. Increased policy uncertainty, as modeled, for example, in Bloom (2009), can also affect aggregate investment and hiring decisions. At the firm level, increases in uncertainty increase the value of real options, including the option to delay investment.

The Fed can also reduce uncertainty by consistently and transparently regulating the banking system. These actions are consistent with financial stability being a goal sought by regulators.[3]

The interaction of markets and policy is actually a full circle. Not only are firm valuations affected by Fed policy, as I have considered

3. Another essential function of the Federal Reserve is to manage the central payment system, which has the potential to be transformed by the distributed ledger technology, as I discussed at the Hoover Structural Foundations of Monetary Policy conference in 2017. See Hodrick (2018).

today, but the Fed also interprets data from the economy, including stock market price levels, as additional noisy signals with which to set its policy. Cieslak and Vissing-Jorgensen (2017), for example, study the impact of the stock market on the Federal Reserve's monetary policy when analyzing the economics behind Greenspan's "Fed put." I expect that the other panelists will discuss this further.

References

Bloom, Nicholas. 2009. "The Impact of Uncertainty Shocks." *Econometrica* 77, no. 3: 623–85.

Campbell, John Y. 1991. "A Variance Decomposition for Stock Returns." *Economic Journal* 101, no. 405: 157–79.

———. 1996. "Understanding Risk and Return." *Journal of Political Economy* 104, no. 2: 298–345.

Cieslak, Anna, and Annette Vissing-Jorgensen. 2017. "The Economics of the Fed Put." Unpublished manuscript, University of California-Berkeley.

Cochrane, John H. 2008. "Financial Markets and the Real Economy." In *Handbook of the Equity Risk Premium,* edited by Rajnish Mehra. Amsterdam: Elsevier.

"Herd Instincts." 2019. *The Economist,* April 20.

Hodrick, Laurie Simon. 2018. "Payment Systems and the Distributed Ledger Technology." In *The Structural Foundations of Monetary Policy,* edited by Michael Bordo, John Cochrane, and Amit Seru. Stanford, CA: Hoover Institution Press.

Pastor, Lubus, and Pietro Veronesi. 2012. "Uncertainty about Government Policy and Stock Prices." *Journal of Finance* 67, no. 4: 1219–64.

Vuolteenaho, Tuomo. 2002. "What Drives Firm-Level Stock Returns?" *Journal of Finance* 57, no. 1: 233–64.

CHAPTER SEVEN

THE FED AND FINANCIAL MARKETS: SUGGESTIONS TO IMPROVE AN UNHEALTHY RELATIONSHIP

Mickey D. Levy

The Fed's relationship with financial markets has become increasingly unhealthy. It's natural for the Fed to look to financial markets as an input to its monetary policy and for financial markets to respond to the Fed's policies and forward guidance. But the Fed's excessive fine-tuning of the economy and financial markets—much of which is unnecessary to achieve its longer-run dual mandate—has created an environment of gamesmanship and "tilts" that have added financial market volatility and harmed economic performance.

This unhealthy relationship has been accentuated by the expanded scope of the Fed's objectives and the broader set of tools it uses to achieve its goals, which have added unnecessary complexities to its operating procedures and communications. Markets are not going to stop responding to what the Fed does and says. The Fed needs to retrain markets but can do so only by breaking some of its bad habits: it must readdress its strategy for achieving its mandated goals, and modify its communications.

Mickey D. Levy is chief economist of Berenberg Capital Markets LLC for the Americas and Asia. The views expressed in this paper are the author's own and do not necessarily reflect those of Berenberg Capital Markets LLC. The author would like to thank Charles Calomiris, Jim Dorn, Peter Fisher, Andrew Levin, Charles Plosser, Roiana Reid, and Scott Richard for their helpful suggestions.

THE FED'S BROADENED SCOPE OF
OBJECTIVES AND POLICY TOOLS

During the Volcker-Greenspan regimes, the Fed made it clear that stable low inflation and well-anchored inflationary expectations were the best contributions monetary policy could make to achieve its dual mandate. That overriding message was clear and the markets understood it. Interest rates were the Fed's nearly exclusive policy tool. Certainly, during the Great Moderation the Fed occasionally deviated from its primary objective—in 1987, in response to the weakening US dollar; in the early 1990s, to the mild recession and slow recovery; and in the 1990s, Greenspan's clear response to the stock market—but the Fed did not persistently fine-tune financial markets.

Since then, the Fed's reaction function has evolved, particularly since the 2008–2009 financial crisis. Subject to its 2 percent inflation target, besides maximizing employment, the Fed now focuses on managing short-term fluctuations in the economy, influencing fluctuations in financial market expectations, and maintaining financial stability. As long as inflation is within the Fed's 2 percent target and inflationary expectations are well anchored, the Fed perceives the flexibility to pursue other objectives. Financial markets are well aware of the Fed's discretionary approach to these broader objectives and respond accordingly, which heightens market volatility.

Many of these Fed objectives have not been well defined, or the Fed interprets and adjusts them for a variety of reasons. The Fed's biggest source of discretion is interpreting its objective of maximum employment; in its official "Statement on Goals and Monetary Policy Strategy," the Fed acknowledges that this "requires assessing a range of indicators and is subject to revision." The Fed earlier linked its interest rate policy to an unemployment rate goal (the Evans rule) and has constantly reinterpreted its goal as its perception of the Phillips curve has changed and Okun's law has fallen apart. It has heightened the labor force participation rate as a focus. It alters its historic estimates of potential growth to improve the statistical fit of its prior forecasts of inflation. International uncertainties have occasionally received significant attention (such as the Fed's accentuated dovish tilts in response to China-related uncertainties in late 2018–early 2019). Financial markets try to anticipate changes in Fed interpretations and focuses.

The Fed has heightened the importance of maintaining financial stability but has not clearly defined the parameters of financial stability or how it fits in with the Fed's dual mandate, nor has it established a strategy for achieving this goal. While history suggests that successfully achieving its dual mandate would significantly reduce the probability of financial instability, the Fed's tendency has been toward fine-tuning financial markets in an attempt to smooth volatility. This may have the adverse impact of adding to volatility in markets and aggregate demand, and distorting economic behavior by constraining the natural fluctuations in interest rates and stock markets that influence economic behavior. In addition, the Fed has responded systematically to declines in the stock market (Cieslak and Vissing-Jorgensen 2018). This happened most recently in early 2016 and in late 2018. Market expectations and valuations reflect these tilts.

THE FED'S "MANDATE CREEP" HAS INVOLVED "POLICY TOOL CREEP"

The Fed's QE1 in late 2008 was an emergency response to a serious crisis that helped to stabilize a serious situation. Although this was an important inflection point in the conduct of monetary policy, the subsequent asset purchase programs—particularly QE3 that was implemented in late 2012 for the express objective of lowering the unemployment rate—reflected a clear shift in the Fed's reaction function that ushered in much more activist Fed policy, an enlarged balance sheet, and a significantly larger role of forward guidance. Its

large balance sheet is now used to accomplish a variety of objectives
and is now part of the Fed's normal conduct of monetary policy.
At the same time, the Fed has dramatically increased its reliance
on communications, and its forward guidance is a critical tool in
financial and economic fine-tuning.

The expanded uses of the balance sheet have heightened the Fed's
involvement in financial markets and poses challenges. In promoting QE3 and forward guidance in 2012, Fed chair Bernanke argued
that they would boost asset prices and encourage risk taking, which
would stimulate economic growth. In the years that followed, these
unprecedented policies clearly contributed to higher asset prices
(stocks, bonds, and real estate) but had little perceptible impact on
nominal GDP growth. If these policies had stimulated growth as
the Fed (and its FRB/US model) had predicted, it would have been
forced to move quicker to normalize monetary policy.

Instead, the sustained slow growth and sub-2 percent inflation
provided the Fed the flexibility to maintain its unconventional
accommodation, but there have been many bumps along the road.
The taper tantrum in 2013—a surprise temporary 100-basis-point
rise in 10-year Treasury bond yields—stemmed from Bernanke's
mention that under reasonable conditions the Fed would eventually taper QE3. While bond yields actually receded during the
actual tapering in 2014, the Fed's subsequent decision to raise
interest rates before unwinding its balance sheet was driven by
the Fed's fears of a negative market response to unwinding the
balance sheet first. Fed chairman Powell's strategy to "keep quiet"
on the balance sheet unwind seemed to work until 2018 Q4, when
the stock market correction and year-end short-term funding
pressures led the Fed to announce the outlines of a balance sheet
strategy.

Significant uncertainty about how the balance sheet affects credit
channels, financial markets, and the economy has muddled the Fed's
communications. The Fed has changed its story, materially reducing

its assessment of the interest rate impacts of QE2 and QE3. Its strategy has evolved toward arguing that maintaining large excess reserves in the banking system helps to manage financial stability and would serve as a buffer in crisis management. Meanwhile, despite uncertainties, financial markets respond to any forward guidance the Fed gives about the schedule of its balance sheet wind down and ultimate size, gleaning evidence on the Fed's hawkish or dovish tones.

Clearly, more research is needed on the balance sheet and also on why the economy did not respond to the Fed's QE3 and forward guidance. Charles Plosser and others argue that the costs stemming from the unnecessary complexity and economic and political risks of maintaining an enlarged balance sheet are understated (Plosser 2019). Research shows that paying interest on excess reserves (IOER) and Fed regulations on commercial bank reserve requirements have affected the demand for bank reserves and bank lending (Ireland 2019). A better understanding of why the money multipliers collapsed (i.e., why the surge in base money did not translate into faster growth of broad money and credit) and why money velocity declined in response to the Fed's asset purchases is important for considering the proper monetary policy responses in the future. Such analyses certainly would be more instructive than the Fed's blanket statement that without QE3 the economy would have faltered.

Markets understand that the Fed is purposely influencing markets, which accentuates the impact of Fed-speak. The Fed's stumble at its December 2018 Federal Open Market Committee (FOMC) meeting is a good example of the negative feedback loop in which the Fed's poor communications initiated a negative market reaction that elicited a subsequent Fed statement aimed at calming markets. In March 2019, JP Morgan issued a report with the following title: "How Much Further Can the Fed Push Markets?" This brings up a host of questions: Why is the Fed pushing markets? Is it necessary to achieve its dual mandate? Might the Fed be undermining its credibility and desired longer-run impacts?

EXTRACTING INFORMATION FROM
FINANCIAL MARKETS

The Fed emphasizes that its conduct of monetary policy is data dependent. As John Williams, president of the Federal Reserve Bank of New York, recently elaborated, data dependence includes consideration of hard economic data, anecdotal evidence provided by business executives, and information provided by financial markets (Williams 2019). But filtering information from stock market behavior is tricky: when is the stock market providing valuable information above that provided by hard economic data and forecasting tools, and when is it misleading? Historically, the stock market has not been a reliable predictor of the economy, and the Fed has "overreacted" to market moves, especially declines.

Why did the Fed respond so aggressively to the stock market correction in late 2018 after being so upbeat on the economy in September 2018 that it expressed the need to raise rates beyond neutral? Although the economic data softened a bit and inflation and inflationary expectations receded, the biggest change was the Fed's dampened expectations in response to the stock market correction and quickly emerging concerns about recession. But the Fed's misguided communications accentuated the stock market correction, which clearly harmed year-end consumer spending. The Fed's subsequent aggressively dovish tilt lifted markets. It is uncertain the value of what the Fed had extracted from the stock market.

The Fed's forecasting track record over the years has been mediocre—its errors in forecasting real GDP have been very large and of magnitudes similar to those of other forecasters (Reifschneider and Tulip 2017). It seems unlikely that its forecasting errors would have been materially different if the Fed had not relied on insights from the stock market. The Fed should be more circumspect about its ability to extract reliable economic signals from the stock market. A more systematic pursuit of its dual mandate would lessen the Fed's intrusions into markets—and unnecessary market volatility.

THE FED'S COMMUNICATIONS: SUGGESTIONS FOR IMPROVEMENT

Although the Fed has elevated its reliance on communications and forward guidance, its efforts to be transparent have been prone to misinterpretation and a source of undesired volatility. The Fed's official Longer-Run Strategy Statement emphasizes that while inflation over the longer run is primarily determined by monetary policy, "the maximum level of employment is largely determined by nonmonetary factors that affect the structure and dynamics of the labor market." Despite this caution, an inordinate amount of the Fed's focus and communications relates to current economic conditions that are beyond its control and have little to do with its dual mandate (Levy 2019).

Fed members provide constant public commentary on economic conditions and appear frequently on TV to assess the just-released monthly Employment Report and other high-frequency government data. The Fed's official policy statement following each FOMC meeting begins with its description of economic conditions and typically (but not always) includes a risk assessment of near-term economic conditions. Small word changes are closely scrutinized for insights into what they may imply for future policy rates. The Fed's quarterly updated economic projections are closely followed as critical forward guidance.

All too frequently, financial market participants wonder or presume that the Fed knows something the markets do not. Following the Fed's further downward growth revisions and explicitly dovish policy statement at its recent March 2019 FOMC meeting, I received an email from an institutional investor: "Why did the FOMC choose to stop early? Is the US economy really that bad?" In reality, the Fed has one important piece of "inside" information: what it is inclined to do with monetary policy. In light of intense market scrutiny, the Fed should be as systematic as possible with its forward guidance about future policies and remember that its economic commentary influences decisions by businesses and households.

One simple recommendation is that FOMC members should cease making public comments immediately following government data releases. Such commentary gives the wrong impression of the Fed's role and mandate. Let private economists, financial market participants, and the media discuss high-frequency data, and how much of the "miss" relative to consensus expectations is due to seasonal adjustments or statistical noise. Being data dependent does not mean responding publicly to high-frequency data. In public speeches and statements, FOMC members should relate their comments on the economy to the Fed's dual mandate. They should carefully distinguish between short-term fluctuations that are beyond the control of monetary policy and intermediate-term trends that the Fed may influence. The Fed's public comments on the stock market should be limited to all but extreme valuations; casual assessments by FOMC members of whether the stock market is too high or too low should be avoided.

THE FED'S POLICY STATEMENTS: RECOMMENDED CHANGES

The Fed's official policy statement following FOMC meetings should be modified in at least three ways. First, every policy statement should begin with an assessment of monetary policy and whether it is consistent with achieving the Fed's statutory mandate, rather than the Fed's assessments of the economy and its subsectors. Reordering of the current format would reinforce the Fed's primary focus on its statutory mandate and policy stance, and properly put current economic conditions in a supporting role rather than the lead role.

Second, the Fed should explicitly convey in every policy statement *separate* balance-of-risk assessments on inflation and on employment and/or the economy. Focusing the risk assessment on the economy, or temporarily dropping the risk assessment and replacing it with nuanced language on inflation and inflationary expectations, only adds confusion. Changes in these risk assessments must be carefully aligned with changes in the Fed's forecasts. Such modifications may have helped to avoid the Fed's communications missteps in December 2018 when the policy statement, Summary of Economic Projections forecasts, and Chair Powell's press conference created confusion while the subsequently released minutes of the FOMC meeting painted a far different picture on the Fed's balance of risks.

Third, the policy statement must include the Fed's strategy on its balance sheet and unwind policy. The Fed's balance sheet strategy cannot simply be ignored or put into an addendum. Even though the Fed has emphasized that interest rates are its primary policy tool, the enlarged balance sheet is nevertheless an important tool, particularly if the Fed were to face the zero lower bound on interest rates.

THE FED'S QUARTERLY FORECAST UPDATES: SUGGESTIONS FOR REVAMPING

The Fed's quarterly Summary of Economic Projections (SEP) draws too much attention to single-point estimates, conveys a sense of certainty, and is prone to misinterpretation. It should be redesigned with three goals in mind: (1) in addition to the Fed's baseline forecast, it should include estimates of forecast uncertainties and appropriate paths of monetary policy associated with them; (2) it should provide a framework for the Fed to analyze and consider monetary policy under different situations and contingency planning; and (3) the forecasts of the appropriate Fed funds rate should not commit the Fed to a policy path.

The current SEPs have the benefit of incorporating the forecasts of all FOMC members, including the inputs of the Bank presidents that reflect their diverse opinions and anecdotal evidence from the districts. However, the SEPs are limited and prone to misinterpretation. The Fed's central tendency and range of forecasts in the SEPs are simply the bands of the baseline ("best") forecasts of the FOMC members (the central tendency throws out the three highest and three lowest forecasts) and do not reflect forecast uncertainties, as they are often perceived.

Since 2010, real GDP growth in the year following the FOMC's December forecasts has been outside the Fed's forecast central tendency in seven out of nine years and outside the range in six years (Levy 2018). The median FOMC member forecast of the Fed funds rate forecast at year-end—the so-called median dot— is too frequently perceived to be a binding commitment. It is noteworthy that in recent years, the futures market has provided more accurate forecasts of the Fed funds rate than the FOMC's median dot.

The FOMC's forecasts may have other problems. Member forecasts may be based on different assumptions about what they consider "appropriate monetary policy," so their individual forecasts may not be comparable and combining them may be biased. The Fed's inflation forecasts may be constrained by its 2 percent target. The Fed knows that its forecasts provide important forward guidance, and this may affect the forecasts provided by the FOMC members. Moreover, the Fed governors may be constrained because their forecasts tend not to stray too far from the senior Fed staff FRB/US model forecasts.

The Fed is aware of these challenges and would like to emphasize the conditionality of monetary policy. Federal Reserve Bank of Cleveland president Loretta Mester has identified key issues in uncertainties and recommended changes, including providing estimates of confidence bands around the SEPs (Mester 2016). Fed researchers David Reifschneider and Peter Tulip analyzed forecasting uncertainties and found that the Fed's median forecasts of real GDP plus or minus the twenty-year moving average of the root mean squared errors (RMSEs) computed from a blend of real GDP forecasts by the Fed and other government and private sector forecasters captured approximately 70 percent of actual outcomes (Reifschneider and Tulip 2017).

Reflecting these observations, the Fed now shows charts of those calculated 70 percent confidence intervals around the FOMC's median forecasts, but they are not included in the SEPs, so they do not get much attention. Instead, they and other measures of uncertainty and balances of risks are included in the back of the FOMC meeting minutes released with a three-week lag.

The optimal solution would be a more systematic approach in which the Fed would publish a single forecast based on a model that is consistent with achieving its dual mandate that would measure how the appropriate Fed funds rate path would vary under different economic and inflation outcomes. However, the Fed has concluded that agreement on a single forecast methodology would be too difficult.

With this constraint, the SEPs should be revamped to incorporate estimates of reasonable uncertainties and the Fed estimates of policies that would be appropriate under alternative economic and inflation outcomes. Rather than ask FOMC members to calculate a confidence interval around their baseline intermediate-term forecasts, the Fed Board staff should provide each member with a calculated 70 percent confidence interval (using the Reifschneider-Tulip methodology), so that before every quarterly FOMC meeting, each FOMC member would submit (1) forecasts for GDP, the unemployment rate, and inflation, along with the high and low bands based on the calculated 70 percent confidence intervals; and (2) three forecasts of the Fed funds rate: one rate appropriate for their baseline economic and inflation forecast and one each for their high and low bands of the confidence intervals. Since the longer-run equilibrium forecasts of the federal funds rate and potential real GDP are unobservable, confidence intervals cannot be calculated. Accordingly, each FOMC member would submit a baseline and a "reasonable range" of that variable deemed to be consistent with achieving the Fed's dual mandate. The Fed's senior staff would also be required to provide its baseline estimates and confidence intervals and three Fed funds rate paths for the intermediate term, along with a baseline and reasonable range for longer-run forecasts.

In addition, the SEPs should include a separate forecast of nominal GDP. This would not be redundant and would serve a valuable purpose. Monetary policy influences nominal spending and production, not real GDP, which is derived from nominal GDP and the Bureau of Economic Analysis's estimate of quality-adjusted inflation, which involves judgment and assumption. Projections of real GDP and personal consumption expenditure (PCE) inflation do not add up to nominal GDP, in part because the PCE index does not include business capital investment or government consumption or investment. Another possible change would be the length of the forecasting period. While the Fed's longer-run forecasts are very instructive, cutting the projection period back to two years from three would eliminate the unnecessary extrapolation into the third year that is beyond the Fed's thinking on monetary policy.

Incorporating a calculated 70 percent confidence interval around baseline economic and inflation forecasts and having FOMC members align their appropriate Fed funds rate forecasts to the upper and lower bands would be a fruitful task. It would encourage the Fed to consider policy responses to a reasonably large band of actual outcomes and to lean against the natural tendency to focus on the baseline forecasts. Also, it would help the Fed clarify its balances of risk assessment at every FOMC meeting and align them with any change in forecasts.

The new SEPs published at the conclusion of each quarterly FOMC meeting would include: (1) the summary table of the medians of the FOMC members' baseline forecasts and the calculated 70 percent confidence intervals over the intermediate-term projection and the medians of their longer-run baseline and reasonable ranges (a prototype with hypotheticals is shown in table 7.1), where the median estimates of confidence intervals for the intermediate-term forecasts would replace the current "central tendency" and "range" forecasts; (2) the Fed's senior staff forecasts, including forecasts of the Fed funds rate; (3) a chart of the median forecasts of the appropriate path of the Fed funds rate for the baseline and upper and lower bands of estimated confidence intervals on the economy and inflation, to replace the current "dot plot" (figure 7.1); and (4) separate charts of the FOMC's median estimated forecasts and confidence intervals (and longer-run ranges) for nominal and real GDP, the unemployment rate, and PCE inflation. In addition, the SEPs would include some of the FOMC's balance-of-risk bar charts that are now in the back of the minutes of each meeting.

Replacing the current confusing dot plot with the median Fed member estimate of the appropriate policy rate for the alternative economic and inflation forecasts would be a step forward. If FOMC members do not want to give up their individual dots and the Fed considers this too controversial and chooses to continue to include the dot plot, it should be shown against the backdrop of the shaded area bounded by the calculated 70 percent confidence intervals (figure 7.2).

One further modification is important: the SEPs should include an addendum on the appropriate size of the balance sheet under the FOMC's median forecast and confidence intervals. It is shortsighted and incomplete to include only the Fed's estimates of an appropriate path of the Fed funds rate. Presumably, under normal conditions and forecasts, the Fed's balance sheet strategy would remain unchanged.

TABLE 7.1. Hypothetical Summary Table: Economic Projections of Federal Reserve Board Members and Federal Reserve Bank Presidents under Their Individual Assessments of Projected Appropriate Monetary Policy, March 2019

Percent

Variable	Median* and 70 Percent Confident Intervals around Forecasts**			Median and Range†	
	2019	2020	2021	Longer run	
Change in nominal GDP	a — b	a — b	a — b	c — d	
December projection	a — b	a — b	a — b	c — d	
Change in real GDP	a 2.1 b	a 1.9 b	a 1.8 b	c 1.9 d	
December projection	a 2.3 b	a 2.0 b	a 1.8 b	c 1.9 d	
Unemployment rate	a 3.7 b	a 3.8 b	a 3.9 b	c 4.3 d	
December projection	a 3.5 b	a 3.6 b	a 3.8 b	c 4.4 d	
PCE inflation	a 1.8 b	a 2.0 b	a 2.0 b	c 2.0 d	
December projection	a 1.9 b	a 2.1 b	a 2.1 b	c 2.0 d	
Core PCE inflation††	a 2.0 b	a 2.0 b	a 2.0 b	c d	
December projection	a 2.0 b	a 2.0 b	a 2.0 b		

Memo: Projected appropriate
policy path

Federal funds rate	a	2.4	b	a	2.6	b	a	2.6	b	a	2.8	c	d
December projection	a	2.9	b	a	3.1	b	a	3.1	b	a	2.8	c	d

Note: Projections of change in real gross domestic product (GDP) and projections for both measures of inflation are percent changes from the fourth quarter of the previous year to the fourth quarter of the year indicated. PCE inflation and core PCE inflation are the percentage rates of change in, respectively, the price index for personal consumption expenditures (PCE) and the price index for PCE excluding food and energy. Projections for the unemployment rate are for the average civilian unemployment rate in the fourth quarter of the year indicated. Each participant's projections are based on his or her assessment of appropriate monetary policy. Longer-run projections represent each participant's assessment of the rate to which each variable would be expected to converge under appropriate monetary policy and in the absence of further shocks to the economy. The projections for the federal funds rate are the value of the midpoint of the projected appropriate target range for the federal funds rate or the projected appropriate target level for the federal funds rate at the end of the specified calendar year or over the longer run. The December projections were made in conjunction with the meeting of the Federal Open Market Committee on December 18–19, 2018. One participant did not submit longer-run projections for the change in real GDP, the unemployment rate, or the federal funds rate in conjunction with the meeting on December 18–19, 2018, and one participant did not submit such projections in conjunction with the meeting on March 19–20, 2019. Forecasts are hypothetical and for illustration purposes only.

* For each period, the median is the middle projection when individuals' baseline projections are arranged from lowest to highest. When the number of projections is even, the median is the average of the two middle projections.

** For each period, "a" and "b" reflect the median economic, inflation, or interest rate forecast minus and plus, respectively, the 20-year moving average of the root mean squared errors (RMSE) computed from a blend of each variable's respective forecasts by the Fed and other government and private sector forecasters.

† A "reasonable range" of the respective variable that may be consistent with achieving the Fed's dual mandate. "c" and "d" are the medians of the lower and upper ends, respectively, of members' estimated ranges.

†† Longer-run projections for core PCE inflation are not collected.

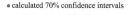

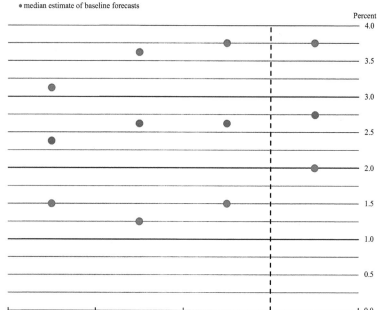

FIGURE 7.1. Hypothetical Dot Plot—FOMC Participants' Assessments of Appropriate Monetary Policy: Median Estimate of Baseline Forecasts and Calculated 70 Percent Confidence Intervals around Baseline Forecasts

Note: Each shaded orange circle indicates the median value of individual participants' baseline judgment of the midpoint of the appropriate target range for the federal funds rate or the appropriate target level for the federal funds rate at the end of the specified calendar year or over the longer run. Shaded blue circles reflect the median baseline forecast minus and plus, respectively, the twenty-year moving average of the root mean squared errors (RMSEs) computed from a blend of forecasts for short-term interest rates by the Fed and other government and private sector forecasters. For the longer-run forecasts, the shaded blue circles are the medians of the lower and upper ends, respectively, of Fed members' estimated ranges of the Fed funds rate judged to be consistent with achieving the Fed's dual mandate. Forecasts are hypothetical and for illustration purposes only.

However, including its balance sheet strategy would definitely be important if the Fed were to face the zero lower bound on rates. Fed chair Powell has changed from characterizing the Fed's balance sheet as being on "auto pilot" to being "in play" under certain circumstances. More policy transparency would be appropriate.

■ calculated 70% confidence intervals
● baseline forecasts

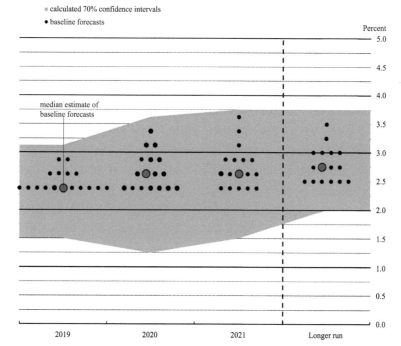

FIGURE 7.2. Optional Hypothetical Dot Plot—FOMC Participants' Assessments of Appropriate Monetary Policy: Baseline Forecasts of Each Participant and Calculated 70 Percent Confidence Intervals around Baseline Forecasts. For the longer-run forecasts, the shaded blue area represents the medians of the Fed members' estimated ranges of the Fed funds rate judged to be consistent with achieving the Fed's dual mandate. Forecasts are hypothetical and for illustration purposes only

CONCLUSION

The Fed must take the lead to break its negative self-reinforcing relationship with financial markets by taking steps to rein in its activist fine-tuning of the economy and financial markets and focus on a strategy for achieving its dual mandate. For starters, the Fed needs to curtail its excessive focus on the real economy and retrain markets to understand that short-term economic fluctuations occur naturally and are beyond the Fed's control. It must strike a symmetrical stance on the stock market and not respond to corrections. Revamping the SEPs by introducing uncertainties and highlighting the conditionality of monetary policy would be consistent with concerns expressed by Fed chair Powell and Governor John Williams and others (Powell 2018; Williams 2018). This has been advocated by Andrew Levin (2014), who urges the Fed to conduct scenario analyses of its monetary policy alternatives—that is, "stress tests" for monetary policy, which would force more accountability and enhance the Fed's transparency.

Market participants may initially balk at the width of the 70 percent confidence intervals, which may be seemingly large compared to the current central tendency forecasts. However, they would soon find them useful in mapping the Fed's conditional policy rate forecasts with alternative reasonable economic and inflation outcomes. Markets are adaptable and would not miss the Fed's dot plot.

References

Calomiris, Charles, and Harry Mamaysky. 2019. "Monetary Policy and Exchange Rate Returns: Time-Varying Risk Regimes." Working paper, Columbia University Business School.

Cieslak, Anna, and Vissing-Jorgensen, Annette. 2018. "The Economics of the Fed Put." Working paper, September.

Ireland, Peter N. 2019. "Monetary Policy Implementation: Making Better and More Consistent Use of the Federal Reserve's Balance Sheet." Position paper. New York: Shadow Open Market Committee, March 29. https://www.shadowfed.org/wp-content/uploads/2019/03/IrelandSOMC-March2019.pdf.

JPMorgan Chase. 2019. "How Much Further Can the Fed Push Markets?" March.

Levin, Andrew. 2014. "The Design and Communication of Systematic Monetary Strategies." In "Frameworks for Central Banking in the Next Century." Special issue, *Journal of Economic Dynamics and Control* 49 (December): 52–69.

Levy, Mickey. 2019. "The Fed's Communications: Suggestions for Improvement." Shadow Open Market Committee, March.

Mester, Loretta. 2016. "Acknowledging Uncertainty." Presented at the Shadow Open Market Committee Fall Meeting, New York City, October 7. http://www.clevelandfed.org/en/newsroom-and-events/speeches/sp-20161007-acknowledging-uncertainty.

Plosser, Charles. 2019. "Balance Sheet: Exposures, Risks, and Financial Difficulties." Paper given at the Shadow Open Market Committee meeting, March.

Powell, Jerome H. 2018. "Monetary Policy in a Changing Economy." Paper presented at the Federal Reserve Bank of Kansas City Jackson Hole Symposium, August 24.

Reifschneider, David L., and Peter Tulip. 2017. "Gauging the Uncertainty of the Economic Outlook Using Historical Forecasting Errors: The Federal Reserve's Approach." Federal Reserve Board Finance and Economics Discussion Series, 2017-020.

Williams, John C. 2018. "'Normal' Monetary Policy in Words and Deeds." Speech delivered at Columbia University, School of International and Public Affairs, New York City, September 28.

CHAPTER EIGHT

MARKET FEEDBACK EFFECTS OF CENTRAL BANK OPERATIONS UNDER AN INFLATION-TARGETING REGIME

Scott Minerd

Central bank inflation-targeting policies have been largely successful, resulting in important positive macroeconomic outcomes, among which is an extended period of well-anchored inflation expectations. These efforts, however, have had significant financial market implications that may ultimately make the central bank's objectives more difficult to achieve. In short, central banks, and the Federal Reserve in particular, have become a victim of their own success. To a significant extent, the term structure of interest rates is driven by inflation expectations. Successful inflation targeting has resulted in a yield curve that is relatively flat and stable, which is reducing the central bank's ability to use market rates as a feedback signal.

THEORIES ON THE TERM STRUCTURE OF INTEREST RATES

Traditionally, there are several theories that explain the term structure of interest rates. The first of these theories is the liquidity preference hypothesis, which states that risk-averse investors demand a premium for holding instruments with longer maturities and bearing interest rate risk that generally causes the yield curve to be upward sloping. Under the preferred habitat theory, different investor types have different maturity preferences and need a premium to shift away from their preferred position in the term structure. Another related theory, the segmented markets theory, states that supply and demand dynamics differ for different maturities, given largely independent investor bases for each point on the yield curve.

Finally, there is expectations theory, which under "pure expectations" theory states that the long-term interest rate is simply the current expectation for future short-term rates, while a looser definition allows for some yield premium that compensates for the risk associated with uncertainty regarding levels of future interest rates. This risk premium related to uncertainty over future rates can be further decomposed into two factors: uncertainty about real neutral short-term rates and uncertainty about inflation.

A THOUGHT EXPERIMENT ON INFLATION EXPECTATIONS

To address the way in which inflation targeting by central banks potentially distorts the feedback signal of the yield curve, let us conduct a thought experiment in which we assume that only expectations theory explains the term structure of interest rates. Furthermore, let us assume that the expected real neutral rate remains constant, so that the primary driver of changes in the term structure is changes in expected inflation.

Making such an assumption is of course a simplification but is not wildly out of step with reality. Over the past forty years long-term interest rates, as represented by the yield on 10-year Treasury securities, have fallen largely because disciplined monetary policy has brought down realized inflation, which in turn has driven down inflation expectations (see figure 8.1). The result is that long-term rates have slowly converged onto long-term inflation expectations.

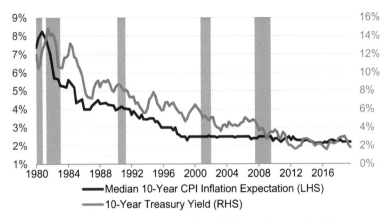

FIGURE 8.1. Long-Term Rates Have Fallen as Inflation Expectations Have Declined: Inflation Expectations and 10-Year Treasury Yield

Sources: Guggenheim Investments and Haver Analytics. Data as of September 30, 2019.

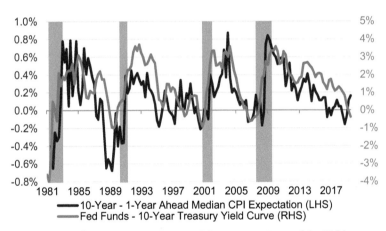

FIGURE 8.2. Inflation Expectations Are a Major Determinant of the Yield Curve: Inflation Expectations and the Yield Curve

Sources: Guggenheim Investments and Haver Analytics. Data as of September 30, 2019.

Similarly, the shape of the yield curve is further driven by inflation expectations (see figure 8.2). Changes in long-term inflation expectations relative to short-term inflation expectations have exhibited a high correlation with yield curve shape in recent decades: as expectations of long-term and short-term inflation converge, the yield

curve flattens, and when longer-term inflation expectations rise
relative to near-term expectations, the curve steepens.

These relationships demonstrate that although a number of factors influence the yield curve, inflation expectations play a major
role in determining both the level and the shape of the curve. This
fact is particularly relevant given that out of the previously mentioned factors that can influence the yield curve, monetary policy
has the greatest influence over long-run inflation expectations.

CONSEQUENCES OF INFLATION TARGETING

In the era of inflation targeting, the Federal Reserve has succeeded
not only in maintaining a low rate of inflation but also in reducing
market expectations of future changes in inflation. A first-order
effect of this reduction in expected inflation changes has been a
consistently lower level of volatility across the term structure of
interest rates (see figure 8.3). Put another way, in a world where
inflation expectations become well anchored at the target rate of
2 percent over a longer horizon, interest rates become more stable

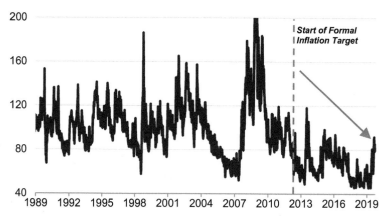

FIGURE 8.3. Volatility of Interest Rates Has Fallen under Inflation Targeting:
Merrill Lynch Option Volatility Estimate (MOVE) Index

Sources: Guggenheim Investments and Bloomberg. Data as of September 27, 2019.

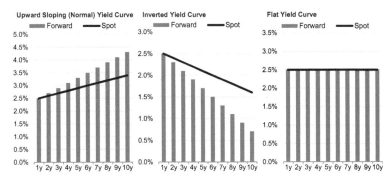

FIGURE 8.4.   Classic Illustration of Spot and Forward Curves

Source: Guggenheim Investments. Data is for illustrative purposes and not actual historical data.

around the 2 percent target. Reduced volatility of interest rates has generally been perceived as a positive development by financial market participants. Many argue that reduction in interest rate uncertainty has allowed for a compression in risk premia across a broad array of markets—from equity to credit to real estate, making capital more affordable.

In our thought experiment where the term structure is driven by inflation expectations, the result of successful inflation targeting is the anchoring of inflation expectations across both short and long time horizons, causing forward rates to converge with spot rates and the yield curve to flatten (see figure 8.4).

This theoretical result is supported by the data. We can observe that periods in which the dispersion of inflation forecasts is high tend to be associated with a higher term premium while periods of low forecast dispersion are generally associated with a lower term premium (see figure 8.5). As the inflation target becomes increasingly credible, long-term inflation expectations converge with short-term expectations, and less of a premium is needed for the uncertainty of not achieving the inflation target. This convergence of inflation expectations results in a flat yield curve at a level consistent with the targeted inflation rate.

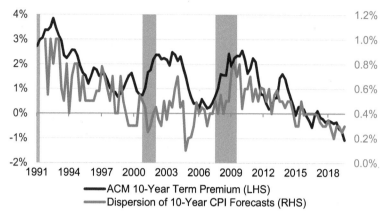

FIGURE 8.5. Stable Inflation Expectations Also Help Explain Lower Term
Premium: 10-Year Term Premium and Inflation Forecast Dispersion
Sources: Guggenheim Investments and Haver Analytics. Data as of September 30, 2019.

In a world where inflation expectations are well anchored at the
2 percent target rate, any temporary overshoot in inflation will be
viewed as transitory, and the yield curve will adjust to reflect any
deviation from the long-term objective. For example, if short-term
rates were to rise to reduce current inflation, and if that increase was
viewed as temporary, there would be an offsetting impact on the term
structure of interest rates based on the expectation that rates will on
average be consistent with 2 percent, causing long-term rates to fall
and the yield curve to invert. Similarly, when short-term rates are
reduced to raise short-term inflation, forward rates will adjust upward
to provide an average rate consistent with the targeted inflation rate
(see figure 8.6). This would explain why a modest increase in short-
term rates could lead to a premature yield curve inversion.

FROM THOUGHT EXPERIMENT BACK
TO THE REAL WORLD

We started this thought experiment by assuming that inflation
expectations are the only influence on the term structure of inter-

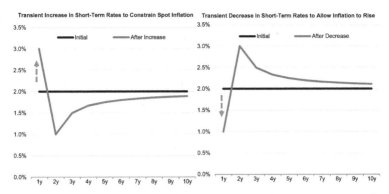

FIGURE 8.6. Effects of Changes in Short-Term Rates on the Term Structure with Anchored Inflation Expectations

Source: Guggenheim Investments. Data is for illustrative purposes and not actual historical data.

est rates. Thus, uncertainty about inflation leads to a premium for long-term yields, and uncertainty—and the term premium for long-term yields—are greatly reduced if not entirely eliminated if inflation expectations are successfully anchored, resulting in a flat yield curve.

Stepping out of the vacuum of our thought experiment and back into the real world, we can see that anchored inflation expectations also affect other investor behavior factors that have been theorized to influence the yield curve. For example, if the yield curve has little slope and uncertainty about future rates is low, investors will have less of a preference for different points on the yield curve, thus muting the impact of habitat preference. This dynamic is precisely what we have witnessed in recent years, as record low-term premia signal reduced uncertainty about future interest rates, resulting in a flattened yield curve.

Similarly, we have seen how inflation targeting has served to reduce the volatility of interest rates. If volatility of interest rates is low, then less of a liquidity premium is required by investors as compensation for holding longer-term securities such as notes and bonds relative to shorter maturity securities such as Treasury bills, since interest rate risk associated with uncertainty and volatility has been reduced. Therefore, the impact of liquidity preference is lessened, which further reinforces a flatter term structure.

MARKET FEEDBACK EFFECTS
OF MONETARY POLICY

Historically, the shape of the yield curve has been an important signal reflecting the market's perception of monetary policy accommodation or restrictiveness. Successful inflation targeting is leading to reduced volatility in long-term rates. With reduced volatility, the ability for long-term rates to signal changes in inflation expectations and the stance of monetary policy is greatly diminished. At the same time, short-term rates are sidelined from providing a market feedback signal, given current policy in which the overnight rate is pegged. Therefore, market participants must look elsewhere for market signals to evaluate the appropriate target of the nominal short-term rate consistent with price stability.

One such alternative signal is monetary aggregates. For example, the growth rate of "true" money supply (currency in circulation plus savings and demand deposits) has reliably slowed in the lead-up to recessions (see figure 8.7). However, this relationship may not be precise enough to guide policy on its own.

Given reduced interest rate volatility, another indicator that has become an important reflection of market perceptions for future Fed policy action is a broader composite of financial conditions, incorporating corporate bond spreads, equity valuations, and the value of the dollar (see figure 8.8). Financial conditions are a relatively strong real-time indicator of nominal growth and may be a guide to future Fed policy as the market perceives a reaction function to financial stress.

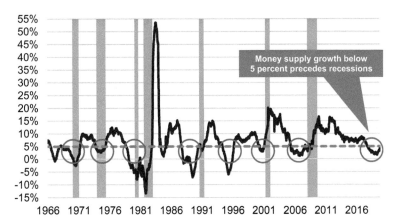

FIGURE 8.7. The Slowdown in Money Supply Growth Warrants Attention.: True Money Supply (Currency in Circulation + Savings and Demand Deposits), Year-over-Year% Change

Sources: Guggenheim Investments and Bloomberg. Data as of September 30, 2019.

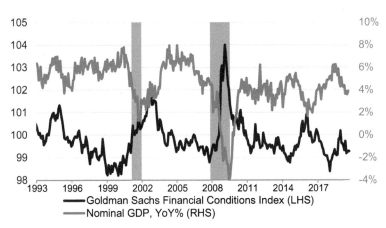

FIGURE 8.8. Broad Financial Conditions Are an Important Signal: Financial Conditions and Nominal GDP Growth

Sources: Haver Analytics and Guggenheim Investments. Data for FCI as of September 30, 2019; for GDP as of August 31, 2019.

Although monetary aggregates and financial conditions provide useful information to market participants, both fail to provide contemporaneous feedback about the degree of monetary accommodation or restrictiveness relative to the Fed's mandate of full employment and price stability on a real-time basis.

IMPLICATIONS AND RECOMMENDATIONS

This analysis has shown how anchored inflation expectations at 2 percent have led to a significantly flatter yield curve at relatively low interest rates. As noted earlier, a short-term overshoot of the inflation target should have little effect on long-term interest rates and increase the likelihood of a yield curve inversion associated with what would otherwise be viewed as a relatively modest increase in rates. Earlier yield curve inversions should lead to shortened rate hike cycles, a dynamic we may be currently witnessing. With shorter rate hike cycles ending in lower rates, efforts to normalize interest rates and escape zero lower bound constraints are becoming more challenging.

At the same time, anchored inflation expectations result in muted volatility of interest rates. Depressed volatility reduces the efficacy of the market signals provided by changes and levels of interest rates, making the setting and timing of appropriate monetary policy adjustments more difficult. Additionally, muted volatility along with a relatively flat yield curve has the unintended side effect of increasing investor complacency, encouraging "reach-for-yield" behavior and compression of risk premia, which increases malinvestment and encourages speculative behavior on the part of investors. These factors heighten the risk of financial instability in the event of exogenous shocks to the system or a cyclical business downturn.

The success of the current inflation-targeting policy regime virtually ensures that interest rate management will be a less effective policy tool going forward, given the proximity to the zero lower bound and the muted feedback mechanism to signal changes in the real economy. This suggests that previously unconventional tools, such as quantitative easing and forward guidance, will remain permanent and necessary features of the monetary policy tool kit. Unfortunately, these unconventional policy tools come with the side effect of further exacerbating instability in financial assets, raising the prospect of more severe boom-bust cycles that damage long-term growth potential.

Well-anchored inflation expectations generally are a positive condition of a healthy economy and a reflection of the Fed's successfully meeting at least one of its dual mandates. The downside of this successful anchoring, however, has dampened market volatility and reduced the efficacy of market feedback. The best solution to this problem may well be to allow more volatility in short-term rates through revised open market operations policy or setting a wider fed funds target range. This would allow short-term rates to more accurately reflect changes in the market demand for credit and reserves. More volatility at the short end of the yield curve would provide a contemporaneous market signal, which would reflect the degree of monetary restrictiveness or accommodation relative to the real economy. Such an approach would remove subjectivity around the appropriate target rate and decrease the risk of unintended errors in monetary policy.

GENERAL DISCUSSION

UNIDENTIFIED SPEAKER NO. 1: I want to address Mickey's point about adding the NGDP [nominal GDP] line to the summary of economic projections. Mickey, I think that's a very good idea. Jeff Frankel's got an article coming out in the *Cato Journal* on that same topic and making the same recommendation. I wanted to ask you a question, because once you think about that, you think about what the value is. And in December, of course, with the rate hike, some people think it was unwarranted. And in January, Powell decided to give a signal of patience, and now there's not going to be any more rate increases. If that NGDP growth target had been in that SEP [Summary of Economic Projections] statement, and if the growth target had been specified, let's say at 5 percent (3 real growth and 2 inflation), they would have seen that the actual growth rate in nominal GDP around that time was pretty much on target, which would have meant no rate increase. And they could project that in the future. And if they have a rule, or at least a quasi rule, that they want to have about 5 percent, it seems like it would lead to more certainty with respect to the conduct of monetary policy. I wondered what you thought about that?

MICKEY LEVY: Jim, I agree. But there are a couple other reasons why you would want to use nominal GDP. One is that it's the broadest measure of economic activity that the Fed's monetary policy affects. Real GDP is derived from nominal, from which they subtract quality-adjusted inflation. The BEA [Bureau of Economic Analysis] estimates of quality adjustment are complex and involve judgment. The Fed must convince itself and the public that its primary role is not to manage the real economy.

In December 2018, the Fed's Policy Statement and Powell's press conference conveyed different information and were inconsistent with how the subsequent minutes of the meeting suggested the Fed members were debating, and they were also inconsistent with the Fed's forecast. This inconsistency would have been avoided with the suggestions I have made on the revamped SEPs and separate risk assessments on inflation and the real economy. It is important that the Fed's forward guidance is easy to understand by markets.

PETER FISHER: I want to thank you all. I think it's been lovely observations in the comments from all four of you. I want to especially compliment Scott for bringing up the awkward thought of volatility being helpful. And I have two lessons of my own from that to share. But I think the most fundamental one is I think if the Fed is trying to stabilize the real economy, then financial variables have to be the shock absorber. And to try to stabilize them both is to do too much.

Now, I at least had the lesson when I managed the fed funds rate, I remember consciously choosing that I had to allow a certain amount of volatility, otherwise the fed funds market wouldn't work. And I probably didn't have a big enough range. But I also remember being challenged by Alan Greenspan once for uttering the thought that we should try to manage the whole yield curve, do something like an Operation Twist, say. And his observation to chide me was, "But then we'd just be looking at ourselves in the mirror."

LEVY: Okay, Peter, that's why they should also not try to manage the stock market and respond excessively to corrections.

UNIDENTIFIED SPEAKER NO. 2: A little bit of more of a philosophical question. As you can guess from my accent, I grew up under a government dictatorship, so I don't like when authorities have too much power. And today at lunch, we were reminded that rules are better than authorities. So, I have a philosophical question. Would it make more sense if the Federal Reserve would vote once a year or whenever on setting up the rules, but not continuously adjusting interest rates? Let it set up rules that

adjust the interest rate, and the Federal Reserve votes on changing the rules but not directly changing the interest rate?

LEVY: It is very important to have rules-based guidelines for the conduct of monetary policy. As Rich Clarida told us this morning,
the Fed should assess the data to see if it is consistent with the
Fed's forecast and that monetary policy is on track for achieving its long-run objective. The quarterly forecast should not
be changed. But the Fed has evolved into becoming a little too
fickle, a little too short term oriented, both on economic fluctuations and financial fluctuations. It is not allowing interest rates
or exchange rates to fluctuate naturally, and this harms the system and affects the Fed's credibility.

SCOTT MINERD: I'd like to respond to the gentleman. I tend to think
that the more we can allow for contemporaneous market feedback in prices, the more it reduces the risk of policy errors based
on, for instance, changes in r^* and other things, which are very
difficult to measure. And I think that the idea of having a targeted interest rate regime, whether it's a corridor system or even
our current system, is failing to allow us to observe how restric-
tive monetary policy becomes. And I think our most recent
incident occurred in the fourth quarter, where we saw short-
term rates reaching IOER [interest rate on excess reserves] as
the Federal Reserve was shrinking its balance sheet. And ultimately the market went into a tantrum, because it perceived that
it was too much. But if short-term rates had been allowed to rise
further, perhaps the central bank would have been more aware of
the fact that quantitative tightening was perhaps having a bigger
effect on the impact of restrictiveness within the markets than it
was measuring because of the regime where IOER tends to try
to suppress the rise in rates.

UNIDENTIFIED SPEAKER NO. 3: I wanted to respond to, or maybe push
back a little bit on, this issue of dysfunctionality that Mickey
raised. I mean, I think it's certainly true that the relationship

between the Fed and the markets does seem a bit sort of dysfunctional at times. But some relationships just sort of have dysfunctionality built into them, and it doesn't mean the relationship isn't valuable and enjoyable in other ways. It seems to me sort of the relationships—I'm speaking as an economist who works in financial markets. It seems to be the relationship just has this dysfunctionality built into it, because the Fed is uncertain about the state of the economy. It knows that there are some signals in financial market prices about the state of the economy. And it also knows that the transmission of its policies goes through the financial markets and, therefore, broader financial conditions are what affects the economy. And so it's kind of inevitable that the Fed pays close attention to market developments. But it's equally inevitable that the market pays close attention to the Fed, right? Because what the Fed does affects all the prices that people or instruments of people are trading. And so, you know, I think some of the suggestions you make are kind of useful, and possibly the Fed at times may communicate too much or may communicate in confusing ways. But sometimes when people in the markets complain about the Fed, what they're really complaining about is the Fed has done something, which has meant they've lost some money. And you know, nobody likes losing money.

LEVY: It's very natural for the markets to respond to everything the Fed says and does, just as it's natural for the Fed to look at the markets. But it is striking that the markets have come to perceive that the Fed's role is to manage the real economy. This is emphasized in the Fed's communications that focus on the real economy and some off-handed remarks about the stock market by FOMC [Federal Open Market Committee] members. When we consider how the Fed tries to extract information from markets, we must ask whether the stock market provides value-added insights about the economy and inflation above what is provided by hard data and anecdotal evidence from CEOs of companies and all the Fed's models. The answer is usually no.

I also emphasize that the Fed relies very heavily on forward guidance, even though nobody knows how it works or how it can work predictably. The Fed also maintains a very large balance sheet, and has changed its explanation for what its balance sheet accomplishes. This is awkward. Yet despite any understanding of the effects of the balance sheet, markets respond when the Fed mentions it. If the Fed would set out to simplify the monetary policy process, it would be better able to achieve its dual mandate with more clarity.

JOHN TAYLOR: So, one of the principles that's come out of research over the years of looking at good rules or strategies for central banks is they rarely include financial variables on the right-hand side. And I think one of the reasons for that is that it adds volatility to whatever they're doing, because there's volatility in markets, which some of you have said is just great. But the point is, there's lots of reasons why just research and models suggest you shouldn't be reacting but doing things the market reacts to. And with this forward guidance, the Reifschneider-Williams approach, it doesn't react. It's basically a rule, which is pretty specific, and it doesn't react to the markets. It's taking advantage of the reaction of the markets to the Fed; term structure of interest rates, for example, is part of that. But I take it your message is from people who are involved in markets is much the same. As much as you can, if there's any kind of a rule or strategy that you're thinking about, it's best not to include the financial variables in that, or at least not very much. At least dampen them. That's what I understand all of you saying, some way or the other. I don't know if that's correct. Certainly, Scott's point of letting the markets work some more is consistent with that. Laurie is consistent with that. George is consistent with that. So it seems to me that's kind of the message.

MINERD: John, I think one of the comments that Mickey made a minute ago is that people think the Fed is managing the real economy, they're responsible for it. I would go a step further as a market participant, and other people around me and the way they behave and talk, they seem to behave in a way that indicates that they think that the Fed has responsibility for managing the markets, which I find very troubling, because obviously I don't see that in the Fed mandate. But I think that the abundance of communication, which may have actually been totally 100 percent necessary during the financial crisis, has changed the perspective of a lot of market participants to think that the Fed has more power than it actually does and has a responsibility that it doesn't have.

JOHN COCHRANE: This was great. I want to expand on your remarks and put it in the context of our big question, the strategies for monetary policy. If we have another financial crisis—*when* we have another financial crisis—it will dwarf everything we've talked about today regarding 2 to 3 percent inflation and r^* and u^* and so on. The Fed has in fact taken on a mandate of financial stability. As Laurie reminds us, however, its tools are a little limited. The link between short-term interest rates and asset prices, even if the Fed wanted to use that, is tenuous at best. How do short-term rates affect risk premiums? Who knows where that comes from.

Scott and Mickey, I think, said that the Fed should talk differently. But the Fed's ability to influence things by talking is even less than its ability to influence things by short-term interest rates.

The Fed is, in fact, running financial markets. The question is, should it go further? Not through its interest rate and monetary policy, through its regulatory arms—its stress tests, "macroprudential" efforts, using the whole Dodd-Frank architecture. Should the Fed be managing the credit cycle and trying to make sure we don't have booms and busts, responding to credit conditions by its regulatory tools? If it thinks there's too much bubble in real estate loans, well, should it clamp down on real estate loans?

I think this is very dangerous. That is, it is the big question about what is the Fed going to do, quite apart from monetary policy. The last time it tried to prick a bubble in asset markets was 1928, and that didn't work out so well.

It is not possible nor advisable to make sure that nobody ever loses money again and no big bank ever fails again. The Fed is not allowing competition and innovation in the banking system. As I think about it, the only answer to this is lots and lots more capital, and then we can let institutions lose money. Otherwise, the next crisis will come. It will be worse than the last one.

LEVY: John, regarding one of your points, since 2010 the Fed has dramatically elevated its priority on financial stability without defining it clearly or what is the Fed's role is in macroprudential risk management, and what tools it has at hand. Also, the Fed emphasizes its transparency, but frequently changes how it interprets past events and policies. It has been very unclear about why the monetary policy transmission mechanism has failed to work, why QE2 and QE3 failed to stimulate faster nominal GDP growth, why the money multipliers have fallen, why money velocity has declined. Good research on this and an open discussion would be very instructive in anticipation of the next recession or crisis, rather than repeating the pat answer, "Oh, we had to do what we did or the economy would have slumped."

LAURIE HODRICK: I'm going to have to jump in on that one. I want to thank both Johns [Cochrane and Taylor] for fairly characterizing my remarks today. One of the main points I was trying to make is that when you look at the channels by which Fed policy can or can't affect firm valuations, it's very clear what the role of uncertainty is. It's not just about the level of uncertainty but also about increases in aggregate uncertainty. Again, while there may be disagreement on this panel, I would argue that an increase in uncertainty is a bad thing. Therefore, a well-disciplined policy that sticks to its knitting, that stays where it belongs, that's clear about what it is, is going to reduce aggregate uncertainty. And that again, if you look at the channels from corporate finance in terms of where Fed policy affects valuation for the firm and then is aggregated into the market, reducing uncertainty is going to enhance firm valuations.

GEORGE SHULTZ: The Fed, I believe, made some mistakes in the last crisis, which I hope they don't repeat, but they probably will. The first mistake was to be part of the bailout mania. When you bail people out, you give the signal that accountability is gone; that is, if you screw up, you don't pay a price. That's devastating and wrong. And if you take the view that this is going to be an orderly bankruptcy, orderly bankruptcies work out all right. Take AIG, for instance. It's a perfectly good insurance company that had this other investment asset that went sour. What you're really doing is bailing out Goldman Sachs and some others that invested in it. It would be better to let an orderly bankruptcy take place and let people who made a bad investment take the penalty. That's the way it should work. Then, they went before Congress, the Treasury, and the Fed together, and they said, "The sky is falling. We need a gigantic amount of money to bail out these securitized mortgages." And everybody knew there was no way they could do it because nobody had the slightest idea how to put a value on them. So they got the money, but they actually used it to bail out big banks, and some of them were forced to take the money by regulatory threats. That was a misuse of the power given to a regulatory agency, and when you do that, you undermine your credibility and you undermine trust. Trust is the coin of the realm. So there were a lot of mistakes made, I think, that I hope won't be repeated.

SYMPOSIUM
"Monetary Strategies in Practice"

Introduction

Charles I. Plosser

I want to start by applauding the Fed's efforts to review its strategies, tools, communications for conducting policy, and how they meet their congressional mandates. I think it's a tremendous effort and that it has an opportunity to bring a lot of insights to the Fed itself as well as the outside world about how the Fed thinks about things. But to seize that opportunity, I really want to stress that I believe the best kind of outcome—and they allude to this in their statement—is communicating at the end of the day how their strategy (whichever strategy they choose), their tools, and their communications all fit together. The coherence of strategy, tools, and communications, the coherence of that message can be vitally important to the Fed in the longer run, regardless of which strategy they choose for the moment. But integrating those things is going to be really important and very useful. And I think, among other things, it will help encourage the Fed and encourage policy to be more coherent, more systematic, and a better communicator in the process.

But I think at the same time, it will matter what strategy they choose. And I'd like to emphasize a couple things with regard to that. The challenge of adopting a new strategy, whatever that may be, will carry with it its own set of challenges. And what I'm afraid of, or what I think could happen if we're not careful, is the Fed could have a new strategy, but if, in the process, they fail to articulate the way the tools and the communications and the strategy all fit together, and how they're going to execute that, then what will happen is the new strategy will look a lot like the old strategy. Too much discretion, too much ability to create leeway between their tools, actions, communications, and strategies will just look like the old discretionary regime. So, tying those pieces together, I think, is going to be an important part of the success of this effort, and the payoff of this effort if, in fact, they can pull it off.

The other point I would make about strategies is that when considering strategies, I think the Fed needs to be very careful about overpromising. They need to understand and accept some humility about what they in fact can deliver on and the precision with which they can deliver it, so that the public will understand what the Fed actually can and cannot do. I think a big danger or risk, if you will, would be the Fed promising some degree of precision in their strategy and then getting frustrated over and over again by not being able to deliver with the precision that markets think they should have. So, I think part of the communications is about setting expectations right with the market in terms of what the Fed is able to do, making sure that there's not too much hubris and that there's some humility in that new strategy, and to communicate that in an effective way. Because otherwise, they'll find themselves lacking credibility, and if they don't have credibility, then whatever new strategy they pick is probably going to fail. Still, I'm very optimistic, and I'm very pleased that this effort's going on.

CHAPTER NINE

Optimal Monetary Policy and Inequality

James Bullard

The remarks presented here are based on "Optimal Monetary Policy for the Masses" (Bullard and DiCecio 2019), which talks about nominal-GDP targeting in a specific framework. In his 2012 Jackson Hole talk (Woodford 2012), Mike Woodford talked about nominal GDP targeting as being the right sort of forward commitment that the central bank needs to make in order to have a better monetary policy and, in particular, to handle monetary policy at the zero lower bound. I'm going to look at nominal GDP targeting here as optimal monetary policy in a different type of model that you're not used to. Part of this comes from my thinking that the profession is overcommitted to the New Keynesian framework, as beautiful as it is and as much as I've written papers about it. We do practically everything in that particular context. There are other models out there in the world. So, let's see what we get out of other models.

Our model is different, but the policy recommendation is similar to that of the New Keynesian model. Because of that I think you might conclude that nominal GDP targeting might be a pretty robust way to approach optimal monetary policy in worlds with the kinds of nominal frictions that we want to talk about. I'm hopeful that we can stimulate more research with the model presented here. I certainly wouldn't take it directly to policy today. On the other hand, I think it is promising. About the discussion and about the framework, what I see happening is that ideas in central banking are gradually shifting. Some of the ideas are brought into the policy discussion and that's how frameworks change over longer periods of time. I think that gives you a better picture of what might happen here, as opposed to the Fed suddenly switching to a different framework on a particular day.

What do we do in this paper? It's a stylized economy. We're going to make simplifying assumptions that will allow for paper-and-pencil solutions. There are going to be private credit markets that are critical and a whole lot of heterogeneity in this economy. I want all of us to work more on heterogeneity, because I think heterogeneous agents are an important frontier for macroeconomics. The role of monetary policy is to make sure that these private credit markets work well, as complete markets, and it's going to look like nominal GDP targeting. The main point of this paper—there are companion papers to this one—is that nominal GDP targeting succeeds in fixing credit market frictions even when there's a whole lot of heterogeneity in the economy, enough to match the Gini coefficients for the US economy (Azariadis et al. 2019).

I'm going to advertise a model by briefly describing the construct and then I'm going to show you some pictures. This is an overlapping generations (OLG) structure. I don't think you should take life and death in the model literally. We're keeping track of people only when they're age twenty; we're not keeping track of them before. We're going to quit keeping track of them when they get to age eighty. They're going to live for 241 quarters, so that we can talk about a quarterly model. Sometimes when people do OLG models, they start to think about long-run issues, but I want to think business-cycle issues. Households have very simple log-log preferences, defined over consumption and leisure.

The key feature is that when you come into this model at age twenty, you're randomly assigned a productivity profile over your lifetime (see figure 9.1). This productivity profile starts low. It rises up exactly in the middle of life, peaks in the middle of life and then goes down to the previous level; this symmetry feature is going to

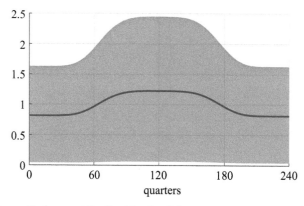

FIGURE 9.1. Endowment Profiles Mass by Cohort

Note: Endowment profiles mass shown as the blue shaded area; the solid line represents a typical endowment profile. The scaling factor is drawn from a uniform distribution. Drawing from a low-normal distribution is harder to visualize, but such a distribution would include arbitrarily rich and arbitrarily poor households.

help us with the math. We are drawing these for the continuum of agents in the incoming cohort from a uniform distribution in the figures below. But you could draw the productivity profiles from a log-normal distribution and have arbitrarily poor and arbitrarily rich households. Elon Musk would be in this economy if we did the log-normal distribution.

The productivity units that you have at every stage in your life are sold in a competitive market at an economy-wide wage. Aggregate production is linear. The economy grows over time at a stochastic rate. So, there's an aggregate shock here. For those of you who are technically minded—a few students in here—this is a heterogeneous-agent economy with an aggregate shock that you can solve with pencil and paper. So that's the technical side of this that is interesting. You could also consider the effective lower bound in this setting. I'm not going to talk about it here so you will have to go to the companion paper for that (Azariadis et al. 2019).

What's going on in this economy? There are peak earning years and the young people aren't earning very much, but they want to

pull consumption forward in the life cycle, so they want to borrow. People who are middle aged want to save for retirement, so
they want to lend to the young people. These forces generate a
big household credit market. You could think of the services that
are being pulled forward in the life cycle by younger households
as housing services. And you could think of the one asset in this
economy as being mortgage-backed securities. Mortgage-backed
securities in the United States are about $9 trillion today, maybe
$10 trillion. Household debt total is about $13.5 trillion today. So,
this is a big private credit market that's out there in the real world.

There's going to be something wrong in this credit market, as
there is in the real world. There's non-state-contingent nominal
contracting, which means that the contracts are set up in nominal
terms and they're not contingent on any shocks that occur in the
economy or among borrowers and lenders. There are two parts to
that. Resources are misallocated because of the non-state contingency. The fact that contracting is in nominal terms means that the
monetary policy maker might be able to do something about that
and fix this problem in the credit market.

Enough about the structure. Let's just go to what you get out
of this. You get a monetary policy that follows a nominal GDP
targeting rule. It delivers complete-markets consumption alloca-
tions, which means it essentially cancels out the uncertainty for the
households going forward. So it's a form of insurance for the households, similar to the findings from Evan Koenig (Koenig 2013).
Kevin Sheedy also has a great paper about this (Sheedy 2014). One
thing out of the Sheedy paper is the crucial role of the non-state-
contingent nominal contracting—nine times more important than
the sticky price friction according to his calibrated model. So, that's
food for thought.

This policy induces equity-share contracting, which means we all
get our own slice of the pie, no matter how much we produce or how
much we get paid on a given day. We all consume the same amounts

because the borrowing and lending works perfectly in this economy, provided the policy maker pursues optimal policy. I'm going to show you cross-sectional pictures, but this is a stochastic economy: consumption does move around, and wages move around, everything moves around, but all in proportion to the real wage. Household consumption growth is equalized across all these agents—rich and poor, young and old, everybody's getting the same consumption growth rate—and it's equal to the aggregate growth rate.

This has really nice properties. The real interest rate is exactly equal to the output growth rate at every date even in the stochastic economy. That's the key theorem in the paper. This is actually a real business cycle economy underlying this model. But you can only get there by pursuing the optimal monetary policy. You could also think of this in terms of the "Wicksellian natural rate of interest." So, what the optimal policy is doing is getting you back to the Wicksellian natural rate of interest. The natural rate of interest is the one that would occur if there were no frictions in the economy, which is the case in the Kydland-Prescott economy. So in that sense, the New Keynesian policy advice and the policy advice coming out of here are exactly the same thing. You want to get the interest rate to be an undistorted interest rate in the economy, the real interest rate.

Because of the preferences we have, all households, rich and poor, will work exactly the same number of hours at each stage in the life cycle (figure 9.2). In figures 9.1–9.4, the horizontal axis goes from zero to 240, i.e., the quarters that you live. But think of this as a cross section. At any point in time, there's a cohort that's just entering the economy. That's the zero over there on the left. And there are other cohorts, like the 120 in the middle, and so on. So, the blue line says that people work more in the middle of the life cycle, and they don't work much at the beginning and the end of the life cycle. We actually ruled out corner solutions here, but they work very little at the beginning and end without retiring. So,

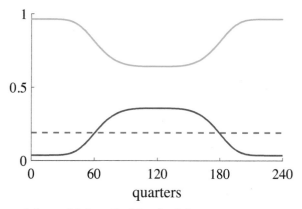

FIGURE 9.2. Labor and Leisure Decisions by Cohort

Note: The blue line shows labor supply by age. The green line represents leisure decisions by age. The red line shows the fraction of time worked in US data, 19 percent. The labor/leisure choices depend on age only. High-income households work the same hours as low-income households at each age.

doctors work forty hours a week. Taxi drivers work forty hours a week. Everybody works forty hours a week in the middle of the life cycle, because that's when you have your peak productivity, and you'd better work while the sun shines.

The credit market reallocates the uneven income (figure 9.3). People work more in the middle of life, when they're more productive, represented here by a blue mass. That's the income section at a point in time in this economy. Notice that the figure portrays only labor earnings and it doesn't show capital earnings. It's very uneven over the life cycle. The red bar and the red box show how much all these different agents are consuming. The way to think of this is to imagine a family of doctors—a young doctor, a middle-aged doctor, the grandfather's a doctor, everybody's a doctor—but only the middle-aged doctor is earning a lot of income. The young doctor's still in medical school and the old doctor is retired. Yet, they're all consuming exactly the same amount because the credit market is working perfectly. So, they are at the very top of the red box there. You could say the same thing about a family of taxi drivers—old

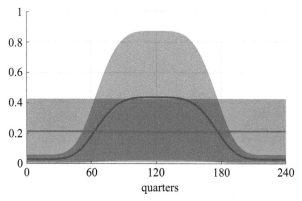

quarters

FIGURE 9.3. Consumption Mass and Labor Income Mass by Cohort

Note: Consumption mass, shown as the red shaded area, and labor income mass, shown as the blue shaded area, along the complete-markets balanced growth path. The red line and the blue line represent a typical consumption and labor income profile, respectively. Under optimal monetary policy, the private credit market reallocates uneven labor income into perfectly equal consumption for each productivity profile. The consumption Gini is 31.8 percent, similar to values calculated from US data.

taxi driver, middle-aged taxi driver, and young taxi driver. Only the middle-aged guy's earning any income, but they're all consuming exactly the same amount. So, if you're on the same life cycle productivity profile, you're going to consume the same amount no matter where you are in the age distribution. These things shift up over time because this is a growing economy, but this is the basic story here. So, the blue line shows the income of the typical guy in the middle and the red line shows the consumption associated with that. We're going to calculate Gini coefficients of labor income and consumption, so that would be off these shaded regions here.

And this is my favorite picture, the net asset–holding mass in this economy (figure 9.4). Maximum indebtedness occurs around period 60, that's like age thirty-five, so you'd be buying your house at that point. Maximum savings is around period 180, that's age sixty-five in this model; after that age, you run down your assets. If you're going to calculate the Gini coefficient off here, it's going to be

318   Bullard

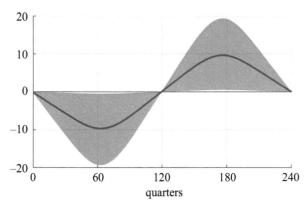

quarters

FIGURE 9.4. Net Asset–Holding Mass by Cohort

Note: Net asset–holding mass shown as the blue shaded area; the solid line represents a typical net asset–holding profile. Borrowing, the negative values to the left, peaks at stage 60 of
the life cycle (age ~35), while positive assets peak at stage 180 of life (age ~65). The financial
wealth Gini is 72.7 percent, similar to values calculated in US data.

TABLE 9.1. Gini Coefficients in the US Data and in the Model

	Wealth[*]	Income[**]	Consumption
US data	80%[†]	51%[††]	32%[§]
Model	72.7%	51.6%	31.8%

Sources: [†] Davies et al. (2011). [††] Congressional Budget Office (2016). [§] Heathcote, Perri,
and Violante (2010).

[*] Wealth is defined as the nonnegative part of net assets.

[**] Income is defined as labor income plus nonnegative capital income.

on the right-hand side of this picture, because we're only counting
positive financial wealth.

If you look at US data, the financial wealth Gini coefficient is
about 80 percent, the income Gini coefficient is 51 percent, and the
consumption Gini coefficient is 32 percent (table 9.1). The model
naturally ranks these Gini coefficients. We can get the income Gini
and consumption Gini almost exactly right. We're a little shy on the
wealth Gini, which is typical of these kinds of models. We do very

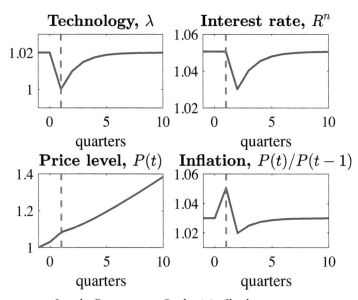

FIGURE 9.5. Impulse Responses to a Productivity Shock

Note: Monetary policy responds to a decrease in aggregate productivity growth by increasing the inflation rate in the period of the shock. Subsequently, inflation converges to its long-run equilibrium value from below. The nominal interest rate drops in the period after the shock.

well at Gini coefficients, even with a very simple, straightforward approach to income inequality.

So, people say, "Jim, why is this nominal GDP targeting?" If shocks were independent and identically distributed (i.i.d.), then you would actually stay exactly on a nominal GDP path at every date. It would actually be perfect nominal GDP targeting. If you have some serial correlation in the shocks, then you're going to go up and down around this path, but you're basically going to return to the nominal GDP path all the time.

People also wonder if this policy looks "weird" somehow? I'm going to show you a picture that says it does not (figure 9.5). Actual policy looks like what central banks already do. Both nominal and real rates fall during a recession. Let me talk to you through this picture, and then we'll get to the conclusions.

On the upper left is the shock in the model to the growth rate of aggregate technology, λ. Let's say that's growing at 2 percent, but you get a shock on day one, so it declines, and then it gradually returns to its mean. The key to optimal monetary policy is that the nominal interest rate there, in the upper right-hand corner, does not fall in the period of the shock. That's the key to nominal GDP targeting. The classic feature of nominal GDP targeting is in the bottom-right corner, where inflation goes up in the period of the shock. Subsequently, inflation falls. Nominal interest rates fall. The real interest rate is below its long-run level. All these features look just like what you would see out of a typical model. I don't think it looks all that different, depending on what you think about the nominal interest rate not falling exactly in the period of the shock. In our model, it falls one period after the shock.

In conclusion, this is a baseline benchmark-type model that could be expanded in many directions. It's based on the idea that actual households have peak earning years. They have to use credit markets to smooth life cycle consumption. There's a friction in that market—non-state-contingent nominal contracting—and the monetary authority can fix that friction. The way the monetary authority fixes that friction is by restoring the Wickesellian natural rate of interest in the model. For the real business cycle people here, that's the stochastic rate of growth of technology. The basic message is that even though there's a lot of heterogeneity in this economy—there are arbitrarily rich people and arbitrarily poor people—they all need the credit markets to smooth life cycle consumption. If you want the credit market to work well, nominal GDP targeting is a way to get the credit market to work well and fix the friction in that market. So, it's optimal monetary policy for the masses.

References

Azariadis, Costas, James Bullard, Aarti Singh, and Jacek Suda. 2019. "Incomplete Credit Markets and Monetary Policy." *Journal of Economic Dynamics and Control* 103 (June): 83–101.

Bullard, James, and Riccard DiCecio. 2019. "Optimal Monetary Policy for the Masses." Federal Reserve Bank of St. Louis Working Paper 2019-009C, April. https://doi.org/10.20955/ww.2019.009.

Congressional Budget Office. 2016. "The Distribution of Household Income and Federal Taxes, 2013," June 8. www.cbo.gov/publication/51361.

Davies, James B., Susanna Sandström, Anthony Shorrocks, and Edward N. Wolff. 2011. "The Level and Distribution of Global Household Wealth." *Economic Journal* 121, no. 551 (March): 223–54.

Heathcote, Jonathan, Fabrizio Perri, and Giovanni L. Violante. 2010. "Unequal We Stand: An Empirical Analysis of Economic Inequality in the United States, 1967–2006." *Review of Economic Dynamics* 13, no. 1 (January): 15–51.

Koenig, Evan F. 2013. "Like a Good Neighbor: Monetary Policy, Financial Stability, and the Distribution of Risk." *International Journal of Central Banking* 9, no. 2 (June): 57–82.

Sheedy, Kevin D. 2014. "Debt and Incomplete Financial Markets: A Case for Nominal GDP Targeting." *Brookings Papers on Economic Activity* (Spring): 301–61.

Woodford, Michael. 2012. "Methods of Policy Accommodation at the Interest-Rate Lower Bound." In *The Changing Policy Landscape: A Symposium Sponsored by The Federal Reserve Bank of Kansas City, Jackson Hole, Wyo.*, 185–288. Kansas City: Federal Reserve Bank of Kansas City.

CHAPTER TEN

Monetary Policies in Practice

Mary C. Daly

My discussion addresses why the Federal Reserve is reviewing its monetary policy framework at this point in time.[1] The first reason is that it's just good practice to review your strategies and tools. The economy changes, and you want to review and revisit these issues. This is something the Bank of Canada does regularly.[2] So I think of this as a best practice, even if we weren't facing some of our current challenges.

But we are facing some challenges. We're more likely to hit the zero lower bound (ZLB) going forward. We've heard this many times throughout this conference. We will frequently find ourselves fighting to push inflation up from below our target, as opposed to trying to pull inflation down to our target. The Fed has been very good at anchoring inflation expectations, but that means they matter more now than perhaps they have in the past. Or maybe they always mattered, but now we really see it. That's going to be increasingly important in the future.

When you put all these things together, we have three potential states of the world. First, we could have inflation that's above our target. We have a long history of knowing how to bring that down

---

1. See Board of Governors (2019).
2. See Bank of Canada (2019).

The thoughts expressed in this presentation are the author's own and do not necessarily reflect those of others in the Federal Reserve System.

to 2 percent. And we have tools and models that suggest we can do it. That's a world we're used to.

The second possible state of the world is the terrible financial crisis we experienced in the last decade, when you have an all-hands-on-deck policy and use every tool you can. But you hope that those financial crises don't happen frequently, so you don't want to necessarily think of the framework review through the lens of a terrible financial crisis.

What we're facing going forward are the following factors: we're more likely to hit the lower bound, we're fighting inflation from below, and we have this really high weight on inflation expectations. That's going to be our new norm for all the reasons that many of the participants here have discussed.

So I want to focus on that third state of the world. What's the best framework if that's the world we're likely to face? These are the factors I think about a lot.

First we're going to have more limited space for funds rate cuts. From the Summary of Economic Projections (SEP), figure 10.1 shows, as Vice Chair Clarida noted,[3] that the median projections by FOMC participants for r-star (r^*), the long-run neutral real interest rate, have been coming down over time. The star variables in general have been trending down, whether you're talking about u-star (u^*), g-star (g^*), or r-star. This is forward looking in many ways, and it just tells you there's less policy space and less funds rate space going forward than we've been accustomed to having in the past.

The second fact you have to look at if you're thinking about making policy going forward is that in recent years, inflation has consistently fallen below our 2 percent target (figure 10.2). That's true whether you look at the headline personal consumption expenditures (PCE) or core PCE index. As Robert Kaplan mentions (see chapter 11), if you consistently fall short of target, it tugs at the expectations. Even if

---

3. See chapter 1 in this volume.

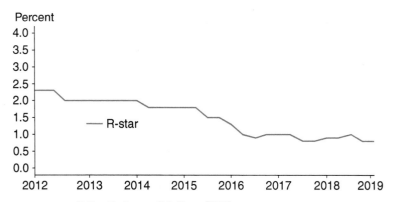

FIGURE 10.1. R-Star Estimates (Median of SEP)
Source: Summary of Economic Projections, Federal Reserve.

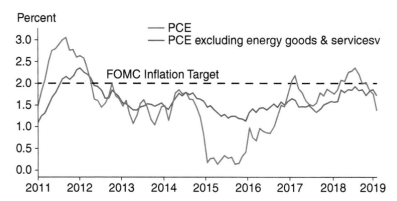

FIGURE 10.2. Core and Headline PCE Inflation, 12-month change
Source: Bureau of Economic Analysis.

expectations haven't become unanchored yet, there's a lot of pressure to tie them to the anchor more closely in the future, as John Williams and Thomas Mertens discussed in their paper.[4]

Another fact that comes from research done by some colleagues at the San Francisco Fed is that inflation expectations matter more today than they used to.[5] Figure 10.3 compares 1997–2007 with

4. See chapter 3 in this volume.
5. Jordà et al. (2019).

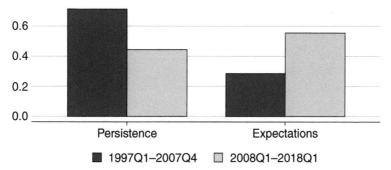

FIGURE 10.3. Coefficient on Lagged Inflation and Inflation Expectations
Source: Adapted from Jordà et al. (2019).
Note: One-year-ahead inflation expectations (for headline CPI) from the Survey of Professional Forecasters.

2008–2018. It shows that if you decompose inflation into persistence versus expectations, the persistence contribution is falling and inflation expectations contribution is rising. We've always worried about inflation expectations, but you can clearly see they're more important now than they have been in the past. This partly reflects the success of our credibility, but it's also something to think about when you wonder if that anchor is going to drift at all.

So if you put those three factors together—low r-star, low inflation, and an increasing role for expectations—and that's the future you face, then it's important to think about new strategies for achieving target inflation going forward. I'd like to discuss three viable alternative strategies when you're at the effective lower bound: nominal income targeting, price-level targeting, and average inflation targeting. I've obviously left out other things we talked about earlier today, such as negative interest rate policies. I'm going to focus on these three types of strategies, or alternatives, because they have something in common.

To start, here is a very stylized depiction of what John Williams and Thomas Mertens showed using quantitative simulations in their paper. The point I'm going to make here is that the three strategies—nominal income targeting, price-level targeting, and

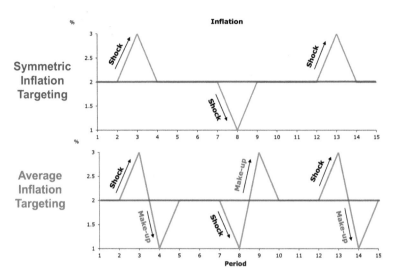

FIGURE 10.4. Targeted Inflation Patterns after a Shock

average inflation targeting—are all meant to have a makeup component that's different from our current symmetric inflation targeting policy. Figure 10.4 shows how the makeup would work if you get a shock. In the first case, we have a positive aggregate demand shock with inflation rising above the target. If you're using symmetric inflation targeting, you simply bring this back to two. If you're away from two, you come back to two.

But if you have average inflation targeting or one of these other strategies, you want to make up for that past miss. In this case, you want to disinflate. That's the makeup strategy.

So this goes forward through aggregate demand shocks, both positive and negative. This is what makeup policies are meant to do. They're meant to offset past misses. And that's very different from our current symmetric inflation target.

Now if you think about these three makeup strategies—nominal income targeting, price-level targeting, and average inflation targeting—they all have the same goal but different ways of achieving it. So we need to evaluate them on those merits. One of the most important evaluation criteria is ease of communication to the public.

I would argue that average inflation targeting would be a bit easier to communicate than nominal income targeting or price-level targeting, simply because people have already accepted that we have a 2 percent inflation target. Thus, average inflation targeting just becomes how we reach and sustain that target. Nominal income targeting and price-level targeting are just harder to communicate. So for that reason I'm going to focus on average inflation targeting.

Even if you choose average inflation targeting as your strategy, there are many open questions. Some of them have been mentioned here today, but I've got a list. First, what is the window length over which you need to average? Do you really need to fully offset, where you potentially commit past the length of the current committee members' terms of office? If your committee's changing, how long do you have to commit for this strategy to be successful?

Another important question is, does this even work if agents in the economy are backward looking rather than forward looking, since so much of this rests on expectations? Does it matter if people do or don't participate in financial markets? Would an average inflation strategy be credible? Could we really deliver on credibility? And, of course, should it be temporary or permanent?

So let me take on those types of questions using a framework developed by my colleague, Sylvain Leduc, and his coauthors, Amano and Gnocchi.[6] What they do is very similar to what John Williams and Thomas Mertens did, using a simple model,

$$i_t = r_t + \phi \frac{1}{n} \sum\nolimits_{k=0}^{n} (\pi_{t-k} - \bar{\pi}),$$

where the weight on the inflation gap (φ) equals 1.5 and the deviations are averaged over a period of $n = 6$ quarters. The point here is

6. Amano, Gnocchi, and Leduc (2019).

to be illustrative, not quantitative, but the illustrative part gives us stack rankings of these different strategies. In this particular model, 20 percent of the households have no access to financial markets, 75 percent of firms are backward looking, and the effective lower bound binds 20 percent of the time. Those are your parameters.

Then the central bank is simply trying to minimize the inflation and output gaps. In this framework, it's going to use an average inflation rule to minimize average inflation around a number of years. The question then is, if you have a ϕ of 1.5, how many quarters does it take?

They ran a number of simulations and came up with six as a good number—six quarters, or one-and-a-half years. The question is, what do you get from those six quarters? If that's all you did, what would you get? Importantly, this is just hitting the effective lower bound and coming back up. It's not staying persistently at the effective lower bound as we did during the financial crisis.

Let's start with just the baseline of inflation targeting (IT). The blue lines in figure 10.5 show what we're all accustomed to seeing. You get a (demand) shock, output goes down, inflation goes down, and it's slow to recover because we're at the zero lower bound in this picture.

What happens if you have average inflation targeting (AIT) using the model framework that I just described? Well, in the model framework they have, the green lines in figure 10.5 show that output recovers a little more quickly. But the important thing is that inflation recovers much more quickly, and that's all because of the inflation expectations term. Agents in the economy know the Fed is going to commit to average inflation targeting, that it's going to get to 2 percent. They see that, and they're forward looking. For one thing, the policy acts as a shock absorber. You don't go down as much because you know inflation is going to come back up, so the shock has less effect on things like pricing decisions. In addition, it's well known and accepted that the Fed is working to stay at this target.

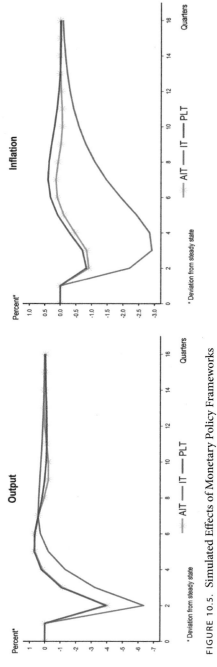

FIGURE 10.5. Simulated Effects of Monetary Policy Frameworks

Source: Amano, Gnocchi, and Leduc (2019)

So how does this compare to price-level targeting (PLT) in the same framework with a full makeup strategy? The red lines in figure 10.5 show that there's not a lot of difference between price-level targeting and average inflation targeting in this framework. And if average inflation targeting is easier to communicate, then it might be the dominant strategy between these two.

As I mentioned, this is a stylized model. This economy is only hitting the zero lower bound episodically and not persistently staying there. But if you expand it in simulations or robustness checks, and if you say you're at the zero lower bound for two to three years, then it means your average inflation target window isn't six quarters. It's more like two to three years. So if you are at the ZLB for two years, it's a three-year target window.

I thought a lot about this. I worried, what if it were something like ten years? How long would we have to go to really make that up? These model simulations say something on the order of six quarters if it's a slight time at the ZLB, and something like three years if it's a longer time.

Let me conclude, though, by talking about some other things that are also very important to credibility. This does not work unless there's credibility, because it all comes through the expectations term. That's why you get the big win: you have to have credibility in order for this to be effective. I would argue that calls for adopting such policies before you hit the effective lower bound—not when you hit the effective lower bound. You lose some of the power you have in this methodology if you wait.

It also implies—and this is the challenging part—that we must have a willingness to disinflate if necessary. That can be challenging for two reasons. One, it's not always popular. And two, we may not find ourselves with that many opportunities to disinflate. So how do we get credibility when that's before us?

I will only say that credibility takes time to earn. Credibility was not something the Fed had immediately when we had the Volcker

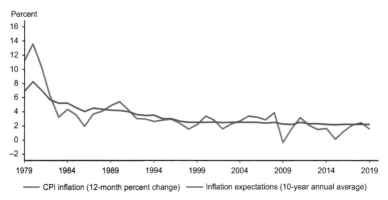

FIGURE 10.6. Inflation and Long-Term Inflation Expectations
Source: Summary of Economic Projections, Federal Reserve.

disinflation. It took a long time. So standing in 2019 and saying we feel like we have credibility is very different from what we heard today, and even in the historical presentation, it just takes time to earn it (see figure 10.6). I don't think we should be pushed off by the fact that credibility is challenging. But you have to be intentional about making sure that's the policy, and then going after it and recognizing it takes a little time.

In summary, with the Fed objectives met—we're close to our inflation target and we've got full employment—our economy is in a good state. So it is a really good time to look at our framework. And this is a best practice anyway.

I find average inflation targeting an attractive option. But credibility keeps coming back as the important thing. I do think the bar for change is high, so it's not enough to say something might work in theory, and we've got some simulations so, why not? Let's do it. The bar is really high because it can be costly to make mistakes in this space.

This framework and all the things we've heard today—the discussion, the debate, the simulations—and many more pieces of research are needed in order for us to make sure we can deliver on the dual mandate's goals for the American people.

References

Amano, Robert, Stefano Gnocchi, and Sylvain Leduc. 2019. "Average Is Better Than You Think: Average Inflation Targeting as a Make-up Strategy." Unpublished manuscript.

Bank of Canada. 2019. "Toward 2021: Renewing the Monetary Policy Framework." https://www.bankofcanada.ca/toward-2021-renewing-the-monetary-policy-framework.

Board of Governors of the Federal Reserve System. 2019. "Review of Monetary Policy Strategy, Tools, and Communications." https://www.federalreserve.gov/monetarypolicy/review-of-monetary-policy-strategy-tools-and-communications.htm.

Jordà, Òscar, Chitra Marti, Fernanda Nechio, and Eric Tallman. 2019. "Inflation: Stress-Testing the Phillips Curve." *FRBSF Economic Letter* 2019-05, February 11. https://www.frbsf.org/economic-research/publications/economic-letter/2019/february/inflation-stress-testing-phillips-curve.

CHAPTER ELEVEN

DISCUSSION OF KEY ISSUES IMPACTING ACHIEVEMENT OF THE FED'S 2% INFLATION OBJECTIVE

Robert S. Kaplan

In our May 2019 meeting, the Federal Open Market Committee (FOMC) left the federal funds rate unchanged in a range of 2.25 to 2.5 percent. In the post-meeting statement, we commented that, on a 12-month basis, overall inflation and inflation for items other than food and energy have declined and are running below 2 percent. The statement also noted that we "continue to view sustained expansion of economic activity, strong labor market conditions, and inflation near the Committee's symmetric 2 percent objective as the most likely outcomes."

BACKGROUND

Headline personal consumption expenditures (PCE) inflation, the Federal Reserve's preferred inflation measure, has been running below our 2 percent target for a substantial portion of the time period since 2012.[1] At the Dallas Fed, we particularly focus on the Dallas Fed Trimmed Mean measure of core PCE inflation, which filters out extreme upside and downside moves in inflation components. We believe this measure is a useful indicator of underlying inflation trends. The trimmed mean is currently running at

---

1. Data are from the Bureau of Economic Analysis (BEA).

approximately 2.0 percent on a trailing 12-month basis and has been in a range of 1.4 to 2.0 percent over the past seven years.[2]

The unemployment rate is currently 3.6 percent and has been below the Congressional Budget Office estimate of full employment for two years.[3] At the Dallas Fed, we particularly focus on the U-6 measure of unemployment, which measures the level of unemployed, plus "marginally attached workers" who indicate that they would like a job but have stopped looking for one, plus people working part time who would prefer to work full time. This measure now stands at 7.3 percent, and is below its 2006 prerecession low of approximately 7.9 percent.[4]

Dallas Fed economists expect GDP growth of approximately 2.25 percent in 2019. While this is slower growth than in 2018, it should be sufficient to further tighten the labor market and cause the rate of wage growth to modestly pick up over the course of 2019. Our economists also expect that, despite some recent weakness in headline and core inflation readings, the headline PCE and Dallas Fed Trimmed Mean measure of core PCE inflation are likely to firm, ending the year in the range of 2 percent.

Some observers have suggested that, with this tight of a labor market, there should be greater wage pressure than the 3.2 percent recent reading of average hourly earnings growth over the past year.[5] They argue that they would have expected wage pressure to have translated into greater price pressure. As most of you know, the Fed has initiated a review of its framework and communication strategy to explore whether there are actions we could take to improve our ability to achieve and maintain our dual-mandate objectives of maximum employment and price stability.

2. As of March 2019. Federal Reserve Bank of Dallas. For a further description of the trimmed mean PCE inflation rate, see Dolmas (2005).

3. As of April 2019. Bureau of Labor Statistics (BLS).

4. As of April 2019. BLS.

5. As of April 2019. BLS.

With all this as background, and in light of our ongoing framework review, I thought it would make sense to step back and explore some of the potential issues raised by recent weakness in headline and core inflation measures. In particular, I will focus my remarks on labor slack, inflation expectations, and structural forces with regard to how they may be impacting the Fed's ability to meets its 2 percent inflation objective.

LABOR SLACK

A number of economists have argued that there may be more slack in the U.S. labor market than standard measurements are capturing. They believe that there may be more scope to attract and retain previously under-represented groups in the workforce. To support this argument, it is worth noting that, since 2015, increases in labor force participation have disproportionately come from under-represented groups. For example, the participation rate of the prime-age female population with less than a high school education has increased significantly, as has the participation rate for black males and Hispanic females.[6]

It is also worth noting that the prime-age labor force participation rate in 2018 was 82.0 percent versus 83.1 percent in 2008 and 84.1 percent in 1998.[7] If we compare U.S. prime-age labor force participation to other developed countries, we find that the U.S. participation rate lags behind many of these countries, although this gap has begun to close somewhat since early 2015.

Is it possible that the strength of the labor market is drawing in workers who have been on the sidelines—particularly under-represented groups—and is also encouraging workers to stay in

---

6. Richter, Atkinson, and Russell (2019).

7. Prime-age indicates 25–54 years old. Yearly value is an average of monthly values. The 12-month average as of April 2019 was 82.2 percent (BLS).

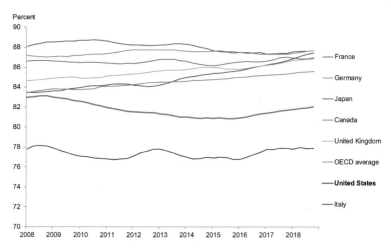

FIGURE 11.1. Prime-Age Labor Force Participation Rates, Ages 25–34

Note: Organization for Economic Cooperation and Development (OECD) average includes data for all OECD countries, except Belgium, Lithuania, and Luxembourg.

Sources: OECD, Haver Analytics.

the labor force?[8] Is it possible that improvements in skills training, child care availability and transportation availability have drawn, and could still draw, more sidelined workers back into the workforce—and keep them in the workforce?

It's important to recognize that gains in labor force participation act to slow the decline of the unemployment rate. Additionally, recent research—including work done by Richard Crump, Stefano Eusepi, Marc Giannoni, and Ayşegül Şahin—has argued that changes in demographics, especially the aging of the workforce, the aging of firms, as well as the increase in the attachment of women to the labor force, may have contributed to a decline in the natural rate of unemployment.[9]

If this is the case, we may look back five years from now and conclude that the natural rate of unemployment was simply lower than

8. Barnichon (2019).

9. Crump et al. (2019).

we had been historically accustomed, and that one of the reasons for the perceived surprising lack of inflation pressure was due to an excessively high estimate of the equilibrium level of unemployment. In this explanation, the Phillips curve may be alive and well, but the intercept is simply lower than we have previously understood. If this is true, central bankers need to be vigilant to the possibility that there is still the potential for inflation readings to firm substantially, with a time lag, if the degree of full employment overshoot becomes more sizeable and persists for an extended period of time.

INFLATION EXPECTATIONS

Another debate relates to the Fed's ability to manage longer-run inflation expectations. As you all know, the Fed has clearly articulated a 2 percent PCE inflation target. Many would argue that the Fed has done a reasonably good job in helping to anchor inflation expectations. They would cite the fact that surveys of professional forecasters' inflation expectations are close to 2 percent, and they would suggest that this is not a coincidence; it is a reflection of the Federal Open Market Committee's policy actions and communications, which have been aimed at achieving and maintaining full employment while anchoring longer-run inflation expectations at our 2 percent objective.

However, other economists contend that, due to an extended period of inflation running below our 2 percent target, expectations may have drifted somewhat lower. This downward drift might be reflected in the University of Michigan survey for inflation expectations over the next five years, which has gone from an average of 2.9 percent in 2013 to 2.5 percent in the twelve months ending April 2019.[10] These economists argue that the Fed may need

---

10. For example, looking across individuals in the University of Michigan survey, Sandor Axelrod, David Lebow, and Ekaterina Peneva find that lower experienced or perceived inflation correlates with lower expected inflation. See Axelrod, Lebow, and Peneva (2018).

to do more to help keep inflation expectations well-anchored. In particular, has the Fed done enough to convince the public that it is committed to a symmetrical 2 percent inflation target? Are there changes to the Fed's policy framework, communication strategy, or other actions the Fed could take to help better anchor inflation expectations at the Fed's 2 percent target?

STRUCTURAL FORCES

An additional area of exploration deals with structural changes in the U.S. and global economies. In particular, are the forces of technology, technology-enabled disruption, and, to some extent, globalization, limiting the pricing power of businesses and muting inflation?

Dallas Fed economists recognize that we are living through a period of acceleration in the trend of technology replacing people. We are also seeing the proliferation of new models for selling goods and services—often technology-enabled (think Amazon, Airbnb, Uber, or Lyft)—that replace traditional models for delivering these goods and services. These new models are often enabling consumers to buy products and services at prices that are dramatically below those of incumbent competitors. To take advantage of this trend, large-platform companies are increasingly bundling products and services—sometimes with little or no gross margin—in order to gain market share.

All this is being facilitated by the fact that the consumer now has in the palm of his or her hand more computing power than most companies did just fifteen years ago. Consumers are able to use this new technology to shop for goods and services at lower prices, often with greater convenience.

The impact of these trends means that companies, depending on the industry, often have much less pricing power than they did historically. In response, companies are investing even more in technology that replaces people and, increasingly, taking actions to achieve greater scale in order to effectively manage the investment and margin implications of these trends. The net result is that, in a range of industries, if there is wage pressure, companies are just as likely to see margin erosion versus being able to pass these costs on to the customer.

As a result of these trends, we are seeing a record level of merger activity by companies in order to get more scale to compete in this environment.[11] Companies are using increased debt issuance to fund merger activities to achieve greater scale and are also using increased debt issuance to fund accretive share repurchases in order to soften the margin dilution they are experiencing.[12] Activist investors are increasingly pressuring companies to take steps to merge and fund accretive share repurchases or face replacement of their boards of directors and/or their executive teams.

The workforce is also experiencing the impact of this trend. Highly educated and skilled workers are often seeing the benefits of technology and disruption—depending on their company or industry. However, those workers with a high school education or less—who lack specific skills training—are increasingly seeing their jobs restructured or eliminated. This is leading to increasing wealth and income inequality.

This discussion would suggest that powerful structural changes in the economy may be an important aspect of more muted price pressures. Further, there may be some evidence in recent productivity statistics that new technology and greater economies of scale could be helping to dampen growth in unit labor costs.

---

11. Thomson Reuters (2018).

12. Data are from Standard and Poor's (S&P) Global Market Intelligence's Leveraged Commentary and Data (LCD). Also see Reuters (2018).

IMPLICATIONS

The Fed's 2 percent inflation target is symmetrical—that is, we don't want inflation to run persistently below or above our 2 percent target. Sustained deviations from our inflation target could increase the likelihood that inflation expectations begin to drift or become unanchored. This could, in turn, make it more difficult for the Fed to achieve its dual-mandate objectives of full employment and price stability.

In this context, the various issues raised in this essay merit further discussion and attention. As the Federal Reserve conducts its ongoing review of our monetary policy framework and communication strategy, the challenge will be to explore potential options for enhancing our policy approach so that we can better achieve our dual-mandate objectives.

References

Axelrod, Sandor, David E. Lebow, and Ekaterina Peneva. 2018. "Perceptions and Expectations of Inflation by U.S. Households," Finance and Economics Discussion Series 2018-073, October. Washington, DC: Board of Governors of the Federal Reserve System.

Barnichon, Regis. 2019. "The Ins and Outs of Labor Force Participation," CEPR Discussion Paper No. DP13481, Centre for Economic Policy Research, January. https://papers.ssrn.com/sol3/papers.cfm?abstract_id=3324216.

Crump, Richard K., Stefano Eusepi, Marc Giannoni, and Ayşegül Şahin, 2019. "A Unified Approach to Measuring u*," Brookings Papers on Economic Activity conference draft, spring. https://www.brookings.edu/bpea-articles/a-unified-approach-to-measuring-u.

Dolmas, Jim. 2005. "Trimmed Mean PCE Inflation." Federal Reserve Bank of Dallas Working Paper 0506, July 25. https://www.dallasfed.org/~/media/documents/research/papers/2005/wp0506.pdf.

Reuters. 2018. "Buybacks to Top Use of S&P 500 Companies' Cash in 2019: Goldman Sachs," October 5.

Richter, Alex, Tyler Atkinson, and Laton Russell. 2019. "Changes in Labor Force Participation Help Explain Recent Job Gains." *Dallas Fed Economics,* Federal

Reserve Bank of Dallas, February 19. https://www.dallasfed.org/research/economics/2019/0219.

Thomson Reuters. 2018. "Mergers & Acquisitions Review; Financial Advisors." *Refinitiv* (full year). https://sales-support.financial.thomsonreuters.com/thesource/getfile/index/f513f65f-ae93-47ed-b2fd-9c21327b12a3.

CHAPTER TWELVE

Improving Our Monetary Policy Strategy

Loretta J. Mester

The Federal Open Market Committee (FOMC) currently uses what has been called a flexible inflation-targeting framework to set monetary policy. It is briefly described in the FOMC's statement on longer-run goals and monetary policy strategy.[1] In my view, this framework has served the FOMC well in effectively promoting our policy goals. A milestone was reached in January 2012 when the United States adopted an explicit numerical inflation goal. Careful analysis and discussions helped the FOMC reach a consensus on the explicit 2 percent goal and the statement that describes the FOMC's approach to setting policy to promote its congressionally mandated goals of price stability and maximum employment.

The FOMC is currently reviewing its policy framework. I am very supportive of this initiative. As a matter of good governance, a central bank should periodically review its assumptions, methods, and models, and to inform its evaluation, it should seek a wide range of perspectives, including those from experts in academia, the private sector, and other central banks. Another motivation to undertake the review now is that the postcrisis economic environment is expected to differ in some important ways from the precrisis world. Based on the aging of the population and the

1. See FOMC (2019b).

The views presented here are the author's own and are not necessarily shared by fellow panelists, other colleagues on the Federal Open Market Committee, or the Federal Reserve System.

expected slowdown in population growth, higher demand for safe assets, and other factors, many economists anticipate that the longer-term equilibrium real interest rate will remain lower than in past decades.[2] In fact, empirical estimates of the equilibrium real fed funds rate, so-called r^*, while highly uncertain, are generally lower than in the past.[3] This means there is a higher chance that the policy rate will be constrained by the zero lower bound and that nontraditional monetary policy tools will need to be used more often. To the extent that these tools are less effective than the traditional interest rate tool or are otherwise constrained, the potential is for longer recessions and longer bouts of inflation well below target.[4] In addition, fiscal policy's ability to buffer against macroeconomic shocks is likely to be constrained, given projected large fiscal deficits and high government debt-to-GDP ratios.[5] This raises the question of whether changes to our monetary policy framework would be helpful in maintaining macroeconomic stability in this environment.

A number of suggestions have been made for alternative monetary policy frameworks that potentially offer some benefits in a low-interest-rate environment. These include setting an inflation target that is higher than 2 percent (an option not being considered by the FOMC in its framework review), using price-level targeting or nominal GDP targeting instead of inflation targeting, targeting average inflation over the business cycle or some other time frame, or using what former chair Ben Bernanke has called temporary price-level targeting (which is essentially doing inflation targeting in normal times and price-level targeting once the policy rate is

---

2. See Mester (2018a).

3. For FOMC projections, see FOMC (2014) and FOMC (2019a). For a review of the literature on the equilibrium interest rate, see Hamilton et al. (2015).

4. Other government policies might also be brought to bear to increase the long-term growth rate and equilibrium interest rate, which would give monetary policy more room to act. Such policies would focus on increasing productivity growth and labor force growth.

5. See Peek, Rosengren, and Tootell (2018).

constrained by the zero lower bound). An idea that has received somewhat less attention is defining the inflation goal in terms of a range centered on 2 percent rather than a point target.[6] Although these alternative frameworks have theoretical appeal, none of them is without implementation challenges. For example, many of them work well in models of perfect credibility and commitment, where the public understands the framework and believes future committees will follow through, and the committee actually does follow through, implying that the committee has control of inflation expectations. Whether these assumptions would hold in practice is an open question. One needs to ask whether it is credible for policy makers to commit to keep interest rates low to make up for past shortfalls of inflation from target even when demand is growing strongly or to act to bring inflation down in the face of a supply shock by tightening policy even in the face of weak demand. It is not clear what actually would happen to inflation expectations in these scenarios despite what is assumed in the models. So the FOMC is going to have to evaluate the assumptions that drive the theoretical appeal of each framework and determine whether in practice the net benefits of any of the alternatives will outweigh those of the flexible inflation-targeting framework, and if not, what, if any, enhancements should be made to our current framework.

Regardless of the framework the FOMC ultimately decides on, the public's expectations about future monetary policy are an important part of the transmission mechanism of policy to the economy. This means effective communication will be an essential component of the framework. I believe there are ways we can enhance our communications about our policy approach that would make any framework more effective. Let me touch on three.

---

6. For further discussion of these monetary policy frameworks, see Mester (2018b) and Mester (2018c).

1. CLARIFY HOW MONETARY POLICY AFFECTS THE ECONOMY AND WHICH ASPECTS OF THE ECONOMY CAN BE INFLUENCED BY MONETARY POLICY AND WHICH ASPECTS CANNOT.

Monetary policy is more effective when the public's and market participants' policy expectations are aligned with our policy decisions. Before this alignment can occur, the public needs to have a basic understanding of our monetary policy goals and what monetary policy can achieve and what it cannot. My concern is that this understanding has diminished since the Great Recession. Regardless of the framework, the FOMC's strategy document should articulate the relationship between monetary policy and our two policy goals of price stability and maximum employment. We should clarify that over the longer run, monetary policy can affect only inflation and not the underlying real structural aspects of the economy such as the long-run natural rate of unemployment or maximum employment. Although this concept is touched on in our current monetary policy strategy document, I do not think that the public fully understands. Indeed, former chair Janet Yellen had to explain in one of her post–FOMC meeting press conferences that in an earlier speech, she did not mean to imply that she favored running a high-pressure economy as an experiment to affect longer-run growth and unemployment.[7]

I think we could do a better job of explaining how monetary policy promotes the economy's growing at potential and operating at maximum employment. In particular, we tend to move our policy rate up when resource utilization tightens and down when resource utilization eases in order to bring our policy rate into alignment with the economy's natural rate of interest, which changes over the business cycle as the economy adjusts to shocks. There doesn't need

---

7. See Yellen (2016, 9).

to be an exploitable Phillips curve trade-off between the unemployment rate and the inflation rate in order for policy makers to want to respond to changes in the unemployment rate, an indicator of resource utilization.[8] The response is not an attempt to actively use monetary policy to affect the longer-run growth rate of the economy or the longer-run unemployment rate. A benefit of explaining things in this way is that it makes it clear that the FOMC is not trying to rob the economy of jobs when it raises interest rates. Another benefit is that it should allay concerns that because the empirical Phillips curve has flattened, monetary policy has become anemic.

Improving the public's understanding of how monetary policy works and what it can achieve would help not only in normal times but also in bad times. The Great Recession was an enormous negative shock, some part of which was likely permanent or very persistent rather than transitory. Monetary policy should not have been expected to make up for that permanent loss. Fiscal policy should have taken on a larger part of the burden.

2. CLARIFY HOW UNCERTAINTY IS ACCOUNTED FOR IN MONETARY POLICY MAKING AND INCORPORATE THIS UNCERTAINTY INTO MONETARY POLICY STRATEGY TO AVOID GIVING A FALSE SENSE OF PRECISION.

According to Voltaire, "Uncertainty is an uncomfortable position, but certainty is an absurd one." In our context, this means it is important to convey that monetary policy makers have to deal with uncertainty in several forms. Monetary policy has to be forward looking because it affects the economy with a lag, but the economy is buffeted by shocks that can lead economic conditions to evolve

---

8. Brainard (2018) discusses the shorter-run neutral rate and longer-run equilibrium interest rate.

differently than anticipated. Moreover, our view of economic conditions in real time can be cloudy because the data come in with a lag and many economic data are revised over time. In addition, there is model uncertainty.

The public needs to understand that given the lags and revisions in the data, incoming information can alter not only the policy maker's view of the expected future evolution of the economy but also his or her understanding of current and past economic conditions. New information could alter the expected future path of policy and might even result in ex post regret of a recent action. Robert Hetzel says that policy making has a flavor of "guess and correct."[9] It is a normal part of monetary policy making that policy makers will always be learning about whether their policy settings are the appropriate ones to promote their goals.

The public has to hold the FOMC accountable for its performance, but it should not hold monetary policy makers to an unrealistic standard. The FOMC took an important step in communicating uncertainty when it began showing 70 percent uncertainty bands around the median projections of FOMC participants, but these are not emphasized. I think they deserve more attention and should be released at the time of the post-FOMC press conference. They are a good illustration of the reasonable amount of deviation to expect between the projections and the outcomes. Some have argued that the FOMC's projections of appropriate monetary policy, the so-called dot plot, should be dropped because actual policy can differ from the projections. I think that would be a mistake. The dots can change over time because of economic developments, but that's a design feature, not a flaw. Omitting the dot plot would not eliminate the uncertainty around the projections, the divergence in views across FOMC participants, or the fact that policy making always entails learning and recalibration, but it would be a significant step back in transparency.

9. See Hetzel (2019).

We need to recognize uncertainty in our broader monetary policy strategy as well. Consider the FOMC's inflation target. After much deliberation, the committee chose a point target instead of a range and a total inflation measure rather than a core measure. Although there were arguments on both sides, the committee was persuaded that a point target would better anchor inflation expectations. Implicit in the choice was that the committee would tolerate small deviations from target given the precision with which we can measure inflation, the precision with which we can guide the economy, and the typical revisions to the personal consumption expenditures (PCE) inflation measures, which tend to be revised up over time.[10] It is interesting to think through whether our policy choices or communications since 2012 might have differed had the committee opted for a range rather than a point target, as some other central banks do, and for a core measure rather than a total measure of inflation. These data revisions and measurement issues, as well as potential difficulties in maintaining anchored inflation expectations during the periods of higher inflation meant to make up for periods of lower inflation, and vice versa, would seem to be amplified in price-level targeting and nominal GDP targeting frameworks.

3. CLARIFY OUR MONETARY POLICY STRATEGY BY TAKING A MORE SYSTEMATIC APPROACH TO OUR POLICY DECISIONS AND IN HOW WE COMMUNICATE THOSE DECISIONS.

Households, businesses, and investors make economic and financial decisions based on their expectations of the future, including the future course of monetary policy, and the FOMC strives to avoid surprising the public with its policy decisions. The communications

---

10. Croushore (2019) finds that the average revision from initial release to first annual benchmark revision to four-quarter PCE inflation over the period 1965Q3 to 2015Q4 was 0.10 percentage point and the average revision to four-quarter core PCE inflation over the period 1995Q3 to 2015Q4 was 0.14 percentage point.

challenge for the FOMC is to give the public a good sense of how policy is likely to respond *conditional* on how the economy evolves without implying that policy is precommitted to a particular policy path *regardless* of how the economy evolves. Essentially, the FOMC needs to convey the strategy it uses to determine its policy actions over time to promote achievement of its policy goals, that is, its reaction function. And this will be true regardless of which monetary policy framework the FOMC ultimately adopts. Ironically, the FOMC's strategy document does not offer much in the way of strategy, and this can lead to a misunderstanding that our policy decisions are discretionary. The term "data-dependent" has been used to explain the FOMC's policy-making strategy, but this term could be potentially misinterpreted as suggesting that policy will react to every short-run change in the data rather than the accumulation of changes that affect the medium-run outlook.

A more systematic approach to setting monetary policy can better align the public's policy expectations with policy decisions and help to reduce some of the uncertainty around how we conduct monetary policy. It can help insulate monetary policy from short-run political considerations, and it can also offer more policy continuity over time as committee members change. In a time of rising public skepticism about "experts," which can undermine public trust in institutions, being systematic will help the public understand how our decisions are actually made, which can enhance the Fed's credibility.

The question is how to ensure that we are setting policy systematically and how to convey this to the public. I have three suggestions. First, although judgment will likely always be a part of policy making, simple monetary policy rules can play a more prominent role in our policy deliberations and communications.[11] The FOMC

---

11. The Cleveland Fed provides updates for a set of monetary policy rules and their outcomes across several forecasts on the Cleveland Fed's website, and the Federal Reserve Board's *Monetary Policy Report* now includes a section on policy rules. See Federal Reserve Bank of Cleveland (March 22, 2019).

has been reluctant to relinquish policy making to following a simple rule, because no one rule works well enough across a variety of economic models and circumstances. But the Board of Governors has begun to include a discussion of rules as benchmarks in the *Monetary Policy Report,*[12] and frameworks that try to build in some commitments and constraints on future policy actions, such as price-level targeting, average inflation targeting, and nominal GDP targeting, are being discussed. This suggests that systematic policy making is garnering more support. As a first step, selecting a few benchmark rules that have been shown to yield good economic outcomes and using these as reference points to aid policy discussions and communicating why our policy may or may not differ from the rules' policy descriptions could go some way in ensuring that our decisions are derived in a systematic way and could help us explain our own policy reaction function to the public.

A second suggestion is to enhance our own FOMC projections by asking the participants to provide a set of economic projections conditioned on a common policy path, in addition to the current projections, which are conditioned on each individual participant's view of appropriate policy. This common path might come from a policy rule. This would be a step toward achieving a coherent consensus FOMC forecast, which has been a challenge but which could serve as the benchmark for understanding the FOMC's policy actions and post-meeting statements, a recommendation I have made in the past.[13]

My third suggestion to help communicate systematic policy making is to make our post-meeting FOMC statement consistent from meeting to meeting and less focused on short-term changes

---

12. See Board of Governors (2019, 36–39).

13. See Mester (2016). Hetzel (2019) also proposes a method to determine an FOMC consensus forecast that would entail the committee's agreeing to its preferred reaction function at the start of each year, and then using an iterative process among FOMC members based on that rule and the board staff's economic model.

in the data released between FOMC meetings and more focused on the medium-run outlook and a consistent set of indicators on inflation, inflation expectations, the unemployment rate, employment growth, output growth, and financial conditions. Each statement could provide the rationale for the policy decision in terms of how accumulated changes in this consistent set of economic and financial conditions have or have not influenced the committee's assessment of the factors relevant for policy, that is, the arguments in our reaction function. The statement would also consistently articulate the committee's assessment of risks to the outlook and other considerations that the committee is taking into account in determining current and future policy. This assessment would be informed by the analysis of alternative forecast scenarios, which are discussed at each FOMC meeting. If we provided more consistency about the conditions we systematically assess in calibrating the stance of policy, the public and market participants would get a better sense of the FOMC's reaction function over time, and their policy expectations would better align with those of policy makers.

I note that all of the suggestions I have made today are relevant regardless of the framework the FOMC ultimately decides to use for setting monetary policy.

References

Board of Governors of the Federal Reserve System. 2019. *Monetary Policy Report,* February 22. Washington, DC: Board of Governors. https://www.federalreserve.gov/monetarypolicy/files/20190222_mprfullreport.pdf.

Brainard, Lael. 2018. "What Do We Mean by Neutral and What Role Does It Play in Monetary Policy?" Remarks at the Detroit Economic Club, Detroit, September 12. https://www.federalreserve.gov/newsevents/speech/brainard20180912a.htm.

Croushore, Dean. 2019. "Revisions to PCE Inflation Measures: Implications for Monetary Policy." *International Journal of Central Banking* 15, no. 4 (October): 41–265.

Federal Reserve Bank of Cleveland. 2019. "Simple Monetary Policy Rules," update of March 22. https://www.clevelandfed.org/en/our-research/indicators-and -data/simple-monetary-policy-rules.

FOMC (Federal Open Market Committee). 2014. "Minutes of the Federal Open Market Committee, March 18–19, 2014," April. https://www.federalreserve .gov/monetarypolicy/files/fomcminutes20140319.pdf.

———. 2019a. "Minutes of the Federal Open Market Committee, September 17–18, 2019," September. https://www.federalreserve.gov/monetarypolicy/files /fomcminutes20190918.pdf.

———. 2019b. "Statement on Longer-Run Goals and Monetary Policy Strategy" (adopted effective January 24, 2012; amended as effective January 29, 2019). Washington, DC: Board of Governors of the Federal Reserve System. https:// www.federalreserve.gov/monetarypolicy/files/FOMC_LongerRunGoals.pdf.

Hamilton, James D., Ethan S. Harris, Jan Hatzius, and Kenneth D. West. 2015. "The Equilibrium Real Funds Rate: Past, Present and Future." US Monetary Policy Forum, February 2015, revised August. https://research.chicagobooth .edu/-/media/research/igm/docs/2015-usmpf.pdf.

Hetzel, Robert L. 2019. "Rules versus Discretion Revisited: A Proposal to Make the Strategy of Monetary Policy Transparent." Unpublished manuscript, March 20.

Mester, Loretta J. 2016. "Acknowledging Uncertainty." Presented at the Shadow Open Market Committee Fall Meeting, New York City, October 7. http:// www.clevelandfed.org/en/newsroom-and-events/speeches/sp-20161007 -acknowledging-uncertainty.

———. 2018a. "Demographics and Their Implications for the Economy and Policy." *Cato Journal* 38, no. 2 (Spring/Summer): 399–413. https://www.cato .org/cato-journal/springsummer-2018/demographics-their-implications -economy-policy.

———. 2018b. "Monetary Policy Frameworks." Presented at the National Association for Business Economics and American Economic Association Session at the Allied Social Sciences Association Annual Meeting, Philadelphia, January 5. https://www.clevelandfed.org/newsroom-and-events/speeches/sp-20180105 -monetary-policy-frameworks.

———. 2018c. "Remarks on the FOMC's Monetary Policy Framework." Panel remarks at the 2018 US Monetary Policy Forum, sponsored by the Initiative on Global Markets at the University of Chicago Booth School of Business, New York City, February 23. https://www.clevelandfed.org/newsroom-and -events/speeches/sp-20180223-remarks-on-the-fomcs-monetary-policy -framework.

Peek, Joe, Eric S. Rosengren, and Geoffrey M. B. Tootell. 2018. "Some Unpleasant Stabilization Arithmetic." Presentation at the Federal Reserve Bank of Boston's 62nd Economic Conference, "What Are the Consequences of Long Spells of Low Interest Rates?" Boston, September 8. https://www.bostonfed.org/news-and-events/speeches/2018/some-unpleasant-stabilization-arithmetic.aspx.

Yellen, Janet. 2016. "Transcript of Chair Yellen's Press Conference," December 14. https://www.federalreserve.gov/mediacenter/files/FOMCpresconf20161214.pdf.

GENERAL DISCUSSION

ANDY LEVIN: Wow. It's a really awesome panel. Thank you, all of you, for your comments and explanations. Two quick comments. First, about earning credibility. Mike Bordo and Chris Erceg and I have a paper that we wrote a long time ago about this. We were looking at the Volcker disinflation and other disinflations, and our conclusion was that the central bank needs to be tough up front to prove it's serious about bringing down inflation, and then it gradually gains credibility. What I worry about is that these makeup strategies rely solely on promises about future policy actions, and there is no way to gain credibility up front, because you're stuck at the zero bound and you can't gain credibility until much later. And I was thinking about this quote: He who hesitates is lost. If the public doesn't believe the commitment while you're at the zero bound, then you don't want to carry it through later, because it was pointless. You didn't get any gain. Why would you do that? And so there's an equilibrium here where they know that, you know they know that, and so the whole thing kind of seems very fragile. And I think Mary mentioned earlier that she's a bit worried or concerned. And I would definitely lose sleep at night worrying that this fragile strategy is the one that the US economy would depend on in a severe adverse scenario.

Of course, that was a statement, but I'd really like to hear your responses to it. Now let me ask a real question. This morning, when we were talking about negative interest rates, Mike made the point that usually what happens is small central banks try things first. For example, in the case of inflation targeting, it was a long, long time before the FOMC [Federal Open Market Committee] was comfortable doing it. And we think, oh, maybe that's what'll happen with digital cash. By contrast, nominal GDP targeting and average-inflation targeting are totally untried and untested strategies, particularly at the zero bound. And so, given that the FOMC is usually so cautious, I honestly don't understand why the FOMC seems so much more willing to take a totally untried and untested strategy, where other innovative approaches seem to be completely off the table?

JIM BULLARD: I agree that you'd be a world leader. You'd be taking the world's top economy and experimenting with a new strategy. You'd want to be really careful about doing that. That was also my argument earlier about why I really don't want the United States to be the first country to move off the 2 percent international standard on inflation targeting. It took decades to get that consensus and you would unleash chaos in global foreign exchange markets, I think, if you did this. I totally agree with you. We should show the same willingness to think about electronic cash. I think there's more going on in the Fed maybe than you appreciate. People are thinking about this. But like nominal GDP targeting, they're not ready to commit to it.

MARY DALY: I'll just add one thing. John Williams, Jim, and I and many others are thinking about these things. That's what we should be doing. That's very different from choosing to change the operating framework. And that's why the bar is high. I don't think all those things are contradictory. Discussing and debating is what we should be doing.

JOHN COCHRANE: Thanks. So, all of these strategies are ways of implementing forward guidance. They rely on the idea that expectations far in the future have stimulative effects today. But that seems quite unbelievable. If you promise lower for longer, then a Fed chair has to go to Congress and say, "Look, I know that the short-term rate should be 5% today, looking at the economy today, but I'm going to keep it at zero for the next year, because I promised three years ago that's what I was going to do in order to stimulate demand back then. So, I'm making good on my promises, even though it's not the right thing for the economy today and will lead to too much inflation." That would be tough. Would anyone believe the Fed would do such a thing? And if not, what good are lower-for-longer promises and speeches?

The Fed had a chance, in fact. There was a long period of talking about lower for longer and forward guidance. And then, starting a couple years ago, the Fed was quite slow to raise rates and got a lot of heat for that. Nobody went to Congress and said, "We're deliberately holding rates lower than they should be, because we want to make good on those forward guidance projects." The chance to build some credibility was lost.

Now let me turn that positive. I think, in response to Andy, there is a way to do it, which is to gain your reputation on the other side—by sticking to a price-level target in the face of too much inflation, not just too little. If inflation goes above target, the Fed can get some reputation by saying it will not just bring inflation back to where it was, but it will run too low inflation for a while to bring the price level back. Getting people to believe one-sided promises is twice as hard.

In that regard, I think Loretta's idea that we're going to make these ideas into a strategy with lots of judgment is not going to work. To tie yourself to the mast this way, you're going to really have to tie yourself to the mast and be much more tied to the rule than you would otherwise want to be. If you use a lot of judgment, fine, but nobody will believe promises that in the future you will deviate from, well, using lots of judgment. It's the only way ex-post to go before Congress and say, "We're holding rates deliberately low even though inflation's increasing," and therefore to get people to believe you'll do that ex-ante. You have to kind of make this policy much more mechanical than you otherwise would. If you don't want to do that for lots of good reasons, then forward guidance is never going to be effective.

MICHAEL BORDO: This comment is for Mary and Robert. About fifteen years ago I wrote some papers on deflation. I did one with

Andy Filardo and some other people. We distinguished between good versus bad deflation. Good meant productivity driven and bad meant collapses in aggregate demand. What we found was that over one hundred fifty years and twenty countries, there were a lot of episodes of good deflation, and they lasted for a really long time. And so, if that's the case, we may be going into one of those situations now. In that case, how does this affect your strategy? It seems like inflation targeting, as we are using right now, really isn't going to work. Maybe we should be following a price-level target, and this just seems like it is not something that should be forgotten.

ROBERT KAPLAN: The reason I've stubbornly raised this third possibility now for more than three years is that I think something structural is going on in the economy. The problem is, it doesn't easily lend itself to academic research. But I can tell, having been in business for a long time and having talked to companies, the economy is going through fundamental, structural change involving technology, technology-enabled disruption, and, to a lesser extent, globalization. And so I don't have the answer to your question, but I want to raise it because it's a third explanation that we have to think about and it will affect how we think about the framework.

And to your last comment—so, then, why aren't we seeing more productivity improvement as a result of these structural changes? That's one of the questions. Why aren't we seeing more productivity improvement? It's one of the questions we've been doing a lot of work on at the Dallas Fed. We don't have all of the answers, but we're trying to think through these questions. We're having a conference, by the way, on this in May—our second one—just to invite the community to consider these questions.

At the Dallas Fed, we believe that productivity is connected to the issue of the adaptability of our human capital. This issue of human capital and adaptability of human capital—it's not the first time in our history we've dealt with it. We believe that workers with a high school education or less are on the receiving end of the effects of these structural changes, as opposed to benefiting from them. I think that is crucial. We believe that the benefits of these trends are being unevenly shared, which may be why you're seeing more uneven productivity results as a consequence of technology. It may also explain the issue of greater income inequality. But we don't have all of the answers. We're asking the questions. And we plan to continue to dig in, and we want to invite the rest of the research community to help us and see if others have good ideas on how to understand and think about these issues.

BILL NELSON: I think this question is for President Daly, but I'd be interested in anyone's views. So, I look out there and I see two-sided risks. I also worry about the fact that, you know, inflation could get anchored on the bad side of two, and the zero lower bound looks kind of close. But at the same time, I worry that historical relationships could reassert themselves. Inflation could start moving up. The Fed could find itself on the accommodative side of r^*, and a flat yield curve, and a flat Phillips curve. Isn't there a risk if the Fed is responding to an average of inflation that it gets behind the curve? I mean, so, it's moving up slowly, because it's responding to average inflation. Meanwhile, real interest rates move down, because expected inflation has gone up, pushing the unemployment rate the wrong way on a Phillips curve whose intercept has also moved up, because expected inflation is higher. I am concerned that adopting an averaging mechanism will put us back in the old days of the Fed getting behind the curve, over-reacting, and adding to business cycle variability.

DALY: That's a great question. Let me start by saying that the discussion I had today is in the context of a broader set of work that many here have done. We just had a monetary policy forum in New York where we talked about this. Is the Phillips curve dead or just hibernating? That was the title of the paper. But I think the even deeper work is, does it have these nonlinearities that surprise us? Or can we see them coming? So if you have a gradual increase in inflation, that's a very different problem than if you're going steadily along at your target and then suddenly have sharp increases, which is when you would worry that you're going to get behind the curve. In average-inflation targeting, if you're using six quarters or three years, you don't have the potential problems associated with averaging over ten years, where you could really get behind the curve and have volatile cyclical swings that we don't offset because we are committed to this long average. It's more heartening that the window length can be short. That you don't have to go to something like full price-level targeting, where you have a full makeup strategy, because then those things do become more prominent. I guess the main thing I want to say is you can't adopt any framework without assessing both sides of the risks. Right now, the prominent risk I focused on is the one we've been talking about a lot. We've got low r^*, slow growth, and low inflation. That's something we're not used to. But we also have to keep studying what happens in our economy when it really heats up. And we just don't have a lot of evidence that charts nonlinearities either in the aggregate data or even in the MSA data, where we have many more experiences of super-hot economies.

ANDY FILARDO: So, I agree that it's really great that the Fed is now regularly reviewing its monetary policy framework. And I appreciate the efforts to try to squeeze a little more performance out of a flexible inflation-targeting regime. However, I'm not sure, based on what I saw today, that there's a clear, urgent case for change. In other words, I don't see compelling evidence of having cleared the high bar that Mary talked about.

My question is about whether the strategies being discussed today are the most urgent now that the shadow of the great financial crisis has largely faded. When many of us heard that the Fed was going to do a strategic review, we thought that it would reflect on some lessons from the past decade about how monetary policy could better address big problems, such as financial crises. I don't think that any of the strategies discussed today would help to prevent a future crisis.

So that leads me to dig into the motivation of the review and the issue of crises. Do you think that monetary policy played a role in the run-up to the global financial crisis? One possibility is that the crisis represented a big one-off shock that came out of nowhere. If so, there is a logic to just focusing on refining the flexible inflation-targeting strategy. Another possibility is that the role of monetary policy in the crisis is still too difficult and early to deal with, and this monetary policy question about how to address crises will be saved for a later date. I also wonder how the Fed's review might fit into the current discussions happening in other venues about moving on to other types of monetary policy frameworks that look at flexible inflation targeting, macro-prudential policies, and the external environment, such as the IMF's [International Monetary Fund's] new focus on integrated monetary policy frameworks.

BULLARD: I can talk about that. I think the "company line" is that in the United States we passed the Dodd-Frank Act, we increased capital requirements a lot for banks, and we put on other types of regulation. That was appropriate, because you don't want to try to react to that with monetary policy. I think there's a fundamental problem on the horizon, or maybe with us today, which is the potential collapse of inflation expectations down to zero. I think that has happened in Japan, and it's been very hard to get off that. It looks like it's happening in Europe and it looks like it's going to be very difficult for them as well. So, I see this discussion as being very relevant to not allowing inflation expectations in the United States to follow in the path of Japan or Europe, and I see that as very much related to the framework discussion.

MESTER: Let me just add that at the upcoming conference at the Federal Reserve Bank of Chicago, there will be a discussion of financial stability and how that relates to the monetary policy part of the framework. So, it is something that we've struggled with in terms of the strategy document. And I can't remember the year that financial stability became part of that strategy document. But it's very terse. So there is going to be a discussion of that at the upcoming conference.

BRIAN SACK: So, one issue I thought would come up today, as part of systematic monetary policy with these threats, would be having the policy rule react directly to inflation expectations. This is related to the question I asked the vice chair this morning. I think that the thing to consider is, in the model that has been used, expectations have been formed consistent with the model. So essentially, expectations are helping you, as you're operating on the path of inflation out in the future. But maybe expectations are also a source of risk themselves, and we don't fully understand how they evolve. They may change because people don't believe the model or see other factors or so on. So, isn't there a case for actually having the policy rule react directly and forcefully to changes in inflation expectations, particularly longer-run inflation expectations?

BULLARD: Yeah. I don't know. In my other work, where I depart from rational expectations, then the expectations become a state variable of the system and you definitely would want to look at that. Some of the literature there does say that you should respond directly to inflation expectations. But I'm also recalling that John's equation one, if I'm not mistaken, actually had inflation expectations as one of the arguments in the policy rule. So, there was a little bit of that today. But I think this is very much an interesting issue. The literature has also talked about the circularity in this and multiple equilibria and stuff like that. But I'm very sympathetic in actual policy making that the state of expectations is a state of the system. It's not the same as the rational expectations that we see in the model.

DALY: I'll just add one thing, recalling something the vice chair mentioned earlier this morning. We have various different measures of inflation expectations right now. But I wouldn't consider any of them perfect. And so, you have to think about how you'd bundle them. If you're going to respond to a variable that you don't measure very well and you really don't understand its formation, that lends itself to more uncertainty. I think it's a very intriguing idea. In fact, when you said it earlier, I wrote it down in my research book. But I think we might not be there yet in terms of understanding how they're formed and how to measure them.

CHARLES PLOSSER: It's been a fascinating panel, as always, and a fascinating day. We've had four presidents plus John Williams talk earlier and the vice chair. I just want to make one comment, and that is, I think listening to the people who've spoken at this conference, particularly the policy makers—and I don't want to exclude Rich [Clarida]—but when you listen to the presidents, we had five of them participating in these comments, you begin to realize, I think, the importance of the Federal Reserve system and the role the presidents in the banks play. They are an important source of new ideas. Their banks are important sources of research in contributing to the formulation of monetary policy and its execution.

I think the other piece I would add is their independence is an important stalwart in part of preserving the independence of the Federal Reserve system and their protection from the politization that can often be pressures. And in this heightened political atmosphere, they are a critical wall, if you will, or support system for preserving the independence of the Fed from either political party, any political influence. So, I think you get a flavor of the contributions that they can make, the ideas that their banks can contribute, as I said. And not taking anything away from the board or from Rich, I think this illustrates how important the Federal Reserve system governance structure is, and its independence is preserved from the bank system, the Federal Reserve bank system.

So, I want to thank all of them for participating, making their contributions—not only their own contributions but the contributions from their research staff. I think it's really important. And a day like today illustrates that importance, I think, and I'm really proud of them and proud of the system for those contributions.

About the Contributors

JAMES "JIM" BULLARD is the president and CEO of the Federal Reserve Bank of St. Louis. In that role, he is a participant on the Federal Reserve's Federal Open Market Committee, which meets regularly to set the direction of US monetary policy. He also oversees the Federal Reserve's Eighth District, including activities at the St. Louis headquarters and its branches in Little Rock, Arkansas; Louisville, Kentucky; and Memphis, Tennessee. Bullard is a noted economist and scholar, and his positions are founded on research-based thinking and an intellectual openness to new theories and explanations. He is often an early voice for change. Bullard makes public outreach and dialogue a priority to help build a more transparent and accessible Fed. A native of Forest Lake, Minnesota, Bullard received his PhD in economics from Indiana University in Bloomington. He holds BS degrees in economics and in quantitative methods and information systems from St. Cloud State University in St. Cloud, Minnesota.

RICHARD H. CLARIDA serves on the Board of Governors of the Federal Reserve System and has been vice chair since 2018, filling a term ending in 2022. Clarida previously served as the C. Lowell Harriss Professor of Economics and International Affairs and chaired the Department of Economics at Columbia University. In addition to his academic experience, Clarida was the assistant secretary for economic policy of the US Treasury, where he was awarded the Treasury Medal in recognition of his service; and served on the Council of Economic Advisers under President Reagan. Clarida has also served as global strategic adviser and managing partner with PIMCO. Clarida is a member of the Council on Foreign Relations. He was previously a member of the National Bureau of Economic Research and served as co-editor of the *NBER International Macroeconomics Annual.* He received a BS in economics from the University of Illinois with Bronze Tablet honors and an MA and PhD in economics from Harvard University.

JOHN H. COCHRANE is the Rose-Marie and Jack Anderson Senior Fellow at the Hoover Institution, a research associate of the National Bureau of Economic Research, and an adjunct scholar of the CATO Institute. Cochrane was previously a professor of finance at the University of Chicago's Booth School of Business and in its Economics Department, and a junior staff economist on the Council of Economic Advisers (1982–83). Cochrane writes about finance, monetary policy, macroeconomics, health insurance, time-series econometrics, and other topics. He contributes editorial opinion essays to the *Wall Street Journal* and other publications and maintains the *Grumpy Economist* blog. Cochrane earned his bachelor's degree in physics at MIT and his PhD in economics at the University of California–Berkeley.

MARY C. DALY is the president and CEO of the Federal Reserve Bank of San Francisco. As a participant on the Federal Open Market Committee, she helps set U.S. monetary policy that promotes a healthy and stable economy. Since taking office in 2018, Daly has committed to making the San Francisco Fed a more community-engaged bank that is transparent and responsive to the people it serves. She works to connect economic principles to real-world concerns and is a sought-after speaker on monetary policy, labor economics, and increasing diversity within the economics field. Daly has served on the advisory boards of the Congressional Budget Office, the Social Security Administration, the Office of Rehabilitation Research and Training, the Institute of Medicine, and the Library of Congress. Daly earned a bachelor's degree from the University of Missouri–Kansas City, a master's degree from the University of Illinois–Urbana-Champaign, and a PhD from Syracuse University.

JAMES D. HAMILTON is the Robert F. Engle Professor of Economics at the University of California–San Diego. He has also taught at Harvard and the University of Virginia. He received a PhD in economics from the University of California–Berkeley in 1983. His research in econometrics, business cycles, monetary policy, and energy markets has been cited in more than 60,000 articles. His graduate textbook on time-series analysis has been translated into Chinese, Japanese, and Italian. Academic honors include research associate with the National Bureau of Economic Research, receipt of the Best Paper Award for 2010–2011 from the International Institute of Forecasters, and a 2014 award for Outstanding Contributions to the Profession from the International Association for Energy Economics. He is a fellow of the Econometric Society and the *Journal of Econometrics* and a founding fellow of the International Association for Applied Econometrics.

LAURIE SIMON HODRICK is a visiting fellow at the Hoover Institution, a visiting professor of law and Rock Center for Corporate Governance Fellow at Stanford Law School, and the A. Barton Hepburn Professor Emerita of Economics in the Faculty of Business at Columbia Business School. Professor Hodrick is known for her groundbreaking research on corporate financial decisions, with a particular interest in corporate cash holdings and capital allocation, including share repurchases and dividends, takeovers, and equity offerings. In recognition, she has been awarded numerous research awards and grants, including the National Science Foundation Presidential Young Investigator Award. She has also received many awards for teaching excellence, including the Columbia University Presidential Award for Outstanding Teaching. Hodrick serves as an independent director for SYNNEX, PGIM Funds, and Kabbage. She received a BA in Economics, *summa cum laude*, from Duke University and a PhD in Economics from Stanford University.

PETER IRELAND is the Murray and Monti Professor of Economics at Boston College, where he teaches courses in macroeconomics and financial economics for undergraduates and doctoral students. His writing and research focus on Federal Reserve policy and its effects on the economy, and has been published in leading academic journals, including the *American Economic Review,* the *Journal of Political Economy,* the *Journal of Monetary Economics,* and the *Journal of Money, Credit, and Banking.* Since 2011, Ireland has also been a member of the Shadow Open Market Committee (SOMC), an independent group of economists first organized in 1973 to monitor and comment publicly on the Federal Reserve and on US economic and regulatory policies. As a member of the SOMC, he contributes monthly editorials to the Manhattan Institute's Economic Policies for the 21st Century (*Economics21*) website. Professor Ireland received undergraduate and graduate degrees in economics from the University of Chicago.

ROBERT STEVEN KAPLAN has served as the thirteenth president and CEO of the Federal Reserve Bank of Dallas since 2015. He represents the Eleventh Federal Reserve District on the Federal Open Market Committee in the formulation of US monetary policy and oversees the 1,200 employees of the Dallas Fed. Kaplan was previously the Martin Marshall Professor of Management Practice and a senior associate dean at Harvard Business School. Prior to joining Harvard in 2006, Kaplan was vice chairman of the Goldman Sachs Group Inc., with global responsibility for the firm's Investment Banking and Investment Management divisions. Born and raised in Prairie Village, Kansas, Kaplan received a bachelor of science degree in business administration from the University of Kansas and a master's degree in business administration from Harvard Business School.

ANDREW LEVIN is a professor of economics at Dartmouth College. His highly influential research on monetary economics ranks him among the top two hundred economists worldwide in terms of citation count. Levin currently serves as a scientific adviser to the central banks of Norway and Sweden (Norges Bank and Sveriges Riksbank) and as a regular visiting scholar at the International Monetary Fund. Previously, he has been an external consultant to the European Central Bank, an external adviser to the Bank of Korea, and a visiting scholar at the central banks of Canada, Japan, Netherlands, and New Zealand; he has also provided technical assistance to the central banks of Albania, Argentina, Ghana, Macedonia, and Ukraine. He received his PhD in economics from Stanford University and worked at the Federal Reserve Board for two decades, including two years as a special adviser to the chair and vice chair on monetary policy strategy and communications.

MICKEY D. LEVY is the chief economist for Berenberg Capital Markets, LLC. From 1998 to 2013, he was chief economist at Bank of America Corporation, where he was on the executive Asset Liability and Finance Committees. Previously, he conducted research at the Congressional Budget Office and American Enterprise Institute. He is a long-standing member of the Shadow Open Market Committee and is on the Advisory Committee of the Office of Financial Research. He is a member of the Council on Foreign Relations and Economic Club of New York. Levy conducts research on monetary and fiscal policies, their interactions, and how they influence economic and financial market performance in the United States and globally. He testifies frequently before the US Congress on various aspects of monetary policy and banking regulation, credit conditions and debt, fiscal and budget policies, and global capital flows.

ANDREW LILLEY is a PhD candidate in Business Economics at Harvard Business School, specializing in international finance and macroeconomics. Prior to commencing his studies, he worked as an interest-rate strategist at UBS for four years. In both roles, he has authored articles on the intersection of central bank policy, capital flows, and the determination of interest and exchange rates. He graduated from the University of Sydney in 2011 with a bachelor's degree with honors in economics.

THOMAS M. MERTENS is a vice president for financial research at the Federal Reserve Bank of San Francisco, where he has been since 2015. Prior to working at the Federal Reserve, Thomas was on the faculty at New York University's Leonard N. Stern School of Business and, during a one-year visit, the Wharton School, University of Pennsylvania. He has taught several courses in finance and continues to teach at the University of California–Berkeley's Haas School of Business. Mertens's research primarily focuses on the pricing of risk and its impact on the macroeconomy. He has published numerous articles in academic journals and contributed to various policy discussions. Thomas received a PhD and MA in Economics from Harvard University and an undergraduate degree in mathematics from the University of Bonn.

LORETTA J. MESTER is president and CEO of the Federal Reserve Bank of Cleveland, where she serves on the Federal Open Market Committee and oversees one thousand employees in Cleveland, Cincinnati, and Pittsburgh. She has more than thirty years of experience in the Fed system, including as executive vice president and director of research at the Philadelphia Fed. Her research focuses on financial intermediation and has been widely published in academic journals. She is managing editor of the *International Journal of Central Banking,* a coeditor of the *Journal of Financial Services Research,* and an associate editor of several other academic journals. An adjunct professor of finance at the Wharton School, University of Pennsylvania, Mester has also taught at New York University. She earned a BA in mathematics and economics from Barnard College of

Columbia University and a MA and PhD in economics from Princeton University, where she held a National Science Foundation Fellowship.

SCOTT MINERD is chairman and global chief investment officer of Guggenheim Investments. Minerd guides the firm's investment strategies and leads its research on global macroeconomics. Prior to joining Guggenheim, Minerd was a managing director for Morgan Stanley and Credit Suisse. Minerd is an overseer at the Hoover Institution at Stanford University and is a board member of RFK Human Rights. He received a BS from the Wharton School at the University of Pennsylvania and completed graduate work at the University of Chicago Graduate School of Business.

DAVID PAPELL is the Joel W. Sailors Endowed Professor in the Department of Economics at the University of Houston, where he has taught since 1984. His fields of expertise are monetary policy, international economics, and applied time-series econometrics. He previously taught at the University of Florida and has held visiting positions at the University of Pennsylvania, the University of Virginia, and the International Monetary Fund. He received a BA from the University of Pennsylvania and a PhD from Columbia University. He has published more than sixty articles in refereed journals, including the *American Economic Review,* the *Review of Economics and Statistics,* and the *Journal of Monetary Economics,* and has served as an associate editor for the *Journal of International Economics,* the *Journal of Money, Credit, and Banking,* and *Empirical Economics.*

MONIKA PIAZZESI is the Joan Kenney Professor of Economics at Stanford University and a research associate at the National Bureau of Economic Research, where she directed the Asset Pricing Program. She is a fellow of the Academy of Arts and Sciences, the Econometric Society, and the Society of Financial Econometrics. Her research is on finance and macroeconomics with an emphasis on fixed income, housing, and monetary policy. She received her undergraduate degree from the University of Bonn and her PhD in economics from Stanford. Prior to joining the Stanford faculty, she taught at the University of Chicago Booth School of Business and the UCLA Anderson School of Business. She also served as monetary adviser at the Federal Reserve Bank of Minneapolis and as coeditor of the *Journal of Political Economy.* She has received the Elaine Bennett Research Prize, the Bernácer Prize, the Zellner Award, and research fellowships from the Alfred P. Sloan Foundation and the Guggenheim Foundation.

CHARLES I. PLOSSER served as the president and CEO of the Federal Reserve Bank of Philadelphia and on the Federal Open Market Committee from 2006 until 2015, during a period of global financial crisis and severe recession, requiring extraordinary action by monetary policy makers. Prior to joining the Fed, Plosser was the John M. Olin Distinguished Professor of Economics and Public Policy and director of the Bradley Policy Research Center at the University of Rochester's William E. Simon Graduate School of Business Administration, where he served as dean. He is also a research associate at the National Bureau of Economic Research. Since 2016, Plosser has served as a public governor for the Financial Industry Regulatory Authority. Plosser earned his PhD and MBA degrees from the University of Chicago. He is a 1970 graduate of Vanderbilt University, where he earned a bachelor of engineering degree, cum laude with honors), and a member of Tau Beta Pi (National Scholastic Honor Society for Engineers).

KENNETH ROGOFF is Thomas D. Cabot Professor at Harvard University. From 2001 to 2003, Rogoff served as chief economist at the International Monetary Fund. His widely cited 2009 book with Carmen Reinhart, *This Time Is Different: Eight Centuries of Financial Folly,* shows the remarkable quantitative similarities across time and countries in the run-ups and the aftermaths of severe financial crises. Rogoff is also known for his work on exchange rates and on central bank independence. Rogoff's 2016 book *The Curse of Cash* looks at the past, present, and future of currency, from standardized coinage to cryptocurrencies and central bank digital currencies. Rogoff is an elected member of the National Academy of Sciences, the American Academy of Arts and Sciences, and the Group of Thirty.

GEORGE P. SHULTZ, the Thomas W. and Susan B. Ford Distinguished Fellow at the Hoover Institution, is one of two individuals who have held four different federal cabinet posts. He has taught at three of this country's great universities and was also president of a major engineering and construction company. Shultz was appointed secretary of labor by President Nixon in 1969 and the next year became the newly formed Office of

Management and Budget's first director. He was secretary of the Treasury from 1972 to 1974. During the Reagan administration, Shultz was chairman of the President's Economic Policy Advisory Board (1981–82) and secretary of state (1982–89). In January 1989, Shultz was awarded the Medal of Freedom, the nation's highest civilian honor. Shultz holds honorary degrees from many universities as well as a PhD from Massachusetts Institute of Technology.

JOHN B. TAYLOR is the Mary and Robert Raymond Professor of Economics at Stanford University and the George P. Shultz Senior Fellow in Economics at Stanford's Hoover Institution. An award-winning researcher and teacher specializing in monetary policy, macroeconomics, and international economics, he served as senior economist (1976–77) and member (1989–91) of the President's Council of Economic Advisers, as undersecretary of the Treasury for international affairs (2001–2005), and, recently, on the G-20 Eminent Persons Group on Global Financial Governance. His book *Getting Off Track* was one of the first on the financial crisis of 2007–08, and he won the Hayek Prize for his book *First Principles*.

VOLKER WIELAND is managing director and holds the Endowed Chair of Monetary Economics at the Institute for Monetary and Financial Stability at Goethe University, Frankfurt. He also is a member of the German Council of Economic Experts. Wieland was previously a senior economist for the Board of Governors of the Federal Reserve System in Washington, DC. Wieland's research interests include monetary and fiscal policy, business cycles, macroeconomic models, and economic dynamics. He has published in leading economic journals such as the *American Economic Review,* the *Journal of Monetary Economics,* and the *Review of Economics and Statistics.* He has served as managing editor of the *Journal of Economic Dynamics and Control* and has received several awards and grants. Furthermore, he has been a consultant to central banks and international institutions. Recently, Wieland has been coordinating the creation of a public archive of macroeconomic models for comparative purposes, the Macroeconomic Model Data Base. Wieland received a PhD in Economics from Stanford University.

JOHN C. WILLIAMS is the president and CEO of the Federal Reserve Bank of New York and the vice chair of the Federal Open Market

Committee. Williams was previously president and CEO of the Federal Reserve Bank of San Francisco. Other positions have included economist at the Board of Governors of the Federal Reserve System, senior economist in the White House Council of Economic Advisers, and lecturer at Stanford University's Graduate School of Business. Williams holds a PhD in economics from Stanford, an MS degree from the London School of Economics, and an AB from the University of California–Berkeley. His research focuses on monetary policy under uncertainty, business cycles, and innovation. He has served on the editorial boards of the *American Economic Review*, the *International Journal of Central Banking*, and the *Journal of Economic Dynamics and Control*.

About the Hoover Institution's Working Group on Economic Policy

The Working Group on Economic Policy brings together experts on economic and financial policy at the Hoover Institution to study key developments in the US and global economies, examine their interactions, and develop specific policy proposals.

For twenty-five years starting in the early 1980s, the US economy experienced an unprecedented economic boom. Economic expansions were stronger and longer than in the past. Recessions were shorter, shallower, and less frequent. GDP doubled and household net worth increased by 250 percent in real terms. Forty-seven million jobs were created.

This quarter-century boom strengthened as its length increased. Productivity growth surged by one full percentage point per year in the United States, creating an additional $9 trillion of goods and services that would never have existed. And the long boom went global with emerging market countries from Asia to Latin America to Africa experiencing the enormous improvements in both economic growth and economic stability.

Economic policies that place greater reliance on the principles of free markets, price stability, and flexibility have been the key to these successes. Recently, however, several powerful new economic forces have begun to change the economic landscape, and these principles are being challenged with far-reaching implications for US economic policy, both domestic and international. A financial crisis flared up in 2007 and turned into a severe panic in 2008 leading to the Great Recession. How we interpret and react to these forces—and in particular whether proven policy principles prevail going forward—will determine whether strong economic growth and stability returns and again continues to spread and improve more people's lives or whether the economy stalls and stagnates.

Our Working Group organizes seminars and conferences, prepares policy papers and other publications, and serves as a resource for policy makers and interested members of the public.

Index

adjusted Taylor rule, 224–25, 236
Adrian, Tobias, 76
Afonso, Gara, 182
Agarwal, R., 54
aggregate demand, 94
    shocks, 327
aggregate growth, consumption and, 315
aggregate production, 313
aggregate shocks, 313
aggregate technology, 320
AIG, 307
AIT. *See* average inflation targeting
Alphabet, 266
Altavilla, Carlo, 50
Amano, Robert, 328
Amazon, 266
American Economic Association, 2
Anbil, S., 183
Andolfatto, David, 215
Armenter, Roc, 182
asset prices, Bernanke on, 272
average inflation targeting (AIT)
    dovish policies and, 120–21
    evaluation of, 327–28
    PLT and, 331
    policies, 106
    Reifschneider-Williams rule and, 134, 165–66
    shock absorption and, 329
    static, 119–23, 129, 145, 145f
    Williams on, 165–66

BA rule, 229
    federal funds rate and, 228f
    measure of, 230f
    performance of, 239–41
bailouts, 307

balance sheet
    of Federal Reserve, 159, 163, 177–78, 272, 284, 302
    Plosser on, 273
    uncertainty and, 272–73
balanced-approach rule, 253–54
    of Federal Reserve, 223
balance-of-risk assessments, of Federal Reserve, 276–77
Ball, L., 219, 237
Banegas, A., 183
Bank of Canada, 323
Bank of Japan, 41, 79–80
Bank of New York Mellon, 185
bank profits, 91
bankruptcy, 307
Banque de France, 24
Basel requirements, 212
BEA. *See* Bureau of Economic Analysis
Benhabib, J., 108, 114
Bernanke, Ben, 20, 36, 94, 107–9, 165, 170
    on asset prices, 272
    on central banks, 37–38
    on QE, 272
    on temporary price-level targeting, 346–47
Bitcoin, 99
Blue Chip Economic Indicators, 232f
Board of Governors, on interest rate rules, 218
bonds
    inflation-linked, 42n8, 45
    nominal, 45
    price pegging program, 28–29
    real, 45
Bordo, Michael, 20, 29, 71, 81, 357, 359–60
Borio, C., 175
borrowed funds, 189

breakeven
    inflation, 12
    inflation expectations and, 46–48
    synthetic, 45, 46f, 69
    vanilla, 46f
Bretton Woods, collapse of, 3
Brunnermeier, M. K., 49
Buiter, W. H., 36, 54
Bullard, Jim, 170–71, 214, 358, 364
Bureau of Economic Analysis (BEA), 280, 300
Burns, Arthur, 260, 261
business cycle theory, 25
    output growth and, 315
    variability in, 361

Caballero, R. J., 56, 175
call options, 67
Calomiris, Charlie, 101
Canzoneri, M., 40
Capital Asset Pricing Model (CAPM), 264
Carney, Mark, 23
cash flows
    discount rate of, 264
    free, 265–66
    future free, 264
cash hoarding, 29–30, 61
cash-arbitrage argument, 156
cashless limit, negative interest rate policy
    in, 50–53
Cato Journal, 97, 300
CBO. *See* Congressional Budget Office
CCTW model, 241
CEA. *See* Council of Economic Advisers
central banks, 3–4, 21, 23
    Bernanke on, 37–38
    core power of, 178
    credibility of, 31, 357
    deviation of rules by, 217–18
    on discretion, 248
    ELB and, 131
    independence of, 33, 163
    inflation and, 40, 329
    inflation targeting by, 31, 289
    interest rates and, 104
    lower bounds and, 105
    output gaps and, 329
    price stability and, 100
    reserve accounts at, 156
    short-term nominal interest rate and,
        110–11
    Taylor on, 304–5
    in United States, 169–70
central payment system, federal reserve and,
    267–68

Chen, H., 175
China, fiscal shocks in, 43–44
Christiano, L., 219, 237–38, 241, 254
Cieslak, A., 268
Clarida, Richard, 20–26, 99, 108, 171–72,
    324, 365
    on Federal Reserve, 302
Cleveland Fed, 352n11
CMR14 model, 241
Cochrane, John, 25, 93, 166, 169, 252, 267
    on financial crisis, 305
    on forward guidance, 358–59
coefficients
    on inflation expectations, 326f
    on lagged inflation, 326f
Coenen, Günter, 167
Cogan, J., 241
cohort
    consumption by, 317f
    endowment profiles mass by, 313f
    labor force participation by, 316f
    labor income mass by, 317f
    leisure decisions by, 316f
    net asset-holding mass by, 318f
commercial paper rate, Federal Reserve and,
    206
Congressional Budget Office (CBO), 5, 227
    output gap, 232
constrained discretion, 20
Consumer Price Index (CPI), 42n9, 44–45
    caps, 69
    synthetic breakevens and, 69
    in United States, 47–48
consumption
    aggregate growth and, 315
    by cohort, 317f
    of households, 315
    life cycle, 320
    monetary policy and, 95–96
    See also personal consumption expenditures
core power, 178
corridor system, 179f
    discount rate in, 200
    interest rates in, 200
    for short-term interest rates, 178–79
cost-push shock, 236
Council of Economic Advisers (CEA), 260
CPI. *See* Consumer Price Index
credibility
    of central banks, 31, 357
    earning, 331–32
    of Federal Reserve, 161, 331–32
    of forward guidance, 40
    Levin on, 357

credit cycle, Federal Reserve and, 305–6
credit market
    household, 314
    nominal GDP and, 312
    reallocation by, 316
Crowe, Chris, 21
Crump, Richard, 76, 338
Cúrdia, V., 175
currency
    dual-currency system, 54
    electronic, 29–30, 54–55
    exchange rates, 54–55
    foreign, 57
    hoarding of, 29–30, 61
    magnetic stripes in, 54
    paper, 53–58, 61–62, 84
    size of, 214
    See also digital cash
The Curse of Cash (Rogoff), 83
Cwik, T., 241

Dallas Fed, 335
    on inflation expectations, 339–40
    on productivity, 360–61
    on structural forces, 340–41
Dallas Fed Trimmed Mean, 335–36
Daly, Mary, 358–59, 361–62, 365
D'Amico, S., 47
data dependence, 5–8
    defining, x, 352
    of federal funds rate, 6–7
    forms of, x
    monetary policy and, 6–7
    in rules-based frameworks, xi
    in United States, 7
    Williams on, 274
Davies, S., 54
debt beta, 265
debt destruction, 36–39
deflation, 359–60
Dell'Ariccia, G., 58
demand shocks, 104, 115–16
    impulse response functions and, 137f
    interest rate rule with, 112n5
    monetary policy and, 154t
    negative, 136
    output gap and, 136–37
    positive, 137
Democrats, fiscal policy of, 39
deposit rates, 167
difference rule, 218
digital cash, 93–95, 357–58
    accounts, 81–82
    design principles for, 81

ELBs and, 83–85
    establishment of, 81
    financial crisis and, 85–86
    financial stability and, 85–86
    implementation of, 97–98
    as medium of exchange, 86
    practical steps for, 86–87
    as store of value, 86–87
digital savings accounts, 95
discount rate
    borrowed reserves and, 182f
    of cash flows, 264
    in corridor system, 200
    federal funds rate and, 179, 180f, 182f,
        200–201
    Federal Reserve, 200
    maturities and, 265n1
    notation for, 265n1
discount window, Federal Reserve, 179–81
"Discretion vs. Policy Rules in Practice"
    (Taylor), 4
disinflation, Volcker, 256, 331–32, 357
disruption, 341, 360
Dodd-Frank act, 305–6, 363
dot plots, 281
    FOMC, 284f
    hypothetical, 285
dovish policies
    AIT and, 120–21
    on interest rates, 118–19
Draghi, Mario, 23
dual-currency system, 54
dual-mandate objectives, 5–6
dynamic first-difference rule, 224
dynamic rules, 170
dynamic stochastic general equilibrium, in
    macroeconomic models, 208

ECB. See European Central Bank
economic expansion, 162–63
economic output, growth in, 162
economic recovery
    adequacy of, 71–73
    Federal Reserve and, 73–81, 85
    QE and, 80f
    regime change and, 161
    in United States, 72f
    V-shaped, 92–93, 101
The Economist, 266
education, labor market and, 337
Edwards, Sebastian, 23, 208–9
effective lower bounds (ELBs), 70
    binding, 116
    central banks and, 131

effective lower bounds (ELBs) (*continued*)
digital cash and, 83–85
mitigation of, 83–85
Eggertsson, G., 39, 109, 175
Eichenbaum, M., 219, 237–38, 254
Eisler, R., 30, 55, 61
ELBs. *See* effective lower bounds
electronic currency, 29–30, 54–55
electronic payments, 156–57
Employment Report, 275
endowment profiles mass, by cohort, 313f
equity beta, 265
equity-share contracting, 314–15
Erceg, Chris, 95–96, 357
EU. *See* European Union
Euler equations
in New Keynesian model, 155
for output gap, 110
Euribor rate, 157
European Central Bank (ECB), ix–x, 81, 178
fine-tuning operations of, 210
on forward guidance, 167
interest rates of, 157
QE by, 35
European Union (EU)
interest rates in, 28, 157
negative interest rate policy in, 49–50,
57–58, 157–58, 167
Eusepi, Stefano, 338
Evans, Charlie, 165, 237–38, 254
Evans rule, 270
excess reserves
federal funds rate and, 183f
interest on, 183f
exchange rates
currency, 54–55
fixing, 167
expectations theory, 290
See also inflation expectations

Facebook, 266
Farhi, E., 56, 175
FD rule
deviations from, 229
federal funds rate and, 228f, 235f
Federal Reserve on, 224
inflation and, 242
measure of, 230f
optimizing, 240
outcomes under, 246
performance of, 239–41
FDdyn, 224
dynamic simulation of, 234
federal funds rate and, 235f

Federal Deposit Insurance Corporation, 183
federal funds rate
BA rule and, 228f
borrowed reserves and, 182f
cuts, 324
daily effective, 187f
data dependence of, 6–7
determination, 181f, 184f
deviations, 226f
discount rate and, 179, 180f, 182f, 200–201
excess reserves and, 183f
FD rule and, 228f, 235f
FDdyn and, 235f
Federal Reserve and, 195
before financial crisis of 2007–2009, 195
Fisher on, 301
FOMC on, 197, 278, 335
forecasts of, 278–80
historical, 232
IOER and, 183f, 184, 186
lending volume and, 187f
longer-run expectations, 15f
market quotes and, 10f
market-implied probability distribution
of, 11
NPP rule and, 228f
PCE deflator and, 233f
PL rule and, 231f, 233f
projections of, 10f
rules and, 228f
setting of, 203–4
T93 rule and, 228f, 231f, 233f
T93adj rule and, 231f, 233f
Taylor rule and, 226f
tri-party repo rate and, 190
Federal Home Loan Banks (FHLBs), 182
lending from, 186
Federal Open Market Committee (FOMC),
5–6, 70, 77, 155, 171, 180, 205–6, 303
accountability of, 350
on central tendencies, 281
confidence intervals of, 281, 284f
dot plots, 284f
on federal funds rate, 197, 278, 335
Federal Reserve and, 275–76
on floor system, 197
forecasts of, 277–78
framework decision of, 347
GDP growth and, 278
on inflation, 8f
inflation outcomes and, 279
on inflation targeting, 346–47, 351
on interest rate rules, 218
mandate of, 5n7

minutes of, 176
on monetary policy, 278, 284f, 345–46
negative feedback loops and, 273
projections of, 324
public comments of, 276
on QE, 74–75
review of, 345
SEP and, 277–78, 281
on uncertainty, 350
on unemployment rate, 72f
Federal Reserve, xiii, xv, 21, 94–95
activist policy of, 271–72
balance sheet of, 159, 163, 177–78, 272,
284, 302
balanced-approach rule of, 223
borrowing of, 209
challenges of, 309–10
Clarida on, 302
commercial paper rate and, 206
credibility of, 161, 331–32
deviations from rules of, 227–35
discount rate, 200
discount window, 179–81
drivers affected by, 265
dual mandate of, 271, 274, 279–80
economic projections of, 282t
economic recovery and, 73–81, 85
on FD rule, 224
federal funds rate and, 195
after financial crisis of 2007–2009, 163
financial markets and, 269, 305–6
financial stability and, 271, 305–6
floor system of, 196–97, 201
FOMC and, 275–76
forecasting of, 274, 277–85
freedom of, 208
Friedman on, 28–29
on futures, 10
during Great Moderation, 270
implementation procedures, 198
improvement of, 275–76
incentives and, 25
independence of, 163–64, 365
on inflation, 100
inflation expectations and, 274, 339–40
inflation targeting by, 342
inside information of, 275–76
on interest rate rules, 222–25, 301–2
on interest rates, 158, 194
macroeconomic models and, 235–47
mandate creep of, 271–73
market perceptions of, 296, 302–3
monetary policy of, ix, 161, 177–78, 195
nominal GDP targeting and, 198

nominal growth and, 296
objectives of, 173–74, 200, 270–71
overnight loans of, 173
overreacting of, 274
ownership of, 38
policy statements of, 276–77, 300
policy tools of, 270–71
preeminence of, 161–62
on price-level targeting rule, 229
QE and, 33–34, 211, 271–72
reserve balances and, 159f
reserves at, 87
review of, ix, xvi, 309, 323
risk assessment of, 280
risk premia and, 267
securities holdings of, 175f
Shultz on, 307
size of, 218
stock market and, 271
strategy selection of, 309–10
sufficiency of, 41
survey data, 9n12
in taper tantrum, 272
toolbox of, 73–81
uncertainty and, 267–68
valuations and, 267–68
weekly liabilities, 189f
Federal Reserve Bank of Chicago, 364
Federal Reserve Bank of New York, 196,
204–5, 274
Ferrero, A., 175
FHLBs. See Federal Home Loan Banks
fiat money system, 195
Filardo, Andy, 213, 360, 362–63
financial crisis, 324
Cochrane on, 305
digital cash and, 85–86
See also Great Recession
financial crisis of 2007–2009, 161
federal funds rate before, 195
Federal Reserve after, 163
monetary policy and, 363
financial markets
Federal Reserve and, 269, 305–6
monetary policy and, 8–13
signals and noise in, 8–13
financial stability
digital cash and, 85–86
Federal Reserve and, 271, 305–6
negative interest rate policy and, 58–59
financial wealth, Gini coefficients, 318
fine-tuning operations, of ECB, 210
firm value, 264
firm-specific risk, 263–64

fiscal councils, 38–39
fiscal policy
    of Democrats, 39
    monetary policy and, 162–64
    of Republicans, 39
    in US, 39
fiscal shocks
    in China, 43–44
    in United States, 43–44
Fisher, Peter, 92, 203
    on federal funds rate, 301
Fixed Income Clearing Corporation, 186
floor system
    of Federal Reserve, 196–97, 201
    FOMC on, 197
    interest rates in, 200
FOMC. *See* Federal Open Market Committee
foreign currency holdings, 57
forward curve, illustration of, 293f
forward guidance, 30–31
    Cochrane on, 358–59
    credibility of, 40
    defining, 39
    ECB on, 167
    inflation targets and, 39–41
    Reifschneider-Williams rule and, 304
Frankel, Jeff, 300
FRB-US model, 221, 254, 255, 256f
    forecasts, 278
free cash flows, 265–66
Friedman, Milton, 14, 21, 56, 81, 94, 99, 199
    on Federal Reserve, 28–29
    on inflation, 2
    on interest rate rules, 220
    on interest rates, 28–29
    on liquidity, 214
    on monetary policy, 2n3
    on unemployment, 2
Friedman rule, 166, 169
Fuhrer, J., 40
future free cash flows, 264
futures
    Federal Reserve on, 10
    interest rates, 9, 11

Galí, Jordi, 108.
GCF. *See* general collateralized finance rate
GDP. *See* gross domestic product
general collateralized finance rate (GCF), 186
    targeting, 215
Germany, 52
Gertler, M., 108, 175
Gesselian stamp tax, 54
Giannoni, Marc, 108–9, 338

Gini coefficients
    calculation of, 317–18
    financial wealth, 318
    labor income mass and, 317
    in United States, 318f
globalization, 360
Gnocchi, Stefano, 328
Goldman Sachs, 307
Goodfriend, Marvin, 54, 91, 180
government debt, maturity structure of, 33–34
government liabilities, QE and, 33
government-sponsored enterprises (GSEs), 212–13
Great Depression, 100, 161
Great Inflation, 256
Great Moderation, 256
    Federal Reserve during, 270
Great Recession, 70, 199n3
    labor force participation and, 72–73
    monetary policy and, 349
    performance during, 227
Greenlaw, D., 176
Greenspan, Alan, 3, 270
    on yield curve, 301
Greenwood, R., 33, 175
gross domestic product (GDP)
    deflator, 231f, 232
    growth, FOMC and, 278
    See also nominal GDP targeting
growth
    aggregate, 315
    aggregate technology, 320
    consumption, 315
    in economic output, 162
    GDP, 278
    nominal, 296
    output, 315
    in take-home pay, 162
    in US, 57–58
GSEs. *See* government-sponsored enterprises
Guha, Krishna, 22, 164–65
Gürkaynak, R. S., 46

Hamilton, James, 175, 177, 194, 200, 203–4, 210–12, 214
Handbook of the Equity Risk Premium (Cochrane), 267
Harlow, Bruce, 261
Harrison, R., 109
Heider, F., 157, 158
helicopter money, 36–39
Hetzel, Robert, 350
Hodrick, Laurie, 306

Hoover Institution, xiv, 71, 99
households
    consumption growth of, 315
    credit market, 314
    debt, 314
    log-log-preferences of, 312
    human capital, 360–61
    hyperactive fiscal policy, 36–39

Iacoviello, M., 241
Ihrig, Jane, 215
IMF. *See* International Monetary Fund
impulse response functions, 133f, 134f
    demand shocks and, 137f
    supply shocks and, 130f, 135f
impulse responses, productivity shocks and,
    319f
IN10 model, 241
incentives, Federal Reserve and, 25
indebtedness, 317–18
inequality, 341
inflation, xvi, 20, 24, 104, 113
    breakeven, 12
    central banks and, 40, 329
    falling, 324–25
    FD rule and, 242
    Federal Reserve on, 100
    FOMC on, 8f
    Friedman on, 2
    gap, 252
    goals, in United States, 345
    lagged, 326f
    longer-run expectations of, 13
    long-term interest rates and, 291f
    macroeconomic models of, 9
    market-based inference of, 13
    model-based inference of, 13
    nominal GDP and, 320
    outcomes, FOMC and, 279
    output gap and, 152–54, 245f
    patterns, 327f
    PCE, 280, 281
    Phillips curve and, 110
    quality-adjusted, 280, 300
    reduction of, 294, 323–24
    regime change, 171
    relative standard deviations of, 242
    shocks, negative, 168
    standard deviation of, 239
    steady-state standard deviation of, 240f
    survey data on, 12–13
    sustained high, 44–48
    T93 rule and, 243f
    true, 170

uncertainty and, 9n11
    unconditional distribution of, 152–54
    unemployment and, 2
    in United States, 170
    variability trade-offs, 245f
    volatility, 166, 219
inflation expectations, 8, 41
    anchoring of, 294
    approximations of, 150
    breakeven and, 46–48
    coefficient on, 326f
    convergence of, 293
    Dallas Fed on, 339–40
    Federal Reserve and, 274, 339–40
    implications, 298–99
    interest rate rule and, 156
    long-term, 42–44, 290–91, 293
    market-derived, 43t
    measurement of, 44–48
    in price-level targeting rule, 149
    real world, 294–96
    relevance of, 325–26
    SAIT and, 145f
    short-term, 291–93
    stable, 294f
    survey data and, 48t
    term structure and, 293
    in United States, 48n12
    upper bounds and, 117–18, 132f, 144f
    well-anchored, 299
    Williams on, 325
    yield curve and, 291f
inflation rate, 110, 115–16
    price-level targeting rule and, 134
    under Reifschneider-Williams rule,
        122–23, 135, 137
inflation targeting
    baseline, 329
    central banks and, 31, 289
    consequences of, 292–94
    by Federal Reserve, 342
    FOMC on, 346–47, 351
    forward guidance and, 39–41
    frameworks, 111–19
    interest rates under, 292f, 295, 298–99
    as international standard, 170
    in Japan, 31
    monetary policy and, 111–16
    negative interest rate policy and, 52
    path amendment of, 40
    rises in, 30–31
    yield curve of, 289
    See also average inflation targeting
inflation-linked bonds, 42n8, 45

inflation-tilting rule, 225
interest
 on reserve accounts, 156, 199
 on reserve balance, optimality of, 159
interest rate on excess reserves (IOER),
  181–84, 187f
 federal funds rate and, 183f, 184, 186
 short-term interest rates and, 302
 tri-party repo rate and, 185f
interest rate rules
 Board of Governors on, 218
 with demand shocks, 112n5
 Federal Reserve on, 222–25, 301–2
 FOMC on, 218
 Friedman on, 220
 inflation expectations and, 156
 Meltzer on, 220
 optimality of, 113n6
 Taylor on, 220
 temporary price-level targeting rule and, 151
interest rates, xi
 central banks and, 104
 in corridor system, 200
 cumulative changes in, 177f
 distribution of, 157
 dovish policies on, 118–19
 of ECB, 157
 in EU, 28, 157
 Federal Reserve on, 158, 194
 in floor system, 200
 Friedman on, 28–29
 futures, 9, 11
 under inflation targeting, 292f, 295,
  298–99
 in Japan, 28, 172
 liquidity premium and, 295
 long-term, 290–91, 291f
 long-term inflation expectations and,
  290–91
 monetary policy and, 155
 natural, 2
 New Keynesian model and, 315
 nominal, 150n12, 156–57
 price stability and, 2
 QE and, 273
 shadow, 226
 short-term, 178–79, 295, 302
 short-term nominal, 110–11
 smoothing, 194, 198–201
 swaps markets, 9
 Taylor rule and, 112, 225
 term structure of, 289–90
 on Treasury bonds, 176f
 on Treasury securities, 290–91

 in United States, 158, 172
 volatility of, 292f, 293, 295
 Wicksellian natural rate of interest, 315
 zero percent, 166
 See also effective lower bounds; negative
   interest rate policy
interest rates on reserves (IOR), 87
International Monetary Fund (IMF), 363
international standards, inflation targeting
  as, 170
investment/savings (IS), 104
IOER. *See* interest rate on excess reserves
IOR. *See* interest rates on reserves
Ireland, Peter, 196n2, 204, 208, 210, 215
IS. *See* investment/savings

Jackson Hole conference, 74
Japan
 financial crisis in, 28
 inflation targets in, 31
 interest rates in, 28, 172
 negative interest rate policy in, 49–50, 57
 QE in, 79–80
JEC. *See* Joint Economic Committee
job creation, monetary policy and, 162–63
Joint Economic Committee (JEC), 76
JPMorgan Chase, 185
junk debt, 35–36

Kaplan, Robert, 324, 360
Karadi, P., 175
Kennedy administration, 260
Kiley, M. T., 58, 109, 170
Kim, Don H., 76
Kimball, Miles, 54
Klee, E., 183
Koby, Y., 49
Koenig, E., 109, 314
k-percent policy rule, 14, 22
Krishnamurthy, A., 76
Kydland-Prescott economy, 315

labor force participation, 26
 by age, 72f
 by cohort, 316f
 Great Recession and, 72–73
 prime-age, 337, 338f
 unemployment rate and, 72f
labor income mass
 by cohort, 317f
 Gini coefficients of, 317
labor market
 education and, 337
 unemployment rate and, 71–72

labor slack, 337–39
Lacker, Jeff, 205
lagged inflation, coefficients on, 326f
large-scale asset purchases
    effects of, 174–78
    QE and, 174
law of one price, 201
LCR. *See* liquidity coverage ratio
Leduc, Sylvain, 328
leisure decisions, by cohort, 316f
Lester, Benjamin, 182
Levin, Andrew, 29, 70–71, 92–96, 177, 238,
    244
    on credibility, 357
    on repo rate, 210
    on stress tests, 286
Levy, Mickey, 95, 300
LIBOR, 59f
life cycle consumption, 320
Lilley, Andrew, 70, 171
liquidity, 12
    Friedman on, 214
    trap, 105n3, 115
liquidity coverage ratio (LCR), 213
liquidity preference hypothesis, 289–90
liquidity premium, interest rates and, 295
log-log-preferences, of households, 312
log-normal distribution, 313
longer-run expectations, of inflation, 13
Longer-Run Strategy Statement, 275
longer-term equilibrium, 346
long-term inflation expectations
    interest rates and, 290–91
    short-term inflation expectations and, 293
long-term interest rates
    determination of, 290–91
    inflation and, 291f
loss ratio, 220
Loungani, Prakash, 70–71, 177
lower bounds
    binding, 169
    central banks and, 105
    equilibrium in, 105n3
    of nominal interest rate, 156–57
    supply shocks and, 169
    zero, 157–58, 323, 331
    See also effective lower bounds

Macaulay duration, 69
Macro Model Data Base, xiv, 218, 221, 248
macroeconomic models, 109–11
    dynamic stochastic general equilibrium
        in, 208
    Federal Reserve and, 235–47

of inflation, 9
of monetary policy, 14–16
nominal interest rates and, 174–75
optimal rules in, 244–47
macroeconomic policy, 3
macroeconomic shocks, 346
macroprudential efforts, 305
Madigan, B., 40
makeup strategies, 327–28
market expectations, 271
market feedback
    monetary aggregates and, 296
    monetary policy and, 296–98
market perceptions, of Federal Reserve, 296,
    302–3
market pricing, 47–48
    of options, 67–71
market quotes, federal funds rate and, 10f
market signals, 211–12
Martin, Bill, 259
maturities, discount rate and, 265n1
maturity structure, of government debt,
    33–34
maximum employment, 73
McCallum, B., 220
medium-scale policy model, 237–38
    output gap in, 236
    trade-off curve in, 246
Meltzer, A., 220
Mendes, R., 108, 114
Merrill Lynch Option Volatility Estimate
    (MOVE), 292f
Mertens, Thomas, 105, 108–9, 114, 158, 170,
    325
Mester, Loretta, 278, 364
Miller, Bill, 259
Minerd, Scott, 302
Miranda-Agrippino, S., 177
Mishkin, Rick, 20, 108–9
modern monetary theory (MMT), 163–64,
    209
Moench, E., 76
monetary aggregates, market feedback and,
    296
monetary paralysis, 31
monetary policy
    benchmark, 139
    calibration, 153t, 154t
    clarification of, 351–54
    consumption and, 95–96
    data dependence and, 6–7
    defining, 195–98
    demand shocks and, 154t
    design, 61–62

monetary policy (*continued*)
dynamic, 132–38
expectations of, 348–49
explanation of, 348–49
of Federal Reserve, 161, 177–78, 195
financial crisis of 2007–2009 and, 363
financial markets and, 8–13
fiscal policy and, 162, 163–64
FOMC on, 278, 284f, 345–46
framework comparison, 127–32, 330f
Friedman on, 2n3
Great Recession and, 349
inflation targeting and, 111–16
interest rates and, 155
job creation and, 162–63
macroeconomic models of, 14–16
market feedback and, 296–98
New Keynesian model and, 155
nominal GDP and, 314
optimal, under discretion, 111–16
outcomes under, 138–40
parameterization of, 127–28
risk-free rate and, 266
role of, 1–5
shocks, 238
simulated effects of, 330f
social losses and, 138f, 140f
static frameworks, 128–32
stress tests, 286
supply shocks and, 125, 135, 153t
systematic approach to, 351–54
uncertainty in, 349–51
Williams on, 158, 286
Monetary Policy Report, 6, 217, 221, 353
analysis of rules in, 252–53
deviations from rules of, 227–35
efficacy of, 248
rules in, 222–25
T93adj rule and, 232
monetary policy rules, xii–xiii
money
functions of, 81
markets, 211
private forms of, 81
See also currency
money supply
slowdown in, 297f
true, 296
mortgages, securitized, 307, 314
Motto, R., 241
MOVE. *See* Merrill Lynch Option Volatility Estimate
Moynihan, Pat, 260
Musk, Elon, 313

Nakamura, E., 177
Nakata, T., 108, 114
National Bureau of Economic Research (NBER), 70, 72f
natural real interest rate, 236
NBER. *See* National Bureau of Economic Research
negative feedback loops, FOMC and, 273
negative interest rate policy
alternatives to, 32
in cashless limit, 50–53
customers and, 157–58
drawbacks, 62
in EU, 49–50, 57–58, 157–58, 167
fairness of, 57
financial stability and, 58–59
implementation of, 28–29, 50–53, 59–60
inflation targeting and, 52
in Japan, 49–50, 57
mildly negative, 49–50
nominal, 52
probability of, 68–69
QE compared with, 32–35
real assets and, 52
on reserve accounts, 159–60
risks of, 52–53
unconstrained, 27, 48–49
in United States, 28, 57
Nelson, Bill, 361
Neri, S., 241
net asset-holding mass, by cohort, 318f
net investment, 265
New Keynesian model, xiv, 104, 109, 218
equations in, 155
Euler equation in, 155
interest rates and, 315
monetary policy and, 155
nominal GDP and, 311–12
nominal short rate in, 156
output volatility in, 219
Philips curve in, 155
small, 236
variables in, 110
Nikolsko-Rhevskyy, A., 220, 221, 225, 226, 254
Nixon, Richard, 260
NK. *See* small New Keynesian model
nominal bonds, 45
nominal GDP targeting, xv–xvi, 169, 358
credit market and, 312
Federal Reserve and, 198
growth, 297f
inflation and, 320
monetary policy and, 314
New Keynesian model and, 311–12

output gap in, 171
QE and, 306
quality-adjusted inflation and, 300
in recessions, 319
SEP on, 280, 300
targets, 300, 311, 320
Woodford on, 311
nominal growth, Federal Reserve and, 296
nominal income targeting, evaluation of, 327–28
nominal interest rate
equations for, 150n12
lower bounds of, 156–57
nominal interest rates, macroeconomic models and, 174–75
nominal risk-free rates, 264
nominal short rate, in New Keynesian model, 156
nonpecuniary costs, 180
non-state-contingent nominal contracting, 314
NPP rule, 225, 229, 254–55, 257
federal funds rate and, 228f
measure of, 230f
performance of, 239–41

Office of Management (OMB), 260
OK. See small Old Keynesian model
Okun's law, 4, 223, 270–71
Old Keynesian model, xiv, 218
output volatility in, 219
small, 237
OLG. See overlapping generations structure
OMB. See Office of Management
open-market operations, 210
operating procedure, 214
Operation Twist, 301
optimal interest rate rule, 120–21
"Optimal Monetary Policy in Closed Versus Open Economies" (Taylor), 23
options, 10
call, 67
market pricing of, 67–71
synthetic, 67
Orphanides, A., 167, 237
output gap, 104, 110
CBO, 232
central bank and, 329
demand shocks and, 136–37
equations for, 150n12
Euler equations for, 110
inflation and, 152–54, 245f
in medium-scale policy model, 236
in nominal GDP targeting, 171

relative standard deviations of, 242
in small New Keynesian model, 236
in small Old Keynesian model, 236
standard deviation of, 239
steady-state standard deviation of, 240f
T93 rule and, 243f
unconditional distribution of, 152–54
variability trade-offs, 245f
output gap-tilting rule, 223, 253–54
output growth, business cycle theory and, 315
output volatility, 219
overlapping generations (OLG) structure, 312
overnight debt, 93
overnight loans, of Federal Reserve, 173

Papell, David, 220, 221, 223, 225, 252, 254
paper currency, 53–58, 61–62
abolition of, 84
Pastor, L., 267
Paulson, Hank, 60–61
payment systems, 55–56
PC index, 25
PCE. See personal consumption expenditures
PCE deflator, 223, 233f
Penn Central, 260
pension funds, 61
personal consumption expenditures (PCE), 80, 232f, 351
core inflation, 325f
headline inflation, 325f
inflation, 280, 281
measurement of, 335–36
Phillips curve, 104, 127–28, 128n11, 270–71, 339, 361–62
inflation and, 110
in New Keynesian model, 155
Piazzesi, Monika, 155–60, 167–68
PL rule
federal funds rate and, 231f
PCE deflator and, 233f
price-level targets in, 229
Plosser, Charlie, 22, 199n3, 365
on balance sheet, 273
PLT. See price-level targeting
polarization, 161–62
policy rate path, 10
Poole, W., 179, 199
Powell, J. H., 272, 284, 286, 300
preferred habitat theory, 290
Prescott, Ed, 25, 94
price stability, 207–8, 336
central banks and, 100
interest rates and, 2
Taylor-type rules and, 4–5

price-level targeting (PLT), xiii, 107, 224–25, 326–27
    AIT and, 331
    algorithm for, 148–50
    Bernanke on, 346–47
    dynamic, 123–25
    evaluation of, 327–28
    Federal Reserve on, 229
    with full makeup strategy, 331
    inflation expectations in, 149
    inflation rate and, 134
    mechanisms of, 168
    parameterized, 139
    PL rule and, 229
    state-level, 125
    supply shocks and, 125
    temporary, 125–27, 134, 151–52, 346–47
prime-age labor force participation, 337, 338f
private banks, 178–79
Prodan, R., 220, 221, 225, 254
productivity, 26
    Dallas Fed on, 360–61
    impulse responses and, 319f
    profile, 312–13
    shocks, 319f
    units, 313
Proulx, K., 175
public comments, FOMC, 276
public debt, 211
public-private partnerships, 97
pure expectations theory, 290

QE. *See* quantitative easing
quadratic loss ratios, 257f
quality-adjusted inflation, 280
    nominal GDP and, 300
quantitative easing (QE), xi–xii, 31, 83
    Bernanke on, 272
    defining, 174
    by ECB, 35
    economic recovery and, 80f
    efficacy of, 74, 78t
    emergency, 35–36
    Federal Reserve and, 33–34, 211, 271–72
    fiscal, 35–36
    fixing, 167
    FOMC on, 74–75
    government liabilities and, 33
    interest rates and, 273
    in Japan, 79–80
    large-scale asset purchases and, 174
    limitations of, 70–71
    negative interest rate policy compared with, 32–35

nominal GDP and, 306
    pure, 32–35
    in US, 34–35
quarterly model, 312
quasi-fiscal policies, 30–31, 60

Reagan, Ronald, 261–62
real assets, negative interest rate policy and, 52
real bonds, 45
real-time measures of discretion, 225–27
recessions, 94–95, 272
    nominal GDP in, 319
reference rate, 121
regime change, 171
Reifschneider, David, 107, 119
    on forecasting, 278–79
Reifschneider-Williams rule, xiii, 107, 121–23, 128, 141
    advantages of, 168
    AIT and, 134, 165–66
    algorithm for, 146–48
    forward guidance and, 304
    inflation rate under, 122–23, 135, 137
    lemma 2, 146
relative standard deviations
    of inflation, 242
    of output gap, 242
repo rate
    Levin on, 210
    private, 190
    reverse, 184–85
    tri-party, 185f, 187f, 190
Republicans, fiscal policy of, 39
reserve accounts
    at central bank, 156
    interest on, 156, 199
    negative interest rate policy on, 159–60
reserve balances
    Federal Reserve and, 159f
    optimality of interest on, 159
residuals, 249
reverse repo rate, 184–85, 187f
Ricco, G., 177
risk assessment, of Federal Reserve, 280
risk premia, 10
    Federal Reserve and, 267
    filtering for, 12, 22
    uncertainty and, 290
risk-free rates
    monetary policy and, 266
    nominal, 264
risk-neutral pricing, 23, 67–71
RMSEs. *See* root mean squared errors
Roberts, J., 58, 109, 170

Rogoff, Ken, 54, 70, 83, 91–102, 171
root mean squared errors (RMSEs), 279
    twenty-year average of, 284f
Rostagno, M., 241
Rotemberg, J., 218
R-star estimates, 325f
Rubin, Bob, 24–25
Rudebusch, G., 219, 237
rule-based international monetary system, 60
rules-based frameworks, data dependence
    in, xi

Sack, Brian, 364
Şahin, Ayşegül, 338
Saidi, F., 157
SAIT. See static average-inflation targeting
San Francisco Fed, 325–26
Schepens, G., 157
Schmidt, Helmut, 260
Schmidt, S., 108, 114
Schmitt-Grohé, S., 108, 114
securities, Federal Reserve holdings, 175f
securitized mortgages, 307, 314
Selgin, George, 97, 169
Seneca, M., 109
Senyuz, Z., 183
SEP. See Summary of Economic Projections
shadow interest rates, 226
Sheedy, Kevin, 314
shock absorbers, 301
    AIT as, 329
shocks
    aggregate, 313
    aggregate demand, 327
    cost-push, 236
    demand, 104, 112n5, 115–16, 136–37,
        137f, 154t
    fiscal, 43–44
    inflation, 168
    macroeconomic, 346
    monetary policy, 238
    productivity, 319f
    supply, 125, 130–31, 130f, 134, 135, 135f,
        141, 151, 153t, 169
short-term inflation expectations, 291–92
    long-term inflation expectations and, 293
short-term interest rates
    corridor system for, 178–79
    IOER and, 302
    term structure and, 295f
short-term nominal interest rate, central bank
    and, 110–11
Shultz, George P., 259–62
    on Federal Reserve, 307

small New Keynesian model (NK), 236
small Old Keynesian model (OK), 237
    output gap in, 236
    trade-off curves in, 246
Smets, F., 237, 254, 255f
Smets-Wouters model, 219, 221
social losses
    monetary policy and, 138f, 140f
    upper bounds and, 132f
Solow, Bob, 260
SOMA. See System Open Market Account
spot curve, illustration of, 293f
static average-inflation targeting (SAIT),
    119–23, 129, 145
    inflation expectations and, 145f
"Steady as You Go" (Shultz), 261
steady-state distribution, 238
steady-state standard deviation
    of inflation, 240f
    of output gap, 240f
Steinsson, J., 177
stimulus, 70–71, 94
stock market, 274
    Federal Reserve and, 271
stress tests, monetary policy, 286
structural forces, Dallas Fed on, 340–41
subsidies, in United States, 158
Summary of Economic Projections (SEP), 7,
    7f, 324
    addendums in, 281–82
    FOMC and, 277–78, 281
    forecasts in, 277, 280
    median of, 325f
    on nominal GDP, 280, 300
    publication of, 281
    revamping, 279
Summers, Larry, 24–25
supply curve, 186
supply shocks, 141
    cutoff, 151
    impulse response functions and, 130f, 135f
    lower bounds and, 169
    monetary policy and, 125, 135, 153t
    negative, 130–31
    positive, 134
    price-level targeting rule and, 125
    responses to, 131
    temporary price-level targeting rule and,
        151
survey data
    Federal Reserve, 9n12
    on inflation, 12–13
    inflation expectations and, 48t
Svensson, Lars, 108, 167, 219, 237

Swanson, E., 175
swaps markets, interest rates, 9
Sweden, 38–39
synthetic breakeven, 45–46
    cap, 46*f*
synthetic breakevens, CPI and, 69
synthetic options, 67
System Open Market Account (SOMA), 75–76

T93 rule, 229, 252–53, 255–56
    federal funds rate and, 228f, 231f, 233f
    inflation and, 243f
    measure of, 230f
    output gap and, 243f
    PCE deflator and, 233f
    performance of, 239–41
T93adj rule, 229
    federal funds rate and, 231f, 233f
    Monetary Policy Report and, 232
    PCE deflator and, 233f
take-home pay, growth in, 162
taper tantrum, 76–77
    Federal Reserve in, 272
targeted inflation patterns, shocks and, 327f
Tase, M., 183
Taylor, John, 4, 20–23, 109, 203–6, 238, 241,
        243
    on central banks, 304–5
    on interest rate rules, 220
    on policy rules, 252
Taylor rule, 4–5, 14–15, 52, 231
    adjusted, 224–25, 236
    defining, 218, 222–23
    deviation, 148
    expression of, 222–23
    federal funds rate and, 226f
    interest rates and, 112, 225
    properties of, 4*n*5
Taylor-type rules
    instrument-rule specification and, 5
    price stability and, 4–5
    Woodford on, 4–5
temporary price-level targeting, 125–27, 134
    Bernanke on, 346–47
    interest rate rule and, 151
    supply shocks and, 151
term premia, 22
    on Treasury, 12
term structure
    inflation expectations and, 293
    of interest rates, 289–90
    short-term interest rates and, 295f
Teryoshin, Y., 221
Tetlow, R., 221

Thornton, D., 177
time-series models, evolution of, 15*f*
TIPS. *See* Treasury Inflation-Protected
        Securities
Tolley, G., 199
transparency, 284
Treasury (US)
    bonds, 45
    debt issuing by, 93
    term premiums on, 12
    yield curve, 11
Treasury and Tax Loan Program (TT&L), 210
Treasury bills, 296
Treasury bonds, interest rates on, 176f
Treasury Indexed Bonds, 45n11
Treasury Inflation-Protected Securities
        (TIPS), 21, 24–25, 42, 85n31
    daily trading volumes on, 47
    launch of, 12*n*13
    market data, 12
    spot rates, 12
Treasury securities, 47, 173
    interest rates on, 290–91
TreasuryDirect, 95
Treasury-Fed Accord of 1951, 162
tri-party repo rate, 187f
    federal funds rate and, 190
    IOER and, 185f
true money supply, 296
TT&L. *See* Treasury and Tax Loan Program
Tulip, Peter, on forecasting, 278
Turner, A., 36

uncertainty, 214
    balance sheet and, 272–73
    Federal Reserve and, 267–68
    FOMC on, 350
    in monetary policy, 349–51
    point estimates and, 16f
    risk premia and, 290
    yield curve and, 295
unemployment, 94
    Friedman on, 2
    gap, 234
    inflation and, 2
unemployment rate, 5
    FOMC on, 72f
    labor force participation and, 72f
    labor market and, 71–72
    longer-run, 7f
    measurement of, 336
    natural, 338–39
    recession and, 21
    in United States, 14–15, 71–72

unicorns
    defining, 266n2
    valuation of, 266
United Kingdom, 38–39
United States (US)
    central banks in, 169–70
    CPI in, 47–48
    data dependence in, 7
    economic recovery in, 72f
    fiscal policy in, 39
    fiscal shocks in, 43–44
    Gini coefficients in, 318f
    growth in, 57–58
    inflation expectations in, 48n12
    inflation goals in, 345
    inflation in, 170
    interest rates in, 158, 172
    negative interest rate policy in, 28, 57
    QE in, 34–35
    subsidies in, 158
    unemployment rate in, 14–15, 71–72
    yield curve in, 24
upper bound, 116–19, 143–45
    binding, 116
    inflation expectations and, 132f, 144f
    inflation expectations with, 117–18
    social losses and, 132f
Uribe, M., 108, 114
US. See United States

valuation, 271
    Federal Reserve and, 267–68
    of unicorns, 266
vanilla breakeven, 46f
Vayanos, D., 175
vector autoregressions, 266
Veronesi, P., 267
Vissing-Jorgensen, A., 76, 268
Volcker, Paul, 3, 168–69, 262
Volcker disinflation, 256, 331–32, 357
Vuolteenaho, T., 266

WACC. See weighted average cost of capital
Waldron, M., 109
Warsh, Kevin, 161–65
weighted average cost of capital (WACC), 264
welfare gains, 120–21
well-anchored inflation expectations, 299
Wenzel, Robert, 168–69
Whelpley, W., 180
Wicksellian natural rate of interest, 315
Wieland, Volker, 166–67, 170, 237, 241, 244, 252
Williams, John, 105–9, 114, 119, 155, 158, 244
    on AIT, 165–66
    on data dependence, 274
    on inflation expectations, 325
    on monetary policy, 158, 286
Woodford, Mike, 4–5, 39, 108, 109, 175, 218
    on nominal GDP, 311
World Bank, 97
Wouters, R., 237, 254, 255f
Wright, I., 76
Wu, J. C., 175

Yellen, Janet, 52, 253–54, 348
Yellen rule, 257
yield curve, 46–47
    factors influencing, 292
    Greenspan on, 301
    inflation expectations and, 291f
    of inflation targeting, 289
    shape of, 291–92
    slope of, 295
    Treasury, 11
    uncertainty and, 295
    in United States, 24
    volatility, 299
Yoldas, E., 183

Zabai, A., 175
zero lower bound (ZLB), 157–58, 323
    time at, 331